PRAISE FOR *THE QUILTER'S COMPUTER COMPANION*

"Finally, out of the haze of computer chaos comes a book to conquer all the cyber confusion and give you the clear, easy-to-understand information you need to make that little gray box your favorite quilting tool . . . Get this book, even if you think you're an expert, but especially if you know you're not."

LYNN LEWIS YOUNG, PUBLISHER/EDITOR, *Art/Quilt Magazine*

"Savvy, sassy, and amazingly comprehensive, this is the indispensable book for computing quilters. When you aren't learning something fascinating and useful, you're rolling on the floor laughing!"

ROB HOLLAND, PLANETPATCHWORK.COM

"*The Quilter's Computer Companion* is an amazing resource, which will benefit both the novice computer quilter and the quilting computer nerd. Whether you want to play with simple designs, create templates, or experiment with color, this book is for you. Undoubtedly, you will be fascinated with *The Quilter's Computer Companion*'s unbelievable compilation of technical information and design ideas."

JOEN WOLFROM, TEXTILE ARTIST AND QUILTMAKER

"Judy and Gloria have done a superb job on their new book. *The Quilter's Computer Companion* will be an invaluable addition to the library of any quilter who combines computing with quilting and should be a staple on every online quilter's bookshelf!"

JUDY SMITH, LIST-OWNER QUILTART
(http://www.his.com/~judy/quiltart.html)
FORUM MANAGER DELPHI'S QUILTING ARTS FORUM
(http://www.delphi.com/quilting)

"The style is very light, readable, and has humor. It is written in language that a quilter who . . . is not yet computer literate can understand . . . A user friendly book!"

JUDY MATHIESON, QUILT DESIGNER AND TEACHER

"*The Quilter's Computer Companion* is a thorough, practical reference book, well illustrated and written with a lively sense of humor. I will use it over and over again."

ANN JOHNSTON, QUILTMAKER

THE QUILTER'S COMPUTER COMPANION

THE
QUILTER'S COMPUTER
COMPANION

Judy Heim & Gloria Hansen

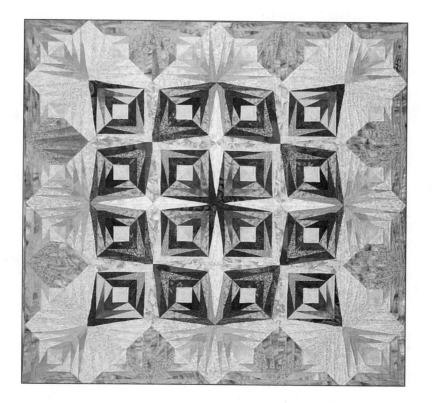

no starch press

San Francisco

Printed in the United States of America

1 2 3 4 5 6 7 8 9 10—99 98 97

Publisher: William Pollock
Project Editor: Karol Jurado
Cover Design: Cloyce Wall, Derek Yee
Cover Photography: Ross Stout (*quilt*), Meredith Chew (*mouse*)
Composition: Derek Yee, Stacie Yamaki, Phyllis Beaty
Interior Design: Margery Cantor
Project Manager and Content Reviewer: Rebecca Pepper
Copyeditors: Rebecca Pepper, Loralee Windsor
Proofreaders: Desne Border, Alice Brzovic
Indexer: Susan Coerr
Author Photos: Mary Langenfeld Photo (*Judy Heim*)

Distributed to the book trade in the United States and Canada by Publishers Group West, 4065 Hollis, P.O. Box 8843, Emeryville, California 94662
Phone: 800-788-3123 or 510-548-4393, Fax: 510-658-1834

For information on translations or book distributors outside the United States, please contact No Starch Press directly:
No Starch Press, 401 China Basin Street, Suite 108, San Francisco, CA 94107-2192
Phone: 415-284-9900; Fax: 415-284-9955; info@nostarch.com; www.nostarch.com

Library of Congress Cataloging-in-Publication Data
Heim, Judy.
        The quilter's computer companion / Judy Heim and Gloria Hansen.
                p. cm.
        Includes index.
        ISBN 1-886411-15-8 (pbk. : alk. paper)
        1. Quilting—Data processing. 2. Computer-aided design.
    3. Internet (Computer network) I. Hansen, Gloria. II. Title.
    TT835.H387   1997
    746.46'041'0285—dc21   97-11527
                                                                               CIP

BRIEF CONTENTS

Our thanks and admiration go to Rebecca Pepper for tirelessly checking every computer keystroke and screen in this book, rewriting many tutorials, correcting our grammar, clarifying quilting lingo, and adding her own quilting perspective to the pages. Thanks, Rebecca! This book couldn't have been possible without your loving care!

We'd also like to thank Ann Johnston, Judy Mathieson, and Sharyn Craig for letting us feature their beautiful quilts, and sharing with us the things they learned while making them with the help of their computers.

Our gratitude goes to Penny McMorris at Electric Quilt and Miriam Neuringer at Quilt-Pro Systems for hand-holding and gentle encouragement. We thank David Aires at Foto-Wear for pointing us in many good directions. Many others provided products and insights, including Phil Hisley of VQuilt-fame, Ricky Ford of QuiltSoft, Rick Sutton of Momentum Software, and Jean Tantra of Meta Theory. Good people in the public relations departments at Adobe, Corel, Claris, Deneba, Wacom, and Canon not only shipped us products, but fielded streams of wacky questions like "Will future versions of your product include a flower-drawing tool?"

Gloria thanks her parents, Robert and Theresa Patrowicz, and her family for their understanding, encouragement, and patience during this long project. She thanks her friends, especially John Swiatek, for their support. And she extends her warmest thanks to her husband, Rich, who always knows just when she needs a hug and who never gasps in horror each time another Macintosh, computer gizmo, or stack of fabric appears in their home. What a guy!

Finally our thanks go to our hyperkinetic publisher Bill ("You need to specify a water temperature in this chapter! You can't tell readers to dunk fabric in water without telling them what its temperature should be!") Pollock for making this book more than an adventure.

We dedicate this book to the friendships that flourish between quilters. We became friends while writing this book, through the miracle of E-mail and regular late night telephone calls. In the process we discovered artistic reservoirs that may have otherwise remained hidden. We hope that you, dear reader, enjoy the same sense of discovery while exploring these pages.

Judy & Gloria

HELP!
THERE'S A COMPUTER BY MY QUILTING ROOM!

Not long ago, Judy Heim wrote a book called *The Needlecrafter's Computer Companion: Hundreds of Easy Ways to Use Your Computer for Sewing, Quilting, Cross-Stitch, Knitting, and More!* (San Francisco: No Starch Press, 1995). Like many computer books, it is a heavy tome of nearly 500 pages. However, that's where its similarity to other computer books ends. Festooned with pictures of angels flying between the computer commands, it was intended as a fun, informative read for stitchers who really don't want to think about computers but who realize there are some pretty nifty ways that a home computer could enhance their creative lives— if only they knew what they were.

The book was, and continues to be, a wonderful success. "Finally, a computer book that I can understand!" many readers have written to say.

At the same time that *The Needlecrafter's Computer Companion* was disappearing from store shelves faster than the latest Word macro book, the rest of the computer press sneered.

"Quilting? I suppose that happens in the Midwest," mused a New York editor at one of those trendy Internet magazines when we suggested he publish a story about quilters communicating via the Internet. Editors at other computer magazines were similarly underwhelmed. "I have a father-in-law in Ohio who makes stained glass, and I think he would like to know how to use a computer," said one, missing the point.

If quilters are misunderstood, their use of computers is even more so. What possible use can an appliance that was born of the need to chart the distance between the earth and the moon have for people who spend their time sewing centuries-old pineapple designs onto fabric?

Faced with such wide-ranging skepticism, we had only one choice: to write a sequel. This book would be just for quilters and would describe in detail how they can best use a computer.

The fact is there are some pretty amazing things that you as a quilter can do with a home computer, and you don't need the latest $4,000 Beyond-Pentium to do it. You can design quilt blocks, templates, appliqué patterns, and stencils. You can print photos on muslin, organize your fabric stash, and prowl the Internet for art to use in your quilt designs. You can exchange e-mail with other quilters around the globe. Heck, you can even put your quilts on display in cyberspace for everyone to see.

There are also some things that you may think you want to do with your computer but that you really shouldn't try. Like scanning all the fabrics in your closet and sorting them into a visual database. Or generating appliqué patterns so complex that even a trained robot with the entire works of Jinny Beyer programmed into neural memory couldn't finish sewing them.

The aim of this book is to tell you what you can use your computer for and the best and cheapest way to accomplish it—and to steer you clear of foolhardy techno-pursuits.

This book is not for everyone. It assumes that the reader possesses a certain degree of computer expertise and some quilting savvy as well. Because of the multiplicity of quilt designing software currently on the market, we couldn't provide tutorials for every software package available for quilters. Instead, we recommend the programs we like, offer tutorials on those, and try to provide general guidance on using the alternatives.

We've also addressed questions we hear over and over from quilters, like, "How can I use CorelDraw to design quilts?" "How can I create an appliqué pattern from a scanned image?" "Should I buy a drawing tablet?" and "Do those cheap inkjet printers that print on fabric really work?"

The opinions that fill this book are ours alone. They come from months of testing, years of experience with computers, and impatience with anything that steals us from the aspects of quilting we really love: poking needle through fabric.

In preparing this book we talked to manufacturers about their products and tried them ourselves. We had our friends and spouses try them. We stayed up all night stirring computer-printed fabrics in chemical baths and drawing Log Cabin quilts on computer screens until our eyes crossed.

Our opinions are often brash because we believe that in the computer world, where ordinarily well-composed people grow giddy over fairytale press releases, good sense is in short supply. We believe that quilters especially need and appreciate good sense. Not everyone will agree with our advice—maybe you won't. But that's okay. We think you're buying this book because you wouldn't mind sitting down one evening with two quilters who've used computers for decades and listening to them prattle on for a few hours about what computer stuff they like to buy and how they like to use it.

By the time you finish reading this book, you may well find that your quilt projects are starting to take over your computer's room. Piles of fabric have replaced stacks of software manuals. Half-basted quilts swaddle the computer boxes. When that happens, you'll know that you have made the cyber-revolution into your own personal artistic revolution. "Help! There's a computer in my living room!" will be but a fading anthem of an anxious past.

We hope you enjoy the discoveries that await you in this book as much as we have enjoyed discovering them. We know that we will never design quilts the same way again—and we hope that the same becomes true for you.

Judy Heim

Gloria Hansen

Quilters use many different kinds of software packages to design quilts. There are currently a half-dozen quilt designing software packages on the market. Quilters also use many brands of drawing programs to design quilts.

Since it's impossible to cover them all, we've focused on the quilting software and drawing programs that we prefer, and the ones that quilters on the Internet use and talk about the most. We've also focused on specific versions of major drawing programs that seem to be in wide use among quilters.

If the software you use is not among the ones we provide specific tutorials for, you'll still find that many of the principles we talk about in this book apply to your software as well. In fact, we've found that most of the general-purpose drawing programs on the market are so similar in their features and design that tutorials for a program like CorelDraw translate almost step-by-step to other drawing programs.

THE STUFF YOU NEED TO BUY

DOES TALK OF GIGABYTES AND RAM LEAVE YOU GLUM? ARE YOU
CONFUSED ABOUT WHETHER TO BUY SPECIAL QUILT SOFTWARE OR A
GENERAL-PURPOSE DRAWING PROGRAM? OUR PRODUCT PICKS TELL
YOU THE HOTTEST STUFF TO BUY TO DESIGN QUILTS.

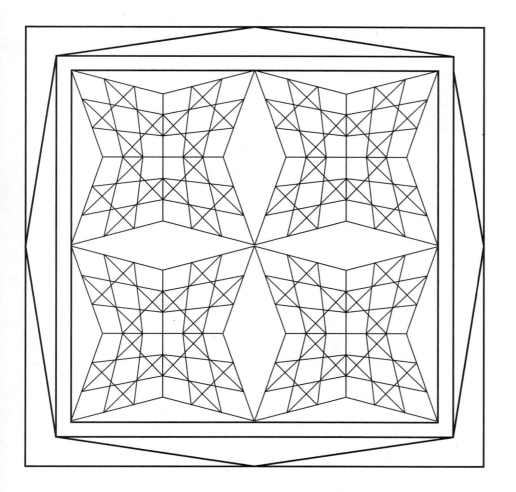

CHAPTER 1

A QUILTER'S COMPUTER STORE ADVENTURES

What happens when you walk into a computer store and ask to buy a computer with which to design quilts? Here's all you need to know to go computer shopping without being ushered out the door with a lollipop.

Walk into a computer store and ask the resident nerd what you'll need to buy to design quilts on a computer and you'll probably get a fuzzy stare. He or she may tell you that you need a CD-ROM drive, a color inkjet printer bundled with craft software, and a drawing pen and tablet to hook to the computer.

The reality is that you don't need any of that.

What you need is a fast and reliable computer, moderately priced. You want one that you can easily upgrade so that in two years you won't be stuck running two-year-old software. You want a monitor with an exceptionally sharp picture, and a fast video card. You want a color scanner, ideally a full-page one. You want a printer that's not going to empty your piggy bank eating up expensive ink cartridges. You want a big hard disk so you don't run out of room when you store all those humongous graphics files or when "junk files" from prowling the Internet clutter your disk.

You'll want to use the computer for things besides quilt designing, of course. Maybe you want to use it in your home business, or perhaps your children want to write school papers on it. Not to worry; the computer we will help you buy will be useful for all of those things.

HOW TO BE A QUILTING COMPUTER NERD

We've both been very busy recently, thanks to the explosion of the Internet. Nearly every weekend a friend, neighbor, or relative stops by to ask us about computers. What should they buy? Can they still use that dusty old computer in their basement? Should they buy a secondhand computer? For many people, shopping for electronics is so anxiety-filled it's a wonder that they own televisions.

Here are our answers to the computer shopping questions we most frequently hear. We've tailored our answers to the computer needs of quilters, and we've included recommendations on buying one of those sewing machines that links to a personal computer. In the next chapter we offer our picks of quilt design and drawing software and tell you the computer hardware you need to run them.

When you shop for a computer, try to get a computer-savvy friend to come along. Look for someone who jumps at the offer, who just loves shopping for computers; then you'll know you've found the right shopping companion.

I WANT A PC. WHAT SHOULD I BUY?

If you're in the market for a PC, head for at least a 133MHZ Pentium or 586. The higher the megahertz, the faster your quilt design or drawing software will run.

- You want 16MB of RAM, also known as memory, and it should be expandable to 128MB; 32MB of RAM will speed up your graphics. (As you'll see in our chapter on printing on fabric, you may need even more memory if you're using lots of high-powered graphics programs.)

- Ask for a motherboard with a ZIF (**zero insertion force**) **socket** so that you can pop in a faster processor when the prices come down. A ZIF socket is an extra CPU socket. Many good computers have ZIF sockets. To upgrade to, say, a 586 or Pentium, all you have to do is pop in a new CPU and deactivate the old one. Anyone with a screwdriver can do it. Without a ZIF socket, you'll be stuck prying out the old CPU with a Swiss Army knife and stuffing some tissue into the hole in the motherboard. That's how our publisher, Bill Pollock, upgrades his computers. This isn't possible, however, if the CPU is soldered in place.

- Ask for at least two but ideally **three open drive bays** so that you can add a new hard drive or tape backup drive if and when you need it.

- Ask for at least **four open slots** on the motherboard so that you'll have enough room to add an internal modem or the special card for a scanner. You can never have too many extra slots, because you never know what exciting new hardware is going to materialize.

- You want at least 2MB of video RAM on your **video card,** sometimes called a graphics card. If you get your choice of video cards, go for a high-end 3-D one with a high refresh rate of 100HZ. Look carefully at different types of images and graphics on the monitor, including black-and-white pictures, text, computer graphics, photos, and gray-scale images. Get the best-quality monitor you can afford. If you can afford a 17-inch monitor, go for it.

- **Hard disks** are relatively cheap (compared to what they sold for only a short time ago), so get a big one—at least 2 gigabytes (GB) or more. If you prowl the Internet and store lots of images to use with your designs, you'll eat up disk space fast.

- Much of today's software comes on CD-ROMs, so at least a quad-speed (4X) **CD-ROM drive** is pretty much a given. (You may also choose to purchase CDs of clip art to use in your quilt designs, though few quilters do). Your kids will probably want to play games that require a CD-ROM drive, but heck, those are expensive (the good ones can run $70 or more). You'll find CD-ROM drives on the market that are much faster than quad-speed drives, but you don't need them unless you want your kids to have more fun with those computer games.

- Do you need a **sound card and speakers?** If you want to play a music CD in your CD-ROM drive and blast it out the PC's speakers, you'll need one. Ditto if you want to listen to music or other sound bites on the Internet or in other software. But if you're cheap like us, spare the expense and spend the money you save on fabric instead.

- Don't pay too much attention to the **software** that comes bundled with the machine, as you'll probably want to buy better stuff. Most of what's bundled may be of little use to you—except for Windows 95. You should get Windows 95.

- Look for at least a **two-year warranty**, but don't pay extra for a longer one— if the computer breaks down it will probably do so in the first year.

- As for **brand names**, we're fond of Micron (**http://www.micron.com**) and Compaq (**http://www.compaq.com**). We're less enthused about Dell and Gateway.

....
T * I * P

Before you buy a computer from a brand name company, read evaluations of the specific machine and the company that makes it. The best ones can be found on the Internet at the C\NET site (http://www.cnet.com/), in PC World magazine (reports are online at http://www.pcworld.com/), and in Consumer Reports. You'll find full Consumer Reports articles on America Online—keywords consumer reports.

SHOULD I BUY A MACINTOSH?

For a graphic artist, nothing compares to an Apple Macintosh, and lots of quilters have them. While not all quilting software runs on a Macintosh (Electric Quilt runs only on a PC), there are many wonderful software tools that you can use to design quilts on the Mac. And many of these are a lot cheaper than comparable software on a PC.

As Mark Twain might have said, the rumors of Apple's demise are greatly exaggerated. Not only does the Macintosh have a loyal following, but thousands of software titles are available for it, for both home and business. Also, after many years of resistance, Apple has finally licensed its hardware technology, so you can now buy clones from authorized makers like PowerComputing.

SHOULD I BUY A MACINTOSH THAT WILL LET ME RUN PC SOFTWARE?

Some Macintosh models come with both Macintosh and PC motherboards in them; some even come with a Pentium chip, so you can run just about any PC software. Press a couple of keys and the Macintosh operating system fades out and DOS or Windows fades in. The problem is that in order to live in both worlds you need a fairly sophisticated understanding of, well, both worlds. Dual systems like this are not for the timid—or easily confused. Another solution if you must run non-Macintosh software on your Macintosh is from the talented people at Connectix who created Virtual PC. This program will run on any currently shipping Mac OS system (meaning you need a PowerPC chip). It gives the Macintosh the ability to run almost any Pentium-compatible operating system, including DOS, Windows (3.x, 95, or NT), IBM OS/2, and even NeXT. This powerful piece of software will cost you about $150. Another option is SoftWindows from Insignia

T * I * P

If you need to run non-Macintosh software on your Macintosh, look into Virtual PC from Connectix. (http://www.connectix.com)

Solutions, which will let your Power Macintosh run DOS, Windows 3.*x*, or Windows 95. If you purchase SoftWindows separately, it will set you back about $300, depending upon which version you buy, though some systems ship with it already installed.

WHAT SHOULD I SHOP FOR IN A MACINTOSH?

For first-time buyers, the Macintosh Performa is a good choice, as it's a snap to set up. Among the clones, the PowerComputing line and the Motorola StarMax (which comes with an amazing five-year warranty) are good choices.

- Ask for a machine with a **PowerPC 603e processor or better** and level 2 cache. A fast chip speed (the higher the number, the faster the chip) is better than a fast MHZ speed. For instance, a machine with a 604e chip running at 132MHZ is actually faster than a machine with a 603e chip running at 150MHZ.

- Sixteen MB of RAM is standard, and anything more is great.

- Get at least a 1.2-gigabyte **hard disk** and an 8x CD-ROM drive.

- Unless you plan to install an extra hard drive or internal Zip drive, don't worry about the number of **expansion bays** the computer has. Similarly, you probably won't need more than the standard number of PCI slots in which you'd install things like video cards. But do note the number of **DIMM** (dual inline memory module) slots and the size of the DIMMs installed. DIMM slots hold your computer's RAM, or memory. If your slots are filled (say your computer has a total of 32MB RAM as two 16MB DIMMs installed in each of two slots), your options for adding more memory are limited. While 32MB of RAM may be plenty for now, you may need more a couple of years down the road. The problem is that, if both available slots are filled, the only way you can add more memory is to remove one of the 16MB DIMMs and replace it with a 24MB or greater DIMM. The 16MB DIMM you've removed is then of no use to you. Moral: If you buy a machine with two slots, buy as much memory as you can afford for the second slot.

- Some Macs come with both Macintosh and PC processors. You don't need this unless you want to run both Macintosh and PC software.

- Look for a machine with **System 7.6 or greater**.

- The Apple extended **keyboard** has a nice click touch that we think is worth the extra bucks.

MY COMPUTER IS AN OLD CLUNKER. CAN I DO ANY QUILTING STUFF WITH IT?

Yes. For example, Electric Quilt, the premier quilt designing software, will work on an old 286 PC running DOS (this was popular in the late 1980s). Many quilters have machines this old and don't want or need anything else. Still, to run some of the drawing programs we talk about in this book, you'll need at least a 386 running Windows, and ideally a 486 or 586.

You can tap into the Internet using literally any computer, even that vintage 1984 PCjr. What you probably won't be able to do, if you're using a relative antique, is tap in very fast or get those splashy graphics. Your interactions with the Internet, and other computer users on it, will probably be restricted to e-mail and slow, text-based interactions. In other words, you type commands into some remote computer, and it answers with cryptic phrases. You won't be able to visit Patchwork Planet on the World Wide Web and view the quilts on display there. You won't even be able to check out the studs on the Stud Muffins of Quilting page. But for many people, all the Internet they want is e-mail. And that may be all you need too. See Chapter 20, "A Quilter's Guide to Cyberspace," for more advice on surfing cyberspace.

SHOULD I TRY TO UPGRADE THAT OLD CLUNKER OR BUY A NEW COMPUTER?

It depends on your needs. As we said, many quilters use 286's and find them perfectly sufficient. If you want to speed up your PC by adding a faster CPU and more memory in order to do more elaborate graphics or Internet stuff, you probably shouldn't bother if the computer is a 486 that's more than two years old. Of course, a lot will depend on the machine, but it is easy to dump a lot of money into new chips and boards for only a minimal increase in performance. It may be wiser to skip the upgrade and buy a new machine instead. If you're thinking of upgrading, you should first have the machine properly evaluated by a technician at a secondhand computer store.

SHOULD I BUY A SECONDHAND COMPUTER?

That depends on how cheap it is. In PC-compatibles we would avoid anything older than a 486. Avoid a 486sx or anything slower—get at least a 486DX/2 66. And, if you're thinking of buying a secondhand 486, be sure you know someone who can properly evaluate and upgrade it for you. You'll probably want to be able to upgrade it to at least 16MB of RAM and add a new, faster CPU. You may want to add a bigger hard disk too. Not all 486's can be expanded. Also, CD-ROM drives can be hard to install in older machines.

If you buy an old Pentium with 8MB of RAM, all you'll probably need to do to upgrade it to a respectable speed is to add another 8MB to bring the RAM up to 16MB. If it has 16MB, don't bother adding any more memory, because you won't get much of a performance boost.

As for Macintoshes, if you can find a used Quadra for $500 or less, grab it. The more memory it has, the better. Look for at least 8MB of RAM, but 16MB is preferable if it's running System 7.5. You'll be very happy with how nicely the Quadra runs programs like Quilt-Pro, Deneba artWorks, SuperPaint, and Canvas 3.5. But unless you're lucky enough to find an accelerated Quadra, don't bother installing Canvas 5.0. If you want to run Canvas 5.0 with ease, look for at least a first-generation Power Macintosh with a Power PC 601 chip.

JUDY & GLORIA'S QUILTER-CHEAPSKATE COMPUTER BUYING TIP

If all you want to do is run Electric Quilt, and tap into America Online, you can pick up an old 386 PC for a couple of hundred bucks, and it will work like a dream for you. The only things you'll be depriving yourself of are speed and the flashy graphics of the Internet.

WARNING!

We visited several secondhand computer stores and asked about the procedures and costs of upgrading various models of computers. Often the store clerks did not know or gave us erroneous (and potentially expensive) advice. If you're planning to go the upgrade route, be sure to find someone knowledgeable who can help you.

WHAT KIND OF PRINTER SHOULD I BUY?

Home computer users are in love with color inkjet printers. They're cheap—from $170 to $280 at the low end—and they come with toys that will keep the kids busy (at least for a while), like software to print comics and greeting cards.

PRINTER BUYING TIP #1

Most laser printers come with 1MB of memory. You'll need to boost that to at least 3MB if you plan to print letter-sized images on fabric. A memory upgrade like that will cost you about $70.

JUDY & GLORIA'S QUILTER-CHEAPSKATE PRINTER TIP

Laser printer cartridges run from $50 to $100 at office stores. You can buy a recycled one for about half that, and depending upon where you buy it, a recycled cartridge may print about 25 to 50 percent more sheets than a brand-new one. See your phonebook for a local firm that sells used cartridges, or check the ads in the back of a computer magazine. Keep in mind that these firms' cartridges can vary a lot in quality, so ask around for recommendations from a local computer users' group. An improperly refilled cartridge may well damage your printer.

PRINTER BUYING TIP #2

Many low-cost printers come with various kinds of drawing and design software, which is sometimes very useful. Some printers come with earlier versions of the popular high-end drawing program for PCs, CorelDraw. That's a good deal.

But if you plan to use your computer for business, a slightly more expensive black-and-white laser printer—around $400 to $500 at the low end—will prove more practical. The print quality, especially for text, will be sharper. A laser printer will print faster (those cheap inkjet printers are sometimes excruciatingly slow).

Laser printers are cheaper to run than inkjets, too. Ink cartridges are pricey, running from about $20 to $40, and they print only a few hundred pages. Laser printer cartridges, in comparison, cost between $50 and $100 and last much longer, printing from 400 to 2,000 or more pages. Also, some low-cost color inkjet printers are designed for home and not for business use. One spits the sheets on the floor as it finishes printing them; it lacks a tray to catch them.

On those rare occasions when you want to print something in color, you can always truck on over to Kinko's or another copy shop with your floppy and rent their high-end desktop publishing printers.

What about those much-ballyhooed T-shirt transfers and fabric sheets you can buy to use with inkjets? Oooh, they're pricey! They cost anywhere from $1.50 to $3 per sheet. There are cheaper alternatives for quilters who want to print images on fabric. See Chapter 17 for our advice on the best ways to print photos and other computer art on fabric.

We hope we've convinced you that buying a cheapo inkjet printer is analogous to buying a Tonka toy truck when what you really need is a sixteen-wheeler with fake tiger fur seats, but we're not ready to give them the Judy & Gloria Seal of Disapproval. Color inkjet printers are fun. They're cheap. We have a good time with them. If you take a look at Chapter 17 and some of the color photos in this book, you'll see what we mean. And if you've got kids in your neighborhood, a color inkjet printer will guarantee your popularity (for better or worse). It's just that we're not ready to trade our laser printers for one.

Should you be concerned about the water-soluble ink from an inkjet printer running on pattern pieces (and fabric) when you're piecing? In general, you don't need to worry (unless you piece a lot of quilts in the fog), but some quilters have reported occasional problems, so this may be a consideration for you.

One final note: If you can get your hands on an old dot-matrix printer (you'll find them cheap at swap meets and advertised for sale in local computer papers), consider buying it. They're great for printing templates. If you're a Macintosh user, look for an Apple ImageWriter II. Gloria found some excellent buys at computer fairs, purchasing a couple for under $25! A nice bonus is that the ink used on the ribbon is waterproof. See Chapter 17 for more ideas and information on a must-have printer driver if you have an ImageWriter II.

No matter what kind of printer you decide to shop for, keep these things in mind:

- Color printers often interpret the colors on the computer's screen in weird ways. Whites may turn into yellows. A mellow pumpkin color may print as a shocking neon orange. Like kitchens decorated in the 1970s, some printers will fill your life with garish tangerines and olives. The color photos on page <xx> show the same T-shirt transfer printed with two different kinds of printer.

- When you shop for a printer, see how it prints different kinds of images. Look carefully at its color interpretations, comparing what's on the screen to what prints on the page. Gray images should be sharp, not fuzzy. Look at the resolution of the printout. The printouts from a 600 dots-per-inch (dpi) printer should be better than those from a 300 dpi one, but be sure to check the print-outs before you buy.

- Keep in mind that stores will probably show you sample printouts of images that are intended to make the printer look good. Bring your own floppy disk of scanned photos, drawings (both gray-scale and color), and quilt blocks to see for yourself.

SHOULD I BUY A DRAWING TABLET?

Drawing tablets like those from Wacom are neat. They look a lot like Etch-A-Sketches and, once they're hooked to your computer, you can draw on them with a special pen and see your drawing on your computer screen. It's a lot easier to draw with a pen on a drawing tablet than it is to push a mouse around on your desk. In fact, professional graphic artists won't do without them.

Drawing tablets work with all the high-end drawing programs like CorelDraw and Canvas. However, they won't work with any of the quilt design programs currently on the market.

Drawing tablets are relatively costly at about $150 to $300 for a small one. You should consider buying one if you plan to design quilts with a drawing program like CorelDraw, because they're helpful for creating freehand-drawn appliqués and stencils. On the other hand, you can get by perfectly well without one. So before you spend the dough, take a look at how you're using your computer to design quilts. If, after a few months, you find yourself spending aggravating hours trying to draw with your mouse, you might be a candidate for a drawing tablet.

JUDY & GLORIA'S QUILTER-CHEAPSKATE DRAWING TABLET BUYING TIP

A color scanner will prove more useful to you than a drawing tablet. You can use a scanner to create quick appliqué patterns, put pictures of your quilts and other stuff on the Internet, and just goof around. Drawing tablets are great toys but they're not a necessity.

BUYING TIPS

Here's what to keep in mind when you go shopping for a drawing tablet:

- Typically, the **smaller** tablets (4 by 5 inches or so) will do fine. But we like the extra room of the 6-by-8-inch ones, which retail for about $300. These tablets run all the way up to 18 by 25 inches in size. You'll probably need a larger one only if you design clothing patterns or trace paper patterns into computer-aided design software. We like the Wacom tablets. You can contact Wacom at 360/750-8882 or 800/922-9348, or at **http://www.wacom.com**.

- Consider the **stylus**. Some pens are heavier than others and need a heavy battery. Our favorite stylus comes with the Wacom tablets. It doesn't need a battery, and it feels like a normal pen. It is pressure sensitive, which means that the harder you press down while drawing the thicker your line, just like with a paintbrush. It also has a plastic eraser on top, which you can use to delete lines on your computer screen. (You can also use the eraser to delete text in word processors and spreadsheets—pretty nifty.)

- Finally, consider the **drawing software** you plan to use with the tablet. All the high-end drawing programs like CorelDraw work with these tablets, but if you'd rather not pay $500 for a drawing program, take a look at FutureWave's SmartSketch, available for about $80 for the PC version and about $70 for the

Macintosh version (800/619-6193), **http://www.macromedia.com/**. (We talk more about SmartSketch in Chapter 2.)

NOTE

None of the dedicated quilt design programs can import scanned images. To work with the images you scan, you'll need to use a drawing program like CorelDraw or Canvas 5.0 and/or a graphics manipulation program like Paint Shop Pro or LView.

Gloria sketched this drawing of her dog by tracing over a photograph on a drawing tablet. (See Chapter 15 to learn how.)

SHOULD I BUY A SCANNER?

JUDY & GLORIA'S QUILTER-CHEAPSKATE SCANNER BUYING TIP

For doing any type of textile design, a cheaper scanner with a lower resolution is preferable to a high-end desktop publishing scanner that will create large, unwieldy scans that may slow down your computer (or even crash it) when you try to fool around with it in your drawing or graphics program.

Definitely. Scanners are handy for getting a picture from a clip-art book, photo album, or drawing pad into your computer. They're also indispensable for getting pictures that you can place on the Internet if you're a store owner; in fact many store owners forgo pricey digital cameras, relying on a scanner instead.

Shop for a full-page scanner with a resolution of at least 300 dots per inch (dpi). (Don't be conned by a claim of a high "interpolated" dpi. Interpolated means that the scanner's real, or "optical," dpi is being boosted by the scanner's software. In other words, the software puts extra dots in your image to make its resolution look higher. Look on the box for the "optical dpi." That's the real measure of a scanner's resolution.) Obviously, you want a color scanner, not a black-and-white one. Shop for one that costs $300 or less. While an $800 full-page scanner with 1,200 dpi optical resolution is dandy, it's overkill for anyone but a desktop publishing whiz or graphic artist.

For about $100 or so, you can get a color handheld scanner, but you'll only be able to comfortably scan a picture the size of a snapshot. If you want to scan larger images with a handheld scanner, you'll have to scan them in strips and then piece them together—and those strips can be nearly impossible to piece together on the computer's screen. The small, cheap scanners that let you feed a single photo may also be all right for you, but we suggest something more versatile.

When you shop for a scanner, look at how it scans both color and gray-scale images. Also look closely at the software that comes with it. Ideally the software should let you manipulate your images by cropping them, adjusting their brightness and contrast, changing their colors, erasing portions, and so on. The software should also let you save the image in all the standard graphic formats, including .JPG, .TIFF, .BMP, and .PCX. Most of the software that comes with the major brands of scanners will probably fit the bill, but if not, download a copy of Paint Shop Pro from **http://www.jasc.com** and use it.

If you want to forgo the scanner, you can always take your pictures to a copy shop or service bureau and rent a scanner. But that can get old fast if you use scanned images regularly. Also, having a scanner on your desk gives you a fun way to play around and learn about computer graphics and image manipulation.

SHOULD I BUY ANY OTHER VIDEO HARDWARE?

Some quilters use video capture boards and video or digital cameras to capture images from their workroom and get them inside their computer. For the average quilter that's a pricey setup and one that is generally unnecessary. Figure on spending a couple of hundred dollars for the video capture card for your computer and another $200 to $500 for a low-end (read: low resolution, mediocre images) digital camera. If you have a camcorder, you can always skip the digital camera and hook the camcorder to a video capture board and snap digital photos that way.

You probably won't need to follow either route unless you're a store owner and you want to create brochures or put a catalog on the Internet. A simple scanner will suffice in most cases if your goal is simply to bring images into your computer. But if you want to post lots of images quickly, consider buying a cheap digital camera. It will provide a much quicker way to do that than having to ship rolls of film off for developing.

WHAT KIND OF MODEM SHOULD I BUY?

If your goal is to tap into online services like America Online and CompuServe or the Internet, you should get the fastest modem you can afford. But at the same time, make sure that your service offers a local phone number that you can connect to at your modem's fastest speed. At this writing, 28.8kbps V.34 modems are the norm (kbps stands for kilobits per second), but the 56.6kbps X2 modems are becoming the de facto standard. If you spring for a 56.6kbps modem, find out how you'll be able to upgrade it to the worldwide 56.6kbps standard—and if so how much it will cost you.

Don't worry about ISDN. Don't worry if the modem has voice mail or a speaker phone (you'll probably never use those things). And faxing with a modem is less relevant to most people's lives than they think. Ignore the software that comes with the modem; it's never any good. You can download better stuff from the Internet.

Buy an external modem (the kinds that sits on your table) if you don't mind paying the price difference (external modems cost about $20 to $50 more than internal ones that you pop inside your computer). External modems are a snap to install—you just plug them into the computer and connect them to your phone line. They're particularly nice because you can watch their flickering lights to see whether data is being transmitted, and they have a separate power switch that you can use to turn the modem off if there is a problem.

If you buy an internal modem, look for a 16-bit card if you have a PC. Before you buy, find out the name of your PC's BIOS and call the computer's manufacturer to find out if it suffers any incompatibilities with internal modem cards.

Consider modems from Hayes, MultiTech, and Motorola; avoid U.S. Robotics. And remember: Modems typically burn out in about three years (except for Hayes modems; they seem to last forever), so get a good warranty.

JUDY & GLORIA'S RULES FOR COMPUTER SHOPPING

RULE 1.   Never buy a computer from a cable TV shopping channel or any retailer that also sells cubic zirconium. Their computers are typically overpriced, and if they don't work you're probably out of luck.

RULE 2.   Shop lots of computer mail-order catalogs. Our favorites are PC Connection (800/800-5555) and Mac Connection (800/800-2222). Their prices are competitive with just about every other catalog, and you'll get great support.

RULE 3.   Never buy computer stuff from people on the Internet unless you absolutely know what you're doing and can see the merchandise first.

RULE 4.   Shopping for a computer is like shopping for a car—do your homework before you walk into a store. Before you start to shop seriously, list all the things you want and get an idea of the going rates, then stick to the list and keep your head. Remember, you can always bargain for lower prices and freebies. And yes, it is a man's world. Test shoppers for one consumer magazine found that women were routinely quoted higher prices than men when shopping for computers.

RULE 5.   Get *at least* a one-year warranty on your computer hardware. If it's going to break it will probably do so in the first year. Warranties that provide on-site service are even better.

RULE 6.   Don't buy the hottest computer on the market—it will be last year's overpriced computer soon enough. Instead, buy a computer that's been on the market for at least six months; that's where you'll find the best buys.

SHOULD I BUY A SEWING MACHINE THAT HOOKS UP TO A COMPUTER?

As if the computer wasn't enough to worry about, now you want to hook a sewing machine up to it! All of the leading sewing machine makers now sell high-end models that connect to home computers. The idea is that you design stitch patterns on the computer—like patterns for machine quilting or elaborate machine embroidery patterns. You transfer or download the pattern to the sewing machine's memory, and then stitch it. When you do the actual stitching, the sewing machine doesn't need to be hooked up to the computer.

These machines are expensive, retailing from $2,000 to $4,000. Some machine quilters and "surface embellishment" fans love them. But before you waltz into a sewing machine store with your credit card to snag one, know that they're not simple to use. What's more, sewing machine stores are often unable to provide the intensive instruction and technical support that these machines and their computer link-ups require (after all, they're not computer stores).

Too, the software you'll need to use to design the patterns on your PC usually isn't that keen. (There's none presently available for Macintosh computers. Some sewing machine stores advise Macintosh users to get SoftWindows so that they can use the PC software on their Macintosh.) For instance, it may be unable to import clip art or photos for you to use as the basis of your stitch design. Or it may import graphics, but it may not do a very good job tracing them with stitches. You'll need to place the stitches yourself by clicking stitch points with the mouse.

Still, lots of quilters on the Internet have and adore sewing machines that link to computers. If you're thinking of buying one, do as much research as possible. Find out if there are any Viking or Pfaff clubs in your area where you can hobnob with owners of these machines. Ask if the sewing machine stores in your city hold classes on working with the model of machine you're interested in buying. And by all means, e-mail quilters on the Internet who use these machines to find out how they like them and what problems they might be having. The "Quilter's Internet Yellow Pages" at the end of this book tells you how to link up with cyberspace support groups for Viking and Pfaff owners.

Join the Pfabulous Pfaff Pfan Club on the Internet and explore the mysteries of the rainbow buttons with Pfaffies around the world. Head to **http://www.kbs.net/** *on the Web. Subscription requires a small fee.*

COMPUTER STORE PEOPLE OFTEN DON'T KNOW A LOT ABOUT QUILTING— AND MAY NOT KNOW MUCH ABOUT COMPUTERS EITHER

What would you hear if you walked into a computer store and asked the clerks what kind of computer you'd need to design quilts? What would they tell you? Feeling impish one afternoon, Judy visited some computer stores to find out.

"What kind of computer would you recommend for designing quilts?" I asked clerks at Circuit City. No one knew. One finally summoned the manager, a wiry fellow with a big grin and oily hair. His name was Al.

"We hear that question all the time," said a grinning Al. "Microsoft has a software package for designing quilts."

"They do?" (Actually, they don't.)

"We don't have it in stock right now," Al said as he ran his hand over a rack, searching for the program, "but we usually do."

"Bill Gates is into everything," I said.

"He is, and this Microsoft quilting software is terrific. You can scan quilts, you can print quilts. You'll probably want a color printer to do that."

"What kind of computer will I need?" I asked.

"Any computer here will run it but all you'll need is something low-powered. You know, a little entry-level Pentium."

I thanked Al and drove to another computer store down the street, where I met Laurie.

Laurie also reported that quilters occasionally asked her to recommend computers, but her advice was the opposite of Al's.

"You'll want a high-end Pentium running Windows 95. Definitely," she said briskly, sweeping between counters of computers. "Something very sophisticated.

You'll need lots of memory and a fast processor. And a 17-inch monitor—maybe even bigger. A machine like that we'd have to special order."

I asked about software.

"You can use Paintbrush in Windows." She demonstrated on a nearby computer by drawing a neon yellow rectangle on the screen with a mouse. "See? You can draw a fabric strip that way."

At a Best Buy in the same shopping strip, I posed the question to two harried teenage clerks. They stopped pushing boxes of computers around to grin at each other, then introduced themselves as Steve and Frank.

"She'd probably want something generic hardware-wise," Steve shot to Frank. "What about software-wise?"

"Software-wise it would be a special order," Frank shot back.

"What about graphic-wise? CAD?"

"Graphic-wise would probably be generic too."

"Not necessarily, if it will be a special order software-wise."

"In that case you can never tell."

"Huh?" I said.

"You might like a Macintosh," piped Frank, leading me to an aisle of tan-colored computers.

"There are so many different ones," I marveled. "What's the difference between them?"

"They're actually all the same," said Frank. "The only difference is that some are faster than others." He added, "That means that when you give them software some go really fast."

"Won't I need a drawing wand or something like that?"

"You mean hardware-wise? You'd have to ask Steve. That's his specialty."

Since Steve had disappeared and Frank was unable to tell me anymore about the Macintoshes, I left, tired, frustrated, and vowing to buy mail order forever after.

CHAPTER 2

A QUILTER'S COMPUTER STORE ADVENTURES, CONTINUED: WHY YOU SHOULD BUY SOFTWARE AND HOW

Should you buy quilt design software? How about CD-ROMs of quilt blocks and fabric scans? Can you download stuff from the Internet? And why do you need to buy software at all?

Without software, a computer is little more than a pagan shrine to obfuscation. You may argue that it is that even with software. What is this software stuff? Software is made up of instructions that drive the computer. It often comes on a disk or CD-ROM. It can be downloaded from the Internet. You can write it yourself, but unless you feel some overwhelming spiritual urge to, you probably shouldn't bother. Software can make your computer into an accounting temp or a word-processing maven, or it can get you on the Internet. It cannot make your computer into a quilter—rest easy—but there are software packages for quilters. There is

- Software for designing pieced quilt blocks and appliqué patterns and printing patterns

- Software with hundreds of traditional quilt block designs that you can size and print

- Software doodads like screen savers of quilt designs and bargello patterns

- Disks of images of real fabric that you can use in your quilt designs

  Which of these should you buy? Wait! You have one more option:

- Drawing software that you can use to design both contemporary and traditional quilts and appliqué patterns

---

A NOTE ABOUT THE TUTORIALS IN THIS BOOK

Quilters use so many different software products for designing quilts, from general-purpose drawing programs to quilt design software, it was hard to assemble a book of design-based tutorials that would help everyone with their particular software. We've tried to focus our tutorials on the quilt design software that quilters like and use the most.

For better or worse, the general drawing programs that quilters use most often are CorelDraw on the PC, and Canvas and SuperPaint on the Mac. As we've pointed out in this chapter, we think there are better and cheaper alternatives. But so far, not a lot of quilters use those alternatives. But the drawing software world is changing. Many new low-cost but high-powered drawing programs are entering the scene. There's also been a convergence in features and interfaces between both high-powered and budget programs, between PC and Mac worlds. Miraculously, most drawing tools work the same in all drawing programs, and increasingly they look the same too. We've built this book around this constancy. So you'll find that the CorelDraw instructions and procedures have parallels in low-cost but less feature-laden programs like SmartSketch for the PC. The directions in this book for Canvas on the Mac will work with Canvas for the PC as well as with our favorite low-cost Macintosh alternative to Canvas, Deneba artWorks.

WHAT SOFTWARE SHOULD I BUY TO DESIGN QUILTS?

At this point you're probably wondering what we recommend. You want a quick answer. You love to shop, but for fabric or patterns. Orbiting kiosks of shrink-wrapped boxes is a big yawn. This is what we think you should buy. As you can see from the table, we're opinionated. Not everyone will agree with our recommendations. But hey, you picked up this book because you wanted our advice, and we're giving it to you. We give addresses for purchasing these and other programs in the table at the end of this chapter.

JUDY & GLORIA'S PICKS FOR QUILT DESIGN SOFTWARE

THE KIND OF COMPUTER YOU HAVE	WHAT YOU SHOULD BUY TO DESIGN QUILTS	WHY
An old PC with an 8088 processor, circa 1987 or earlier, running DOS	Your choices are limited. You may be able to find a simple drawing program in a secondhand computer store, but we recommend that you trade this dinosaur in for a newer beast.	You'll drive yourself bonkers trying to find a way to design quilts on a machine like this.
An 80286- or 80386-based PC running DOS	If you're new to computer quilt design, buy the $64.95 BlockBase from The Electric Quilt Company. Electric Quilt, for $110, is another fine choice. It would not be unwise to consider buying them both.	Electric Quilt is the niftiest quilt design software on the market. It comes with over a thousand built-in pieced block and appliqué patterns, and it also lets you draw your own. You can lay out your blocks in oodles of quilt layout schemes, and you can color them with hundreds of fabric designs that you'll find in stores. You can create stencils and border designs. You can even put your pattern into a brochure together with instructions to pass out at classes. BlockBase is not actually a design program. It's a collection of 3,500 quilt patterns—a computerized version of Barbara Brackman's *Encyclopedia of Pieced Quilt Patterns*. You can size the blocks, color them with fabric designs, and print their patterns. But you can't lay them out in a quilt design or draw your own blocks. You can use BlockBase's patterns with Electric Quilt but not with other programs.
A PC running Windows 3.x or Windows 95	If you don't mind running DOS programs, try Electric Quilt or BlockBase from Electric Quilt. If you prefer Windows, buy Quilt-Pro ($95) by Quilt-Pro Systems. CorelDraw by Corel Corp. The latest version lists at about $700 (ouch!). Corel has discontinued its practice of selling older versions for under $100, but it is still possible to find these old versions bundled with some low-cost printers. Now that's a buy. Comparable, but cheaper, high-end drawing programs are Macromedia's Freehand and Canvas 3.5 for the PC. Both list for about $400. If you're not familiar with pricey programs but are interested in using a drawing program, start by downloading from the Internet some of the trial versions of lower-cost drawing programs mentioned later.	In addition to Electric Quilt and BlockBase described above, you should also consider Quilt-Pro by Quilt-Pro Systems. Quilt-Pro is similar to Electric Quilt except that it's a Windows program. (In other words, it uses the Windows interface, letting you cut and paste between it and other programs.) Some quilters prefer its more vibrant graphic style. It offers more than a thousand built-in block styles. As with Electric Quilt, you can lay them out in numerous styles, color them with fabric fills, calculate yardage, and print stencils. Many quilters prefer a high-end drawing program like CorelDraw. The drawback is that such programs are tough to learn, and you have to draw everything from scratch—they come with no predrawn Maple Leaf blocks. That can be a grind. You can lose patience fast. We recommend that if you're starting out designing quilts on a computer, you get a copy of a quilt design program and later supplement it with a drawing program.

THE KIND OF COMPUTER YOU HAVE	WHAT YOU SHOULD BUY TO DESIGN QUILTS	WHY
A Macintosh 68020 to 68040 running System 7 or higher with 8MB RAM	Deneba artWorks ($49.95) SuperPaint from Adobe Systems ($50) Canvas 3.5 from Deneba Corp. ($399) Quilt-Pro for Macintosh from Quilt-Pro Systems ($95)	We highly recommend Deneba artWorks. It's inexpensive and has all of the important drawing tools you need. You can also create some great texture fills with ease. SuperPaint combines drawing, painting, and some image-processing capabilities. It is also a great bargain. Creating quilt blocks is a snap; there are great tools for curved lines, appliqué shapes, and special effects; and the painting program gives you the ability to create some nifty fabric-like fills. If you have the extra money, Canvas 3.5 is worth the investment. It has a great assortment of tools for quilt design, layers, multiple-level zoom, great special effects, and more. Quilt-Pro is our top choice for Macintosh quilt-specific software because, in addition to creating geometric blocks, laying out, calculating yardage, and printing templates for blocks and paper piecing, you can also create appliqué designs. It has an arc and a Bezier Curve tool, plus other features we think you'll enjoy.
A Macintosh with a PowerPC chip and at least 16MB RAM	Canvas 5.0 ($599), as well as any of the above software	Canvas version 3.5 is still a good choice, but buy an upgrade version if you can. We like working with the easy-to-customize palettes.

How about all those other goodies, like disks of digitized fabrics and quilt block screen savers? Skip 'em. You can make your own screen splash with a quilt block pattern (you'll find directions at the end of this chapter). You can also scan your own fabrics (Chapter 16 shows you how) and use them in quilt designs. But while Hoffman prints dancing around a computer screen may elicit "Oooh"s from fellow quilt guild members, it's not all that practical to design with calicos swimming over your screen. You'll never get the color and print density of the fabric as it appears on the computer screen to match the way it will actually look in a quilt. We also believe it's often wiser to design a quilt in shades of gray, at least initially, and worry about the colors later. We talk about that in Chapter 10.

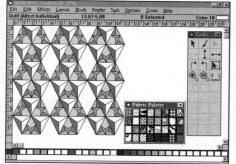

Designing quilts is a snap in quilt design programs like Quilt-Pro.

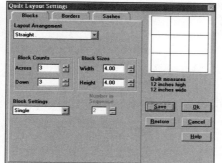

To lay out a quilt in Quilt-Pro, you merely "tab" through the folders, click on the design elements, and specify their number and size.

DENEBA ARTWORKS

The artWorks tool box with the Bezier curve option selected.

If you're a Mac user and you haven't yet purchased a drawing program, Deneba artWorks is the one you want. We think Deneba artWorks is the best-kept secret in the Mac quilting world. It retails for $49.95 and includes a CD-ROM with 500 fonts and 8,000 clip-art images. It contains all of the needed drawing tools—line, rectangle, oval, arc, polygon, and Bezier curve, among others. It has snap-to-grid, rulers, zooming features, and auto-trace abilities. This program even has the ability to work in layers. It's made by Deneba, the people who make Canvas.

The Canvas opening screen.

The opening screen for Deneba artWorks.

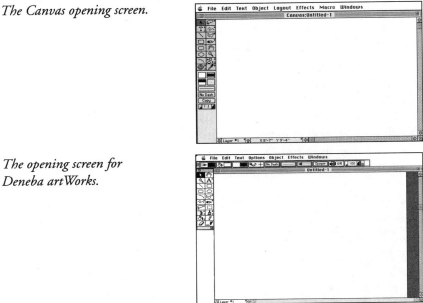

Compare the artWorks opening screen to the Canvas 3.5 screen, and it's easy to see that artWorks is essentially a baby Canvas 3.5. Look at the menu bar. The Macro menu is missing from artWorks, and there is an Options menu instead of a Layout menu. But by opening up the menu bar items, you'll discover that the features that make Canvas 3.5 such a joy to design quilts with are included in artWorks.

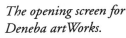

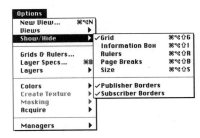

Show/hide opened under the Options menu in artWorks.

Managers opened under the Options menu.

The Object menu with the Arrange submenu showing the shuffling options.

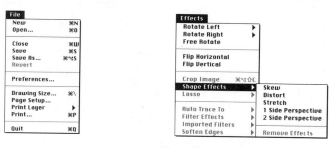

The File menu.   *The Effects menu.*

The Options menu is where you go to set up your grids and rulers and to display them. You'll also find the Managers command on the Option menu. This is where the Auto-Trace tool is located. The Object menu contains selections for scaling, shuffling items, grouping, and so on. The Drawing Size command is located on the File menu. Just as in Canvas 3.5, the Effects menu contains commands for rotating, flipping, and special shape effects—skew, distort, stretch, and one- and two-point perspective.

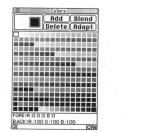

The color palette showing the option buttons.   *The Color Manager.*

The color and pattern fills, pen width, dashed lines, and zooming features all work essentially the same as in Canvas 3.5, but the palette for these items is located along the top of the document. You won't find a Pantone® color palette, but by "tearing off" the Color palette to keep it open, you'll discover buttons for color options. Clicking on the Add button brings up the Color Manager, where you can mix whatever color you need, so you'll never miss the Pantone® colors (unless you're a professional illustrator).

We are so impressed with this program that we recommend it to any Mac computer owner even thinking of designing a quilt on the computer. Sure, it's missing the more advanced tools—things like the smart mouse feature, parallel tool, dimensioning tools, and the x and y coordinates that are a part of Canvas 3.5. But we believe the average quilter will not miss these features. Many of the tutorials for Canvas 3.5 in this book can be applied to artWorks.

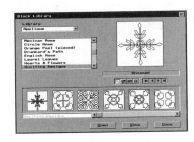

Quilt-Pro (and Electric Quilt) calculates the fabric you need for the quilts you design.

You'll find over a thousand traditional and innovative quilt block designs in Electric Quilt's block library.

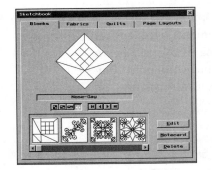

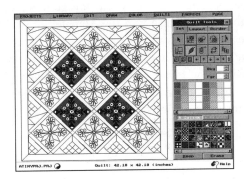

In Electric Quilt you select blocks, fabrics, and quilt layout elements from the program's library, saving them in a sketchbook. You create a sketchbook for each project that you design, and you then select elements from the sketchbook as you lay out and refine your quilt.

Laying out and coloring quilts in Electric Quilts is a snap. You can test different color schemes and fabric patterns, as well as change the layout and blocks as you work.

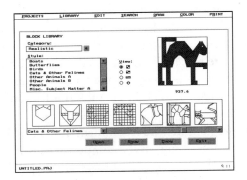

BlockBase is an electronic version of Barbara Brackman's Encyclopedia of Pieced Quilt Designs, *with more than 3,500 quilt block patterns. You can use the patterns with Electric Quilt or color them, resize them, and print them. You can also use them with other programs that support their file format, but not all do.*

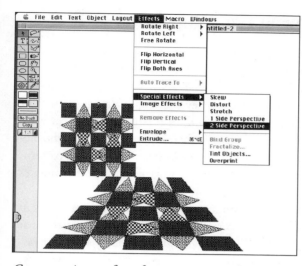

Canvas 3.5 is one of our favorite programs for quilt design on the Macintosh. Tools like two-point perspective can create very interesting effects.

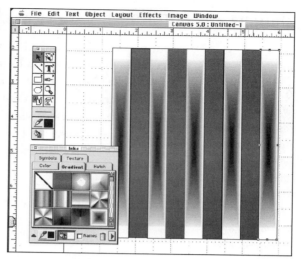

Canvas 5.0 has inks, textures, and gradient fills that version 3.5 lacks. But if you don't have a PowerPC chip, don't bother getting it—it will be too slow! Besides, some of the fun tools, like two-point perspective, are not included in Canvas 5.0.

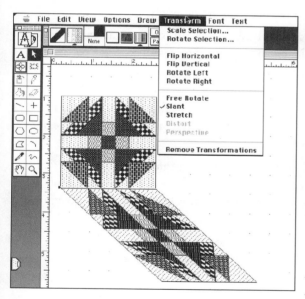

Inexpensive SuperPaint has unique draw and paint layers that make it a great choice for quilters with Macs. Fun tools like the slant, stretch, distort, and perspective allow you to give your blocks a whole new angle.

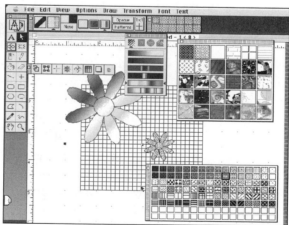

SuperPaint has great fill patterns, tools for creating fun shapes, and an easy way to create good-looking fabric fills.

SHOULD I BUY QUILT DESIGN SOFTWARE OR DRAWING SOFTWARE?

Your major decision when buying software for quilt design will be whether to buy specialized quilt design software like Electric Quilt or general-purpose drawing software like CorelDraw or SuperPaint.

The advantage of quilt design software is that everything is already drawn for you. The pieced block designs (think of it, thousands of them!), appliqué patterns, stencils, borders, even the layouts and fabrics are there. You simply pick the elements you want, lay them out, color them, and voilà! You have your quilt pattern. Electric Quilt and Quilt-Pro will even calculate fabric yardage and print templates for you.

What's more, Electric Quilt and Quilt-Pro are easy to learn to use. And if you call for tech support, not only will someone answer the phone (a rare occurrence at some computer companies), but they will offer advice and sympathy (another rarity at some companies). They may even give you quilting advice, because these companies hire quilters to answer tech support calls—something you can be sure they don't make an effort to do at Corel Corp.

But quilt design packages have their drawbacks too, namely,

- They pretty much restrict you to designing quilts with square block designs, though there are exceptions. You can do some fancy stuff in Electric Quilt and Quilt-Pro (see some of the design chapters to see what we mean), designing innovative quilt tops. But the drawing tools are otherwise pretty limited.

- They won't let you import a scanned image or clip art to use as the basis of a quilt or an appliqué design. You might want to do that to design appliqué patterns.

- They won't let you transform quilt blocks or designs in some of the ways that drawing programs are capable of, like pulling the design around the screen, overlapping it with other parts of the design, or transforming its perspective. Electric Quilt and Quilt-Pro let you do some of these things to a certain extent, but not like drawing programs do.

- Their drawing tools are basic. You get lines and a Bezier tool to draw curves, and that's about it. You also can't draw in layers like you can in a high-end drawing program, something that comes in handy, especially when drawing appliqué patterns.

- You can't easily export your designs to use in other quilt design or drawing programs. Quilt-Pro lets you export block designs, but they don't come through cleanly—lines and colorings tend to vanish, and sometimes the block breaks into pieces.

- They're quirky. Sometimes Electric Quilt behaves badly in the presence of certain mouse drivers. In Quilt-Pro it can be hard to "group" patches to create a block and then move the block without having it fall to pieces. On the other hand, these packages are the products of home-based businesses, and for what they do they're *pretty darn impressive*.

Still, these nits aside, for under $150, these quilt design programs are a great buy.

What about drawing programs like CorelDraw? Drawing programs give you far more powerful drafting and image-manipulation features than quilt design software does, but holy cowabunga, they can be a pain to learn to use. Not only that, but you have to draw all your quilt blocks from scratch. And your stencils. And your borders. Some computer quilting nerds don't mind that. They pride themselves on their ability to extract a nine-patch from any $500 drawing program, no matter how illogically it functions. And face it, these drawing programs can be pretty powerful design tools. Many quilt artists couldn't live without them.

Drawing programs can be expensive. CorelDraw currently lists for about $700. It became popular with quilters because Corel used to sell superseded versions of the program for under $100, but it's since discontinued the practice. You'll still find older versions of CorelDraw bundled with many printers and computer systems, though.

STEPS TO HELP CHEAPSKATES BUY GOOD DRAWING SOFTWARE

DOWNLOAD DEMOS FROM THE INTERNET. Our software chart at the end of this chapter lists the Web sites for all the major drawing software companies whose products we think are suited for quilt design. Several offer nearly full-featured downloadable demos of their products—a good way to try out the program to see whether you like it.

TRY ONE OF THE LOW-COST DRAWING PROGRAMS FIRST. You can buy copies of the more expensive stuff later. Claris offers a free downloadable demo of ClarisDraw for PCs and Macs (about $130) at **http://www.claris.com/**. Another good low-cost program for PCs is SmartSketch (under $50) from FutureWave (now owned by Macromedia) (**http://www.futurewave.com**). Macintosh users should try Deneba artWorks (under $50).

OLDER VERSIONS OF SOFTWARE ARE SOMETIMES BETTER THAN THE NEW ONES. We put the latest versions of various high-end drawing programs through their paces and discovered that, when it comes to quilt designing, old versions at least suffice and are often superior to the latest versions. (This makes sense. Once a software publisher has a good product, it often updates it by just stuffing it full of more and more frivolous features that few people need.)

Take Canvas, for example. Canvas 5 has many features we doubt you'll use. It's expensive and intimidating for the novice user. Canvas 3.5, however, is more user-friendly and less expensive. We think CorelDraw 7 is overkill and has more gewgaws than we need; versions 5 and even 3 were in some ways better suited for quilt designing because of their simplicity. Those old versions of CorelDraw still pop up on occasion. You can sometimes find them bundled with low-cost printers—we think that's a bargain. If you happen to spot one and need a printer, snap it up.

Some software companies like Deneba sell old versions of their high-end programs at a significant discount. Always ask if such versions are available.

SHOP AT SECONDHAND COMPUTER STORES OR BUY OLDER VERSIONS OF SOFTWARE FROM OTHER QUILTERS. Secondhand computer stores can be great places to pick up old but perfectly sufficient versions of drawing software.

DO YOUR HOMEWORK. Talk to other quilters about what they're using to design quilts.

BOTTOM LINE. If you're just getting started using your computer to design quilts and you have a PC-compatible, we recommend Electric Quilt's BlockBase. If you're a more seasoned computer user, and if you have money to spend, get a copy of Electric Quilt and consider supplementing it with a low-cost drawing program, if you want a little more design capability. If you have a Macintosh, get a copy of Deneba artWorks.

DESIGNING QUILTS WITH A DRAWING PROGRAM VERSUS A PAINT PROGRAM, OR WHY CORELDRAW LACKS A SPRAY CAN AND AN ERASER

Understanding the difference between drawing programs and paint programs will help you both select the proper program and learn to use it.

When you whip out CorelDraw or another similar drawing program for the first time, you'll probably feel a profound sense of irritation after squiggling the pencil tool over the screen for a few minutes. Why does the program keep deleting entire lines when you want to erase only portions of lines? Why does it keep coloring the entire quilt block that you've drawn when you only want to color a patch? And why isn't there a spray can with which you can spray color over portions of your drawing?

Welcome to the world of drawing programs.

There are two different types of programs with which you can draw, and they're as different as North and South America:

- Paint programs draw by placing individual dots, or pixels, on the screen. They're called "bit-mapped" because they define objects as collections of bits. Think of them as being like crayons. You have your "fat bits" of crayons and your "little bits," etc.

- Drawing programs draw by defining each line as a separate mathematical entity. They're called "vector-mapped" because they draw by defining paths between points. Think of them as the precision drafting tools of an architect or engineer.

The Paint program built into Windows is a paint program. CorelDraw and other high-end drawing programs that quilters like to use are drawing programs. SuperPaint for the Macintosh is a pleasant combination of the best of both worlds, which makes it easy for newcomers to computer graphics to use.

What difference does this make to quilters? If you draw a square in a paint program, the computer considers it a collection of dots. They may be white dots, or they may be purple. If you draw a square in a drawing program, the computer regards it as a mathematically defined line.

You can draw squares in a paint program, but you can't manipulate them.

With a drawing program, each object you draw can be moved and manipulated independently of the other objects on the screen.

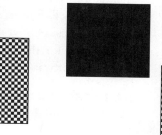

Draw a second square on top the first in a paint program, and the computer thinks you are simply adding more dots to your image. But draw a second square on top of the first in a drawing program, and the program will think that you're adding another separate line, or object, to your drawing.

In the case of the paint program, no matter what you add to the drawing, the computer thinks of it as a single, unified image or collection of pixels. But each time you add something new to a drawing in a drawing program, the program regards it as a new and distinct object.

The difference between the two becomes clear when you try to change your drawing. In the paint program, you can't click on a square or other shape and resize it or move it, but you can in the drawing program. However, in the paint program, when you want to delete something, you pull out the eraser tool and rub it over the screen and the pixels vanish. You can't do that in a drawing program. You must select an individual line or element to delete, and the program will delete the whole thing.

What this means to you is that while you can technically draw a quilt block in a drawing program like Windows Paint, it's going to be a lot like drawing with those big chunks of pastel chalk that the kids draw with on the driveway. You can't do things like snap lines to a dimensional grid, or resize and reshape elements, or even form patches—feats that are essential to computer quilt designing. You're going to need a drawing program. But it also means that you're going to have to learn your way around that peculiar vector world of drawing programs, and that can take time. As many quilters have found, however, it's not too hard, so long as you give up looking for an eraser tool.

IS THERE OTHER SOFTWARE I SHOULD BUY?

T * I * P

You probably got Internet software of some sort with your computer. If you didn't, head to Chapter 20 for our recommendations.

As we mentioned in the last chapter, we tend to be underwhelmed by the surprise boxes full of second-rate software and CDs that come with computers these days. If you are disappointed with what came with your computer, here are some recommendations for programs we couldn't live without. They are listed in the order in which they will find relevancy in your life.

Be skeptical of anything else you might be inclined to buy when taking a computer home for the first time. And remember, you can download demos of just about any software you're interested in from the Internet.

HANDY SOFTWARE FOR PC-COMPATIBLES

Here's a list and description of software you'll want to add to your collection.

PAINT SHOP PRO BY JASC, INC., 800/622-2793 OR 612/930-9800

You'll need this shareware program to crop and spruce up images like photos as well as to convert them to different graphic formats, whether for use in quilt design or for putting pictures on the Internet. You can download it from the Internet at **http://www.jasc.com/**. If you like it, the company asks that you send them $69. Do it. Paint Shop Pro is indispensable.

VIRUSAFE FROM ELIASHIM

ViruSafe scans files and disks for viruses, nasty things that can turn your computer into digital cacciatore. It also monitors your computer's memory for invaders. Use it to scan disks that you bring home from work or borrow from friends, as well as files that you download from the Internet. Lots of home computers are infected with viruses through these channels. There are many commercially available virus scanners, but ViruSafe is consistently better at detecting viruses than lots of name-brand products and it's free. Look for it on the Internet at **http://www.virusafe.com/**.

LOTUS ORGANIZER BY LOTUS

If you're a quilt teacher, author, or frequent show-goer, personal information manager, or PIM, software can provide a indispensable way of keeping track of classes and projects. These programs include calendars, phone books, and various project organizers. The best is Lotus Organizer, with a street price of about $80.

MICROSOFT WORD

If Windows Works came bundled with your PC, its built-in word processor may be sufficient for your needs. But if you're designing quilt patterns to sell or have a store for which you want to design brochures, you'll find that the desktop publishing features in Word (about $300 street price) can't be beat. You can incorporate into Word documents quilt designs created in Quilt-Pro, as well as ones from CorelDraw or other high-end drawing programs. You can also add clip art and other froufrous. (Electric Quilt 3 and later versions offer a pattern layout feature that lets you combine instructions with patterns designed in EQ. If you have EQ that may be all you need.) You can even use Word's drawing feature to design quilts if you like (although it's not as easy as with a drawing program).

QUICKEN BY INTUIT

Want to keep track of those mounting fabric bills? Okay, you'd rather not. But perhaps you have other financial chores, like squeezing something out of the monthly budget for food and heat. You can use the spreadsheet feature in Microsoft Works to track bills and expenses, and that may be all you need. But if you want to feel truly in control of your mounds of bills and do things like draw pie charts of how much money is being sucked out each month by mail-order swatch clubs, Quicken's for you. It's also great for bookkeeping chores of small businesses. You can download a demo version at **http://www.intuit.com/**. The full version costs $25 to $40 street price, depending on the package.

HANDY SHAREWARE FOR MACINTOSHES

Here's a list of Macintosh shareware you'll want to add to your collection. The quickest way to download these programs is to go to C|Net's shareware library at **http://www.shareware.com**.

SHAREDRAW BY PIERCE SOFTWARE, INFO@PIERCESW.COM

This is an amazing, full-featured drawing program, including grids, textures, and drawing tools such as polygons, squares, arcs, and so on. It requires System 7 or later. Shareware: $29.95.

GRAPHIC CONVERTER BY LEMKE SOFTWARE, 100102.1304@COMPUSERVE.COM

This is a must-have for converting graphic files into various formats, including JPEG/JFIF, MacPaint, PICT, TIFF, BMP-Windows, ESPF, GIF, and many others. It requires System 7 or later.

The file name to download is **mac/multimedia/graphiccon27.sit.hqx**. Shareware: $35.

GIFCONVERTER BY KEVIN MITCHELL, KAM@KAMIT.COM

This program lets you view GIF, TIFF, RIFF, JPEG, RLE, PICT, and other graphic file formats. It also lets you save to any of these formats or print them to any Mac printer. Download from **http://www.kamit.com/gifconverter.html**. Shareware: $30 for key to remove reminder message, $45 for disks and manual.

DISINFECTANT BY JOHN NORSTAD, J-NORSTAD@NWU.EDU

Virus protection, scanning, and removal. And it's free! Requires System 7 or later. Download from **http://www.shareware.com**.

STUFFIT EXPANDER BY ALADDIN SYSTEMS

Another must-have, and it's free! This program decompresses files in any of the StuffIt formats and Compact Pro format. Requires System 7 or later. General info: **http://www.aladdinsys.com**; download from **http://www.aladdinsys.com/consumer/updates.html**.

ZIPIT BY TOM BROWN, TBROWN@DORSAI.ORG; THOMAS.A.BROWN@YALE.EDU; TOMMY6@AOL.COM; 70314.3342@COMPUSERVE.COM

A Zip utility for the Mac. This program creates and decompresses PKZip files, the popular PC compression program. Requires System 7 or later. Shareware: $15. Download from **ftp://ftp.awa.com/pub/softlock/mac/products/zipit/zipit-135.hqx**.

COLORDESIGN 1.2 FOR THE MACINTOSH BY MOMENTUM SOFTWARE

ColorDesign is a fun program, great for quilters who love to explore symmetry and color. It basically works like this: You select a shape, symmetry, and color, then click with the mouse inside the work area. The program generates the shape in the selected symmetry and color. Click again to create more shapes and colors. You're literally clicking your way into all sorts of interesting designs.

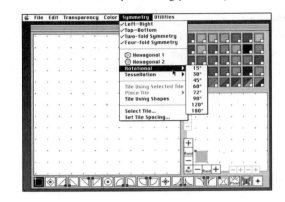

ColorDesign symmetry options.

With a click on a submenu selection, you can choose two-fold symmetry, four-fold symmetry, and rotational and tessellation effects.

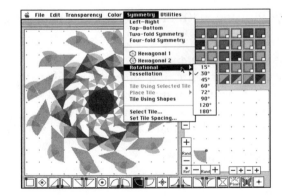

A design created with ColorDesign.

You can select a simple shape and orientation (such as a square or triangle) from the shape menu that runs along the bottom of the program window. Or you can select a shape and customize it. You can tile shapes and generate kaleidoscopic designs. Colors can be transparent or opaque, or you can choose blends and tints. You can select the color you want to work with or let the program select it for you at random. (The color palette is based on your computer, meaning that if you have 24-bit color, you have access to millions of colors.)

Canvas 3.5 users will recognize the Xor setting in the transparency menu for creating positive/negative designs.

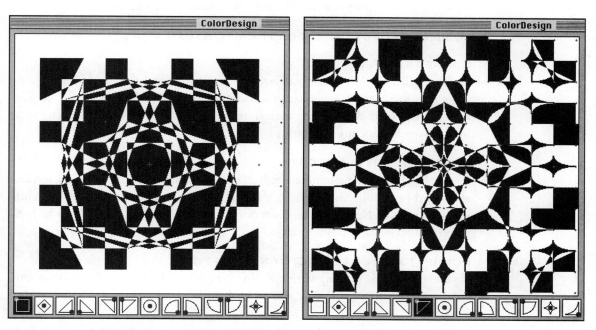

Designs created with the Xor setting in ColorDesign.

There are a few patterns fills you can work with, and the program can generate some textures—the very clear manual explains exactly how it all works.

As fun as this program is to play with, it is not quilt-specific—for example, it doesn't create templates or calculate yardage. It's also not a drawing program. You can't, for example, select a portion of the design and delete it. You also cannot select a shape and drag it to alter it; instead, you need to select buttons to make changes to a shape.

You can print your designs (you'll want a color inkjet printer), but you cannot save a design as anything other than a PICT file. Nor can you copy and paste any of your creations. To translate a design into a usable quilt pattern, it's best to stick with shapes you're comfortable working with, like squares or triangles, and to keep the image simple. To play with your creations further, you can import the PICT file into Canvas or SuperPaint. We experienced no problems with exporting or importing.

ColorDesign quickly creates designs based on repetition, shapes, and color. It's a fun, addictive tool—great for igniting the imagination. It won't replace your quilt design or drawing program, but it certainly is a nice addition.

See the table "Where to Get Quilt Design Software (and What It Costs)" on page <xx> for information on purchasing ColorDesign software.

URL MANAGER PRO BY ALCO BLOM

This program helps maintain all of your favorite Internet addresses in a hierarchical database. It supports the Mac's drag-and-drop capability. Requires System 7 or later. Shareware: $25. Download from **http://www.shareware.com**.

COMMERCIAL SOFTWARE FOR THE MACINTOSH

QUICKEN BY INTUIT

See the earlier section on PC software for a description of this bookkeeping software. Requires a 68030 or better processor; 6MB RAM with System 7.0 or 7.1; 8MB RAM with System 7.5 or later; and 12MB free disk space. Intuit's Web site is at **http://www.intuit.com/**. About $40.

CLARISWORKS BY CLARIS CORP.

If your Macintosh came bundled with this program, use it. It contains very serviceable word-processing, spreadsheet, drawing, database, and web page design software, as well as Netscape Navigator for Internet access. Claris's Web site is at **http://www.claris.com**. About $100.

NOW UP-TO-DATE & CONTACT BY NOW SOFTWARE

If your calendar is bulging with teaching schedules, class schedules, notes about what quilts are in what shows, and all of the other to-dos in life, you'll want this program.

It's a user-friendly personal information manager (PIM) that includes calendars, alarm reminders, and to-do lists. It also keeps track of names, addresses, and phone numbers, and there are e-mail links for Eudora, America Online, and other services. You can download a demo from **http://www.nowsoftware.com**. About $100.

ADOBE PHOTODELUXE

This is inexpensive image-editing software, perfect for novice users. For under $100, you have access to tools such as brightness/contrast, hue, and saturation and excellent interactive tutorials.

T * I * P

Computer mail-order catalogs like PC Connection (800/800-5555) and Mac Connection (800/800-2222) offer the lowest prices on software packages from big-name vendors. You'll often find the "street prices" for software packages to be hundreds of dollars lower than the manufacturer's listed retail price in catalogs. While catalogs are the places to shop for that pricey drawing program, they unfortunately don't carry any of the quilt design programs.

WHERE TO GET QUILT DESIGN SOFTWARE (AND WHAT IT COSTS)

The table in this section tells where you can find out about and purchase the quilt design software we discuss in this book. For our top recommendations, see "Judy & Gloria's Picks for Quilt Design Software" at the beginning of this chapter. A few of the companies listed here sell demos (or at least were planning to as this book went to press). Give them a call and ask about a demo before you buy. Also ask about a money-back guarantee, since some of the companies offer one.

HOT TIP!

Find out what folks on the Internet are saying about the latest versions of these programs at Planet Patchwork http://www.planetpatchwork.com/qltprogs.htm.

NOTE

Product information changes like the tides. Before sending money to any of these companies, call to ask for recent prices as well as shipping fees, and to verify system requirements.

PRODUCT	COMPANY	PRICE	DOWNLOADABLE VERSION OR DEMO?	COMPUTER REQUIREMENTS	COMMENTS
QUILT DESIGN PROGRAMS					
Electric Quilt	The Electric Quilt Company 1039 Melrose St. Bowling Green, OH 43402 800/356-4219 or 419/352-1134 http://www.wcnet.org/ ElectricQuiltCo/ equiltco@wcnet.org	$110	No	PC-compatible with 286 or higher processor, DOS 5.0 or later, 640KB RAM, VGA or higher graphics, 10MB free hard disk space. Runs under DOS, Windows 3.x, or Windows 95.	A top recommendation. See "Judy & Gloria's Picks."
BlockBase	The Electric Quilt Company (see above)	$64.95	No	PC-compatible with 286 or higher processor, DOS 3.0 or later, 640KB RAM, VGA or higher graphics, 6MB free hard disk space. Runs under DOS, Windows 3.x, or Windows 95.	A top recommendation. See "Judy & Gloria's Picks." 3,500 quilt patterns that you can resize, color, and print.
Quilt-Pro	Quilt-Pro Systems P.O. Box 560692 The Colony, TX 75056 214/625-7765 or 800/884-1511 http://www.quiltpro.com/ salamon1@airmail.net	$95	No	PC version: 386 or higher processor, Windows 3.0 or later, 4MB RAM, VGA or higher graphics, 10MB free hard disk space. Mac version: Mac II or higher with System 7 or later, 4MB RAM, Color Quick Draw.	A top recommendation. See "Judy & Gloria's Picks."
QuiltSoft	QuiltSoft P.O. Box 19946 San Diego, CA 92159 619/583-2970	$99	Yes	PC version: Windows 3.x or 95; 486 or higher processor, 8MB RAM, 8MB free hard disk space. Mac version: System 7 or later, 4MB RAM, 2MB free hard disk space.	Good for creating quick block patterns. Includes layout and yardage calculation. Prints patterns and templates.
VQuilt	Computer Systems Associates P.O. Box 129 Jarrettsville, MD 21084 410/557-6871 pnh@clark.net	$39.95	No	PC-compatible with 286 or higher processor, 500KB RAM, DOS 3.0 or greater.	Simple, DOS-based design program; inexpensive and without lots of frills. Has lots of fans, for good reason.
PCQuilt	Nina Antze 7061 Lynch Rd. Sebastopol, CA 95472 800/731-8886 http://www.pcquilt.com/ antze@pcquilt.com	$75 for PC version; $35 for Mac version	Mac demo available for $5 by mail or from America Online (look in Computer/Macintosh/Graphics).On the Internet, download it from ftp.hawaii.edu / mirrors/ info-mac/app/ pc-quilt-demo.hqx or ftp.luth.se /pub/ mac/demo.	PC version: Windows 3.x or 95; 386 or higher processor; 8MB RAM. Mac version: System 7 or later.	A no-frills quilt block design program. Make changes to a block and see them appear instantly in the quilt layout. Limited block and fabric selection, but elegant interface. And you can try the Mac version before you buy it. PCQuilt was the first computer quilt designing program ever, and it's matured nicely.

PRODUCT	COMPANY	PRICE	DOWNLOADABLE VERSION OR DEMO?	COMPUTER REQUIREMENTS	COMMENTS
PC Patch for DOS	Stitch Designs 5523 South 700 West Murray, UT 84123 801/269-1948	$80 for PC	Demo is $5 plus $2 s/h by mail.	PC: 386 or higher processor.	Generates geometric designs and prints templates.

GENERAL-PURPOSE DRAWING PROGRAMS

PRODUCT	COMPANY	PRICE	DOWNLOADABLE VERSION OR DEMO?	COMPUTER REQUIREMENTS	COMMENTS
CorelDraw	Corel Corp. 1600 Carling Ave. Ottawa, Ontario, Canada CD K1Z 8R7 800/772-6735 http://www.corel.com/	$695 for current PC version; the company no longer sells older versions, but some printer makers bundle CorelDraw 3 with their printers. $399 for Mac version	No	PC version 5: Windows 3.x, 386 or higher processor, 8MB RAM. PC version 7: Windows 95 or NT, Pentium 60 or faster processor, 16MB RAM, 40MB free hard disk space. Mac version 6: PowerPC processor, System 7.5 or later; 20MB RAM, 40MB free hard disk space; 256-color monitor.	A top recommendation. See "Judy & Gloria's Picks."
Freehand	Macromedia 600 Townsend St., Suite 310 W San Francisco, CA, 94103 800/989-3762 http://www.macromedia.com/	$399.95	No	PC version: Windows 95/NT, 486/50 or higher processor, 16MB RAM, 70MB free hard disk space. Mac version: System 7 or later (System 7.5 for xRes), 68040 processor, PowerPC processor or higher for xRes, 16MB RAM, 70MB free hard disk space.	An excellent drawing program, and much cheaper than CorelDraw, but it takes a lot of learning. Still, it's popular with quilters.
Adobe Illustrator	Adobe Systems 1585 Charleston Rd. Mountain View, CA 94039 800/833-6687 http://www.adobe.com/	$495 for PC version; $595 for Mac version	No	PC version: Windows 3.x with 4MB RAM or Windows 95 with 8MB RAM, 386 or higher processor. Mac version: System 7 or later, 60820 or higher processor with 6MB RAM or Power Mac with 7MB RAM.	This is an excellent drawing program but with a steep learning curve. It's popular with quilters who really know their way around their computers.
Adobe SuperPaint	Adobe Systems (see above)	$99 for deluxe CD; $50 for regular version	No	Macintosh: System 6.0.7 or later, 2MB RAM, or 4MB RAM for System 7 or later.	A top recommendation. See "Judy & Gloria's Picks."
Canvas 3.5	Deneba Software 7400 SW 87th Ave. Miami, FL 33173 800/622-6827 http://www.deneba.com	$399	Yes; Mac and Windows demos available at company's Web site.	Windows 95 version: 486 or Pentium processor. Windows 3.x version: 286 or higher processor. Mac version: System 7 or later; 8MB RAM recommended.	A top recommendation for the Macintosh. See "Judy & Gloria's Picks." PC users should consider it as an alternative to CorelDraw.
Canvas 5.0	Deneba Software (see above)	$599	No	PC version: Windows 95 or NT, Pentium processor, 16MB RAM for Windows 95 or 24MB for Windows NT, VGA monitor and 8-bit display or better. Mac version: PowerPC 601 processor or higher, 16MB RAM, System 7 or later, color monitor with 8-bit display or better.	A top recommendation for the Macintosh. See "Judy & Gloria's Picks." PC users should consider it as an alternative to CorelDraw.

PRODUCT	COMPANY	PRICE	DOWNLOADABLE VERSION OR DEMO?	COMPUTER REQUIREMENTS	COMMENTS
Deneba artWorks	Deneba Software (see above)	$49.95	No	Any Macintosh, even old ones running System 6!	A top recommendation. See "Judy & Gloria's Picks." We think of it as a baby Canvas 3.5.
ClarisDraw	Claris Corp. 5201 Patrick Henry Dr. Santa Clara, CA 95052 800/544-8554 http://www.claris.com	$129 for PC version; $199 for Mac version	Yes; Mac and Windows demos available at company's Web site.	PC version: Windows 3.x or 95, 386/25MHz or higher processor, 8MB RAM for Windows 3.x; 16MB RAM for Windows 95. Mac version: Mac Plus or higher, 4MB RAM for System 6.0.7 or 8MB RAM for System 7 or later.	Simple, low-cost drawing program; PC users should download the trial version and seriously consider it.
ShareDraw	Pierce Software, Inc. 1417 Selborn Place San Jose, CA 95126 http://shareware.com	$29.95	Shareware	Macintosh: System 6.0.7 or later.	An amazing full-featured drawing program that includes textures, polygons, grids, etc.
SmartSketch	Macromedia 600 Townsend St., Suite 310W San Francisco, CA 94103 800/457-1774	$59.95 for the PC version; $49.95 for the Mac version	Yes; demos of Windows and Mac versions available at: http://www.futurewave.com.au/smartsketchtrial.htm. Highly recommended!	PC version: Windows 3.x with 386 or higher processor, 8MB RAM, 7MB free hard disk space. Mac version: System 7 or later, 68020 or higher processor (68040 recommended), 8MB RAM, 7.5MB free hard disk space.	A fun drawing program that includes on-screen tutorials, shape recognition, and simple-to-use drawing tools. PC users intimidated by the high price of CorelDraw should definitely download the demo version from the Web site. For the Mac, we still suggest artWorks or SuperPaint, but this is a fun addition.
MacDraft	Microspot 12380 Saratoga-Sunnyvale Road, Suite 6 Saratoga, CA 95070 800/622-7568 http://www.microspot.com	$295	No	Macintosh: System 6.0.5 or later (accelerated for Power Macintosh); 1.5MB RAM.	This full-featured drawing program includes an excellent tool palette.
Adobe Streamline	Adobe Systems 1585 Charleston Rd. Mountain View, CA, 94039 800/833-6687 http://www.adobe.com/	$199 PC and Mac	No	PC version: Windows 95 or NT, 486 or higher processor; 16MB RAM; CD-ROM drive. Mac version: System 7.5 or later; 68030 or higher processor; 4MB RAM; CD-ROM drive.	Use this superb program to convert scanned images, like photos, into vector drawings so you can edit the lines. It's great for creating appliqué patterns, although many of its features can be found in high-end drawing programs. See Chapter 15 for more information.
GENERAL-PURPOSE PAINT PROGRAMS					We recommend vector-based drawing programs, but we know there are quilters, especially appliqué artists, who use paint programs.
Fractal Design Expression	Fractal Design Corp. 5550 Scotts Valley Drive Scotts Valley, CA 95067-6959 800/ 846-0111 http://www.fractal.com/	$449 for Windows and Mac; sidegrade $149	Yes; download at company's Web site.	PC version: Windows 95 or NT, 486 or higher processor; 12MB RAM; color display; CD-ROM drive. Mac version: System 7.1 or later; 68030 or higher with FPU or PowerPC, 8MB RAM for 68030; 12MB RAM for Power PC; CD-ROM drive.	An excellent paint program for the advanced user. This program does have some hybrid vector drawing abilities.
Fractal Design Dabbler	Fractal Design Corp. (see above)	$69 for Windows and Mac	No	PC version: Windows 3.1 or 95; 486DX or better; 8MB RAM; CD-ROM drive; color display. Mac version: System 7.0 or higher; 68030 or better (FPU required for some effects); 8MB RAM; CD-ROM drive; 13" color monitor.	This paint program comes with interactive tutorials for leaning how to draw with different media (like pastels, pencils, and different types of papers).

PRODUCT	COMPANY	PRICE	DOWNLOADABLE VERSION OR DEMO?	COMPUTER REQUIREMENTS	COMMENTS
Fractal Design Painter Fractal Design Poser	Fractal Design Corp. 5550 Scotts Valley Drive Scotts Valley, CA 95067-6959 800/ 846-0111 http://www.fractal.com/	Painter is $549 for Windows and Mac; Poser is $249 for Windows and Mac; $69 upgrade	Yes; you can download demos of both Painter and Expressions at the company's Web site.	PC version: Windows 3.1 or 95; 486 or Pentium processor, 8MB RAM, math coprocessor required for some effects. Mac version: System 7.0 or later, 68030/40 or higher processor, Macintosh or Power Macintosh; 8MB of application RAM (16MB or more recommended); System 7.0 or later. PC: 80486 or Pentium PC compatible; 8 MB of RAM (16MB or more recommended), Windows 3.1 or Windows 95; Math coprocessor required for some effects; CD-ROM drive recommended.	Both are excellent paint programs for the advanced user. Poser creates the human form in 2-D and 3-D images.

THE KING OF IMAGE EDITING PROGRAMS

PRODUCT	COMPANY	PRICE	DOWNLOADABLE VERSION OR DEMO?	COMPUTER REQUIREMENTS	COMMENTS
Adobe Photoshop	Adobe Systems 1585 Charleston Rd. Mountain View, CA 94039 800/833-6687 http://www.adobe.com/	$895 for Windows and Mac; $179 upgrade; $279 LE upgrade	Yes, from company's Web site.	Windows: 3.1w/DOS 5.0 or later; 95 or NT; 16MB RAM (32MB recommended); CD-ROM drive. Mac: System 7.1 or later; 68030 or higher (PowerPC recommended); 16MB RAM (32MB recommended); CD-ROM drive.	For sophisticated computer-using quilters, nothing compares to the image-editing abilities of Photoshop. Unfortunately, it's super-pricey. For the average quilter, the lower-priced Paint Shop Pro or LView is perfectly sufficient.

DOODADS

PRODUCT	COMPANY	PRICE	DOWNLOADABLE VERSION OR DEMO?	COMPUTER REQUIREMENTS	COMMENTS
Terrazzo	Xaos Tools, Inc. 600 Townsend St., Suite 270E San Francisco, CA 94103 415/487-7000	$15	Yes; download from http://www.share.com. Search for "quilts" and download terrazzo-demo-1.0.sit.hqz.	Any Macintosh program capable of using an Adobe Photoshop plug-in tool; 1MB RAM more than host program requires; System 7 or later.	This tool produces regular patterns based on the seventeen symmetries.
Quilter's Aid	Little Patches 154 S. Via Lucia Alamo, CA 94507	$5 (write for avail-ability)	QUILTX.SEA	Macintosh	Shareware HyperCard stack calculates yardage for quilt with up to six fabrics.
Bargello Designer 32	AyerSoft Co. 5305 Laguna Ct. Byron, CA 94514 510/634-6022 bargello@ayersoft.com http://www.ayersoft.com/bargello	$45	Shareware; download BARGELLO.ZIP from company's Web site.	PC-compatible running Windows 95, 486 or higher processor; 8MB RAM.	Super-nifty program for designing bargello quilts. Prints templates, calcu-lates yardage, can do quilt layouts.
QUILTS.EXE	Cascoloy Software 4528 36th St., N.E. Seattle, WA 98105	$20	Shareware; look for it online or write to ask about availability.	PC-compatible running Windows 3.x.	Quilt screen saver for Windows 3.x. (Not for Windows 95.)
ColorDesign	Momentum Software 57 Sawmill Rd., Suite B New Fairfield, CT 06812 203/746-8637 rsutton@nai.net	$89.95	No	Macintosh II or higher; System 6.0.3 or later; 3MB RAM; color monitor.	Not a drawing or quilt-specific pro-gram, but a good tool for exploring color, shape, and symmetry.

PRODUCT	COMPANY	PRICE	DOWNLOADABLE VERSION OR DEMO?	COMPUTER REQUIREMENTS	COMMENTS
QuiltText and QuiltBlock Fonts	The Electric Quilt Company 1039 Melrose St. Bowling Green, OH 43402 800/356-4219 or 419/352-1134 **http://www.wcnet.org/ ElectricQuiltCo/** equiltco@wcnet.org	$9.95 to $14.95 per disk	See company Web site for sample graphics.	Any.	Quilt block and quilt text TrueType fonts. Can be used with any PC or Mac word processor or graphics program.
Quilt-Pro Fabric Disks	Quilt-Pro Systems P.O. Box 560692 The Colony, TX 75056 214/625-7765 or 800/884-1511 **http://www.quiltpro.com** salamon1@airmail.net	$19.95 per disk	See company Web site for sample graphics.	Any machine running Quilt-Pro.	Extra block patterns, fabric patterns, and border designs for use with Quilt-Pro for the PC or the Mac.
QuiltSoft Fabric Disks	QuiltSoft P.O. Box 19946 San Diego, CA 92159 619/583-2970	$22.95 per disk	No	Any machine running QuiltSoft, Quilt-Pro, or drawing software.	Beautiful scanned fabric collections from Hoffman, Kona Bay, P&B Textiles, and Clothworks.
Professional Block Library	QuiltSoft (see above)	$14.95	No	Any machine running QuiltSoft.	Extra block designs to be used with QuiltSoft.
MECC's Tesselmania! Deluxe	Minnesota Educational Computing Corp. 6160 Summit Drive North Minneapolis, MN 55430 612/569-1500 **http://www.mecc.com/**	$39.95 Windows or Mac	Yes, available from **http://www.mecc.com/ products/lang/tmd/ tmd.html.**	Windows: 3.1 or higher; 486/50MHz or higher processor; 4MB RAM; 256-color SVGA monitor; 2x CD-ROM drive; sound card. Macintosh: 68040 or PowerPC; System 7.1 or later; 5MB RAM; 2x CD-ROM drive.	This fun program creates tessellated designs.
Patchwork-9	Meta Theory 1678 Shattuck Ave., #243-A Berkeley, CA 94709 510/540-0822 or 510/848-4478 MetaTheory@aol.com or meta@lanminds.com	$40	E-mail or write author Jean Tantra for demo download site, or check American Online library.	Macintosh running System 7.5 or later.	Quilt screen saver for use with After Dark screen saver software.
KaleidoscoPix (AKA 8th-er, Cookie Cutter)	Meta Theory (see above)	Distributed free as a promotion for Patch-work-9.	E-mail or write author Jean Tantra for demo download site, or check America Online library.	Macintosh running System 7.5 or later.	A fun utility that creates a kaleido-scope image on a portion of your screen.

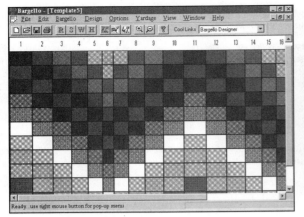

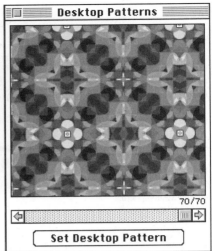

*Bargello Designer 32 lets you create scrumptious bargello quilt patterns. You can download it from the AyerSoft Web site at **http://www.ayersoft.com/ bargello** to try before you buy.*

A desktop pattern created using KaleidoscoPix from Meta Theory.

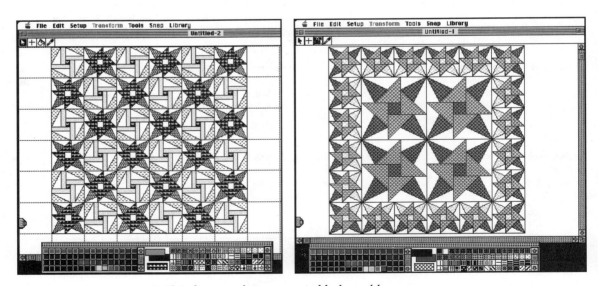

QuiltSoft's strength is geometric blocks and layouts. It's easy to create lovely designs. The program calculates yardage, prints templates, and prints blocks for paper piecing. It is available for both PCs and Macs.

CREATE QUILT-PATTERN WALLPAPER FOR WINDOWS 95

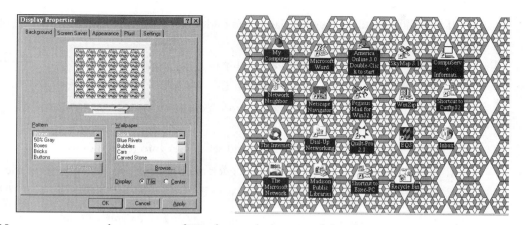

Now you too can make your copy of Windows 95 look positively revolting!

It's easy to give Windows 95 a quilt-pattern splash screen, also known as wallpaper. Take a quilt block from a drawing program or quilt design program and save it as a .BMP file. (In Quilt-Pro you need to select it, then use the Export feature. Quilt-Pro saves it as a .WMF file, which you need to pull up in a graphics program like Paint Shop Pro and save in BMP format. In BlockBase, you'd print the block to disk as a PCX file, then open it in a graphics program and resave it as a .BMP one.)

Click the **Start** button, and select **Settings • Control Panel**. Click on the **Display** icon. In the **Display Properties** box, tab to **Background**. Under the **Wallpaper** setting, click **Browse**. Click your way to the saved BMP quilt block file and click **OK**. Click **Tile** to tile the block on the screen, or **Center** to plop it in the middle of the screen. Click **Apply** when you're done.

There's an even easier way to get a quilt block splash screen. If you're on the Internet and happen upon a quilt block that you like, center the cursor over it and click the right mouse button. A menu will pop up. Select **Set as Wallpaper**. Just make sure that you get permission to copy the block from whoever drew the block originally.

CREATE QUILTING DESKTOP PATTERNS FOR YOUR MACINTOSH

If you're using System 7.5, it's easy to create desktop patterns with a quilting theme. Create a design in any drawing or quilting program. Then copy it to the **Clipboard**. Head over to the Apple menu, select **Control Panels**, and select **Desktop Patterns**. Then just paste the design into the window and click **Set Desktop Pattern**.

We used ColorDesign to create this wild desktop pattern.

CREATE QUILT ICONS IN YOUR MACINTOSH

If you'd like a quilt icon to replace a file folder or some other icon on your screen, here's how to do it.

1. Create a small quilt design in a drawing or quilt program.

2. Copy it to the Clipboard (**COMMAND-C**).

3. Return to the Finder and click once to select the icon you want to change (don't launch it, just select it).

4. In the Finder, go to the **File** menu and select **Get Info** (**COMMAND-I**).

5. In the information box that appears, click to select the icon that appears in the upper left (a box will appear around it).

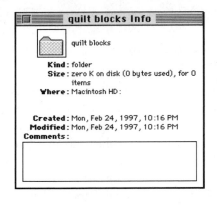

The Get Info box for a file we created called "quilt blocks." The folder is selected.

6. Choose **Paste** from the **Edit** menu to create the new icon (**COMMAND-V**).

The Get Info box with the new quilt icon pasted in.

quilt blocks

7. When viewing your items by icon or small icon, your new icon will appear.

Our quilt blocks file with a custom icon.

That's it!

GETTING STARTED DESIGNING
QUILTS ON YOUR COMPUTER

WHETHER YOU DESIGN WITH A DRAWING PROGRAM OR QUILT DESIGN
SOFTWARE, LEARNING TO USE THE SOFTWARE EFFECTIVELY CAN BE A
CHALLENGE. OUR QUICK STEPS WILL HAVE YOU DRAWING AND COLORING
QUILT BLOCKS PAINLESSLY WITH WHATEVER SOFTWARE YOU USE.

CHAPTER 3

QUICK-START TIPS AND SNEAKY WAYS TO DRAW QUILT BLOCKS WITH QUILT DESIGN SOFTWARE

Give yourself a pat on the back if you bought quilt design software. You won't have to get an advanced degree in vector theory in order to draw a nine-patch. These tips will get you started.

Remember how, when you were a kid, you used to sit on the floor with a scissors and snip shapes out of paper? You'd cut squares, snowflakes, hearts, and circles (lopsided ones), then you'd line them up on the floor and try to figure out what to do with them next.

Many quilters struggle through the same process with their quilt design software. After many hours grappling with the line, Bezier, and arc tools, they end up with a circle or perhaps a misshapen heart on their computer screen. Beyond this, creativity taps dry. It's late, the sun has set, one's hand has grown weary from pushing the mouse around its pad, and anyhow reruns of *Murphy Brown* beckon. Dreams of artistic fulfillment are abandoned for the day. We quilters are a preternaturally patient breed. But it is often the most patient members of a civilization on whom computers wreak their greatest psychological stresses.

Think of it: A computer is the only artist's tool that can tire the artist so that a brisk hour of house painting seems relaxing in contrast. Crayons won't exhaust you this way. And watercolors are so soothing they've been used in mental institutions for years. Computers would never be used to soothe patients in a mental institution.

It is with dread of the malaise that comes from trying to figure out where on the screen to put the Bezier tool that we write this chapter. It is not intended as a replacement for your quilt software's manual. We simply want to show you a few tricks we've learned about using programs like Electric Quilt and Quilt-Pro, some fast ways to get started so that you don't have to read through the entire manual before drawing a nine-patch. We'll also share some discoveries about the programs.

JUDY & GLORIA'S SHOCKING COMPUTER REVELATION

We assembled this chapter by gathering together all the Really Dumb Confusions we had when using these programs. Where is the drawing pad? What do I do once I've drawn a patch? That sort of thing. The manuals for both Electric Quilt and Quilt-Pro are outstanding, and you should take time to work through them. But even in the presence of superior software documentation, someone will whine, "But what do I do once the mouse moves the cursor off the screen?" We were that person. The amazing thing is, in the course of trying to find answers to our dumb questions, we discovered some undocumented features in these programs. Consider this a crib sheet for computer klutzes— plus a little more.

There are two ways to get your quilting software to cough up a quilt block: You can use a ready-made block design from the software's library, or you can draw the block from scratch.

Obviously, the first method is going to be easier, and you should avail yourself of it whenever possible. Both Electric Quilt and Quilt-Pro offer over a thousand block designs in their libraries. Designs range from prosaic four-patches to fantastical house and cat-shaped appliqués. You can reshape them, resize them, and print patterns for them in a snap.

USING QUILT BLOCKS FROM THE PROGRAM LIBRARIES

Many computer-loving quilters never bother to draw quilt blocks from scratch; they find enough inspiration in their quilt design software's block patterns. They can color them, reshape them, and lay them out in different sizes and patterns. Here's how to find your way to the quilt block pattern libraries in our favorite quilt design programs, plus tips on how to make quick use of them.

A JUDY & GLORIA WARNING: DON'T TRUST THE ACCURACY OF TEMPLATES PRINTED WITH YOUR QUILT SOFTWARE

Nothing is more frustrating than cutting out a zillion patches and then discovering that they don't fit together accurately when you sew them into a block. It's not uncommon to come across inaccurate template patterns in books and magazines. But you also run across them in quilt software. Although most block patterns found in the libraries of quilt programs are extremely accurate, there are glitches—especially in the patterns of complex blocks.

To avoid aggravation, we suggest that before you print templates for a block pattern, you first print a foundation block in the size that you want the finished block to be. Once it's printed, pull out a ruler and do some measuring. You may find that patches that you think are a repeat of a certain shape actually differ in size. (This is especially true with some of the more complex block patterns in Quilt-Pro.)

How can you fix the problem? You can always redraw the block. Otherwise, you'll need to piece the block according to the "map" of its patch lay-outs that some programs like Quilt-Pro print with each pattern.

HOW TO FIND THE QUILT BLOCK LIBRARY IN ELECTRIC QUILT

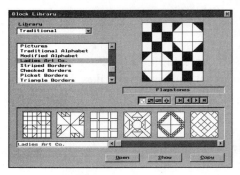

1. From the **Library** menu, select **Block Library**. In the screen that appears, use the scroll bars to sift through the different libraries and their block designs. Click the **Copy** button to copy a block design to your design Sketchbook in Electric Quilt. You can copy to your Sketchbook as many blocks as you like.

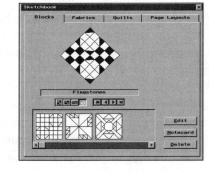

2. The Sketchbook is where you store fabrics, blocks, and quilt layout designs for a project. To get to it, press F8 or select **Draw** menu and choose **Sketchbook**.

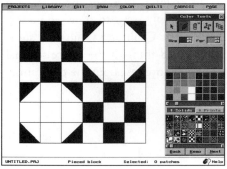

3. To color the block, select the **Blocks** tab in the Sketchbook. Click on the block pattern to select it, then click the **Edit** button. The block appears on the coloring board, with the color tools.

HOW TO REDRAW, COLOR, TWEAK, AND TINKER WITH QUILT BLOCKS FROM ELECTRIC QUILT'S LIBRARY

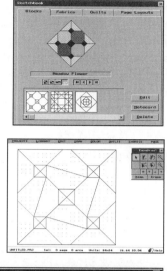

1. Select a block from the library and add it to your Sketchbook according to the steps above. From the **Draw** pull-down menu, select **Sketchbook** or press **F8**. Click the **Edit** button and the quilt block will appear in the sketchpad.

2. You can use any of the editing and drawing tools to change the quilt block. Asymmetrical lines have been added to this Meadow Flower block to give it an off-kilter look. Click the **Keep** button to save your new block.

NOTE

See our tips for using Electric Quilt's drawing tools later in this chapter.

3. When you click the **Keep** button, it adds your new block to the Sketchbook. When you open the Sketchbook, tab to the **Blocks** folder to see the blocks that you have accumulated. You can display them in on-point and "flattened" variations by clicking the appropriate button. Here our renovated Meadow Flower appears flattened. The block isn't actually transformed, though. This just gives you an idea of how the block will look if it's shaped that way.

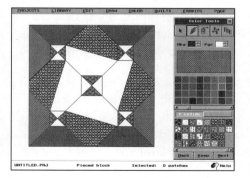

4. Color your new block by pulling down the **Color** menu and selecting **Toolbox**. This coloring toolbox can be a bit baffling to use. Notice the **Solids** and **Prints** buttons two-thirds of the way down. Above these buttons you see solid colors. Below these buttons you see fabric prints (which you can change by using Electric Quilt's fabric libraries and packets, but more on that in Chapter 16). To color a patch with a solid color, click on the **Paintbrush** tool, click on the patch to select it, then click the **Solids** button and click on the color. To color a patch with a fabric print, you'd click the **Prints**

button instead and select a print pattern, right? Yes, but there's one more step if you're using a print. See those BKG and FGR scroll buttons? They stand for "background" and "foreground," and you need to use them to select the background and foreground colors of the fabric print.

HOW TO FIND THE QUILT BLOCK LIBRARY IN QUILT-PRO

1. From the **Block** menu, select **Open**. Make sure that Blocks is selected under Libraries. You should see a list of block types on the right. Double-click on a block type to display a list of all of the blocks of that type. Click [..] to return to the list of block types. When you find a block you want, highlight it, and click **OK**. The block will appear on the gridded drawing screen.

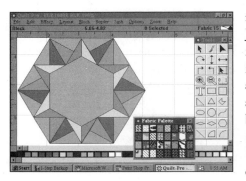

2. You can color and resize the block. Just remember that in order to move or resize it as a whole you must first group its individual patches into a single whole so that the patches don't go fluttering about. Select everything on the screen by pressing **CTRL-A**, or select the **Select** tool from the toolbox. Use it to lasso the box—click outside one of the corners of the block and, holding the left mouse button down, drag the mouse to draw a dotted line around the whole block.

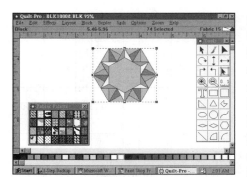

3. When you release the mouse button, the band should snap around the selected block, and black handles will appear around it. From the **Effects** menu, select **Group**. You can resize the block or distort it by moving these black handles. You can also move the block by moving the cursor to the center of the block (the cursor becomes a hand), holding the mouse button down, and dragging the block to its new position. Now that the block is grouped, you can also duplicate it

(**CTRL-C**). But to color the block's patches, you must first *ungroup* the block (select the block, and from the **Effects** menu select **Ungroup**). You'd then color the individual patches and group them again when you're done.

DRAWING YOUR OWN QUILT BLOCKS FROM SCRATCH

Let's say that you can't find the quilt block you want in the five zillion patterns in your quilt design software, so you decide to draw it yourself. The drawing tools in quilt programs are remarkably similar to those in full-blown drawing packages, except that they're much simpler to use. Isn't that a relief? They've also been tailored for use in drafting quilt blocks.

The steps to follow before you start drawing are pretty much the same in quilt software as they are in a drawing program:

1. You set up your drawing area's grid.

2. You activate snap-to-grid so that the lines and patches you draw align to the grid and don't squiggle around.

3. You display the on-screen ruler if one is available.

The process of drawing the block is also similar:

1. You draw your quilt block by drawing lines (Electric Quilt) or patches (Quilt-Pro).

2. You make sure that the points of your patches align properly.

3. You group your patches into a block.

4. You size your block or otherwise transform its shape.

5. If you want to color the block, you ungroup its patches so that you can color them individually (so that you don't end up with one single-colored square).

Depending upon your quilt software, you may not need to follow the last three steps.

HOW TO DRAW A PIECED QUILT BLOCK IN ELECTRIC QUILT

Drawing original blocks in Electric Quilt is extremely easy. The program offers two drawing boards: One is for pieced blocks; Electric Quilt takes whatever you draw on this pad and turns it into a piecing pattern. The other is for appliqué; in it you can draw closed shapes like leaves and flower petals and layer them as you would fabric in appliqué.

In Chapter 14 we'll talk more about designing appliqué in Electric Quilt. For now we'll just talk about the drawing tablet for pieced blocks.

Electric Quilt's manual offers excellent, easy-to-follow tutorials on using its pieced block drawing tablet. To get you started, here are some little-known tricks that might not be so obvious about drawing in Electric Quilt.

REMEMBER

Before you start drawing anything, always have in mind a clear conception of what you want to draw. A hand-drawn sketch of a quilt block will save you time fooling around at the computer.

WHERE TO FIND THE PIECED BLOCK DRAWING PAD

Pull down the **Draw** menu and select **EasyDraw**. To see the dimensions of what you're drawing, head back to the **Draw** menu and select **Show Rulers**.

SETTING UP YOUR DRAWING AREA

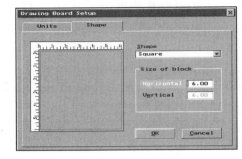

*You can set the size and shape of your drawing board by pulling down the **Draw** menu and selecting **EasyDraw Setup**. In the box that appears, click on the **Shape** tab. There you can specify your block's dimensions and its shape. You can set it up as a square, rectangle, diamond, or freehand shape. Click **OK** to apply your choices.*

WHAT ARE GUIDES?

Guides are like gravity points. As you draw, your lines align to their nearby lines and intersections. They make it easy to draw perfectly symmetrical designs.

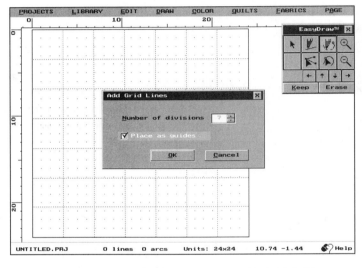

*You can add grids and guides to your drawing pad by pulling down the **Draw** menu and selecting **Add Grid Lines**. Electric Quilt will ask you for the number of grid divisions in your block. Place a check beside **Place as Guides**, and Electric Quilt will turn the grid into drawing guide lines.*

HINTS FOR DRAWING A BLOCK

Drawing in Electric Quilt is a far more straightforward deal than it is in a typical drawing program. Its Line tool always behaves and draws straight lines, instead of squiggling to kingdom come. There is an Arc tool for when you want to draw a curved line, and when you try to reshape the curve, the arc editing tool doesn't stretch it into a double-jointed noodle with fifty vanishing points and then disappear, as it does in certain drawing programs (we won't name names).

Yes, everything is fairly straightforward in Electric Quilt's drawing board. Best of all, you don't have to tussle to join lines together to create patches or group patches together before your block falls apart. All you have to do is draw your lines and color them. Electric Quilt takes care of making them into a patched quilt pattern for you.

Here are our tricks, discoveries, and insights into drawing with Electric Quilt.

T * I * P

*As you draw, you might want to convert all or part of your drawing into guides. Doing so will make it easier to align lines and "snap" them to the block's intersection points to get the precision pieced patches that you want. To select your entire drawing, go to the Edit menu and click on **Select All**. Or click on the Pointer tool and use it to click on the individual line or group of lines that you want to convert to guides. You can also select all of the lines in an area by clicking on the Pointer tool and then dragging the mouse over the area with the mouse button held down. This draws a rubber-band box around the lines. Once you have selected the lines you want to convert to guides, pull down the **Draw** menu and select **Convert to Guides**.*

A MEMORY TRICK TO REMEMBER WHAT'S IN THE TOOLBOX Do all those buttons in the EasyDraw toolbox look the same to you? They do to us, especially when our rhinestone pince-nez are askew. Just remember, the top row of buttons is for doing something (notice the pencil for drawing straight lines and the curve tool for drawing arcs). The bottom row is for undoing or correcting something (the Edit Line tool and the Edit Arc tool).

THE MOST IMPORTANT THING TO REMEMBER ABOUT DRAWING IN ELECTRIC QUILT Electric Quilt is actually much smarter than any of us. This may not be immediately apparent, because the program masquerades under a clumsy interface, but it's true. One very smart thing that Electric Quilt does is try to make patches from anything you draw, no matter how lopsided your drawing. Unlike other drawing and quilt design programs, you don't have to tell it where and how to make patches; it just does it on its own. And it invariably succeeds.

The only thing you need to remember as you draw with Electric Quilt is that your lines must either end at the sides of the drawing canvas, meet the ends of other lines, or intersect other lines. That way you and Electric Quilt will be in agreement about how you want your patches drawn.

If you're ever unsure of the results of this unspoken agreement, click the **Keep** button, then head to the Sketchbook, found in the **Draw** menu, and, in the color view (the larger box showing the selected block), you'll see the patches that Electric Quilt has saved. Electric Quilt won't save lines or portions of lines that it can't turn into patches.

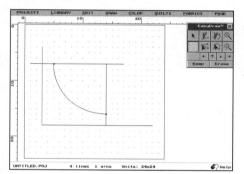

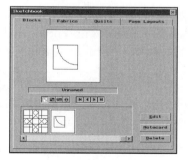

Drawing Drunkard's Path blocks is easy in Electric Quilt, even when you're tipsy. That's because Electric Quilt fashions patches even from lines that overrun their bounds.

DELETING LINES WITHOUT ERASING THE ENTIRE QUILT BLOCK   If you've just pulled Electric Quilt from its box, one of the things you probably noticed is that when you click the Erase button, everything on the drawing board disappears. What a downer. And you must have spent forty minutes trying to draw a nine-patch that didn't look like a tornado blew through it. The moral: Keep away from the Erase button unless you want to start your drawing from scratch.

To erase a line in Electric Quilt, click on the Pointer tool, then click on the line so that heavy black handles appear on its ends. To get rid of the line you've selected, press the DELETE key on your keyboard.

You can also delete groups of lines by drawing a rubber-band box around them with the Pointer tool to select them and then pressing DELETE.

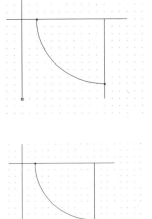

COMPUTER QUILTING SUPER-KLUTZ SAVER

Did you erroneously click the Erase button and cause your entire quilt block to disappear? Not to worry. If, at any time in your struggle with the drawing tools, you clicked the Keep button, you'll find the then-current version of your quilt block stored in the Sketchbook. To get it back, pull down the Draw menu and select Sketchbook. All of your saved versions of the quilt block will be there. Select one and click the Edit button.

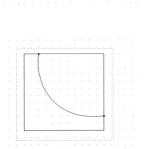

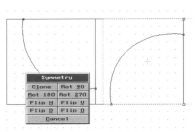

EDITING LINES To clean up some of those lines in our inebriated Drunkard's Path piece, start by selecting the Edit Line in the toolbox. Click on the line and pull the black handles that appear at each end to change the length of the line.

MOVING LINES To move a line, draw a rubber-band box around the line with the Pointer tool. Then "pick up" the line by moving the mouse cursor to the center of the selected area and pressing and holding down the mouse button. With the mouse button still held down, drag the line to its new location and let go of the mouse button.

EDITING CURVES Let's put a little more curve into that pie quarter! Select the Edit Arc tool by clicking on it in the toolbox. Click once in the center of the curve. A "tent" will appear. Pull on the apex of the tent while holding down the mouse button to stretch the curve.

COPYING, ROTATING, AND FLIPPING PATCHES

1. To transform the entire patched piece, draw a rubber-band box around it by first selecting the Pointer tool from the toolbox and holding the mouse button down while stretching the box around the group of patches.

2. Click twice on one of the selected piece's black handles to pop up the Symmetry menu. Click on buttons to duplicate (clone) the selected pieces, mirror them, or rotate them.

YOU WILL FIND ALL OF YOUR ATTEMPTS TO DRAW DRUNKARD'S PATHS IN THE SKETCH- BOOK. As you can see, Electric Quilt saves only those attempts at which lines actually intersect. And it's a good thing. In the sorry excuses for patches shown here, Electric Quilt "trimmed" off the dangling ends of the arcs. That's because it will try hard to form patches from even the most chaotic drawing, and it often does a good job of it too.

ACTIVATE THE SECRET CURVE EDITING MENU! Here's a nifty trick. To edit a curve once you've drawn it, select the Edit Arc tool from the toolbox. Click on the curve so

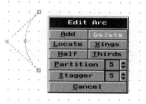

that a broken-lined triangular "tent" appears around it. Now double-click on the apex, or point, of that tent. The Edit Arc box will pop up. You can use it to alter the shape of your curve by adding nodes (those little black squares) to it (click **Add**). Click **Locate** to add a node to the precise point you want on the curve. The **Partition** button will break the line into a number of even intervals that you specify. STAGGER will add evenly spaced nodes beginning a half-step into the arc. Once you've added nodes to your arc, you can edit them.

GET PHYSICAL WITH THE POP-UP SYMMETRY MENU! Feel in the mood to flip, rotate, and replicate? Select the Pointer tool,

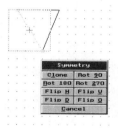

and then select the line or group of lines that you'd like to dupli- cate or flip. (Do this by drawing a rub- ber-band box around the lines or clicking on a line.) Now double-click on one of the black handles of your selected object and the Symmetry menu will pop up. You can duplicate the object, rotate it, or flip it. The crosshairs on the selected object tell you where its center is; the object will rotate around this center.

....

T * I * P

Turn off snap-to-grid when you're drawing curves or appliqué pieces. Keep snap-to-grid on when you're drawing patches with straight lines.

——

NOTE

If you can't see the on-screen ruler, pull down the Options menu and choose Show Ruler.

HOW TO DRAW A QUILT BLOCK IN QUILT-PRO

Quilt-Pro offers some pretty sophisticated drawing tools for drawing quilt blocks. Click on a patch icon, then click and drag the cursor over the screen, and a patch appears. Different types of drawing grids make it a snap to draw uniquely shaped blocks precisely. Here are some tips:

SETTING UP YOUR DRAWING AREA

Activate snap-to-grid by heading to the **Options** menu and putting a check beside **Grid Snap** or by pressing CTRL-G (COMMAND-G on a Mac). This will cause all the patches you draw to align with the grid you set up.

Set up your grid by pulling down the **Options** menu and clicking on **Screen**. Set the grid to ⅛ inch by clicking the **Size** setting down to 0.125 inch.

You can set up the grid under Grid Type to be square, circular, isometric, or eight-pointed.

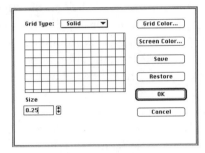

The square grid is for drawing blocks with square or rectangular patches, like nine-patches. Here "Solid" means that the grid appears as solid lines. You can also specify dotted lines.

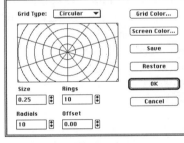

The circular grid is for drawing blocks with circular patterns, like Mariner's Compass. You can increase the number of arms (radials) and alter the size of the concentric circles in Quilt-Pro's circular grid to draw more elaborate star or circular blocks.

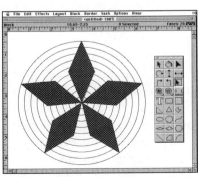

An example of a pattern drawn with a circular grid.

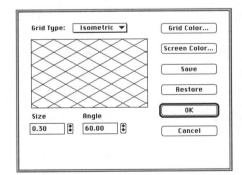

The isometric grid is for drawing blocks with hexagons, diamonds, or triangles. This is also the grid you'd use to draw isometric baby blocks. Change the angle and size of the isometric grid to draw optical illusion quilts.

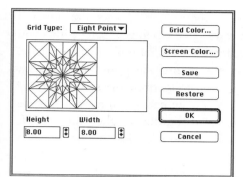

The eight-point grid is for drawing eight-pointed star blocks such as Lone Star. It makes drawing star-shaped blocks easy.

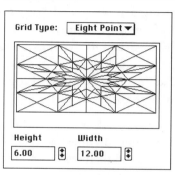

Change the height and width settings of the eight-pointed star grid to create blocks with distortions.

DRAWING A BLOCK

The important thing to remember when drawing in Quilt-Pro is that you need to draw blocks one patch at a time, and each object must be a closed patch. To accomplish this, you can either

- Use the patch drawing tools like the square, rectangle, triangle, and so on.

- Draw your patch with the Straight Line or Arc tool. Make sure the lines meet. Then select the lines by drawing a rubber-band box around them with the Select tool. Press CTRL-J (COMMAND-J on a Mac) or select **Effects/ Join** to join them into a patch. You can tell that your patch has achieved patch status if you can color it.

Ideally, you want to use the patch drawing tools whenever possible, because that will make your life easier.

Here are some other things to keep in mind:

If your patch is straight-sided but irregularly shaped, use the Polygon tool to draw it.

You can change the shape of a patch with the Edit tool. Select the tool by clicking on it, then move the fat cursor to the corner you want to alter and hold the left mouse button down. Drag the corner to the place you want it to be. You can also short or lengthen lines and curves with the Edit tool.

In order to color a patch, duplicate it, or move it, you must first select it. To select a patch, click on the Select tool, then click on the patch or draw a rubber-band box around it by holding the mouse button down as you drag the cursor around the block.

When you want your patches to align to each other rather than to the grid, turn off snap-to-grid (CTRL-G) (COMMAND-G on a Mac), and use snap-to-point instead. (To use snap-to-point, simply click the right mouse button when drawing, instead of the left mouse button. On a Mac, click the mouse button when drawing and hold down the OPTION key.) Snap-to-point will align the points of patches that you draw with the Polygon tool. (If you draw patches with other tools, like the square, it will align only the beginning and end points.) Snap-to-point is tricky, however. To get two patches to align, you must draw the second one by starting at the point on the first where you want the patches to align, this time clicking the right mouse button on each corner as you draw (rather than the left button, as you would normally do). Remember to double-click the mouse when you're done drawing a patch with the Polygon tool.

When you're finished drawing your block, select and group the patches by clicking on the Select tool and drawing a rubber-band box around the whole block or by choosing **Select All** from the **Edit** menu (Mac users can use COMMAND-A to choose Select All). From the **Select** menu, click on **Group** to make them into a whole. You can now duplicate the block, flip it, distort it, and do other wonderful things. Remember that in order to color the patches or change individual patches, you'll need to ungroup the block.

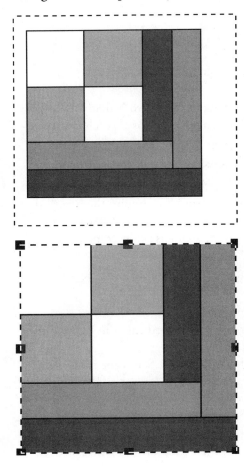

1. Select your blocks by clicking on the Select tool and drawing a rubber-band box around them while holding down your mouse button.

2. When you release the mouse button, black handles will appear around the selected block. From the **Select** menu, choose **Group** to make the individual patches into a whole.

USE BLOCKS IN QUILT-PRO'S LIBRARY AS STARTING POINTS
FOR YOUR OWN EXCITING VARIATIONS

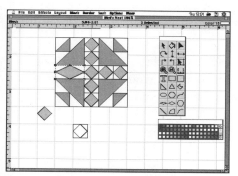

1. We took the Bird's Nest block from the Five Patch.

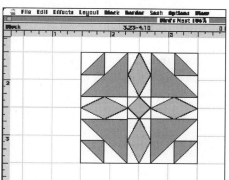

2. We ungrouped the block, dragged some pieces to the outside of the block, and stretched the remaining shape.

**A JUDY & GLORIA WARNING:
DON'T TRUST THE ACCURACY
OF YARDAGE ESTIMATES
MADE BY YOUR QUILT SOFTWARE**

Before you strike off to the fabric store with your list of fabric needs for the quilt pattern you created with your quilt software, take a second look at the yardage requirements. While they may be accurate, you may actually end up needing more fabric, depending upon how you lay out your templates and cut your patches. So always check the software's yardage estimates yourself with your calculator. Or play it safe and buy an extra half-yard of each fabric (that may sound like a lot, but we love fabric).

3. This is the new variation.

1. We took the Arrowhead Star block from the hexagon folder.

2. Using the Polygon tool, we redrew an area to create this variation.

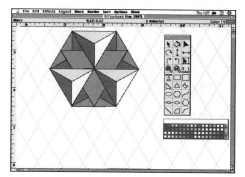

1. First we set up a 30-degree isometric grid. We used the Polygon tool to draw a series of wedges inside a 30-degree triangle. We repeated the triangle to form a hexagon.

2. We repeated the hexagon and added some borders. Wouldn't this make a great paper-pieced wall hanging?

We drew a traditional block on a 60-degree isometric grid, creating a diamond-shaped block.

Use the Polygon tool to draw unconventional stars. Set up an eight-pointed grid, and activate snap-to-grid. Draw your patches by clicking on the center of the star and then clicking on each corner of the patch. Click twice on the corner where you started drawing to finish the patch. Now go on to outline the next patch.

CHAPTER 4

HOW TO SET UP YOUR DRAWING AREA AND DRAW A QUILT BLOCK WITH DRAWING SOFTWARE

Drawing quilt blocks in drawing software is easy if you follow these simple steps.

In Chapter 2 we compared quilt design software to general-purpose drawing programs. Quilt programs come with literally thousands of predrawn quilt patterns, layouts, and stencil patterns built in. No drawing is necessary on your part (although they let you draw if you wish). Still, many quilters prefer drawing programs because of their flexibility. You can import art and draft some truly innovative quilt designs with them. But drawing programs can be daunting to master. Indeed, a friend who manages a graphic arts company comes home each night with her ears ringing from the screams of artists frustrated by these sometimes confounding tools.

In this chapter you'll find tutorials for getting started drawing quilt patterns in the most popular drawing programs used by quilters. The drawing programs on the market are so similar that the concepts and tutorials for programs covered in this and subsequent chapters translate fairly easily to other drawing programs like SmartSketch or Deneba artWorks. In the tip sheet at the end of each section in this chapter you'll find general steps for accomplishing the same feats in literally any drawing program. (In fact, you can even use these steps to design quilts with the drawing features of some high-end word processors like Microsoft Word.)

DRAWING PROGRAM BASICS

Most drawing programs are designed similarly. They give you a selection of tools like pens, boxes, and circles. A eraser is often conspicuously—and maddeningly—absent.

That's because drawing programs draw by defining each line as a mathematical path between points. Paint programs, in contrast—which always have erasers—draw by spraying dots, or pixels, over your drawing area. To a newcomer, this is one of the most confusing things about drawing programs. In order to erase a line, you must first select it and then press the DELETE key. When you do this, the entire line vanishes. You can't just rub an eraser over the portion of the line that you wish to erase, as you can in a paint program. Similarly, in order to change a line, you must work with the whole line, moving or editing it. You can't just erase part of it and redraw it.

This penchant of drawing programs to define elements in a drawing as paths rather than as "painted" areas leads to some peculiarities. For instance, if you draw a quilt block by drawing lines and then attempt to color its "patches," the drawing program will probably regard the entire block as one entity and color the whole thing green or purple or whatever. You need to draw each individual patch as a closed path in order to color it separately. Also, when you try to move your quilt block, if you haven't "grouped" all of its assorted paths properly, the lines will probably scatter about.

We talk more about these phenomena in subsequent chapters. For now, we'll introduce you to the basic steps and concepts for drawing a quilt block.

REMEMBER!

Don't confuse drawing programs with paint programs, which are more like coloring with crayons on a computer screen. If the distinction between the two still seems fuzzy, reread our discussion of the differences between them in Chapter 2.

HOW TO SET UP YOUR DRAWING AREA

NOTE

All CorelDraw directions will work with both versions 7 and 5 of the program. Differences in CorelDraw 7 are noted in brackets.

We all know that quilt blocks are easier to draw on graph paper than on a blank sheet of paper. That's why the first thing you need to do to draw quilt blocks in a drawing program is to make your drawing area look like graph paper by turning it into a grid—and giving it a few intelligent features. Here's how to set up Corel-Draw, Canvas, and SuperPaint to draw quilt blocks.

SET UP YOUR DRAWING AREA IN CORELDRAW

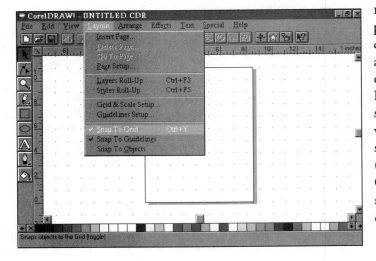

1. First, to display the on-screen ruler, pull down the **View** menu (ALT-V) and choose **Rulers**. A check mark should appear next to it, and you will see rulers on the edges of the drawing window. Now you want to specify snap-to-grid, so that your lines will snap into place when you draw them. In CorelDraw 5, simply pull down the **Layout** menu (ALT-L), and click to check **Snap to Grid** [In CorelDraw 7, you specify snap-to-grid in the **Grid & Ruler Setup** dialog box; see step 2].

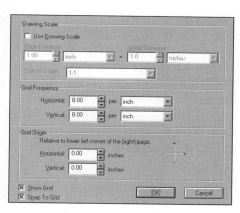

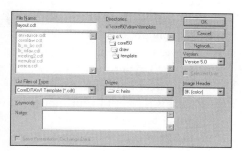

2. From the **Layout** menu (**ALT-L**), select **Grid & Scale Setup** [or **Grid and Ruler Setup** in CorelDraw 7]. This box will appear. Under **Grid Frequency**, type **8** per inch for both the Horizontal and the Vertical settings. (Some quilters like to set their grid to 4 squares per inch, claiming that it's easier to use.) In the lower left-hand corner of the box, click to check the box beside **Show Grid**. (If you checked Snap to Grid in the Layout menu earlier, the Snap to Grid box should already be checked.) [In CorelDraw 7, go to the **Grid** tab and check the boxes beside both **Show Grid** and **Snap to Grid**.] Click **OK** to save the settings.

3. Save your new settings as a template so that you can load them easily the next time you want to design a quilt. Pull down the **File** menu (**ALT-F**), and select **Save As**. This box will appear. In the **List Files of Type** box, scroll to CorelDraw Template (.cdt). Beneath **File Name** type **layout.cdt**. In the **Directories** box, be sure to click to the **Draw/Template** directory so that you can find your template when you need it. Click **OK** to save the settings. The next time you want to design a quilt, you can load these settings by pulling down the **File** menu (**ALT-F**) and selecting **New from Template**. From the list of template files, select **layout.cdt**.

SET UP YOUR DRAWING AREA IN CANVAS 5.0

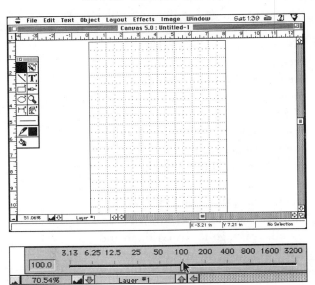

1. To display the on-screen ruler, pull down the **Layout** menu, slide down to **Display**, and slide over to select **Show Rulers**. To display the grids, repeat the same steps, but select **Show Grids**. To turn on snap-to-grid, pull down the **Layout** menu, slide down to **Snap To**, and slide over to select **Grids** (it defaults to a ⅛-inch grid).

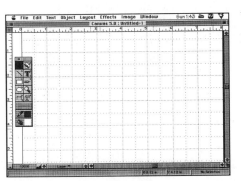

2. You'll notice that your work area is within a small page sitting in the middle of your computer screen. The default in Canvas 5.0 is to display the document at 50 percent of its size, but you'll probably prefer to have the working area cover the screen. To do this, pull down the **Layout** menu, slide to **Views**, and select **Zoom In**. Another way to do this is to hold your mouse button down on the **Scale** window, which is located on the bottom left of your work area, to display the sliding bar (shown here). Slide over and select **100%**. You'll notice the Scale window change from 70.54%, the default display, to 100%.

Your work area should now cover your screen.

T * I * P

*In both Canvas 5.0 and 3.5, selecting **Retain Selected Tool** in the **General Preferences** box saves you from having to reselect the same tool over and over again.*

3. To save your selected tool, pull down the **File** menu and select **Preferences**. Click the **General** tab. Then click to check the box next to **Retain Selected Tool**. Click **OK**.

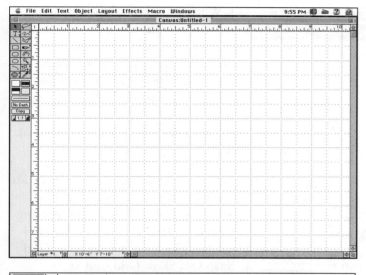

4. Save these settings as a template called Layout Page. Pull down the **File** menu and select **Save As**. This box will appear. Click on the arrow in the **File Format** box, and, holding the mouse button down, slide to **Canvas 5.0 Template**. Then type **Layout Page** in the **Save Current Document As** box. Save the document in your Canvas 5 folder. The next time you want to begin designing a quilt, just open this file.

SET UP YOUR DRAWING AREA IN CANVAS 3.5

1. To display the on-screen ruler, pull down the **Layout** menu, slide down to **Show/Hide**, and slide over to **Rulers**. To display the grids, repeat the same steps, but select **Grid** (it defaults to a ⅛-inch grid). To turn on snap-to-grid, pull down the **Layout** menu and select **Snap to Grid**.

2. The default in Canvas 3.5 is to display the document at 100 percent of its size. You can use your mouse to zoom in or zoom out by clicking on the magnification/reduction box located on the bottom of the palette icons display.

3. To save your selected tool, pull down the **File** menu and select **Preferences**. Scroll in the box on the left until you see General. Click on **General** to highlight it, then check the box next to **Retain Selected Tool**. Click **OK**.

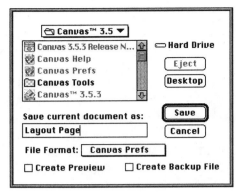

4. Save these settings as a template called Layout Page. Pull down the **File** menu and select **Save As**. This box will appear. Click in the **File Format** box and hold down the mouse button to display a list of file formats, then slide to **Canvas Prefs**. Finally, type **Layout Page** in the **Save Current Document As** box. Save the document in your Canvas 3.5 folder. The next time you want to begin designing a quilt, just open this file.

MACINTOSH SYSTEM 7 USERS TAKE NOTE!

Make an alias of your layout file and insert it into your Apple menu.

SET UP YOUR DRAWING AREA IN SUPERPAINT

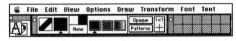

1. When you open a SuperPaint document, it defaults to the Paint layer of the program, but you'll need to work in the Draw layer. To get to the Draw layer, click the compass icon in the upper left corner of your screen. You'll know you're in the Draw layer because the word "Draw" appears in the menu bar instead of the word "Paint."

2. Display the on-screen ruler and grids and turn on snap-to-grid by pulling down the **Options** menu and selecting **Grid & Rulers**. You will see this box. Click to check the boxes next to **Grid Snap On**, **Show Grid**, and **Show Rulers** to turn these features on. Click **OK** to close the box. Your screen will look like the box shown here.

3. The default in SuperPaint is to display the document at 100 percent of its size. You can zoom in and zoom out by selecting these options on the **View** menu.

```
┌─────────────────────────────────────────┐
│  ▱ Aldus SuperPaint 3.5 ▼                │
│  ▨ 10/7                    ⊏ External #1  │
│  ▨ 11/29/95 #5 colored     156,920K available │
│  ▨ Aldus SuperPaint        ┌──────────┐  │
│  ▨ big mouth               │  Eject   │  │
│  ▢ Clipart Folder          └──────────┘  │
│                            ┌──────────┐  │
│                            │ Desktop  │  │
│  Save document as:         └──────────┘  │
│  ┌─────────────────────┐   ┌──────────┐  │
│  │ Layout Document     │   │   Save   │  │
│  └─────────────────────┘   └──────────┘  │
│                            ┌──────────┐  │
│  ○ SuperPaint  ● Save as:  │ Cancel   │  │
│                ┌──────────┐└──────────┘  │
│                │Stationery│              │
│                └──────────┘              │
└─────────────────────────────────────────┘
```

4. Templates you create in SuperPaint are called Stationery. Save your settings as a Stationery document called Layout Page. Pull down the **File** menu and choose **Save As**. This box will appear. In the box next to **Save As**, click and hold down the mouse button to display a list of file types. Select **Stationery**. In the box under **Save Document As**, type **Layout Document**. Save the document in your SuperPaint folder.

NOTE TO MACINTOSH USERS

Each time you use your Layout Page stationery, you'll need to make the grid visible again. For some reason, that command does not hold.

TIPS FOR SETTING UP YOUR DRAWING AREA IN OTHER PROGRAMS

Follow these steps to set up your drawing area for designing quilts with any drawing program.

1. Turn on the ruler so that inch measurements appear on your screen.

2. Turn on the "show grid" feature.

3. Set the grid to ⅛ inch.

4. Activate "snap-to-grid" so that the lines you draw align with the grid.

5. Turn on the "retain selected tool" option if one is available, so that you can save the selection of drawing you like.

Once you have made these settings, save them as an individual file—or as a template—with a name like "Layout." Whenever you want to draw a new design, load your Layout file and begin sketching. When you're done, save the file with a new name (use the Save As command) so that you don't overwrite your original template. Better yet, save it with a new name before you begin sketching, so that you don't forget.

HOW TO ENLARGE YOUR PAGE SIZE (OR GET RID OF THE PAGE COMPLETELY)

When you fire up most drawing programs, you see an image of an 8½-by-11-inch page on the screen. But what if you want to draw a quilt block that's 10 inches square or design an entire bed-sized quilt? It won't fit on that page, will it? And that page always seems to get in the way as you're drawing.

It turns out that you don't need that image of a page (until it actually comes time to print). You have several options for creating a larger drawing:

JUDY & GLORIA'S RULE #1 FOR DRAWING QUILT BLOCKS

Don't think that you have to draw your quilt block to scale. Draw it to a size that you can work with easily on your computer screen. You can always resize it later.

• You can scroll down the screen to get away from the page. You draw somewhere else, in other words.

• You can tell your drawing program to lose the page. (It's a menu option.)

• You can ignore the page and draw as much outside it as you need to. When it comes time to print your drawing, select your drawing program's "tiling" feature to have the program automatically split the design across several pages.

GET RID OF THAT ANNOYING PAGE IN CORELDRAW

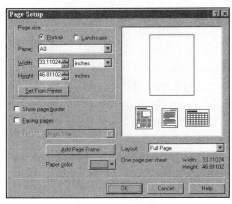

In CorelDraw 7, pull down the **Layout** menu and select **Page Setup**. Remove the check beside **Show Page Border**. Click **OK**. If, when you return to the drawing area, black handles surround the page, signifying that it's selected, press the **DELETE** key to remove the page.

In earlier versions of CorelDraw, pull down the **Layout** menu and select **Page Setup**. Click on the **Display** tab in the dialog box, and remove the check beside **Show Page Border**.

When you want to print your design, return to the **Page Setup** dialog box and check **Show Page Border** to redisplay the page so that you can see how your design will fit on the printed page.

ENLARGE YOUR DRAWING AREA IN CANVAS 5.0

From the **Layout** menu, select **Document Setup**. Type the size of the page you want to work with into this box.

ENLARGE YOUR DRAWING AREA IN CANVAS 3.5

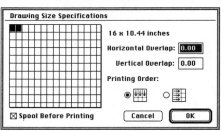

From the **Layout** menu, select **Drawing Size**. You will see this box. The grid represents 81 square feet, with each block in the grid equal to one page. When you open a new document, the upper left box is black, indicating that the document consists of one page. To increase the size of the document, click another white box on the grid. As you click, the blocks turn black and the document's size appears to the right of the grid. The Printing Order options let you print the pages in vertical columns or in horizontal rows—important if your design is large and you want to print a specific page.

MACINTOSH TIP

In all Macintosh drawing programs, the size of your working page is determined by the page size you select in the Page Setup box (which you'll find under the File menu). Consider using legal-size paper for designs or blocks that are between 11 and 14 inches.

ENLARGE YOUR DRAWING AREA IN SUPERPAINT

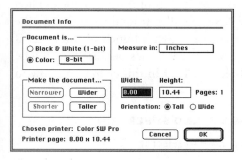

From the **File** menu, select **Document Info**. You will see this box. Type in the width and height of the document you want to work with. Use the scroll bars to move around in your document.

Now you're ready to start drawing!

HOW TO DRAW A LINE

The easiest way to draw a quilt block is to draw it with your drawing program's freehand or straight-line tool. But using it can be a bit more complicated than simply moving your mouse cursor around the screen. Remember that in a vector drawing program, as opposed to a paint program, each line is a discrete object. When you draw a line in a paint program, if you want to delete it you simply rub over it with the program's eraser tool. The eraser rubs out each of the line's pixels. It's not so easy in a drawing program. You must first select the line with the appropriate tool, and then you can delete it.

Drawing in a drawing program can take a bit of getting used to. Here are tips to get you over the bumps. Spend an evening doodling with the drawing tools to build your confidence.

DRAW A LINE IN CORELDRAW

1. Find the pencil or Freehand tool on your screen. Click on the pencil icon and hold down the left mouse button to display the "flyout" menu of choices. Select only the Freehand tool (you can slide your cursor slowly over the menu and see descriptions of the tools' functions at the bottom of the screen).

2. Once the tool is selected, move your mouse to the drawing window (it should change into crosshairs). Click on the screen where you want to start the line, release the mouse button, and then click on the screen where you want the line to end.

FUTZ WITH A LINE

To shorten or lengthen a line you've drawn, first click on the Pick tool in the toolbox to select it. Then click on the line so that "handles" (eight black squares) appear in a box around it; these tell you that it's selected. To lengthen or shorten the line, click on one of the handles, hold down the mouse button, and move the handle in the direction you want. You can also move the entire line this way. Note that you can also distort the line this way (intentionally or otherwise), so you want to be careful how you pull those handles. You can also lengthen or shorten the line by clicking on the Shape tool and pulling or pushing the line's end nodes.

JUDY & GLORIA'S RULE #2 FOR DRAWING QUILT BLOCKS

The computer artist's maxim is that anything that's hard to draw on a computer is easy to draw on paper and vice versa. For example, the preliminary sketch for an appliqué flower will probably be easier to draw on paper than on a computer. On the other hand, drafting a geometrical quilt block with perfectly straight lines is easier on a computer than it is on paper. So make life easy on yourself: Start by sketching your quilt block on paper, but don't worry about getting it perfect. Once you have an idea of what you want to draw, sit down at the computer. Rely on the computer to do the things that you find hard to do on paper, like drawing straight and perfectly symmetrical lines, resizing, and drawing to scale.

JUDY & GLORIA'S RULE #3 FOR DRAWING QUILT BLOCKS

CorelDraw's Freehand tool is many cyber-quilters' undoing. Lines end up crooked, and large segments of their designs disappear when they try to delete just one line. Here are some tips:

- *To draw straight lines, click and release the mouse button once where you want your line to start. Use the mouse to slide the crosshairs over your drawing area, and click and release again to end the line.*

- *For freehand drawing (that is, to make crooked lines), hold the mouse button down as you draw.*

- *To draw a series of connected lines, click once to start the line, then double-click on the spot where you want your line to end and the next line to begin. When you're finished drawing lines, click once to end it.*

DELETE A LINE

To delete a line that you've drawn, click on the Pick tool in the toolbox. Then click on the line to select it (you will see handles around it) and press the **DELETE** key. (You may notice after you've drawn a bunch of lines that if you try to delete just one a whole mess gets deleted. That's because CorelDraw thinks that the lines are joined. See the directions later in this chapter on how to unjoin them.)

DRAW A LINE IN CANVAS 5.0, CANVAS 3.5, AND SUPERPAINT

 1. Click the Line tool on the Tools palette to select it.

2. Move your mouse to your drawing page (it should change into crosshairs). Click where you want to start the line. Hold down the mouse button, slide the mouse to create the line, and release the mouse button to end the line. To draw another line connected to the first, click and hold down the mouse button on the end of the line you just drew, sliding the mouse to create the line as before.

FUTZ WITH A LINE

To shorten, lengthen, or change the direction of a line, first click on the Selection Arrow in the Tools palette, then use it to click on the line you want to change. You'll notice small, black squares, called handles, at the ends of the line; these tell you that the item is selected. Move the arrow over one of these handles. In Canvas, the Selection Arrow changes to crosshairs when it is on top of a handle; in SuperPaint it does not. Click and hold down the mouse button while you drag the mouse to lengthen, shorten, or change the direction of the line. As long as snap-to-grid is on, the line will remain straight.

DELETE A LINE

Click on the Selection Arrow in the Tools palette, and use it to select the line you want to delete. (The handles indicate that the line is selected.) Press the **DELETE** key.

TIPS FOR DRAWING A LINE IN OTHER PROGRAMS

Follow these steps to draw quilt blocks with the line tool in any drawing program:

1. Turn on the snap-to-grid feature so that lines will be straight.

2. Click the icon that looks like a straight line or a pencil.

3. Click the spot on your drawing canvas where you want the line to begin, and then click where you want it to end.

4. To erase the line, select it with the program's selection tool, then press **DELETE**.

Use the zoom tool in your drawing program to zoom in on areas of your drawing and make sure that lines start and end where they're supposed to. Don't worry about drawing your quilt block to scale initially—you can always resize it later.

HOW TO JOIN AND UNJOIN LINES AND DELETE MORE LINES YOU DON'T WANT

When you want to join two seams in a quilt, you might tack them together with a small stitch. That's also what your drawing program does when it puts two lines together. It stitches them together and thinks of the two lines as forming a single path.

But sometimes it does this in strange ways—and when you don't expect it. You try to delete part of a block, and the program deletes a large portion of it. Or you try to move a line, and all its neighbors move with it.

That's why you need to know how to join lines, as well as how to unjoin them.

JOIN AND UNJOIN LINES IN CORELDRAW

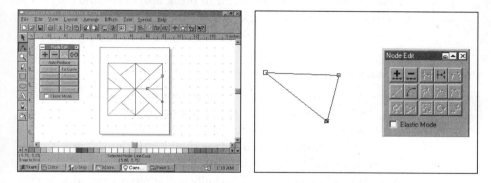

The Node Edit Roll-Up in CorelDraw 5 (left) and in CorelDraw 7 (right)

Drawing programs like CorelDraw make you deal with *nodes*. Nodes are small squares that mark junctures, bends, and joinings of lines, and sometimes they just magically appear in the center of a line. Like gremlins in the Steven Spielberg movie, nodes can multiply wildly. That's why it's important that you master the Node Edit menu (or Roll-Up, for you Corel experts).

To get at a line's nodes, select the line with the Pick tool. Big squares should appear. Now click on the Shape tool, and little transparent squares should appear on your selected line. These are the nodes. Head back to your drawing area and double-click on the node you want to fool with, or press CTRL-F10. The **Node Edit Roll-Up** should pop up, and the node you've selected will appear solid black. (If you're trying to do this for a square, triangle, or other closed object—like a quilt patch—first select the object and, from the **Arrange** menu, select **Convert to Curves**, or press CTRL-Q. Then click on the Shape tool and proceed as above.) To get rid of the selected node and its corresponding line segment, click the "minus" button. To add a node, click the "plus" button.

Why would you want to add a node? You might do so if you wanted to break a line—perhaps to move or delete a segment. You'd first add a node to the line and then click the break-apart button in the Node Edit Roll-Up.

The break-apart button in CorelDraw 5 (left) and in CorelDraw 7 (right).

You could then press DELETE to remove a segment or drag one of the nodes to move it and adjust the shape of the line.

For more control over where you add a node, you can click on the Shape tool and then double-click on the line where you want to add a node. The **Node Edit Roll-Up** will appear. Click the "plus" button to add a node in the selected location.

T * I * P

To delete more than one line at a time, hold down the SHIFT key while using the **Selection Arrow** to select each line. All of the lines you click on will be selected. Then press DELETE to delete all of the lines at once. This works in almost all Macintosh drawing programs.

WATCH OUT!

To erase a line, first select it with the selection tool, then press DELETE. If your drawing program highlights more than one line when you try to select only one, the program thinks the lines are joined. You can "unjoin" them (see directions in the next section) to delete only one, but sometimes it's easier to delete them all and then redraw the proper lines.

WHAT ABOUT DRAWING QUILT BLOCKS WITH A DRAWING TABLET?

Drawing tablets are fun, but it's easier to draw quilt blocks with the tools in your drawing program, like the straight-line tool. It's much easier to draw perfectly straight lines and curves with your drawing program than it is with a drawing tablet. (Chapter 15, which is about creating appliqué designs, talks more about using drawing tablets.)

NOTE TO MACINTOSH USERS

Luckily, most Macintosh drawing programs have no nodes to deal with.

A related button in some incarnations of CorelDraw looks like something you'd find in a wedding ring quilt. It's the "join" button. To use it, select two nodes and click this button to join them. Note that joining them does not draw a line between them; it creates a single node at a point halfway between the two original nodes.

Drawing programs like CorelDraw insist that "open" paths be "closed" in order for you to color them. In other words, all their nodes must be joined. Say you draw a quilt block and try to color individual patches of the block. You'll discover that CorelDraw will insist on coloring the entire block the same color. In order to color patches individually, you must draw each one as a closed path. We'll learn how to do that in Chapter 6.

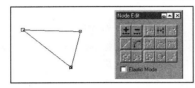

In CorelDraw 7, you can pop up the Node Edit Roll-Up by pressing **CTRL-FIO**. Use this menu to break apart lines and curves by selecting the Shape tool, clicking on a node in your patch, and then clicking on the appropriate Node Edit button to transform it.

USE CORELDRAW 7'S KNIFE TO CUT LINES

CorelDraw 7 has a nifty Knife tool that you can use to cut lines. To use it, hold your mouse button down on the Shape tool so that the flyout menu appears.

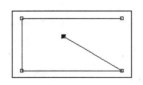

Click on the Knife button. Your cursor should turn into a little X-acto knife. Use your "knife" to break lines by clicking on the spot on the line where you'd like to break it. The knife will insert a new node at this point. Next, click the Shape tool and use it to break the line. You can use the Knife tool to cut curves as well as straight lines—and you can use it to cut squares into triangles and circles into half-moons.

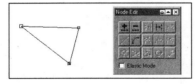

This started as a rectangle. We used CorelDraw 7's Knife tool to split the corner, then used the Shape tool to pull one of the rectangle's sides.

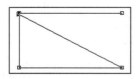

Here we have a triangle, and a lonely line shooting off into space, from what started as a rectangle.

HOW TO GROUP LINES INTO A BLOCK

No, we're not ready to create patches yet. Nor are we ready to start coloring. Those tasks require skills that are a bit more advanced. Right now we need to learn how to "group." You can group lines. You can group objects. When you group a bunch of stuff, the drawing program regards it as a single entity. When you draw a quilt block, you group the lines. If you don't group them, when you try to move the block—or expand it, duplicate it, squeeze it, or push it through virtual reality—the lines will scatter. Your drawing area will look like a tornado blew a scarecrow across Kansas.

Sometimes, however, you'll need to ungroup your quilt block in order to pull apart lines or edit portions of it.

T * I * P

If you want to group only some lines but not all of them, hold down the SHIFT key while selecting each line. Then group. This works in almost all Macintosh drawing programs.

GROUP OBJECTS IN CORELDRAW

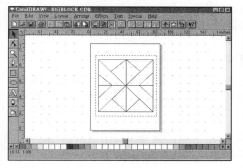

To group items in CorelDraw, you'll first need to select them. To do so, first click on the Pick tool. Draw a broken-line selection box (a box made up of dashed lines), or "rubber band" your quilt block by placing the cursor on a corner of the drawing area well outside the block. Press and hold the left mouse button and drag the cursor to the opposite outside corner of the drawing to select all of it. When you release the mouse button, black handles should appear around the block, telling you that it's been selected in its entirety. (If they appear around only a portion of the block, try again.) Head to the **Arrange** menu and click on **Group**. Or press CTRL-G. (Follow the same steps to ungroup the block, except select **Ungroup** from the **Arrange** menu or press CTRL-U.)

Once you have grouped your block, you can duplicate it (select it with the Pick tool and press CTRL-D), resize it (select it and pull on a corner handle), and perform on it other amazing transformations we'll learn about in future chapters.

GROUP OBJECTS IN CANVAS 5.0 AND 3.5

To group items in Canvas, first click on the Selection Arrow tool. Use the mouse to place the arrow on the upper left corner of your block. Now, holding down the mouse button, drag the arrow to the lower right outside corner. You should see a broken-line selection box appear around the block as you drag your arrow. When the block is encircled, release the mouse button. You should now see black handles on the lines, indicating that they are selected. Go to the **Object** menu and select **Group**, or press COMMAND-G to group the lines. Canvas should now treat the individual lines as one object—the handles should appear on the outside corners and midpoint of the block.

To ungroup the block, click on it with the Selection Arrow tool. You'll see handles around the block to indicate that it is selected. Now select **Ungroup** from the **Object** menu, or press COMMAND-U. The handles should now appear on the individual lines telling you that the block has been ungrouped.

Now that you know how to draw a basic quilt block, you can perform sophisticated transformations to it, like perspective warps. Or you can simply duplicate it, resize it, and flip it to create interesting variations. We talk more about these techniques in future chapters.

SUPER-QUILTER TIP!

Many quilters use quilting programs like Electric Quilt or drawing programs to verify the accuracy of quilt patterns in magazines. (Magazines are notorious for printing inaccurate templates.) By quickly redrawing a pattern on a grid, you can tell if it will sew up properly. And if it won't, you can adjust the pattern pieces accordingly.

QUICK BLOCKS

*Tired of fooling around with the pencil tool? Start by drawing a square with the rectangle tool. Import a piece of clip art into your drawing program. (Most high-end drawing programs come with a nice selection that you can use.) Stars work well. Select the clip art and size it to fit in the block properly. Use the rectangle tool to draw a box around it. Select the box with the selection tool, then use the drawing program's **Send to Back** command to move the box to the back of your star or other clip-art image. With the selection tool, draw a rubber-band box around the entire drawing, then group it. Voilà! It's a quilt block. Now they tell me!*

GROUP OBJECTS IN SUPERPAINT

Grouping in SuperPaint works exactly as described for Canvas 5.0 and 3.5, except that the Group and Ungroup commands are located on the Draw menu.

TIPS FOR GROUPING OBJECTS IN OTHER PROGRAMS

Follow these steps in any drawing program to group your block, so that its lines don't scatter when you duplicate it, resize it, or perform other transformations.

1. Click on the selection tool.

2. Use it to draw a rubber-band box around the quilt block. Or, if you're using a Macintosh program, hold down the SHIFT key and use the arrow to select each line that you want to group.

3. Select the **Group** command.

Now that you know how to draw a basic quilt block, you can perform sophisticated transformations to it like perspective warps. Or you can simply duplicate it, resize it, and flip it to create interesting variations. We talk more about these techniques in future chapters.

CHAPTER 5

BEYOND PALE LINES

A field guide to rectangles, ovals, arcs, Bezier curves, and other handy drawing tools.

You may have noticed that your drawing program offers other tools besides the Line or Freehand tool. Tools like a rectangle and an oval and all manner of arcs and curves. An especially problematic one is the Bezier tool—scary because it's named after a French mathematician, and you can never seem to get it to work right.

This chapter assumes that you've found these tools in your drawing toolbox. You initially avoided them, because the demands and responsibilities of the straight-line tool overwhelmed you. But you're feeling braver now. You'd like to venture into new areas. We'll show you what you can do with them and how to do it.

WHAT ARE THOSE BLACK LUMPS AROUND MY DRAWING, AND WHAT DO I DO WITH THEM?

Perhaps most disconcerting to newcomers to drawing programs is the concept of handles. Handles are the black squares that appear around a line or other drawn object when you have selected it. Before you can move, resize, skew, or otherwise transform a line or group of lines, you must first select it. You know that it is selected when you see the handles.

SELECTING AND TRANSFORMING OBJECTS

TO SELECT AN OBJECT. Click on the selection tool, and then use the fat arrow to click on a line of the object you wish to select. Handles will appear around the object to tell you that it's selected.

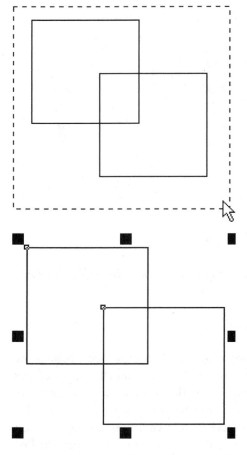

TO SELECT SEVERAL OBJECTS. Click on the selection tool. Holding the left mouse button down, draw a rubber-band box around all of the objects. (This box is also known as a marquee, selection box, or lasso.)

When you release the mouse button, black handles will appear around all of the objects, to show you that they've been selected. If the black handles don't appear around all the objects, try selecting them again.

TO SELECT YOUR ENTIRE DRAWING. Most drawing programs have a **Select All** feature on their **Edit** menu that will select everything on your drawing canvas.

TO MOVE A SELECTED OBJECT. Move the cursor to one of the lines of your selected object, hold the left mouse button down, and drag the object to where you want it.

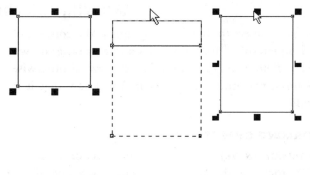

TO RESIZE A SELECTED OBJECT. Point the arrow at one of the big black handles framing the selected object. Hold the left mouse button down and drag the drawing to stretch it. Dragging a corner handle while pressing the **SHIFT** key will resize the object proportionally.

TO DELETE A SELECTED OBJECT. Select a line or portion of your drawing and press the **DELETE** key.

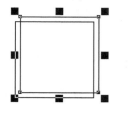

TO DUPLICATE A SELECTED OBJECT. Select a line or object, then press the duplication key combination (**CTRL-D** in most **PC** drawing programs). To move your new copy away from the original, move the cursor to one of the lines of the copy. Press the left mouse button and drag the object to where you want it.

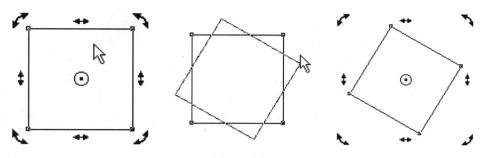

TO ROTATE A SELECTED OBJECT. Move the cursor to one of the lines of the selected objects, and click a second time so that the black handles turn into arrows. (Or simply click twice in order to select the object and display the arrows.) Point the cursor at one of the corner sets of arrows, hold the mouse button down, and "pull" the object either clockwise or counterclockwise in order to rotate it.

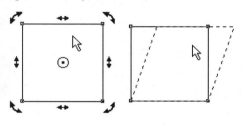

TO SKEW A SELECTED OBJECT. Point the cursor at one of the lines of the selected objects, and click a second time so that the black handles turn into arrows. (Or simply click twice in order to select the object and display the arrows.) Move the cursor to an arrow in the middle of a boundary line (in other words, not a corner set of arrows). Hold the mouse button down and drag that side of the object to skew it.

THE VERSATILE RECTANGLE

It hovers in the center of your toolbox like a freeway sign. You know that if you click on it you'll get what you want: a rectangle or square. Nothing weird will happen.

DRAW A SQUARE

To use the square tool, click on the square tool, click on your canvas, and drag the mouse while holding the mouse button down. When you release the mouse button you should have a square. If you hold the CTRL key down while you drag the mouse—the SHIFT key if on a Mac—you'll create a perfect square. To resize your square, select it so that handles appear around it and then drag the handles. Drag a corner to enlarge or shrink it and keep it perfectly square.

WHAT YOU CAN DO WITH SQUARES

Draw a square and duplicate it to make a whole bunch. Push them together to make a nine-patch. Select them by drawing a rubber band around them, and group them together to form a block. Resize them, duplicate them, and pull them around as a group so that you get some of the interesting quilt layouts shown here.

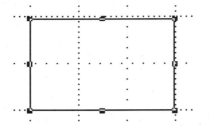

To turn your square into a rectangle, click on it to select it, and then pull one of the handles with your mouse.

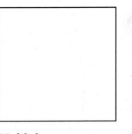

Hold down CTRL while dragging your mouse—or the SHIFT key on a Mac—to create a perfect square.

Use the rectangle tool to quickly make a nine-patch. Be sure to group the individual squares so that the patches stick together.

After duplicating your nine-patch, stretch it into rectangles of different sizes.

The nine-patch in the center of this quilt layout is the same as the nine-patch that was duplicated to create the above figure. Only this time, two-point perspective was applied to it, and it was duplicated multiple times and rotated.

THE ORNERY OVAL

Ovals aren't a part of many traditional quilt block designs, but they should be because they're so versatile. They can be hula hoops one minute, flower petals the next. No matter where you put an oval it's never out of fashion.

DRAW AN OVAL OR A CIRCLE

To draw an oval or a circle, click on the Oval or Ellipse tool, click on your screen where you want to place the oval, and drag the crosshairs while holding the mouse button down. Release. For a perfect circle, hold down the **CTRL** key while you're dragging, or the **SHIFT** key on the Mac. Hold it down until after you've released the mouse button.

WHAT YOU CAN DO WITH CIRCLES AND OVALS

Fill your circles with a color or fill pattern from your drawing program. Make lots of ovals in various sizes and shapes and put them together to get a quilt design. Overlap them to get old-fashioned quilt block designs like Clamshell.

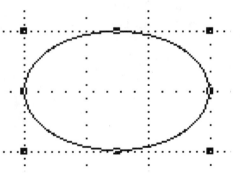

Anyone for clams? You can create an old-fashioned clamshell effect by tiling and layering circles. Fill them with your drawing program's fill patterns to simulate cotton prints.

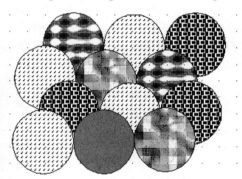

Use the selection tool to select your oval so that handles appear around it. Drag the handles with your mouse to stretch the oval.

1. We lined up circles of the same size.

2. With the drawing program's snap-to grid option activated and the grid set to ⅛ inch, we compressed each circle horizontally in successive increments of ⅛ inch, pushing the circles together so that they just meet.

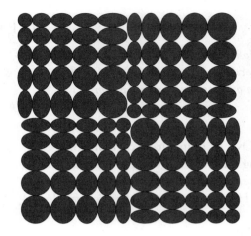

3. We repeatedly duplicated the row and then grouped and dragged the new row upward, compressing each new row vertically in ⅛-inch snap increments. The result is this optical illusion design.

THE ADAPTABLE ARC

If your drawing program offers an arc tool, you're a lucky duck. Mac programs do, but PC programs like CorelDraw often don't. An arc tool makes it easy to draw blocks like Orange Peel and Drunkard's Path because you can use it draw quarter-ovals and quarter-circles. Arc tools are also handy for drawing stencils.

DRAW AN ARC

To draw an arc, click on the Arc tool. Move the crosshairs to the spot where you want to begin drawing. Click and hold the mouse button down while you drag the mouse. To draw a quarter-circle, hold the **SHIFT** key down while dragging.

To change the size of the arc, select it and then drag any of its handles. (If you're using SuperPaint on the Mac, you can change the size of the arc by selecting and dragging a handle. You can also reshape the arc. Select the arc and pull down the **Draw** menu. Select **Reshape Arc**, or press **COMMAND-R**. Now drag one of the two handles to reshape the arc. Note that the reshaping is limited to the outline of the oval of which the arc represents one quarter.)

This is what your arc should look like.

T * I * P

*Canvas users can hold down the **OPTION** key while dragging to an arc from the center out. In Canvas 5.0, the Arc tool is on the Oval tool menu.*

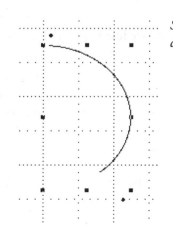

Select the arc and drag any of its handles to change its size and shape.

WHAT IF YOU USE CORELDRAW AND DON'T HAVE AN ARC TOOL?

Dump your PC and buy a Mac. No, seriously, if you're a Corellian (someone who is constantly being tortured by CorelDraw), cozy up to the Oval tool, described earlier. You'll also need to make friends with the Node Edit Roll-Up.

There are several ways to draw a perfect arc in CorelDraw, though none are as straightforward as using an arc tool. (Are you sure you don't want to buy a Mac?) The easiest way to draw an arc is to draw a circle or an oval and then chop it into bits. (Remember the node editing rigmarole in the last chapter? Now it's starting to make sense.) Here's how:

Use your Oval tool to draw a circle or oval. With the circle selected, click on the Shape tool. When you move the now-bloated cursor over your circle, a little box or node should appear on the rim of the circle. Click and drag the node around the circle with your mouse to remove as much of the circle as you want. If you drag your cursor outside the circle, you'll get an arc. If you drag it inside the circle, you'll get a pie piece (which you can later color or make into a patch).

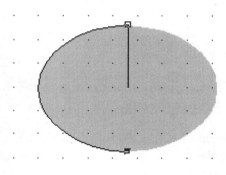

In CorelDraw, you can make an arc by beginning with a circle and using the Shape tool to move its node into an arc.

To change the size and shape of your arc, click on the Pick tool. Click on the arc to select it, then drag any of the handles to change the arc's size and shape.

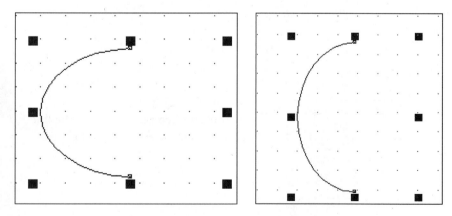

To change the arc's shape, select it and pull the handles.

CORELDRAW CURVE-DRAWING TRICKS

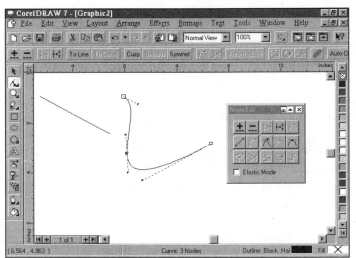

CorelDraw gives you some easy ways to draw and manipulate curves. First, you need to familiarize yourself with the Node Edit Roll-Up (CTRL-F10). What you can do is use the Freehand tool to draw a straight line, convert the line to curves, and then use the various curve-editing buttons on the Node Edit Roll-Up to twist and bend it. Here's how:

 Draw a straight line with the Freehand tool.

 Click on the Shape tool. Use the big, fat arrow cursor to click on the transparent box-shaped handle at each end of the line.

Now click on the button in the Node Edit Roll-Up that will convert the line to curves. New black bumps or nodes should appear on the line. You push and pull these bumps to make your line into an arc. Use the arc-editing tools in the Node Edit Roll-Up to shape your arc.

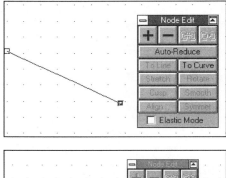

1. In CorelDraw 5, click on the To Curve button to convert your line to curves.

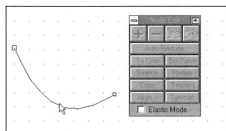

2. You can then push and pull the line around as if it were a piece of elastic.

WHAT YOU CAN DO WITH ARCS

Once you've mastered the art of drawing arcs, a whole new world opens for you. No more will your quilt blocks be restricted to dippy triangles and squares—you can plunge off into the realm of Orange Peels, Hearts-and-Gizzards, and even appliqué. Use the Rectangle tool to draw a box around your arc. Put two arcs together and multiply them to make leaves and petals. Or arrange arcs in a circle to make a perfectly symmetrical Whig Rose. Here are some examples.

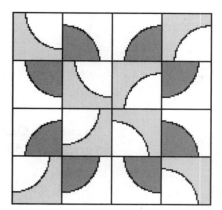

Drunkard's Path

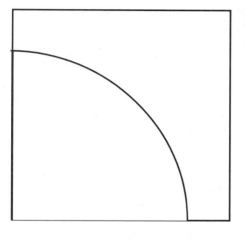

1. Use the arc tool to create a pie piece. Then draw lines around your arc to box it in.

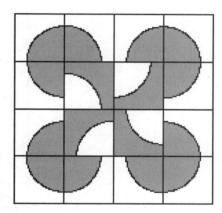

Wonders of the World

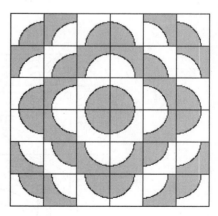

Love Ring

2. Duplicate, stretch, and flip your pie pieces to create this quilt layout.

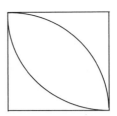

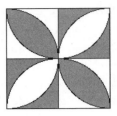

1. To create an Orange Peel block, start by drawing an arc. Add a second arc to it.

2. Using the Line or Freehand tool, draw the rest of the box.

3. Duplicate the box, put them together, and rotate them to create an Orange Peel block.

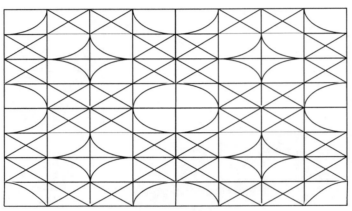

Combine blocks drawn with arcs with ones made up only of straight lines for an interesting effect.

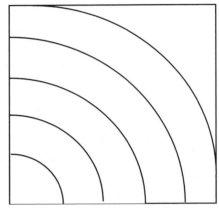

1. Draw a series of symmetrical arcs to create a block that looks fairly ordinary but offers a wealth of possibilities.

2. Duplicate, stretch, and rotate the block to make what could either be a lovely multicolored quilt layout or a quilting stencil.

THE FOOTLOOSE FREEHAND CURVE

In the previous chapter we avoided talking about drawing curves with the Freehand tool because they always come out looking a bit ragged. You can spruce them up a bit, but they still sometimes look a bit mangy. In most instances, you should reserve the freehand curve for appliqué.

T * I * P

Remember to turn snap-to-grid off when making curved lines.

DRAW A FREEHAND CURVE

To draw a freehand curve, select the Freehand tool. Hold your mouse button down and drag it to form the desired line on your screen. Release the button. To make the line smoother or a bit curvier in CorelDraw, select the Shape tool. Then, with the enlarged cursor, push the line's nodes (those transparent boxes) to form the shape you desire. Give the line extra nodes by double-clicking on one of the nodes to pull up the Node Edit Roll-Up. Click on the "plus" button to add a node to the line. You can use your mouse to stretch it around.

Use the Node Edit Roll-Up in Corel-Draw to add nodes to your freehand curve, which will make it easier to bend and shape.

USE THE SMOOTH POLYGON TOOL IN
CANVAS 3.5 TO DRAW FOOTLOOSE FREEHAND CURVES

To draw freehand curves with Canvas 3.5, first select the Freehand tool and slide over to select **Make Smooth Polygon**. Position your mouse in the document where you want to begin your curve, and then hold the mouse button down while dragging the mouse to establish your curve. Release the mouse button when your shape is complete. Your curved line will be as accurate as your ability to draw and control the mouse. To edit the curve, select the Selection

Arrow tool. Then place the arrow on the curve and double-click your mouse button. This brings up a line of small boxes called edit points that make up the path of the curve. Use the arrow to select an edit point. While holding the mouse button down, drag the box to reshape the curve. You can resize the curve with ease, but you'll quickly find that reshaping it is *much* more tedious.

WHAT YOU CAN DO WITH FREEHAND CURVES

In most instances, freehand curves are a bit perilous when plied outside of the dainty world of appliqué. When you need more symmetrical curves for blocks like Drunkard's Path, you're better off using the Arc tool, or even the dreaded Bezier curve.

TALES OF THE BEZIER MONSTER

Say you want to draw a curve with a little more personality than a standard arc. The curves you draw with the freehand tool always come out frumpy looking. When you want a smooth curve, one that swirls like the edge of a cloud, use the Bezier tool. The Bezier tool can be a bear. It never seems to work logically. It pops dashed lines that work like levers all over your screen. What's more, it's *alleged* to be guided by mathematical precepts. So is the atom bomb.

NOTE

The Bezier tool operates by the same principles of most drawing programs. Every curved segment has four points: one at each end (called anchor points) and two that hover around the curve—sometimes called control handles. You pull these control handles to reshape the line. Although the Bezier tool is awkward to use at first, it's incredibly handy, especially for drawing appliqué. Learning to use it well is worth your time.

CREATE A BEZIER CURVE IN CORELDRAW

To draw a Bezier curve in CorelDraw, position the cursor on the Freehand tool, and hold the left mouse button down until the flyout menu appears.  Select the Bezier tool. Now move your cursor to the spot on the screen where you want the curve to start. Press and hold the mouse button. A dark box should appear where your curve is going to start.

Drag the mouse in the direction in which you want to draw the curve. As you drag the mouse, two points should appear and move in opposite directions from the node. The distance between them and the node determines the depth of the curve. Their angle will determine the curve's slope.

Release the mouse button when these two points are in the proper position.

Now move the cursor to where you want the curve to end. Press and hold the mouse button. A second node should appear with a line connecting it to the place where the line is to start. Holding the mouse button down, pull the second set of points out, to establish the curve of the line, as shown here. When you release the mouse button, the curve should be drawn. You can continue in the same manner, drawing curves connected to this one. Press the spacebar twice to start drawing a new, unconnected curve.

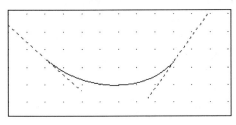

Think of your Bezier curve as a piece of elastic that's being pulled and stretched by two levers with dashed lines.

CREATE A BEZIER CURVE IN CANVAS 5.0

There are two tools in Canvas 5.0 that let you create Bezier curves: the Freehand tool and the Curve tool. The Freehand tool works almost like the Bezier tool in Canvas 3.5. (see the next section). To use it, select the Curve tool from the toolbox and, while still holding the mouse button down, slide over to select the Freehand tool. Position the crosshairs on your screen where you want to begin your curve. Hold the mouse button down and drag your mouse to establish your curve. Release the mouse button when your shape is complete. To edit the curve, click on the Selection Arrow tool, then place the arrow on the curve and double-click the mouse button. The anchor points should appear. Follow the instructions for Canvas 3.5, in the next section, to edit your curve, or see the Canvas manual for its excellent editing instructions.

The 5.0 manual claims that the Curve tool is more versatile than the Freehand tool. We think it takes some getting used to. To use it, select the pen-shaped Curve tool from the toolbox. Position the crosshairs on your screen where you want to begin the path for your curve. Click your mouse to set the first anchor point, but before releasing the mouse button, drag the mouse to set the first tangent line. Each anchor point defines where a path segment begins and ends. The tangent line controls the shape of the curve. Changing the length of the tangent line changes the depth of the curve.

Continue creating your curve this way, double-clicking on the last anchor point to complete the shape.

To edit the curve, choose the Selection Arrow tool. Place the arrow on the curve and double-click your mouse button—the anchor points should appear. Follow the instructions below for Canvas 3.5 to edit the curve, or see the manual for its excellent editing instructions.

CREATE A BEZIER CURVE IN CANVAS 3.5

To create a Bezier curve in Canvas 3.5, click the Freehand drawing tool in the toolbox, and select **Make Bezier Curves**. Position the crosshairs where you want the curve to start. Hold the mouse button down and drag it to establish where the curve should be. Release the mouse button to finish the shape. To resize your curve, click on the Selection Arrow tool, then click on the curve to select it. Drag the handles that appear around it to resize the curve.

To edit the curve, select it and press **COMMAND-E** to place it in Edit mode. Anchor points should appear along the curve. To change the curve, you can move an anchor point or its tangent line to reshape it. Click on an anchor point to display its direction points and tangents.

Change the length of a tangent line to change the size of the curve. To do this, click on the direction handle at the end of the tangent line and, holding the mouse button down, drag the line.

Add a point to the curve by holding down the **OPTION** key (the cursor will change to a plus sign) and clicking the mouse where you want to add the point.

Delete a point from the curve by holding down the **OPTION** and **SHIFT** keys (the cursor will change to a minus sign) and clicking the mouse on the point to be deleted.

T * I * P

There's a more user-friendly way to make a Bezier curve with the Curve tool in Canvas 5.0. Select the Curve tool from the toolbox. Position the crosshairs on your document where you want to begin your path. Click your mouse button to set the first anchor point, then release the button, move the mouse, and click the mouse button to set the second anchor point. Continue clicking without dragging in this way, and when you're done, double-click on the last anchor point to complete your shape.

This method of using the Curve tool produces only anchor points—it won't produce tangent lines. (No fun when it comes time to reshape the curve.) But you can easily add tangent lines to make reshaping easier. To do this, choose the Selection Arrow tool, then place the arrow on the curve and double-click to put the curve into Edit mode. Select an anchor point by clicking on it. Now press and hold the TAB key. At the same time, position the pointer inside the anchor point box and press and hold the mouse button. Still holding the mouse button down, drag away from the anchor point to create a tangent line. Voilà! A tangent line right where you want it!

T * I * P

If your drawn curve is not as smooth as you'd like, try lowering the speed setting of your mouse.

It is much easier to create smooth, flowing curves with fewer anchor points. In drawing an S curve, this illustration has the Freehand Tolerance set too tight. Notice all of the anchor points—this is no fun to edit.

Here the tolerance is set too loose—there are only two anchor points, not enough to edit into a smooth curve unless you add another point or two.

Here the tolerance is set one notch to the left of loose. We've found this setting to be the best to work with.

After selecting the Edit mode, we easily shaped the curve into a smooth "S" shape.

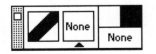

Before you draw a Bezier curve in SuperPaint, the Area Fill box must be set to None. Otherwise, the program will automatically close your curved line.

When you edit a Bezier curve in Canvas, the curve will display the anchor points along its path. Selecting an anchor point will display its tangent line. A direction handle is at each end of the tangent line.

You can change the size of the curve by dragging the tangent line's direction handle toward or away from the anchor point. By dragging the tangent line's direction handle at an angle, you can change the size of the curve segment.

SET THE FREEHAND TOLERANCE

Under **File**, select **Preferences**. Select **Bezier & Polygon** from the left scroll box, and under Freehand Tolerance, click the circle to the left of Loose. Practice making large "S" shapes to get the hang of using the Bezier curve.

CREATE A BEZIER CURVE IN SUPERPAINT

To draw a Bezier curve in SuperPaint, start in the Draw layer. Select the Freehand tool from the Tools palette. (In order to draw a curved line, the Area Fill box must be set to None.)

Position the crosshairs where you want your curve to start. Hold the mouse button down and drag it to establish where the curve should be. Release the mouse button to finish the shape. To resize your curve, click on it with the Selection Arrow to select it. Handles will appear around it. Drag the handles to make the curve larger or smaller. To edit the curve, select it and choose **Reshape Bezier** from the **Reshape** menu (it appears in place of the Draw menu). You can drag the anchor points themselves or drag the reshaping handles, as the tangent lines are called. To add an anchor point, hold down the **OPTION** key and then click where you want to add it. To delete an anchor point, click on the point you want to delete and then press the **DELETE** key. When you're done reshaping the curve, click outside it. The Reshape menu will revert to the Draw menu.

WHAT YOU CAN DO WITH BEZIER CURVES

Because Bezier drawing is so precise, it's a quick way to draw patches (or closed objects) that can be colored or filled with patterns. When you get the hang of it, it's especially useful for drawing curved, symmetrical patches, as well as lovely curved appliqué designs.

JUDY & GLORIA'S TIP FOR SMOOTH BEZIER CURVES

Using longer tangent lines to shape your curves is more effective than using shorter ones.

THE POWERFUL POLYGON

With the Polygon tool you can quickly and accurately draw many-sided geometric patches. Because drawing programs recognize patches drawn with the Polygon tool as closed objects, you can color or shade them with fill patterns without messing around with node joining tools and other such nonsense.

But the Polygon tool works differently in every drawing program. While in many drawing programs you can use it to draw all kinds of shapes and patches, including triangles and hexagons, in CorelDraw 7 you can use it to draw only true polygons and stars. And the Polygon tool is completely absent from earlier versions of CorelDraw. Here's how it works in different drawing programs.

JUDY & GLORIA'S AMAZING POLYGON TIP!

Be sure that snap-to-grid is activated so that you can draw your polygon patches accurately to a grid. Also, activate snap-to-object, if your program has it, so that your patches align with each other.

CREATE AND EDIT A POLYGON IN CORELDRAW 7

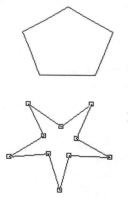

1. You can use the Polygon tool only to draw polygons and stars, but that doesn't mean you can't have a lot of fun with it. Draw a polygon, turn it inside out by pulling on its nodes with the Shape tool, and you get a star.

2. Convert your star to curves and you can create a wavy star.

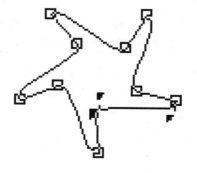

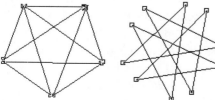

3. Turn your polygon inside out, and spin the corners around to make a star with patches.

CREATE AND EDIT A POLYGON IN CANVAS 5.0

To draw a polygon in Canvas 5.0, click the Curve tool with the mouse and, while holding the mouse button down on the Curve tool, slide over to select the Polygon tool. Position the crosshairs on your document where you want to begin your polygon. Click once. A small, hollow square, which we'll call a point, will appear, indicating the beginning of your shape. Move the crosshairs, without holding the mouse button down, then click to establish the second point. The two points should connect to form a line. Continue in this manner until your shape is complete. If you end at the beginning point, your shape will automatically complete itself. If you want to create an open-ended polygon, double-click the last point to finish.

To resize a polygon, click on the Selection Arrow tool. Place the arrow inside the polygon and click once. Handles will appear around the outside of the polygon, and a dashed line will enclose the shape. Grab a handle and drag it to the desired new shape.

To edit a polygon, select the Selection Arrow tool. Place the arrow inside the polygon and double-click. Only the points on the polygon will appear. To edit a point, click on it and drag it to the desired location.

CREATE AND EDIT A POLYGON IN CANVAS 3.5

To create a polygon in Canvas 3.5, select the Polygon tool and follow the instructions given in the previous section for Canvas 5.0. Creating and resizing are the same.

To edit a polygon, use the Polygon submenu. To see this menu, hold the mouse button down on the Polygon tool. The Polygon submenu allows you to edit, add, and delete points. Selecting **Edit Points** allows you to grab a point and move the line to a new location. Selecting **Add Points** will turn your crosshairs into a plus symbol, and selecting **Delete Points** will turn your crosshairs into a minus symbol. To use either option, select it and place the plus or minus symbol on your shape where you want to add or delete points.

CREATE AND EDIT A POLYGON IN SUPERPAINT

To draw a polygon in SuperPaint, go to the Draw layer and select the Polygon tool. Position the crosshairs on your document where you want to begin your shape. Click once, then move the crosshairs, without holding the mouse button down. You should see a line following your crosshairs. When the line is the length you want, click your mouse to set it. Then move the crosshairs again and click to create the second line. Continue in this manner until you are ready to complete your polygon. To stop drawing, double-click your mouse.

To resize a polygon in SuperPaint, select it and then drag any of its handles. You can also reshape the polygon. Select the polygon and pull down the **Draw** menu. Select **Reshape Polygon**, or press **COMMAND-R**. Multiple reshaping handles will appear. Select a handle to reshape your polygon. To exit the Reshape mode, click outside the polygon, or just select another tool.

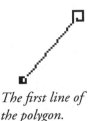

The beginning of the shape.

The first line of the polygon.

The completed polygon.

T * I * P

*By default, Canvas 3.5 has you define each point on the shape by clicking and releasing the mouse button rather than by dragging a line. To change this default so that you see the line being drawn, go to the File menu and select **Preferences**. Then select **Bezier & Polygons** in the left column and click to check the box next to **Canvas 2.1 Polygon Creation**.*

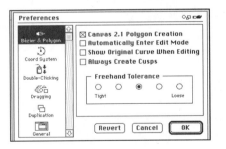

T * I * P

Before you draw a polygon in SuperPaint, the Area Fill box must be set to None. Otherwise, your shape will fill with whatever color or pattern is in the Fill box.

CHAPTER 6

PATCHES, PATCHES, AND MORE PATCHES!

How to turn all that junk on your computer screen into real quilt patches.

"What? They use *paper* pieces? You mean they cut out all these patches from paper?"

That's what one of us (we won't admit which one) gasped when she was learning to quilt. She had grown so thrilled with slicing up yards of fabric in minutes with a rotary cutter that the idea of assembling a quilt any other way seemed slow and primitive.

Whether quickly pieced with a sewing machine and foundation papers or meticulously hand-pieced with the help of paper templates, patches are the foundation of quilts—we don't have to tell you that. But getting a drawing program to draw a patch is more complicated than merely drawing the lines with a mouse. (If computers were really advanced they would include special keyboard buttons that would let you pop a patch onto the screen whenever you wished.) Here are some things you need to know about drawing patches with your computer.

You need to draw your patch as a *single, closed object*. That means that the line around it must make one continuous path and that the lines that make up the sides of the path must be joined. This is starting to sound like high school geometry, isn't it?

A patch needs to be a single, closed object in order for you to

• Color it

• Print a template for it

• Group it together with other patches to create bigger quilt designs

If all this seems complicated, think of a patch lying on your sewing room floor. It is a single, unbroken cosmic entity. You can pick it up. You can throw it around. You can step on it. That's what a patch on your computer screen should be: a unique cosmic entity.

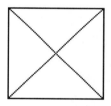

If you take a square and draw diagonal lines from corner to corner, it might look like you have made four triangles, but they are not really closed patches.

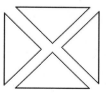

In order to make closed patches, you need to draw each triangle individually.

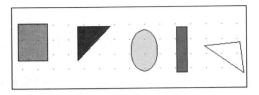

Patches.

A HIGHER COSMIC PURPOSE FOR PATCHES

Let's say you've already drawn a quilt block. It looks magnificent sitting there on your screen. But when you head for the bucket tool to color it, the whole thing turns into one blazing magenta square.

Why does this happen? Because you need to turn the lines of your block into closed objects, or patches, in order to color them individually. The easiest way to do this will depend upon your drawing program, and it's easier in some than in others.

There's another reason to make patches. If you've been drawing for more than fifteen minutes with a drawing program like CorelDraw, you know how hard it is to get all the little pieces of your quilt block perfectly symmetrical and even. By creating patches with the rectangle or oval tool, you have more control over the shape and dimensions of a block's patches than you do when you draw them with the freehand or straight-line tool.

You can make one patch "to spec," then quickly duplicate it, push all your duplicates into blocks, group your blocks, and voilà! You have a neat little quilt block. You can then duplicate that block, pull it, stretch it, resize it, lay it out into a quilt top, add seam allowances, and other wonderful things. You'll learn all about these techniques in the chapters that follow this one. But first you need to know the basics: how to create and fill in patches.

CREATING PATCHES

There are a number of ways to make patches. The method that works best for you will depend upon your style of designing. You can

- Draw patches with the freehand or line tool, then embark upon the laborious process of joining their lines to close them.

- Quickly outline patches with the Bezier straight or curve line tool and let the Bezier tool join the lines for you. Or you can draw them with the polygon tool, if your drawing program has one.

- Place your original drafted quilt block on one layer in your drawing program and turn it into "guides" (broken lines that look like seams, with which lines drawn on other drawing layers will align). You then trace your patches on top of the guides—on another drawing layer—making each into a closed object as you trace. You'd use the freehand or line tool, the Bezier tool, or the polygon tool.

- Use the rectangle and oval tools to draw a patch, then push and pull the patch to the size and shape you want.

- Some combination of the above.

Here are the easiest ways to create patches in your favorite drawing programs.

CREATE PATCHES IN CORELDRAW

CorelDraw, like many other sophisticated drawing programs, lets you draw things on different layers. Most people will never use this feature unless they like to, say, draw airplane engines in their spare time. But we quilters are not most people. You can use these different layers to work with patches by drawing your quilt block on one layer and then tracing its patches on another. That way you can quickly draw your patches as closed objects and then color them or print them as templates.

CorelDraw has another useful feature called "guides." When you designate an object as a guide, you can have the lines of objects that you draw on a different layer "snap to" or align with the lines of the guide on the layer below. So you can take your drafted quilt block, turn its lines into guides, and then trace your patches on a different layer. Here's how:

1. Draw and group your block (select it and press **CTRL-G**, as explained in Chapter 4), then display the Layers Roll-Up by pressing **CTRL-F3**.

2. Press **ALT-E-A**, or pull down the **Edit** menu and choose **Select All**.

The first step in turning a quilt block into patches in CorelDraw is to turn your block drawing into guidelines. You do it with the Layers Roll-Up (CTRL-F3). (The CorelDraw 5 Layers Roll-Up is shown here.) Not only can you turn the block into guides with this menu, but you can also use it to move between the different layers of your drawing.

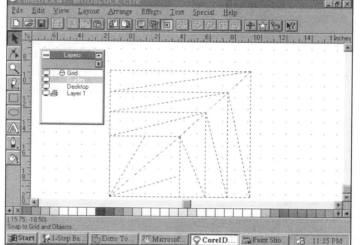

T * I * P

You select objects in CorelDraw 7 by selecting the Pick tool and then clicking on the center of the object or on one of its outer lines. In earlier versions of CorelDraw, you select unfilled objects by clicking on an outer line only.

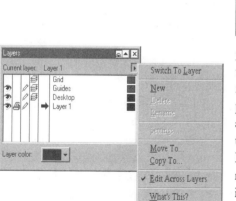

3. In the Layers Roll-Up, click on the tiny right-pointing arrow in the top right-hand corner. In the menu that pops up, click on **Move To**. A fat arrow will appear. Move the arrow to the **Guides** entry listed in the Layers Roll-Up, and click on it. This should move your quilt block from the drawing layer to the guidelines layer and turn it into a set of guides, as evidenced by broken lines.

T * I * P

When drawing with the Freehand tool, you need to double-click on each corner of the patch while drawing it. When drawing with the Bezier tool, you have to click only once on each corner.

IMPORTANT CORELDRAW TIP!

It's easiest to draw patches with the Bezier tool because it's more precise than the Freehand tool and *because the Bezier tool makes it easier to draw your patches as closed objects.*

DESIGN TIP

As you draw patches, fill them with color so that they're easier to see. Color fills also make it easy to tell when a patch has become a closed object—if it's not closed you won't be able to color it. To color a patch, click on the Pick tool, then click in the center of the patch (or the outside line of the patch if you're using a version of CorelDraw prior to version 7) so *that square handles pop up around it. Now click on a color on the bottom of your screen to fill it with color.*

BE CAREFUL!

Do not join any of the patches together as you draw them. Instead, make each patch an individual entity by tracing around it. Think of your drawing line as a thread. Once you've drawn one patch, "break off the thread" by clicking once on the corner where you began drawing if you're drawing with the Freehand tool, double-clicking if you're drawing with the Bezier one.

4. Return to the drawing layer to draw your patches by double-clicking on **Layer 1** in the Layers Roll-Up menu. You should be presented with a pop-up menu asking all sorts of questions. Just make sure **Visible** and **Printable** are selected. [In CorelDraw 7, simply make sure the eye icon and the printer icon are not dimmed in the Layers Roll-Up.] Click **OK**.

5. Turn on the Snap to Guidelines feature by pulling down the **Layout** menu (press ALT-L) and clicking a check beside **Snap to Guidelines**.

6. Now you're ready to draw your patches by tracing over the guidelines to make closed objects. You can use the Freehand, Bezier, Rectangle, and Oval tools to quickly form closed patches.

If you're using the Freehand or Bezier tool, trace patches one at a time, joining their nodes to close them. To do that, click on the Freehand or Bezier tool. (You get to the Bezier tool by holding your mouse button down while the cursor is sitting on the Freehand tool. The Bezier tool will appear in the flyout menu that pops up.) When your cursor changes to crosshairs, move the crosshairs to a corner of a patch. Click the corner to start, and release the mouse button. Pull the line to the next corner of the patch and click on the corner twice if you're drawing with the Freehand tool, once if you're using the Bezier tool. Pull the line to the next corner, and so on. When you've traced all around your patch, click once on the corner (or node) where you started drawing to "break off" your drawing line with the Freehand tool; double-click to break off if you're drawing with the Bezier tool.

You need to trace around each patch in this way. Use the Zoom tool to zoom in on corners to make sure they line up with those of your original design.

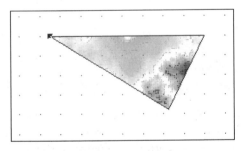

Drawing patches in CorelDraw is easy with the Bezier tool. Click the corners of the patch, and the Bezier tool will connect the corners as you go. If you have selected a default color or fill pattern by clicking on the Fill tool with no object selected, the patch will fill with color once it's a closed object.

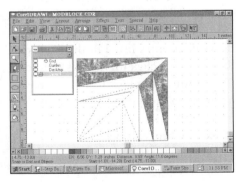

Once your drafted block has been converted to guides (with broken lines), switch to the drawing layer and trace around each patch with the Freehand or Bezier tool, clicking (with the Bezier tool) or double-clicking (with the Freehand tool) on the corners.

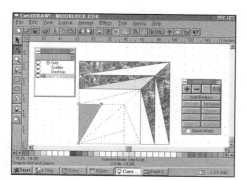

You can make a triangular patch by using the Rectangle tool to draw a square, then using the Node Edit Roll-Up to delete one of the square's corners.

CREATE PATCHES IN CANVAS 5.0, 3.5, AND SUPERPAINT

Whew! In Canvas and SuperPaint there are no nodes to fuss with. Instead, drawing patches is simply a matter of using the tools described in Chapter 4. Just be sure that your shape is closed.

Our favorite way to create patches for quilt block design is with the Polygon, Square, and Oval tools. See Chapter 4 for how best to use these tools.

We often start a design using the line tool—it's a fun way to doodle and experiment. But when it comes time to make templates or to use color and fill, you'll appreciate making patches and working in layers. Place your original line drawing on one layer. Then, using the Polygon tool, trace the shapes you need into patches on another layer. Here's how to use layers in the various programs.

WORK WITH LAYERS IN CANVAS 5.0

Drawings made in Canvas are automatically made on Layer 1, but you can work with additional layers by using the Layers menu. To do so, pull down the **Layout** menu, slide down to **Layers,** and slide across to choose a function of the Layers menu.

You can move from layer to layer, or you can view the **Layer Info** box, where you can create a new layer, hide layers, or show layers.

Another way to work with layers is by using the Current Layer box at the bottom left of your document window. Press and hold the mouse button down in the box that tells what the current layer is. This brings up a list of your layers inside the Layer Info box. Click **New** to create a new layer.

To change the name of a layer, highlight the layer name inside the Layer Info box and type a new name. As long as a layer name is highlighted, you can click on the Options button for additional ways to modify the selected layer—you can change a color, make the layer visible, lock it, password-protect it, or make it printable.

When it's time to print a layer, choose **Print** from the **File** menu (or press **COMMAND-P**) to bring up the Print dialog box. Click on the arrow in the box next to **Print**, and slide to select **Layers.** This brings up another box where you can select the layers you wish to print.

WORKING WITH LAYERS

CORELDRAW PATCH-MAKING POWER TIP!

This trick comes from CorelDraw quilt design expert Jan Cabral: To draw a triangular patch quickly, use the Rectangle tool. Select the Rectangle tool and move the crosshairs to a corner of a patch on your drafted quilt block. Click on the corner, and, holding the left mouse button down, drag the square so that three of its corners line up with three corners of the patch guides. Release the mouse button when they're perfectly aligned. Click on the Pick tool, and click on the square to select it. In CorelDraw 7, press CTRL-Q to convert its lines to curves. Press CTRL-V in earlier versions of CorelDraw.

Double-click on the Shape tool to bring up the Node Edit Roll-Up, or press CTRL-F10. Click on the node on your square that you'd like to delete. You want to delete the one that's not lined up with a corner on the guides. (You remember nodes, don't you? Those boxy outlines sitting on the corners of your square?) When you click on the node, it will turn to solid black, indicating that it is selected.

Now click on the "minus" button in the Node Edit Roll-Up. The selected node should disappear, and you'll be left with a triangular patch. Cool, huh?

REMEMBER

The Line tool creates lines, not closed shapes. So even if you make what appears to be a closed shape using the Line tool, it's not going to accept a fill unless you convert your entire drawing to a bitmap (see Chapter 10).

DESIGN TIPS

• For precision patches, turn on the grid and show the rulers.
• Use COMMAND-D to duplicate patches.
• Turn snap-to-grid off and experiment with odd-shaped polygons for interesting new designs.

NOTE

Although SuperPaint does have a Draw layer and a Paint layer, they serve different purposes. SuperPaint does not support working in drawing layers.

After selecting Layers from the Print dialog box, select which layers you want to print from this box.

WORK WITH LAYERS IN CANVAS 3.5

Like Canvas 5.0, a new drawing created in Canvas 3.5 is automatically on Layer 1. To work with different layers, use the Current Layer box located at the bottom left corner of the document window.

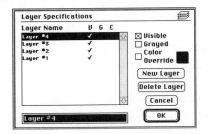

The Current Layer box is located at the bottom left corner of your document. A new document automatically starts on Layer #1.

To create a new layer, press and hold the mouse button down in the Current Layer box. Drag the mouse up to **Layer Specs**. You can also pull down the **Layout** menu and select **Layer Specs** or use the key combination **COMMAND-B**.

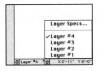

In the Layer Specifications dialog box, click on the New Layer button. The new layer is highlighted. You can keep the default name (Layer #2) or name the layer something obvious so that you'll know what it contains.

Here are some more tips for working with layers:

- Each layer can be made visible or grayed, or can be a color. You can delete a layer by selecting it and clicking the Delete Layer button.

- To work in a particular layer, press and hold the mouse button down in the Current Layer box. While still holding the mouse button down, slide up to select the layer name. You can also click on the up and down arrows on either side of the Current Layer box to move between layers.

- If the document has several layers or becomes very large, consider saving individual layers. Choose **Save Layer As** from the **File** menu to save an individual layer as a separate document.

- To print a single layer, pull down the **File** menu. Slide down to **Print Special** and select **Layer**. The Layer dialog box will appear. Click to check the layer or layers you want to print, then click **Print**.

COLORING PATCHES

Face it, black-and-white patches are no fun, but there may be good reasons to hold off on coloring your blocks. In upcoming chapters we'll show you why you may want to wait, shading them instead with "values" of grays and blacks until your design is complete. But for now, we know you're itching to splash some color on your screen. Here's how to do it as Picasso might have done.

COLOR PATCHES IN CORELDRAW

1. To color patches in CorelDraw, first be sure your patches are "closed" objects with joined lines. To color them, click on the Pick tool. Move your cursor to the center of the patch and click to select it, or click on one of its outside lines if you're using a version of CorelDraw prior to version 7. Black boxes will appear around the patch to show that it's selected.

2. Click on a color in the Color palette at the bottom of the screen. The patch should fill with the color. (If it didn't, either you didn't select the patch, or else it's not a closed object.)

3. Click on the up arrow or the right arrow on the very bottom right-hand corner of your screen to display the colors in CorelDraw's palette.

COLOR PATCHES IN CANVAS 5.0

1. To color the inside of a patch in Canvas 5.0, first click on the Selection Arrow tool, then click in the center of the patch you want to color. Black handles will appear around the patch to indicate that it's selected.

2. Click and hold the mouse button on the Fill Ink tool, and slide over to select the **Color** tab on the **Inks** palette. Select a color and release the mouse button. The color should fill your patch.

CUSTOMIZE COLORS IN CANVAS 5.0

1. Hold the mouse button down on the Current Fill Ink box until the Inks palette appears. While continuing to hold down the mouse button, slide the mouse over to the **Inks** palette and drag the palette to the right. This will separate it (or tear it) from the Current Fill Ink box and allow you to customize it.

CORELDRAW COLORING TIP

Say you've grouped a bunch of patches into a block. When you go to color them, all the patches turn the same color. That's because you need to ungroup the patches in order to color them individually. (Select the whole block, then choose Ungroup from the Arrange menu, or press CTRL-U. You may need to ungroup several different areas of the block if you grouped it multiple times while you were assembling it.) You should then be able to select each patch and color it individually. When you're done, regroup your patches into a block by selecting the whole block and pressing CTRL-G.

NOTE

Clicking on the X on the bottom left of your screen will drain the color or fill pattern from the selected patch.

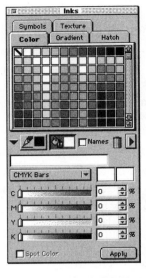

2. Click the triangle at the lower left of the Inks palette to open the **Color Manager.** Of the six color reference systems you can select, we'll look at CMYK. CMYK stands for cyan (C), magenta (M), yellow (Y), and black (K); this is the four-color process used in printing. Although you may not be a printing professional, CMYK lets you create custom colors simply by sliding the bar that appears next to each color—an excellent way to experiment with color mixing. After you a mix a new color, you can add it to the Inks palette. To do this, click the preview box in the Color Manager (it's next to the box that shows the current fill ink) and, while holding the mouse button down, slide the color from the preview box to the color palette. When you release the mouse button, the color should appear in your palette.

COLOR PATCHES IN CANVAS 3.5

1. To color the inside of a patch, first click on the Selection Arrow tool, then click in the center of the patch you want to color. Black handles will appear around the patch to indicate it's selected.

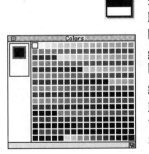

2. Find the Color Fill box and click and hold the mouse button down on the bottom white box to change the background color (the background is any blank space inside your patch, the foreground color is the outside line of the patch). Holding down the mouse button, slide to select a color, and then release the mouse button. The shape should fill with the color you chose.

You can also use Pantone® colors to color your patches. Pantone® is a popular spot color system. It allows a designer to select colors that can be reproduced, or matched, with a single ink color or converted to CMYK equivalents for printing. To use Pantone® color, pull down the **Windows** menu and select **Pantone® Colors**. The Pantone® Colors palette should appear in a window. Select the center of your patch with the Selection Arrow tool, and then select a color from the Pantone® Colors palette while holding the **OPTION** key down to fill it with that color. To change the foreground color to a Pantone® color, do not hold the **OPTION** key down.

COLOR PATCHES IN SUPERPAINT

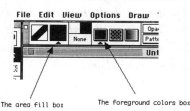

The area fill box

The foreground colors box

1. To color the inside of a patch, first click on the Selection Arrow tool, then click in the center of the patch you want to color. Black handles will appear around the patch to indicate that it's selected. Click on the **Area Fill** box.

2. Click once inside the **Area Fill** box. A small black triangle pointing to the box should appear beneath it, indicating that it's been selected.

3. Press and hold the mouse button down on the **Foreground Colors** box to the right of the black Permanent Fill box, and select a color from the pop-up color palette. Release the mouse button to fill the patch with the color you selected. (This color should also appear in the Area Fill box.)

WHAT IF MY DESIGN IS MADE UP ONLY OF LINES? CAN I FILL IT THIS WAY?

In most drawing programs, if your design is made up only of lines, instead of closed patches, you won't be able to fill the areas of your drawing as described here. But if you're using SuperPaint, all is not lost! You can copy your drawing into the Paint layer (select it and choose **Copy to Painting** from the **Edit** menu) and then use the Paint Bucket tool to pour color into the shapes. (See the SuperPaint manual for more information, and be sure to save the original line drawing as a separate file.) Keep in mind that once you are working in the Paint layer, you are working with bitmapped images, not vector images. So editing your shape is not as easy. Of course, you can also group the entire drawing, draw polygons on top, and then fill the polygons with color, as in other drawing programs.

USING FILL PATTERNS

Instead of using solid colors, you can color your patches with patterns. A pattern can be black and white, such as a series of dots or lines, or it can be a gradient fill, which means that the color will graduate from light to dark in a pattern that you specify. You can change the colors in the pattern to make them look more like fabric, or you can customize patterns. Here's how to do it.

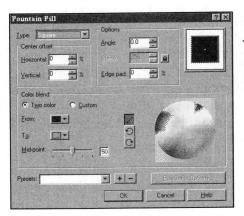

In CorelDraw 7 you can create a gradient fill pattern with the Fountain Fill dialog box. The color will graduate from light to dark in a pattern that you set, such as a square or conical one.

USE FILL PATTERNS IN CORELDRAW

CorelDraw comes with oodles of fill patterns, both colored and black and white. They have names like Coral Forest and Heavenly Clouds. Most of these patterns look modernistic and tie-dyed, but some of the black-and-white patterns look like calicos. You can also change the colors and intensity of these patterns. to make them look more like fabric. In Chapter 16 we'll talk more about how to create and find fill patterns that look like fabrics in CorelDraw. For now, here are some tips to get you started coloring patches with fills:

Click on the Fill tool icon to pop up a menu with fill options. If you slide your cursor over this menu, explanations of each option will appear at the bottom of CorelDraw's screen.

Use the Fill Roll-Up to preview and change fill patterns. To get to it, hold your mouse button down with the cursor over the Fill tool. Slide the cursor to the button that looks like a menu. You'll know you're in the right place when your cursor moves over a button and "Opens Special Fill Roll-Up" appears at the bottom of your screen. Once you've selected a fill, select the patch and then click **Apply**.

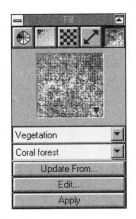

The Fill Roll-Up in CorelDraw 5.

The Fill Roll-Up in CorelDraw 7.

 *The Texture Fill menu lets you edit, change, and preview fill patterns. To get it, hold your mouse button down with the cursor over the Fill tool. Slide the cursor to the Texture Fill button and release it. Choose a texture from the* **Texture List** *and click* **OK**.

USE FILL PATTERNS IN CANVAS 5.0

Canvas 5.0 includes some really nice symbols, textures, gradients, and hatch patterns that you can use to fill your patches (you'll find them on the Inks palette).

1. To fill a patch with a pattern, first click on the Selection Arrow tool, then click in the center of the patch you want to fill. Black handles will appear around the patch to indicate that it's selected.

 2. Hold the mouse button down on the Fill Ink tool, and select either the Symbols, Textures, Gradients, or Hatch tab. Release the mouse button on your selection to choose a pattern. The pattern should fill your patch.

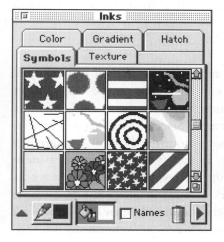

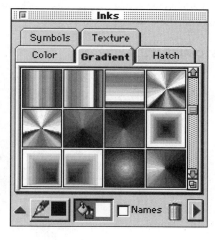

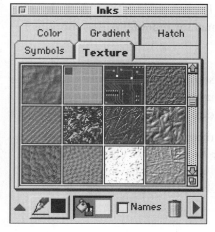

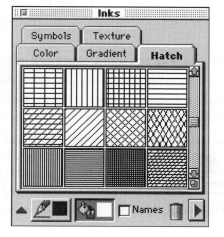

USE FILL PATTERNS IN CANVAS 3.5

1. To use a pattern to fill the inside of a patch in Canvas 3.5, first click on the Selection Arrow tool, then click the center of the patch you want to fill. Black handles will appear around the patch to indicate that it's selected.

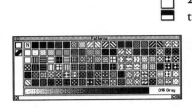

2. Click and hold down the mouse button on the Fill Patterns box (found above the Foreground/Background color fill boxes) and select a pattern from the menu. Release the mouse button on your selection to choose a pattern, and the pattern should fill your patch.

CHANGE THE COLORS OF THE FILL PATTERNS

To change the colors used in a fill pattern, press and hold down the mouse button to select a pattern, and then click on the Foreground Color box (the black half of the box). Keep holding the mouse button down while you select a color. The foreground (black area) of the pattern should change to your selected color. Now hold your mouse button down on the Background Color box (the white half of the box) to select a color in it. The background (white area) of the pattern should change to the color you select.

CUSTOMIZE FILL PATTERNS

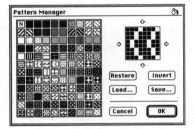

To modify one of the fill patterns, pull down the **Edit** menu and select **Managers** and then slide over to **Patterns**. Select the pattern you want to modify from the Pattern Manager box that appears (you should see the pattern in the preview box). In the preview box, click on a black square to turn it white, or click in the white area to add a black square. When you're finished, click **OK**. Your customized fill will appear in the Fill Pattern palette. (See the Canvas 3.5 manual for more fill pattern options.)

USE FILL PATTERNS IN SUPERPAINT

1. To fill patches with patterns in SuperPaint, start in the Draw layer. Click on the Selection Arrow tool, then select the patch you want to fill with a pattern. Black handles should appear around the shape to indicate that it's selected.

2. Select the Area Fill button. You should see three Permanent Fill boxes—white, black, and none—to the right of the Area Fill box. This nice feature gives you quick access to these three fills without having to open the color palette. If your area fill is not black, click inside the black Permanent Fill box to change it to black.

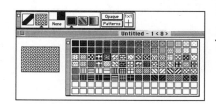

3. Hold the mouse button down on the Patterns box (located under the menu bar) to fill your patch with the pattern you select. (The Area Fill button should fill with the pattern you've selected.)

CHANGE THE COLORS OF THE FILL PATTERN

To change the color used in a fill pattern, click to select a pattern, then select the Foreground Color box (the solid box to the right of the black Permanent Fill box). Hold your mouse button down to select a color and change the black pattern to the color you select. To change the background color, hold the mouse button down on the Background Color box (the space surrounding the three Foreground boxes). This brings up the same color palette as before. Select a color.

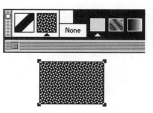

We used the same fill but reversed the background and foreground. Notice that the fill in the square is darker. Also notice that the Foreground Color box is white and the Background Color box is black.

FILL A PATCH WITH TEXTURE

To fill a patch with texture, select a patch with the Selection Arrow tool, then click to select the Area Fill box. Hold the mouse button down on the Textures box (to the right of the Foreground Color box) to bring up the Textures palette, and select a texture. Release the mouse button on the texture you select, and that texture should fill your shape. (In Chapter 16, we'll show you how to create custom textures and add them to your Textures palette.)

CHAPTER 7

MOVING PATCHES AROUND YOUR SCREEN
TO CREATE BIGGER DESIGNS

Drawing and coloring patches is only the start. Duplicate them and push them around to make more blocks and designs, plus learn some template printing magic.

In Chapter 4 we explained how to draw quilt blocks with a drawing program. But there's another way to create them—and even to create entire quilt designs—that some quilters find easier. They start by drawing one or two patches and grouping them together to create bigger ones. They then duplicate, stretch, and resize their patches to create bigger blocks, and they put different sizes and forms of them together to make interesting combinations.

See Chapter 9, "The Log Cabin Block: A Case Study," to see what you can do starting with only a single square patch. Chapter 8, "Use Computer Tools to Transform an Old-Fashioned Quilt Block into Something Really Cool," explains the different computer design techniques you can use to transform a quilt block.

DUPLICATING AND MOVING PATCHES

Here's what you need to know to start making your own patch-based quilt designs.

DUPLICATE AND MOVE PATCHES IN CORELDRAW

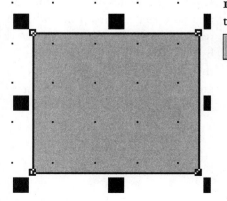

1. Draw a patch with the Rectangle tool. Select it by clicking on the Pick tool, then clicking on the patch to select it.

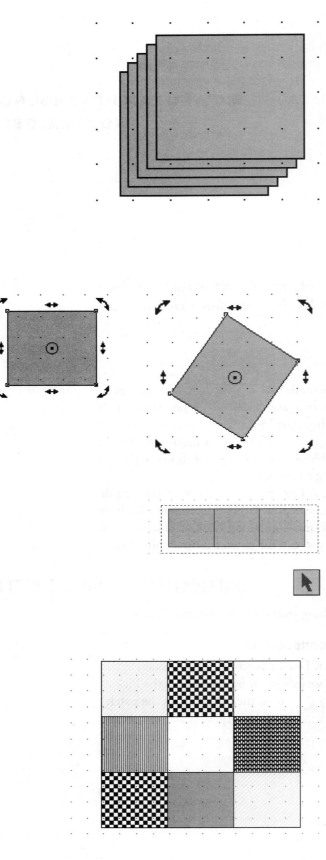

2. Duplicate the selected patch by pressing **CTRL-D**. To move your duplicates in CorelDraw 7, select one, move your cursor to the center of the patch, and hold down the mouse button so that your cursor turns into a cross. Move it to where you want to place it and release the mouse button. (In earlier versions of CorelDraw, move the patch by placing the cursor on one of the lines of the patch, holding the left mouse button down until the cursor turns into the sort of **X** that might mark a pirate's treasure map, and dragging the patch to the new position.)

3. Rotate the patch. To do this, double-click on one corner of the patch. When double-headed arrows appear around the patch, hold your mouse button down on one of the corner sets of arrows and slide the mouse. (Pulling one of the sets of arrows on the sides of the patch will skew it.) Release the mouse button when you're done.

4. Arrange the patches into a block. When your patches are in position, select them by clicking on the Pick tool and drawing a rubber-band box around the entire group (don't leave any out!). Group the block by pressing **CTRL-G**. Be sure you have **Snap to Grid** and **Snap to Objects** activated (they're in the **Layout** menu) so that your blocks align precisely.

5. Become a group player. Remember that it's easier to line up two or three patches than it is to line up six. Work by grouping a few blocks together, then duplicating the group. Push groups together, then group them and duplicate them.

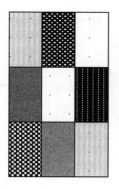

6. You need to group to resize, but ungroup to color. You can resize your grouped block by selecting it and pulling the black handles that appear around it. However, if you want to color individual patches, you'll need to ungroup the block. Select the block and ungroup (**CTRL-U**) each grouped segment. Be sure to regroup (select the block and press **CTRL-G**) when you're done.

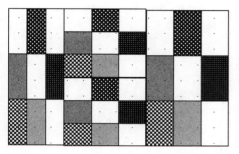

7. More fun in groups: Push different grouped segments of blocks of different sizes together to make interesting designs. Be sure to group the whole caboodle when you're done.

DUPLICATE AND MOVE PATCHES IN CANVAS 5.0, 3.5, AND SUPERPAINT

The following steps show how to copy and move patches in Canvas or SuperPaint to make an Ohio Star pattern. In SuperPaint, remember to start in the Draw layer.

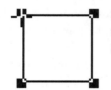

1. Draw a square with the Rectangle tool and then select it with the Selection Arrow tool.

2. Duplicate the selected patch by pressing **COMMAND-D** as many times as you need to (four times in this example).

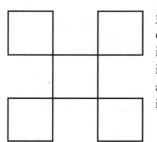

3. To move your duplicates, first click on the Selection Arrow tool, then click inside the patch, but instead of releasing the mouse button, hold it down and drag the patch to where you want it. Then release the mouse button.

T * I * P

Remember, it's quicker and easier to line up and place grouped patches than individual ones. Hold the SHIFT key down while clicking to select more than one patch.

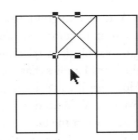

4. Use the Polygon tool to draw a triangle, then duplicate the triangle, flip it (by choosing **Flip** from the **Effects** menu in Canvas or from the **Transform** menu in SuperPaint), and drag it into place. Repeat to make a square containing four triangles.

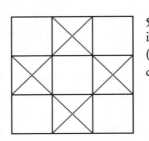

5. Select the triangles and group them into one unit. Duplicate the unit (**COMMAND-D**) and drag it into place to create the Ohio Star block.

"I KNOW! I'LL TURN MY COMPUTER INTO A FABRIC WALL!"

If you're thinking, "Hey, why don't I save some time and, instead of drawing quilt blocks, just draw a whole mess of patches. Then, I'll move them around the screen and fit them together. It will be just like pinning fabric patches to a fabric wall, then shuffling them around." Some computer quilters like to do this, and you can too, but if your patches aren't as symmetrical as you think, you're in for trouble. (And pushing little patches around the screen into quilt blocks can try anyone's patience.)

But if you want to try it for yourself, here are some hints: Be sure to turn on your drawing program's snap-to-grid feature. Also turn on snap-to-object, if your program has it, so that the patches align with one another when you push them together. Use the zoom tool to zoom in on patch corners to make sure they align. If the patches don't align, you may end up with a quilt block that's slightly askew—a real pain when it's time to duplicate it and lay it out into a quilt on the screen, just as it is when you try to lay out real quilt blocks that are askew.

PRINTING PAPER TEMPLATES OF PATCHES

AN IMPORTANT WARNING FROM JUDY & GLORIA!

Before you print five zillion paper templates, be sure to check with a ruler the measurements of the first batch you print. Your printer may not be printing to scale with perfect accuracy. Inkjet printers in particular are notorious for printing things just slightly out of dimension.

Whether you want to print templates of individual patches for piecing or for appliqué, it's easy with a drawing program once you get the tricks down. You can print your templates with or without ¼-inch seam allowances, and you can print them on freezer paper, computer paper, or even special template plastic that you feed right through your printer (it works great for speedy rotary cutting). You can print templates one at a time or by the hundreds. (Computers are better at mindless, repetitive tasks than we are.)

PRINT PAPER TEMPLATES IN CORELDRAW

There are two ways to add a seam allowance in CorelDraw. You can use the Contour Roll-Up to add a ¼-inch border to the patch, or you can create a seam allowance by changing the width of the "pen" used to draw the outline.

Regardless of the technique you plan to use, you first need to move your patches away from the block itself. To do this, select the patch you wish to use as a template by clicking on the Pick tool and then moving the cursor to the center of the patch. Holding down the left mouse button, drag the patch to an area outside your drawing. (In versions of CorelDraw prior to version 7, move the patch by positioning the cursor over one of the patch's outside lines and then, holding the left mouse button down so that the cursor turns into an **X**, dragging the patch to where you want it.)

ADD A SEAM ALLOWANCE WITH THE CONTOUR ROLL-UP

A contour, or border, can be applied to only one patch at a time. To add a simple ¼-inch border to a single patch, follow these steps:

1. Use the Pick took to select the patch. With the patch selected, pull down the **Effects** menu and select **Contour** in CorelDraw 7, **Contour Roll-Up** in CorelDraw 5. The Contour Roll-Up appears.

2. Click to check the **Outside** option, specify an **Offset** of 0.25 inch, and specify 1 for the **Steps** option. If you like, click on the pen icon (in CorelDraw 7, click on the color wheel to see it), and specify gray for the color of the cutting line.

3. Click **Apply**. The selected patch will be surrounded by a ¼-inch seam allowance.

ADD A SEAM ALLOWANCE BY WIDENING THE OUTLINE

You can also add a ¼-inch seam allowance to a patch by giving it a ½-inch-wide drawing line. It might seem counterintuitive to create a ¼-inch seam allowance by giving the patch a ½-inch drawing line, but it's necessary because half of the drawing line (or ¼ inch) will fall outside the patch you drew, and ¼ inch will fall inside the patch. Don't worry, though: You can hide the part of the outline that falls inside the patch behind a white fill, so that you can see the true size of the patch. With this technique, the entire seam allowance will be gray, making it easy to distinguish. It can also be applied to more than one patch at a time, which means it is much faster if you need to add seam allowances to numerous patches. Here's how it's done:

1. Click on the Outline tool and then, in the toolbar that appears, click on the **Pen Roll-Up** icon to display the Pen Roll-Up.

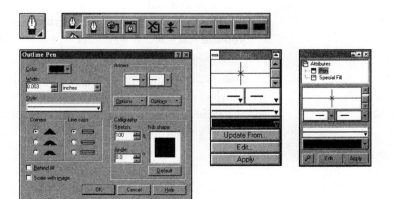

2. Click **Edit** to display the Outline Pen dialog box.

3. Set **Width** to 0.500 inch (to give you a ¼-inch seam around the template).

4. Set the color to gray by clicking on the box next to **Color** and selecting gray from the palette.

5. Click to check the **Behind Fill** box.

6. You can give your templates snipped-off corners by selecting the blunted corner pattern in the **Corners** box. Click **OK**.

7. Head back to your patch and make sure it's selected. If it is not, click on the Pick tool and click in the center of the patch so that handles appear around it (click on an outline of the patch in versions of CorelDraw prior to version 7).

8. Back in the Pen Roll-Up, click **Apply**. If your patch already has a fill, you should see a gray ¼-inch border. If it is not filled, you'll see a ½-inch border. You'll need to add a fill to hide ¼ inch of the outline (see the next step).

9. To fill the patch, select it, click on the Fill tool, and select the **Fill Color** icon. Click on a color (white will work just fine), and click **OK**. You should now see a filled patch with a ¼-inch border.

PRINT THE TEMPLATES

10. You can print one or more templates without printing the rest of the block by first selecting them and then pulling down the **File** menu, clicking on **Print**, and choosing **Selection** (in CorelDraw 7) or **Selected Objects** (in CorelDraw 5). Be sure to click **OK**.

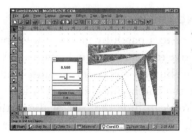

To make a template, drag a patch to an area outside your design, and then use the outline tools to give it a seam allowance, if you want one.

PRINT PAPER TEMPLATES IN CANVAS 5.0

To add seam allowances to your templates with Canvas 5.0, you need to create a ¼-inch double line and load it into the Strokes palette. Creating this double line allows you to make a sewing line and a ¼-inch seam allowance line simultaneously. It takes several steps, but it's worth it because you only need to do it once. Then you can just select it whenever you want to make templates. Here's how to do it.

1. Hold down the mouse button on the Strokes tool until the Strokes palette appears. While continuing to hold down the mouse button, slide the mouse over to the palette box and drag the Strokes palette to the right. This will separate the Strokes palette from the Strokes tool and allow you to customize it.

2. Click on the **Parallel** tab at the top of the **Strokes** palette to bring up the **Parallel** palette.

3. At the bottom left of the palette is a small triangle pointing upward. Click on it so that the arrow points down to open the **Parallel Manager**.

4. Type **2** in the **Parallel Lines** box. Type **18** for the number of points in the **Spacing** box (there are 72 points to an inch; 18 points is ¼ inch). Select **Above** in the **Eccentricity** box.

The Parallel palette with the Parallel Manager opened and the settings for two solid lines.

5. If you want the outside cutting line to be dashed, click on the top line in the box on the right to select it. Then click in the small dashed-line box and, while still holding the mouse button down, select the type of dashed line you want.

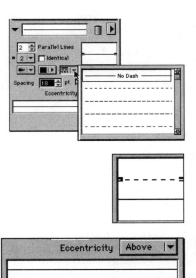

Holding the mouse button down on the small dashes box brings up the dash selection box.

The top line is now dashed.

6. The most important step is adding the customized parallel line setting to the palette. Under the word Eccentricity is a long box called the Preview box. It now shows only one line going through its center, but it's the double lines you just created. Take our word on this. Click and hold the mouse button down on this box, and you should see the border of the Preview box turn to dotted lines.

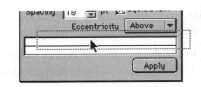

Holding the mouse button down on the Preview box turns it into a box with dotted lines.

7. When you see the dotted lines, drag the box up to the **Strokes** palette, then release the mouse button. The parallel line style you created should show up in the palette.

The customized line is now added into the Parallel palette.

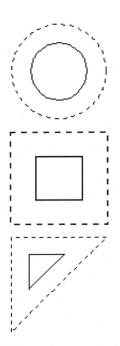

Using the customized stroke tool and the oval, square, and polygon tools to make patches with ¼-inch seam allowances.

8. Click the small triangle to close the Parallel Manager, and then click in the upper left of the Strokes palette to close it.

Whew!

Now, any time you want, you can use the customized stroke that you just created to add a seam allowance to your patch. To use it, first select your drawing tool. Then click and hold your mouse button down on the **Strokes** tool, select the **Parallel** tab, and select the new line style you created. A ¼-inch seam allowance will automatically be added to your shape. To add a ¼-inch seam allowance to a shape that you have already drawn, first select it. Then select the customized line that you added to the Parallel palette.

PRINT PAPER TEMPLATES IN CANVAS 3.5

Canvas 3.5's Parallel Polygon tool is great for creating seam allowances, but to use it you'll first need to select some settings to make it work best.

 1. Select the Parallel Polygon tool from the Object Tools menu.

2. Double-click on the Parallel Polygon tool to bring up the **Parallel Lines Manager** dialog box. (You can also bring up this dialog box by pulling down the **Edit** menu, sliding down to **Managers**, and selecting the **Parallel Lines Manager** from the menu that appears.)

T * I * P

When you finish making templates with ¼-inch seam allowances, remember to go back to the Strokes palette, select Pen, and click on a pen stroke width so that you can go back to drawing shapes with a single outline.

Parallel Line Manager dialog box. These settings will create a dashed line for the cutting line and a solid line for the sewing line.

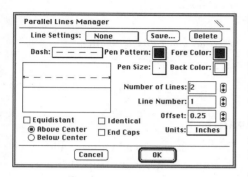

3. Type **2** in the **Number of Lines** box. Type **2** in the **Line Number** box and type **0.00** in the **Spacing** box. Then go back to the **Line Number** box and type **1** in it and type **0.25** in the **Spacing** box. This instructs the manager not to offset line 2 by any increment but to offset line 1 by ¼ inch. Then select **Inches** in the **Units** box. The **Above Center** option circle will be highlighted, and two lines should appear in the preview box.

4. We like the outer line to be made with dashes to indicate the cutting line. To change the outer line from solid to dashed, first click on the top line to select it. Then hold the mouse button down on the **Dash** box and select a dashed line. To change a dashed line back to a solid line, select **No Dash** from the Dash box. Click **OK** to continue. Now you're ready to create a template with a ¼-inch seam allowance. Here's how to do it on top of a block that is already drawn.

5. Select the Parallel Polygon tool from the Object Tools menu. The arrow will turn into crosshairs. Line up the crosshairs with a point on your patch and click, then move the mouse and click at the next point. Continue until the shape is complete.

Using the parallel polygon tool to create a template with seam allowance.

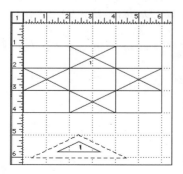

6. To move the template, click on the Selection Arrow tool, then press and hold the mouse button down inside the template. Drag the template to the bottom of your page and release the mouse button. Number the block and the patch, using the Text tool, to make it easier to keep track of which patch goes where.

······················

T * I * P

*Your ¼-inch parallel settings will remain as the default until you change the settings. Or you can save the settings. Click the **Save** button at the top of the manager, and call it "¼ setting." Then when you want to use the ¼-inch setting, just select it from your **Line Settings** box in the Parallel Lines Manager.*

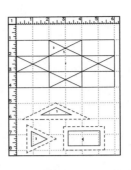

7. Continue making templates until you have all of the shapes you need for your block.

Original block and templates.

PRINT PAPER TEMPLATES IN SUPERPAINT

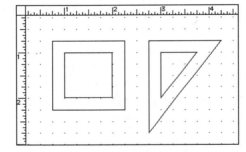

The easiest way to add a seam allowance to your patches with SuperPaint is to draw it with the Line tool. To do this, select **Grid & Rulers** from the **Options** menu. Type **0.25** in the **Grid Spacing** box, and check the boxes next to **Grid Snap On**, **Show Grid**, and **Show Rulers**. Then select the Line tool and draw a second line ¼ inch away from the edge of the patch.

A ¼-inch seam allowance added to some patches.

SUPERPAINT TIPS

• To add a seam allowance to odd shapes, turn off Grid Snap On. Then use the small guidelines on the ruler to indicate the position for your seam allowance.

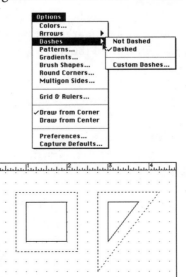

• To make the outside line dashed rather than solid, pull down the **Options** menu, select **Dashes,** and slide to select **Dashed**.

The Options menu in SuperPaint with the Dashes option highlighted.

The seam allowance as a dashed line.

MORE TIPS AND IDEAS FOR PRINTING TEMPLATES

- Sometimes it's easier to print your block full size and cut templates from it. If you do, remember to turn on the ruler and activate snap-to-grid to accurately resize the block on your screen. After you have printed the block, check its dimensions with a ruler to make sure the size is accurate.

- Number your templates by typing a number on each patch in your quilt block, using the text tool, and then typing a corresponding number on each template that you print. Otherwise, it's easy to forget which patch goes where.

- If the block is large, copy and paste the templates into a new document and then switch between the two documents, to make it easier to work with the block.

- If your drawing program supports layers, place the quilt block on one layer and create your templates on a second layer.

- Give your templates dashed lines to designate cutting lines.

WHAT SHOULD YOU PRINT YOUR TEMPLATES ON?

You can always print your templates on plain white paper, but here are some alternatives:

- The dull side of freezer paper works great, especially for appliqué templates. If you have an old dot-matrix printer, use it to print your templates. It will give you dotted, semiperforated lines that will be easy to cut. Freezer paper is pretty hard to feed through laser printers, but it has been done. And no, the printer's heat won't melt the paper.

- The paper side of fusible web. But be sure to buy a web that doesn't separate easily from the paper.

- Templar is quilt template plastic that you can put through a laser printer. It's available for $8.25 for six letter-sized sheets from Heirloom Stitches, 626 Shadowood Lane, S.E., Warren, OH, 44484.

- If you plan to use the paper piecing technique, use good-quality tracing paper in your printer. It will make an enormous difference in how accurately you can piece the block.

- Worried that ink from the templates might run on your fabric as you stitch? If you printed your templates on a laser printer, you have nothing to worry about, since the ink used is a powder that can be rubbed off fabric with water. If you have an inkjet printer, chances are good that the inkjet's black ink cartridge is water resistant (you can find out in your printer's manual if it is), meaning that the ink will be harder to get out of fabric. If you have such a printer, print your templates with the color cartridge instead; the ink in the color cartridges is more water soluble.

DESIGN STRATEGIES
FOR QUILTING NERDS

USE YOUR KNOWLEDGE OF THE AGE-OLD METHOD OF DRAWING
QUILT BLOCKS TO POINT AND CLICK YOUR WAY INTO THE FUTURE OF
QUILTING. IN THIS SECTION WE SHOW YOU HOW TO BECOME A TRUE
INNOVATOR IN QUILT DESIGN!

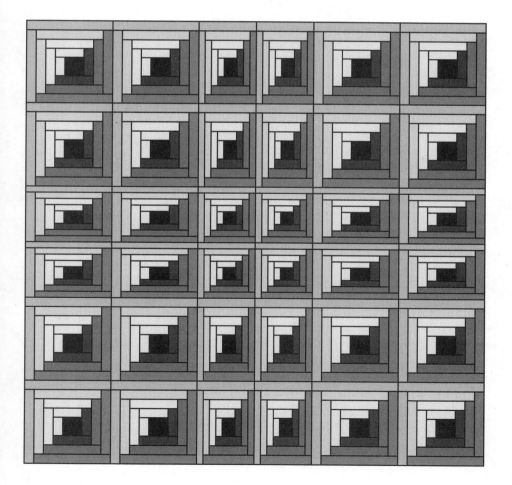

CHAPTER 8

USE COMPUTER TOOLS TO TRANSFORM AN OLD-FASHIONED QUILT BLOCK INTO SOMETHING REALLY COOL

Use simple techniques like stretching, resizing, and repetition to create quilt designs you've never dreamed of before.

One of the wonders of designing on a computer is that you can quickly transform an unassuming little quilt block into a pile of twisted variations. Take an Ohio Star. You can stretch it, spin it, resize it, push it through virtual reality, and map it to a sphere. You can even paste other Ohio Stars on the sphere with it. Try to do the same thing with a copy machine and scissors and you'll be snipping out paper triangles until cows rain on Paducah.

Of course, you need to use a drawing program or quilt design software to launch these radical transformations, though the capabilities of quilt design programs like Electric Quilt are limited compared to the CorelDraws of the world.

Whichever program you have, rest assured that you no longer have to settle for an Ohio Star that looks like a star beaming down on a perfect world. Just a few mouse clicks and it can be an airplane, a bottle rocket, or even—heaven forbid—a hundred snips of fabric falling from the sky.

MILLION-DOLLAR SPECIAL EFFECTS FOR QUILT BLOCKS

It is said that all great things start with a quilt block, and, in fact, life itself may have sprung from a quilt block (but who knows; that is theology). An easy way to begin designing is by drawing a quilt block, especially if you use drawing software. If you use quilt design software you can select a block from the software's library. The block can be as traditional as Log Cabin or a modern, Dadaistic confection. Don't pay too much mind to what it looks like initially. When we get done, it may be unrecognizable anyway. Don't worry about what size it is either.

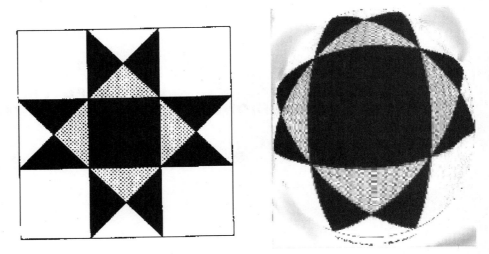

Here is an example of the sort of nonsense you will tootle with for hours when you become symbiotically linked to your computer. On the left you see an Ohio Star; on the right you see it mapped to a sphere in Corel Photo-Paint.

Look at your quilt block as if you were a Hollywood special effects artist. Would you like it to look like it's riding a roller-coaster? Or standing in front of a funhouse mirror? Maybe you want it walking down a long, dark hallway. Or perhaps you'd prefer an explosion in the corner.

By manipulating a quilt block with the simplest of computer drawing-board effects, you can create astonishing transformations to a pattern. These are some of the tools you have at your disposal:

- Repetition
- Distortion
- Skewing
- Overlapping
- Resizing
- Stretching
- Mirroring

These things seem obvious, don't they? Who doesn't know how to resize or repeat a block? But this leads us to our first Rule of Quilt Block Transmogrification (see the margin).

For example, on page 294 the quilt *Breaking Free* is fashioned of quilt blocks that are similar to the blocks that make up *Awakenings,* the quilt on the cover of this book. But if you look closely, you'll see that there are three versions of the block: a large one, a small one, and a rectangular, or "stretched," one. These are simple variations of the same block, but together they create a very different quilt from the one on the book's cover.

The quilt *Dancing Shadows* on page 305 is another example. All of its blocks are essentially the same, except that some are smaller than others. A fabric strip has been added to them to square them off with the bigger blocks.

Follow our tips in the remainder of this chapter to see how simple changes to an ordinary quilt block can lead to dramatic design changes in your quilt.

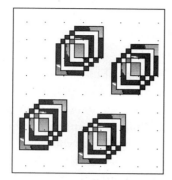

By simply overlapping squares, you can create whimsical block designs.

SPECIAL REMINDERS FOR THOSE USING DRAWING SOFTWARE

If you're using a drawing program, remember that once you finish drawing the block you should group it. That turns its individual lines into a single object—a whole, if you will—that you can push and pull around your screen without its lines (or patches) fluttering into a million fragments. To group in CorelDraw, click on the Pick tool, draw a rubber band around the block with your mouse, and press CTRL-G. You group the same way in Macintosh drawing programs, except that you press COMMAND-G.

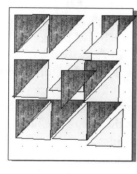

Tsk, tsk. This is what's going to happen to your quilt block if you don't group it.

T * I * P

You can also group a group of blocks to create an even bigger block that you can twist and pull around your screen. Or you can duplicate a group of blocks, then stack different sizes of your block group together for an intriguing quilt layout.

Select the block by clicking on the Selection Arrow or Pick tool and clicking on the block. Black squares will appear around the block. Size the block so that it will fit on your screen by using your drawing software's scaling feature or by pulling one of the corner handles with your mouse.

TRICKS FOR TRANSFORMING A QUILT BLOCK WITH A DRAWING PROGRAM

- **TO CLONE A BLOCK** in any Macintosh or PC drawing program, select the block by clicking on the Selection Arrow or Pick tool and then clicking on the block so that black handles appear around it. Press CTRL-D on the PC or COMMAND-D on the Mac, or choose **Duplicate** from the **Edit** menu. Or you can press CTRL-C or COMMAND-C to copy the block to the Clipboard, and CTRL-V or COMMAND-V to paste the new block into place. Keep pressing CTRL-V or COMMAND-V to paste more copies onto your drawing area.

- **TO MOVE A BLOCK**, select the block by clicking the Selection Arrow tool or Pick tool and clicking on the block so that black handles appear around it. Then click anywhere on the block except directly on the handles and, holding the mouse button down, drag the block to its new position. Try overlapping portions of quilt blocks to create unique effects.

IN ELECTRIC QUILT YOU MAKE NEW INTERPRETATIONS OF OLD QUILT PATTERNS IN THE QUILT LAYOUT GRID

With a drawing program you blend and distort quilt blocks on a blank screen. In Electric Quilt, the best place to do it is on the quilt layout grid, not on the drawing board. While Electric Quilt offers a drawing pad, its drawing tools pretty much limit you to sketching one block at a time. While you can't create the really wild blocks and combinations of blocks with Electric Quilt that you can with a drawing program, you can still create some pretty snazzy variations of traditional blocks and designs by stretching them and rejiggering them around the layout grid.

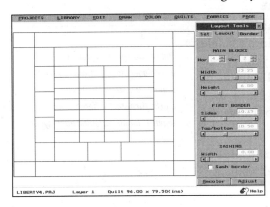

The best place to start your experimentations with different-sized blocks in Electric Quilt is in the Quilt toolbox. Here you specify the number of your blocks and borders, their sizes, and layout. Once you've set up a grid like this, you can start experimenting by placing different blocks in the grid and borders and flipping and mirroring them. You can also color them with fabrics.

- Start by creating a blank quilt layout grid. To do this, choose **New Quilt** from the **Quilts** menu. Then pull down the **Quilts** menu again, select **Toolbox**, and click on the **Layout** tab. On the Layout tab, you can set the number of blocks in the quilt and their size. On the Border tab you specify the number, size, and style of borders. Give your grid several borders, with a number of blocks in each border. (Click on the **Style** options in the **Border** tab to change the number and type of blocks in the border.) Don't worry too much about the size of the blocks and borders; you can always adjust these things later.

- Add a wide variety of quilt blocks to your Sketchbook. You can sketch them yourself by pulling up the drawing pad—pull down the **Draw** menu and select **EasyDraw**. Or you can load them from the quilt block library—pull down **Library** and select **Block Library**. When you find a block you like by scrolling and clicking through the selections, click **Copy** to add it to your Sketchbook. This is where it's handy to be able to flip through a copy of the *EQ3 Block Book,* which is a paper version of what's in Electric Quilt's libraries.

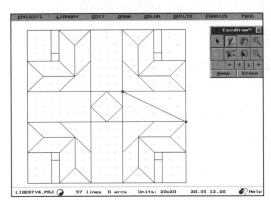

You can create your own blocks or edit any of the ones in Electric Quilt's enormous block library.

- You can also alter any of the blocks in Electric Quilt's block library. Pull down the **Draw** menu and select **EasyDraw**. To edit a block from the block library, pull down the **Library** menu and select **Block Library**. Click and scroll through the blocks. Select the one you like by clicking on it, then click **Copy** to copy it to your Sketchbook. Close the Block Library box by clicking on the **X** in the top right-hand corner. Now open your Sketchbook by pulling down the **Draw** menu and selecting **Sketchbook**. Click on the **Blocks** tab. With your mouse, select the block you want, and then click **Edit**. The block will appear in the EasyDraw sketching area. You change any of its lines or add your own design to the block. Be sure to click the **Keep** button to save the block. When you go to lay out your quilt, the new block will be waiting for you in your Sketchbook.

The block patterns in this quilt layout are fairly traditional, but all have been flipped or stretched for an almost Bauhaus look (okay, it's not exactly Bauhaus, but if you add some orange . . .). The pattern in the outer border is an elongated Lotus Blossom block. That's one of the intriguing things you can do with Electric Quilt: stretch a block pattern into an entire pieced border.

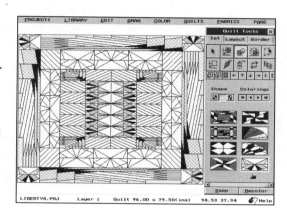

- Add blocks to your layout grid by heading to the Quilt toolbox (choose **Toolbox** from the **Quilts** menu) and clicking on the **Set** tab. You should see all the quilt blocks you added to your Sketchbook displayed at the bottom of the toolbox's Set page. To place them on the grid, click on the block, click on the Set tool, and then click the square in the grid where you want to place the block. You can keep clicking to place the same block multiple times.

- To rotate or mirror a block on your grid, click on one of the rotation icons, then click on the block.

*Electric Quilt's country set layout lets you lay quilt blocks on a "blank page" set up as a quilt. You can resize the blocks, flip them, and rotate them. To use the country set layout, pull down the **Quilts** menu, click on **New Quilt** to create a new quilt, and, in the dialog box that appears, scroll to **Country Set** and click to select it. Then click **OK**. You can then drag any block from your Quilt toolbox onto your quilt layout. This quilt was created by stacking and resizing one block design.*

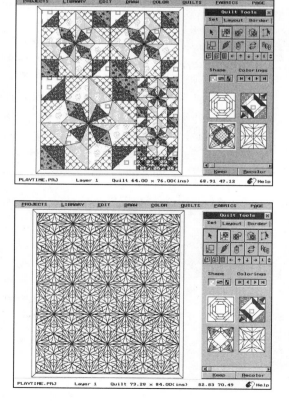

You can create some pretty spectacular designs in Electric Quilt by laying out line drawings of quilt block designs onto a baby blocks layout. (The baby blocks layout is another choice when you pull down the Quilts menu and click on New Quilt.) This quilt design was created with that ho-hum block design in the bottom right corner of the Quilt toolbox.

SHUFFLE AND STRETCH PATCHES IN QUILT-PRO TO CREATE ASTONISHING QUILT BLOCK TRANSFORMATIONS

Quilt-Pro offers a variety of tools for making basic changes to quilt blocks, including mirroring, overlapping, resizing, and rotating blocks with extraordinary ease. Because Quilt-Pro lets you color blocks with fabric as you go, you can see how color works with your design.

Here are some tips for altering quilt blocks in Quilt-Pro for the PC as well as the Mac:

- Begin by either taking a block from Quilt-Pro's block library (pull down the **Block** menu and select **Open**) or drawing your own. Group the block by selecting it with the Select tool, then choose **Group** from the **Effects** menu. Remember that in Quilt-Pro it's easier to create blocks by placing patches on the grid than to do it by drawing with lines, as you would in a drawing program.

- Zoom out. Throughout your designing, use the zoom feature regularly, since Quilt-Pro's screen is cramped. On the PC, pull down the **Zoom** menu and choose **Reduce** to zoom out. On the Mac, zoom out by pulling down the **View** menu and selecting **Reduce**.

- Duplicate your block by selecting it with the Select tool in the toolbar and then pressing **CTRL-D** (**COMMAND-D** on a Macintosh). Make a number of duplications. In the Mac version, you'll need to duplicate the block one at a time and avoid multiple duplications. This is because blocks tend to break up, reverting to scattered patches. Yes, it is a pain.

- To resize or stretch a block, make sure that it is grouped and then select it with the Select tool. Click and drag one of the black handles. Drag a corner handle to resize the block while maintaining the same shape. Drag on a side handle to stretch the block to a new shape. You can also specify a precise size by selecting the block and then choosing **Resize To** from the **Effects** menu.

- To mirror or rotate a block, select it with the Select tool, then click on one of the flip or rotate tools in the toolbar.

Snap tool.

Edit tool.

- Quilt-Pro's skew or reshape feature will stretch only one line or patch point at a time. To use it, click on the Snap tool in the toolbar. Then click the Edit tool. Point to the corner of the patch you want to change. Hold the mouse button down and stretch the corner. This tool is really best used for creating patches in nontraditional shapes. If you don't care whether the shapes snap to the grid, don't bother clicking on the Snap tool first.

- As you work, group blocks regularly into larger block segments to create a larger design, unless you're using the Mac version. It seems as though any time you do anything to a grouped block in the Macintosh version of Quilt-Pro, it inconveniently ungroups. You'll want to stick to smaller block groups and keep regrouping as the need arises.

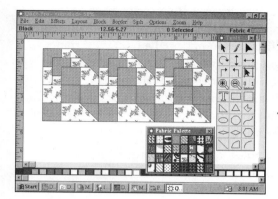

We began by putting four squares together into a four-patch. We grouped it. We duplicated it three times. We overlapped the blocks. We used the Edit tool to elongate one of the patches (it's the light patch on the bottom row). We added a couple of extra triangular patches. We grouped the resulting block into a big block then we duplicated that two times. To create an even larger design, we could duplicate this group and mirror or rotate it.

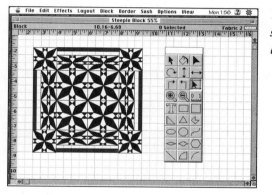

You can scale and stretch blocks in Quilt-Pro. This design started with the Steeple Block in Quilt-Pro. Adding a border completes the design.

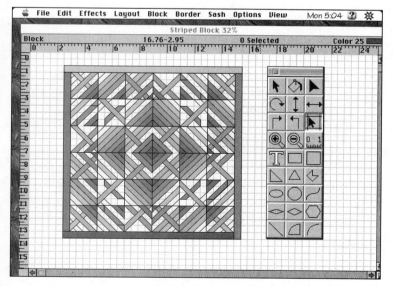

BE CAREFUL!

When you open a block in Quilt-Pro's library, it's ungrouped. You'll need to group it before you stretch or spin it, or you'll have an awful mess of fluttering patches on your screen. We've also found that sometimes when you ungroup a set of blocks, the blocks revert to individual patches instead of blocks in a set. (Early versions of Quilt-Pro for the Mac suffer a terrible grouping problem that causes blocks to revert to loose patches as they're moved around. Try to get a version that's later than 2.0.)

This quilt was created with the Striped Block pattern found in the Misc folder on the PC or the Miscellaneous folder on the Macintosh. We duplicated the block nine times. Some blocks were ungrouped so that patches could be deleted or rotated. All nine blocks were then grouped, duplicated, rotated, and repeated.

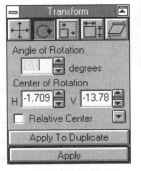

- **TO CHANGE THE SIZE OF A BLOCK,** click on the Pick or Selection Arrow tool, click to select the block, and press and hold down the mouse button on a corner handle of the block. Drag the block to its new size. Be careful! You can drag a square block into a rectangle this way. If you want to resize the block without distorting it, simply drag a corner handle in CorelDraw, or use the **Transform Roll-Up** (on the **Effects** menu in CorelDraw 5, the **Arrange** menu in CorelDraw 7) to indicate a precise size. In Canvas, hold down the **SHIFT** key while dragging a corner handle, or choose **Scale** from the **Object** menu for precise sizing. In SuperPaint, drag a corner handle, or choose **Scale Selection** from the **Transform** menu to resize a block. Enter the same percentage in both the Horizontal and Vertical boxes to resize it without distorting it.

- **TO CREATE A MIRROR IMAGE OF A BLOCK,** copy your original block, and select it with the Pick or Selection Arrow tool. If you're using CorelDraw, move your mouse to one of the side handles of the block. The cursor should change into crosshairs. Holding the mouse button down, drag the handle to the opposite side of the screen. This will flip the block around to create a mirror version. You can also use the mirror selections in the **Transform Roll-Up** (on the **Effects** menu in CorelDraw 5, the **Arrange** menu in Corel-Draw 7). If you're using Canvas on the Macintosh, choose **Flip Horizontal**, **Flip Vertical**, or **Both Axes** from the **Effects** menu. In SuperPaint, pull down the **Transform** menu and choose **Flip Horizontal**.

- **TO ROTATE A BLOCK,** click on the Pick or Selection Arrow tool, and click on the block to select it. In CorelDraw 5, pull down the **Effects** menu and choose **Transform Roll-Up**. Click on the **Rotate** icon. Type in the angle of rotation and click **Apply**. [In CorelDraw 7, pull down the **Arrange** menu, choose **Transform**, and slide to **Rotate**.] You can also double-click on a corner to display the rotation handles and then drag a corner of your block. In Canvas 3.5, pull down the **Effects** menu and choose **Rotate Right** (or **Rotate Left** or **Free Rotate**, if you prefer). In Canvas 5, choose **Rotate** or **Freeform** from the **Effects** menu. To rotate a block in SuperPaint, choose **Rotate Selection** from the **Transform** menu. You can select the degree of rotation, for example, 90 degrees. You can also choose **Free Rotate** and drag the selection with the mouse.

- **TO SKEW A BLOCK,** use the Pick or Selection Arrow tool to select the block. In CorelDraw 5, choose **Transform Roll-Up** from the **Effects** menu. Click the **Skew** icon in the Transform Roll-Up. Type in the number of degrees by which you want to skew the block, and click **Apply**. [In CorelDraw 7, pull down the **Arrange** menu, choose **Transform**, and slide to **Skew**.] You can also double-click on a corner to display the rotation arrows and then drag one of the side arrows. In SuperPaint, choose **Slant** from the **Transform** menu. If you're using Canvas 3.5, pull down the **Effects** menu and select **Transform**, then slide to **Skew**. Hold down the mouse button while dragging a handle of the selected block to skew it. You can also use the one- or two-point perspective option in Canvas 3.5 by selecting **1 Side Perspective** or **2 Side Perspective** from the **Effects** menu.

- **TO DISTORT A BLOCK,** click on the Pick or Selection Arrow tool, and click on the block to select it. In CorelDraw 5, choose **Transform Roll-Up** from the **Effects** menu. [In CorelDraw 7, pull down the **Arrange** menu and choose **Transform** to see the transform options.] In Canvas 3.5, pull down the **Effects** menu and select **Special Effects,** then slide to **Distort.** In Canvas 5.0, pull down the **Effects** menu and select **Envelope.** The Envelope dialog box will appear. Select **Distort,** click **Apply,** and drag a handle. In SuperPaint, first create your block in the Draw layer. Save it, then select the block and choose **Cut to Painting** from the **Edit** menu. Use a selection tool to select the block (see your manual if you need assistance with these tools). Then pull down the **Transform** menu, select **Distort** or **Perspective,** and drag a handle. Select your finished block and choose **Cut to Drawing** from the **Edit** menu.

DESIGN TIP

One-point perspective elongates one corner of a block to a vanishing point, while two-point perspective stretches it to two vanishing points. This is fun to experiment with. Try applying one-point perspective to a block and then applying two-point perspective to a copy of it.

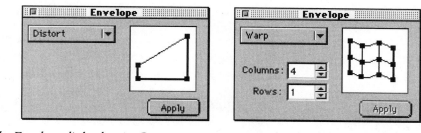

The Envelope dialog box in Canvas 5.0 presents several options for distorting, warping, and reshaping your blocks.

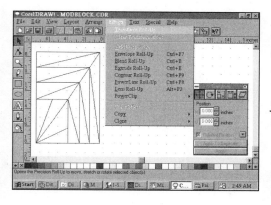

*The Effects menu in CorelDraw offers many opportunities for duplicating and distorting quilt blocks. You can have the most fun with the Transform Roll-Up. This is where you mirror, rotate, stretch, and skew objects. [In CorelDraw 7, choose **Transform** from the **Arrange** menu. Click on any of the transform options to display the **Transform Roll-Up.**] Start by selecting the block with the Pick tool. You can stretch and resize the block in various ways by pulling on the black handles around it.*

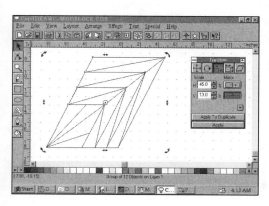

Click on the object to change the black selection handles to double-handled arrows. If you pull on one of these with your mouse, you can rotate the block or skew it.

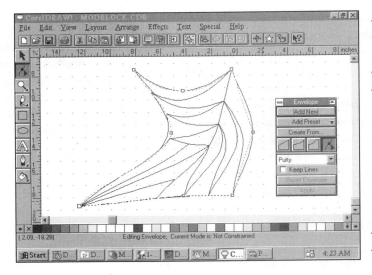

Now this is what you call pushing a quilt block through virtual reality! Use CorelDraw's envelope editing tools to twist and squeeze your block. Press CTRL-F7, or select **Envelope Roll-Up** from the **Effects** menu [**Envelope** from the **Effects** menu in CorelDraw 7]. Click the **Add New** button in the roll-up. Click one of the envelope editing buttons to choose straight-line mode (the block will maintain straight lines between its handles); single arc mode (an arc will form between each pair of handles); double arc mode (a rippling wave will form between the handles); or unconstrained mode (that's freehand; you can do whatever you like). When you're done pushing the handles of your quilt block around, click **Apply**.

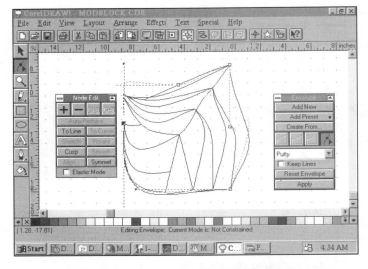

For additional bending and distortion, use the **Node Edit Roll-Up** to add or delete nodes, as described in Chapter 4. Be sure to ungroup your block first.

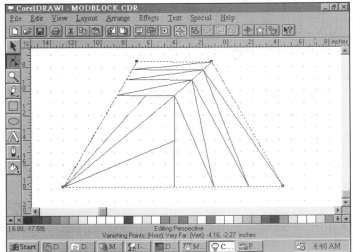

You can change your block's perspective in CorelDraw by selecting the block, then pulling down the **Effects** menu and selecting **Add Perspective**. Drag the handles to the dimensions you want.

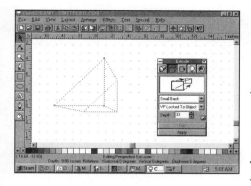

*Why, it's a quilt patch rotating in 3-D space! Choose **Extrude Roll-Up** from the **Effects** menu [**Extrude** from the **Effects** menu in CorelDraw 7]. Select your quilt patch with the Pick tool. Click **Edit** in the **Extrude Roll-Up**. The **X** on the screen is the vanishing point. You can move the vanishing point around with your mouse to elongate or shorten the 3-D patch, or type a value from 1 to 99 in the **Depth** box to see what happens. You can click on the lightbulb to add shadowing to your 3-D patch and all sorts of other fancy things. Note that the extrude effects work only with one object, or patch, at a time, not with multiple objects, such as a grouped block.*

JUDY & GLORIA'S RULE #2 OF QUILT BLOCK TRANSMOGRIFICATION

Never do to one quilt block what you can do to two. Or three, or four, or five.

JUDY & GLORIA'S RULE #3 OF QUILT BLOCK TRANSMOGRIFICATION

The repetition of pattern in a quilt is what gives it a soothing rhythm. But you'll find that the most intriguing designs are ones that temporarily disrupt the rhythm of things, supplanting it with another rhythm, if only temporarily. This is true in freehand drawing design, but it's especially true in computer design.

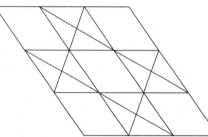

Here is our Ohio Star skewed.

Distortion gives you a slightly different, off-balance effect. This was accomplished with the Skew tool in Canvas 3.5.

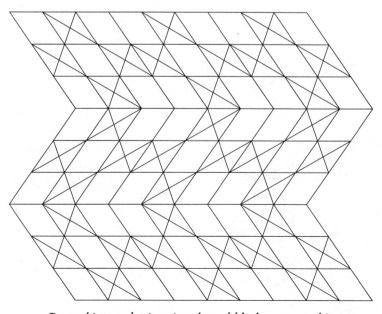

By stacking and mirroring skewed blocks, you get this.

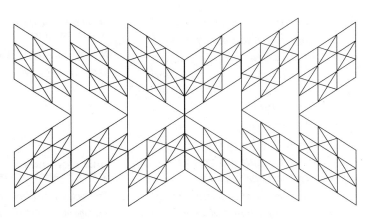

Butt skewed blocks end to end and mirror the rows for a "house of mirrors" effect.

Distort a block, mirror it, stack four together, and you have stars that are ready to break out of the sky.

Duplicate and mirror your skewed Ohio Star in the opposite direction for a geometric petal effect.

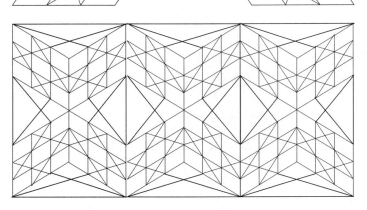

By adding a few lines to the mirrored, skewed blocks, you get this astonishing block.

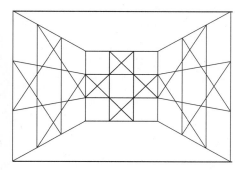

1. Take two Ohio Stars skewed with two-point perspective, add an ordinary Ohio Star, and you get a Bow Tie variant.

T * I * P

Create a library of your favorite block designs and variations. Save each block individually to a file, naming it in such a way that you'll know what it is later, like GOOFBALL.BLK. If you're using a Mac, store sets of variations in individual folders.

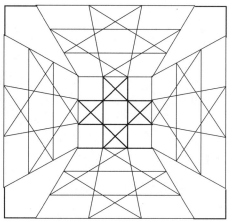

2. Add two more blocks, and your block looks like you're walking down a long tunnel of Ohio Stars.

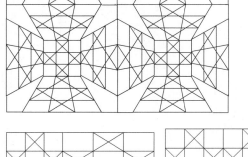

3. Put four of these blocks together and you're really cooking.

JUDY & GLORIA'S RULE #4 OF QUILT BLOCK TRANSMOGRIfiCATION

Never stop experimenting!

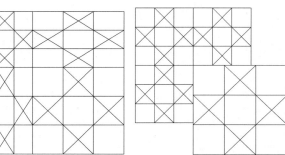

You don't need to use complex perspective-distortion techniques to create intriguing blocks. Simple resizing, stretching, and overlapping can create hundreds of eye-enchanting effects.

CHAPTER 9

THE LOG CABIN BLOCK:
A CASE STUDY

It started life as a plain Jane, but our simple makeovers give it cyber-age sparkle.

The Log Cabin block is probably responsible for the start of more quilting careers than any other quilt block design. It's so simple—scrap fabric strips, or logs, spiraling around a center square. Anyone who can sew a straight seam can whip one up—and even if you can't, the block is so forgiving of rumples and tucks that even a child can piece together a beautiful quilt of logs.

You don't have to push a Log Cabin block through a virtual reality keyhole in order to use your computer to generate lovely variations of this old-fashioned favorite. All you need to know is how to draw a square on your computer screen, and you're off.

BUILDING A LOG CABIN

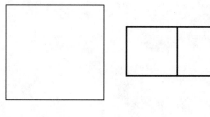

1. Start by drawing the center square. Use the rectangle tool, and be sure to draw a perfect square. Add a second square to it, and put them side by side.

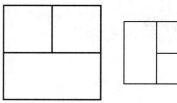 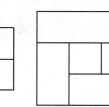 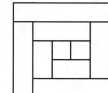 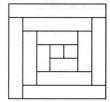

2. Using the rectangle or polygon tool, create your first log. Continue to add logs, adding them around the center of your square in a clockwise fashion.

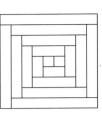

3. When your block is done, select it and group it. Be sure to save your completed block.

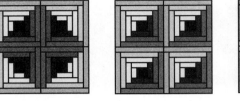

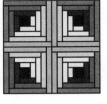

4. You can color it by selecting individual logs and using fills or colors in your drawing program.

REMODELING WITH LOGS

Experiment with your Log Cabin block by flipping, stretching, and resizing it. Group together blocks of different sizes and shapes, then duplicate them and flip them around.

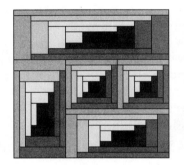

Step 1

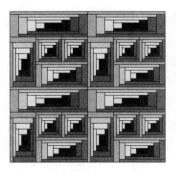

Step 2

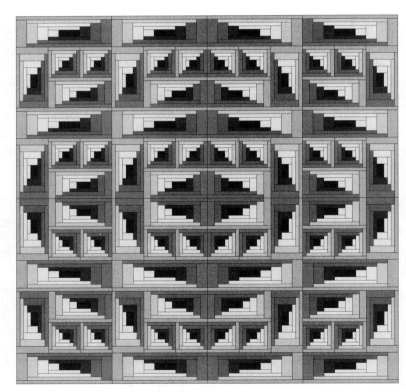

Step 3

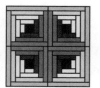

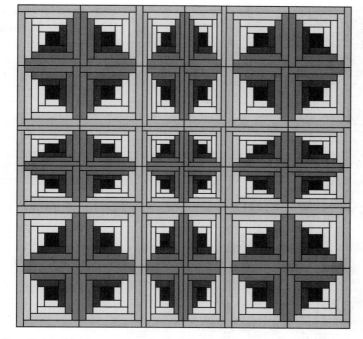

Four of our original Log Cabin blocks are placed with the dark corners together. The center of the design is duplicated and stretched. Notice the larger corner squares.

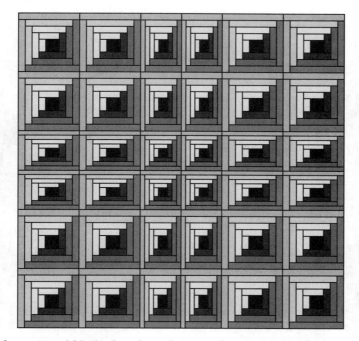

We are still using the four original blocks, but their placement has changed. What a remarkable difference in design this makes! The design was made by ungrouping the entire arrangement, then regrouping it into four quarter-segments. The segments were then flipped.

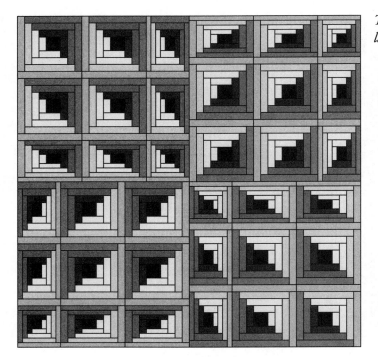

This is another variation of the same layout, again flipped and stretched.

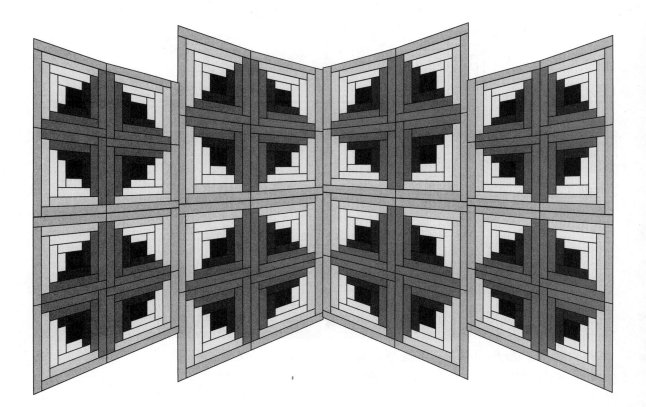

Here is our original block, this time distorted with the drawing program's distortion features.

Here we used the same four Log Cabin blocks. We duplicated the unit and then applied two-point perspective. We then repeated the resulting block and flipped it around a central four-block square.

The design is duplicated three more times to create a stunning effect.

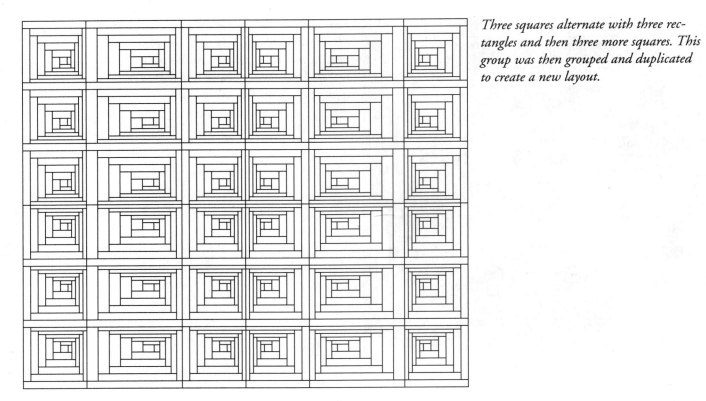

Three squares alternate with three rectangles and then three more squares. This group was then grouped and duplicated to create a new layout.

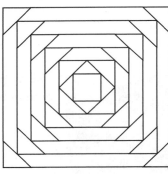

Draw different styles of Log Cabin blocks to experiment with.

Use the skew feature to make a diamond-shaped Log Cabin.

Combine different sizes of Log Cabin blocks to see where you end up.

T * I * P

An overhead projector is another tool for enlarging a design. Print your design onto transparency film—available for inkjet and laser printers—then project the image onto a wall and trace it.

We printed out a Log Cabin perspective design onto white paper. The paper was placed in the projector and enlarged onto a wall for tracing. Consider using a projector to enlarge designs for tracing when they are too cumbersome to print in pieces.

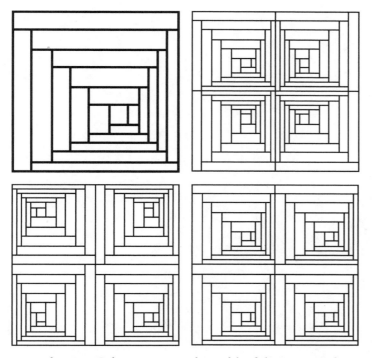

An easy way to alter Log Cabins is to vary the width of their strips. This is not so easy on paper, but with a drawing program it's a snap. In the quilt block at the top left, half the logs are drawn at half the width of the other logs. By grouping the block, duplicating it, and rotating it, you can achieve a variety of different looks.

CHAPTER 10

EXPLORING SHADOW, SHADE, AND COLOR

How to use your computer to play with color value and contrast to create spectacular quilt designs.

One of the virtues of a computer is that you can use it to draw a myriad of design experiments that would take hours to visualize with a pencil and a pile of fabric. You can play with color, toy with shapes, and apply light and contrast to one area of your quilt and then zoom back to survey it from afar.

This chapter explores a grab bag of tricks.

THINK VALUE, NOT COLOR

Have you ever bought a pile of beautiful fabrics, only to find that when you took them home and sewed them into a block the result looked wretched? Your first thought is that the colors are wrong. Then you wonder if it's the pattern that's at fault. In actuality it's usually the play of value and contrast in the fabrics that is undermining your design.

VALUE IS SIMPLY HOW LIGHT OR DARK A COLOR IS

The light value of a color can be represented by a shade of gray. The scale of grays that a color can correspond to is referred to as its value scale or gray scale. Black has a value of 100 percent, while white has a value of 0. You can dilute any pure color in graduated amounts by adding white to create a range of lighter colors, or tints; pink is a tint of red. Similarly, you can add black to create shades of a color; burgundy is a shade of red.

The difference between values is known as contrast. A light value and a dark value will have a high degree of contrast, and two medium values will have a low degree of contrast.

Color values can be represented as a scale of grays from white to black.

Gray looks darker when it's beside white.

What does this mean when you're designing quilts? Basically, it means that it's important to have a palette of fabric colors that represents a full range of color values. In other words, you need a good assortment of light, medium, and dark fabrics in your stash.

Here's an exercise: Try sorting your fabric collection by value. Compare your fabrics to the gray scale shown here. If you have trouble determining a fabric's value, try squinting and holding it at arm's length. Hold up one fabric beside another.

It's harder to determine the value of printed fabrics than it is solid-colored ones. If you're having trouble, try looking at a small portion of the print. If you still can't determine its value, it's probably because the print contains lots of high-contrast light and dark images. Such fabrics tend to be more difficult to work with than ones having an even value.

VALUE CAN PLAY TRICKS ON THE EYE

Just as the eye-play of an optical illusion depends upon value and pattern, so does the beauty of a quilt, even an old-fashioned one. Here are some things to keep in mind:

- The value and contrast of a color are relative to what lies beside it. A color can appear lighter or darker depending upon the value of the color next to it. If you place a gray fabric next to a white one, the gray looks darker than if you place it next to black fabric.

- Value placement defines shape, and shape in turn defines pattern. Log Cabin quilts are excellent examples. If you don't properly alternate the light and dark fabrics, the Log Cabin pattern is lost. Color plays a role, but it's less important than the value placement, for that's what creates the pattern and distributes the weight of the design.

- Strong contrasts between value create visual tension that advances the design. Dark areas of your quilt appear heavy, solid, dense. Light areas can look airy and translucent. It's the dance between them that creates your design. You can weaken the tension and create a softer design by softening the contrast of values. Simply by changing a value or its placement, you can change the emotional impact or mood of your design.

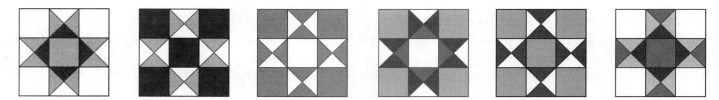

The mood of the Ohio Star block changes as you change the value of its patches.

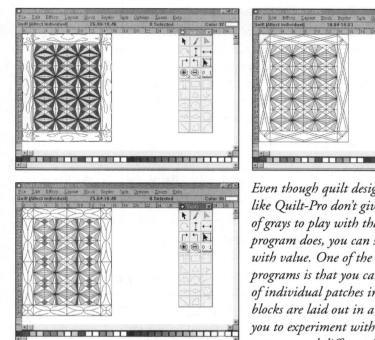

Even though quilt design programs like Quilt-Pro don't give you the range of grays to play with that a drawing program does, you can still experiment with value. One of the virtues of these programs is that you can change the value of individual patches in blocks after the blocks are laid out in a quilt. This allows you to experiment with different contrast patterns and different flows of movement in your design.

IF YOU REMEMBER NOTHING ELSE FROM THIS BOOK!

Throughout the earlier chapters of this book we've been telling you that adding color to your quilts is fun. So is filling blocks with scanned and digitized fabrics. But the very best way to design is to work with values of gray, not color. That's the best way to explore the visual play of your design.

DESIGN TIP

Keep the lines of your block very simple. That way you can play with value to get the most interesting effects.

T * I * P

If you're filling polygons, hold the SHIFT key down while clicking to select multiple patches. It's quicker to fill multiple shapes simultaneously with the same value than it is to fill them individually.

CONVERT YOUR LINE DRAWING TO A BITMAP TO PAINT IT FASTER

Let's say you've drawn a beautiful quilt layout in your drawing software. You want to start filling it with shades of gray. Unless you trace the entire thing into patches, however, you won't be able to color patches with different gray values. A quick way around this dilemma is to convert your line drawing into a bitmap. (See "Designing Quilts with a Drawing Program Versus a Paint Program, or Why CorelDraw Lacks a Spray Can and Eraser" in Chapter 2 for a discussion of how a bitmap drawing compares with a line or vector one.) Here are some tips:

- Keep a version of your original line drawing by saving it under a different name. Once you convert it to a bitmap, you're not going to be able to change it back to a vector line drawing, meaning that you won't be able to start ungrouping lines and changing areas if you decide to modify the design.

- Before converting your drawing to a bitmap, make sure that all its lines meet and there are no small gaps. Otherwise, when you pour the fill, the color will leak outside the lines into areas that you don't wish to be filled.

- If you pour a value into areas of your design where you don't want it, head to the **Edit** menu and select **Undo**.

- When, before duplicating a block's patches, you group it, don't forget to ungroup it when you want to change its color.

CONVERT TO A BITMAP IN CORELDRAW

It is possible to convert a line drawing to a bitmap in CorelDraw, but it's a pain, and it won't work as well as it will with other drawing programs. In CorelDraw 7 you simply pull down the **Bitmaps** menu and click **Convert to Bitmap**. (Save your drawing under a different name first.) Specify **16** colors and a resolution of **75** dpi to keep the drawing small. Then proceed to paint the drawing in Photo-Paint, as described in step 4 below. In earlier versions of CorelDraw, follow these steps:

1. Select your block, then pull down the **Arrange** menu and select the **Combine** command.

2. Head to the **File** menu and select **Export**. Under **File Name**, give the file a new name, then add the extension **.BMP** to specify bitmap format.

3. You need to keep your drawing as small as possible so that Corel's Photo-Paint program can handle it. In the **Bitmap Export** dialog box, specify **16** colors and set the pixel height and width to something small, like **100 by 100**.

4. Save the drawing with a new file name. Start Photo-Paint, pull down the **File** menu, and choose **Open** to open the drawing. You can then paint individual portions of your design with the bucket fill tool in Photo-Paint. When you're done painting, save your drawing, close Photo-Paint, and head back to CorelDraw.

5. Pull down the **File** menu and choose **Import** to import the painted quilt blocks. (They're going to look kind of grainy.)

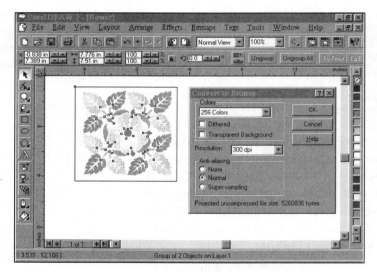

In CorelDraw 7 you can convert vector drawings to bitmaps, but do you want to? For most people it's going to be more trouble than it's worth. Note the projected size of the bitmap shown here—more than 5 megabytes! Use fewer colors and lower resolution to keep files to a manageable size.

CONVERT TO A BITMAP IN CANVAS 5.0

Follow these steps to convert a line drawing to a bitmap in Canvas 5.0:

1. Use the Selection Arrow tool to select the block or design you want to convert.

2. Pull down the **Image** menu, select **Area**, and slide over to **Render**. The Render Image dialog box will appear. Use the default settings and click **OK**. Your line drawing is now a bitmap painting.

3. Now click on the Paint Object Creator tool at the top right of the tool-box. This brings up the Paint toolbar. Select the Bucket tool.

4. Select the value you want to work with from the **Inks** palette. Use your mouse to place the bucket icon inside the area you want to fill, then click to fill it.

CONVERT TO A BITMAP IN CANVAS 3.5

1. Use the Selection Arrow tool to select the block or design you want to convert.

Group Specifications		(Unit: ')
Number Of Objects: 8		Group #: 6
Top: 1.5	Height:	1.5
Left: 2	Width:	1.5
☒ Convert To Paint Object		
Depth: 8 Bit	DPI:	72
Cancel		OK

2. Pull down the **Object** menu and select **Group Specs**. The Group Specifications dialog box will appear. Check the **Convert to Paint Object** box (we like to use 8-bit definition). Then click **OK**. Your line drawing is now a bitmap painting.

EGO BOOST

If you own quilt design software, you don't have to go through this rigmarole. You can paint large portions of your quilt design with just a few clicks of the mouse.

3. Press and hold down the mouse button on the Lasso tool. Slide over to select the Bucket tool.

4. Select the value you want to work with from the **Back Color** palette. Use your mouse to place the bucket icon inside the area you want to fill, then click to fill it.

CONVERT TO A BITMAP IN SUPERPAINT

1. Use the Selection Arrow to select your drawing. Then, from the **Edit** menu select either **Cut to Painting** or **Copy to Painting**. We like Copy to Painting in case we want to go back to the original drawing and modify it.

2. Click on the Paint Layer icon to go to the Paint layer. Your drawing is copied (or cut) to this layer as a painting.

3. Select the Paint Bucket tool, then select the value you want to work with from the **Colors** palette. Use your mouse to place the bucket icon inside the area you want to fill, then click to fill it.

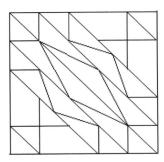

This is the block from the Directions quilt, pictured in the color gallery of this book.

We've duplicated the block and its value placement.

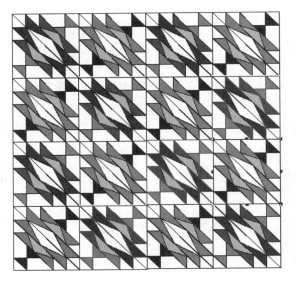

We've changed the values in certain areas to create a different emphasis in the design.

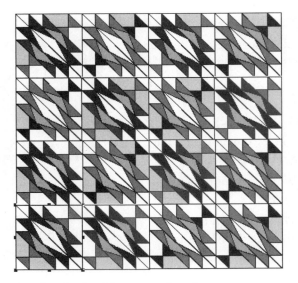

Another look with more value changes.

Here we kept the same values but flipped some of the blocks. Notice that the darker values make the center cross pop.

Here's a repeat of the block with darker values.

Here we merged the darker blocks from one layout and the central blocks from another.

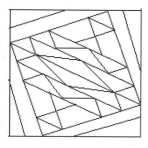

Just for fun, we took the block, rotated it within a larger square, and added a border.

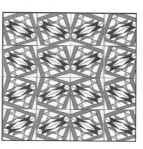

For the quilt layout we repeated the blocks and flipped them. Adding value to the layout makes it come alive.

The same block arranged differently, with value.

Look at the change of emphasis in the design we created just by darkening certain values.

CHAPTER 11

GOOD STARS ABOVE!

Using grids to draw stars, suns, and other heavenly bodies.

If you've spent more than ten minutes trying to draw quilt blocks in your drawing or quilt design software, you've probably discovered that it's darned hard to draw stars or any quilt block with a circular motif. The points of your star are never symmetrical, and when you try to arrange patches or lines in a circular design, it never comes out looking even.

To draw these things, you need a special grid. In Chapter 4 we showed you how to set up a drawing grid that looks like graph paper on your computer screen. It's easy to draw patches on a square grid because they "snap to" or align with the grid's lines or gravity points. But sometimes you need a grid that's circular, not square; you might even want to draw on a grid that's a little bit, well, warped to create unusual blocks and designs.

You can create a grid of any shape—circular, star-shaped, diamond-shaped—and draw on it. Here are our strategies for creating and drawing on grids.

JUDY & GLORIA'S GRID-SAVVY TIPS

- All drawing programs have a dialog box that you can use to set up a grid. Usually the only grid you can create automatically is a square one. However, high-quality quilt design programs like Quilt-Pro and Electric Quilt also let you configure a drawing grid. And Quilt-Pro includes built-in circular and star-shaped grids.

- If your drawing program lets you draw on different layers, you can draw a special grid like a circular one on one layer, then transfer it to the grid or guides layer or simply transfer it to a different drawing layer. You would then draw your block on another layer.

SOBERING GRID REALITIES

Quilt-Pro is the easiest software with which to create unique grids for drawing quilt blocks. Take a look at the instructions for setting up a drawing area in "How to Draw a Quilt Block in Quilt-Pro" in Chapter 3 to see what we mean. Electric Quilt lets you draw only on a conventional square grid.

- If your drawing program doesn't let you draw on different layers, once you've drawn your grid, change its color to pale gray or blue to make it easy to draw over.

- When you finish drawing a special grid, group the entire grid and save it as a separate file; then you can use it to draw on whenever you get the urge.

- For real design fun, create a grid in which the lines intersect at unusual angles, and try drawing on it.

- If you're using a PC drawing program, don't forget to turn on snap-to-grid or snap-to-guides before you start drawing on your grid.

GRID FUN!

Okay, we warned you. You'll never be able to look at boring square graph paper the same way again. Here is a vivacious variety of tutorials to give you a sense of the possibilities of grids.

CREATE A QUICK STAR-SHAPED GRID IN CORELDRAW

In CorelDraw there are two ways to set up grids:

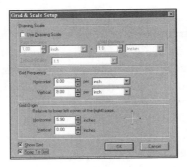

*You can find the Grid & Scale Setup dialog box in CorelDraw 5 by pulling down the **Layout** menu and clicking on **Grid & Scale Setup**. Here's where you specify the orientation of your grid's graph paper–like lines.*

- You can use the Grid & Scale Setup dialog box to set up a square grid, but that's about all. To see how to do this, refer back to "Set Up Your Drawing Area in CorelDraw" in Chapter 4.

- You can draw your own grid with circles, lines, and so forth. Then select it, group it, and move it to the guides layer. This turns it into a sort of grid. When you draw on other layers, your drawing lines snap to the guide lines below.

We're going to use the second method to create a star-shaped grid with the guides feature. You can use this guide to draw a variety of star-shaped blocks.

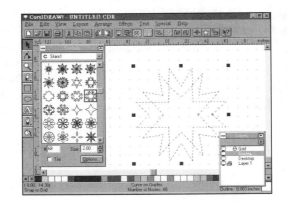

1. In CorelDraw 5, pull down the **Special** menu and select **Symbols Roll-Up**. Find the **Stars** library, select a star, and drag it to your drawing area. Make it the size you want your block to be.

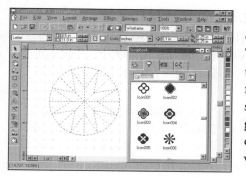

In CorelDraw 7, put your Corel clip art CD-ROM in the drive, pull down the **Tools** menu, and select **Clipart**. Search through the folders on the CD-ROM to find **Designs**. You'll find a variety of stars and symbols that work well as grids. Drag the one you want to your drawing area and make it the size you want your block to be.

2. In CorelDraw 5, pull down the **Layout** menu and select **Layers Roll-Up**, or press CTRL-F3. [In CorelDraw 7, pull down the **Layout** menu and select **Layer Manager**.] This is the roll-up you use to move between drawing layers and to move objects between layers.

3. Using the Pick tool, select the star so that black handles appear around it.

4. In the **Layers Roll-Up**, highlight the drawing layer that you're presently on—in this case Layer 1. Click on the right-pointing arrow in the upper right corner of the roll-up to pop up a little menu. Select **Move To** (Hint: Move To will appear only if an object on your drawing layer is selected.) A fat arrow appears. Use the arrow to point to **Guides** and click on it. This will move your star from the drawing layer to the guides layer.

5. Now you need to tweak some of the settings. In CorelDraw 5, double-click on **Guides** in the Layers Roll-Up to open a dialog box with various settings. Select **Visible** and **Locked**. The latter setting will keep your guides and drawing from separating as you work. [In CorelDraw 7, click on **Guides** and click on the right-pointing arrow in the top right corner to open the dialog box. Click **Settings** to display the Guides Settings dialog box. Check **Visible**. If there is a check next to **Editable**, remove it.] There are still a few more settings to make. Click the **Setup** button. Select **Show Guidelines** and **Snap to Guidelines**. Click **OK** twice to return to the Layers Roll-Up.

CREATE A DIAMOND-SHAPED GRID IN ANY DRAWING PROGRAM

To create a diamond-shaped grid in almost any drawing program, first draw a line with a 30-degree angle, then duplicate it with a .25 offset. Create as many duplicates as you need to fill the screen. Create a second set of parallel lines like this and mirror it horizontally. Duplicate this set and mirror it vertically. Detailed directions for doing this in CorelDraw appear below.

6. To move back to your drawing layer, in the Layers Roll-Up, click on the name of your drawing layer—usually Layer 1. [In CorelDraw 7 you also need to make sure the pencil beside the name of your drawing layer is darkened. Click it if it isn't. Click to dim the pencils beside all the other layer names.] Now you can begin drawing.

7. Use the Zoom tool to help you place your lines precisely as you draw. You don't need to draw a star exactly like the one you're using as a guide. Experiment by drawing different kinds of star designs. The advantage of the guides is that they establish some symmetry for your work.

CREATE A DIAMOND-SHAPED GRID IN CORELDRAW

1. To create a diamond-shaped grid, first draw a single line. Use the Freehand tool to draw a straight line at a 30-degree angle. (The angle appears in the center of the status bar at the bottom of the window.)

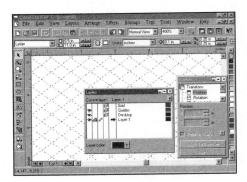

2. In CorelDraw 5, pull down the **Effects** menu and choose **Transform Roll-Up**. [In CorelDraw 7, pull down the **Arrange** menu and select **Transform**. Click on **Position**.] In the roll-up that appears, set **H** and **V** to **0.25** inch. Click **Apply to Duplicate** to draw copies of the line at ¼-inch intervals across your screen.

3. Duplicate your set of lines as follows. Pull down the **Edit** menu and choose **Select All** to highlight everything on the screen. Press **CTRL-D** to create a duplicate of your set of parallel lines.

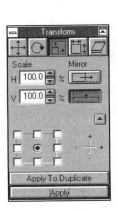

4. Mirror your duplicate set of lines. In CorelDraw 5, click the scale button on the Transform Roll-Up. Under **Mirror**, click on one of the options (it doesn't matter which), then click **Apply**. [In CorelDraw 7, click on one of the mirror buttons (it doesn't matter which) at the top of the screen. The mirror buttons are blue and appear under the View list box. They appear only when an object in your drawing area is selected.] When you click on a mirror button, your duplicate set of parallel lines should flip around to create a diamond pattern.

5. Group all your lines. Pull down the **Edit** menu and choose **Select All** to highlight everything on the screen. Press **CTRL-G** to group your lines.

6. Move the grid to the guides layer. Everything on your screen should still be selected. (If not, pull down the **Edit** menu and choose **Select All**.) Pull down the **Layout** menu and select **Layers Roll-Up** in CorelDraw 5 or **Layer Manager** in CorelDraw 7 to get at the Layers Roll-Up, or press **CTRL-F3**. Highlight **Layer 1** on your drawing layer. Click on the right-pointing arrow in the top corner of the dialog box. In the menu that pops up, click **Move To**. With the fat arrow that appears, click on the guides layer.

7. To save your grid as an individual file, pull down the **File** menu and select **Save**. Whenever you want to draw a star or isometric block, open this file. Before you start drawing, be sure to activate snap-to-guides. Also make sure that you're drawing on a drawing layer and not the guides layer itself by checking the Layers Roll-Up (press **CTRL-F3**). In CorelDraw 5, you should see a lock icon next to all layers except your drawing layer. In CorelDraw 7, the pencil icon beside the name of your drawing layer should be darkened, and the other pencil icons should be dimmed beside the names of the other layers.

CREATE A DIAMOND-SHAPED GRID IN CANVAS

Here's how Macintosh users can create a diamond-shaped grid in Canvas 5.0 or 3.5.

1. To create a diamond-shaped grid in Canvas, first use the Line tool to draw a single line. As you are drawing the line, look at the coordinates at the bottom of the page. Change the angle of the line until the coordinates indicate that it is a 30-degree angle. It helps to zoom out and draw one line across the length of your page.

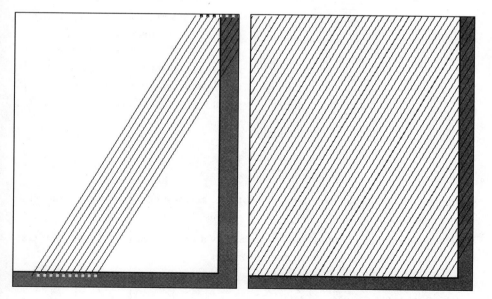

2. Duplicate the line. In Canvas 5.0, select the line and then choose **Replicate** from the **Edit** menu. In Canvas 3.5, select **Duplication** from the **Edit** menu. Set the number of copies to **10** (or however many lines you want). Offset each copy by .25. Group, duplicate, and overlap the first and last lines so they line up perfectly.

3. Select the group, duplicate it, and choose **Flip Horizontal** from the **Effects** menu. This fills your entire page with diamonds.

4. Group the grid and save it. Then use it whenever you need it.

Canvas has a Smart Mouse tool. Activating this powerful tool snaps the pointer to specified angles or objects. Read on to see how to set up the Smart Mouse to snap to the 30-degree grid you just created.

USING CANVAS 5.0'S SMART MOUSE

1. To use the Smart Mouse in Canvas 5.0, first open your saved grid.

2. Pull down the **Layout** menu, select **Layers**, and slide over to **Layer Info**. Click **New** to create a new drawing layer.

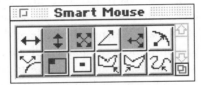

3. Pull down the **Layout** menu again, and select **Smart Mouse**. The Smart Mouse palette appears.

4. Double-click any constraint icon to open the **Smart Mouse Manager**. Inside the **Current Constraints** window, click next to **30° Angle** to select it (the other constraints should be unselected). Click the **Source Lines** and **Pointers** boxes to select them. Click **OK**.

5. Pull down the **Layout** menu, select **Snap To**, and slide over to **Smart Mouse.** Turn off Snap To Grid.

6. Select the Line or Polygon tool. As you draw a line, the Smart Mouse pointers will guide you, and the line will snap into place.

USING CANVAS 3.5'S SMART MOUSE

1. To use the Smart Mouse in Canvas 3.5, first open your saved grid.

2. Pull down the **Layout** menu and select **Layer Specs.** Click **New Layer** to create a new drawing layer, then click **OK.**

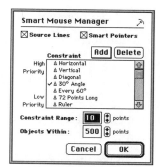

3. Pull down the **Edit** menu, select **Managers**, and slide over to **Smart Mouse**. The **Smart Mouse Manager** appears. Click the **Source Lines** and **Smart Pointers** boxes. In the **Constraint** window, click next to **30° Angle** to select it (the other constraints should be unselected). Click **OK**.

T * I * P

When you're finished, remember to turn Smart Mouse off.

4. Pull down the **Layout** menu. Turn Snap To Grids off, then select **Smart Mouse**.

5. Select the Line or Polygon tool. As you draw a line, the Smart Mouse pointers will guide you, and the line will snap into place.

TRIMMING GRID LINES FROM THE EDGES OF THE PAGE

When you're making a grid, lots of lines go off the page. It would be nice to have a rotary cutter tool and just slice down the sides for a neat trim. While there's no such tool in Canvas, there is a Scissors tool.

One way to change the size of a line is to select and resize it. If you don't want to risk changing the angle of the line, or you want to remove a specific portion of a line, you can snip it with the Scissors tool. To trim the edges of your grid to fit your page, first ungroup the lines and delete the whole lines that are outside your page. Then use the Scissors tool to trim the rest. Here's how.

1. Select the Scissors tool from the Effects Tools palette in the toolbox. Move the pointer to a line you want to snip. The scissors icon on your screen will turn to crosshairs when a snip can be made.

2. Click to create a break, or snip, in the line.

3. When you're done snipping the lines, use the Selection Arrow to select the portion of the line you don't want, then delete it.

CREATE A DIAMOND-SHAPED GRID IN SUPERPAINT

1. To create a diamond-shaped grid in SuperPaint, in the Draw layer, turn **Grid Snap** on, and draw one horizontal straight line.

2. Pull down the **Transform** menu and select **Rotate Selection**. In the dialog box that appears, type **30** in the **Degrees** text box, and check **Counterclockwise** and **Rotate Around Lower Left**. Click **OK**. You now have a line at a 30-degree angle.

3. Select the line. Pull down the **Edit** menu and select **Replicate**. In the Replicate dialog box, choose **10** copies (or however many you want) next to **No. of Copies**. Under **Move Each Copy**, specify **0.25** inch to the right. Leave the scale at **100%** and the Rotate Each Copy box at **0** degrees. Click **OK**.

4. Pull down the **Edit** menu and choose **Select All**, then choose **Group** from the **Draw** menu. Duplicate the lines (choose **Duplicate** from the **Edit** menu), then choose **Flip Horizontal** from the **Transform** menu. This creates the grid.

5. Continue to duplicate and group until the grid covers your work area.

6. When your grid is complete, pull down the **Edit** menu and choose **Select All**, then choose **Group** from the **Draw** menu.

7. Select the grid, then select the **Line Fill** button and choose a light color so that your grid is not distracting.

8. Select your grid, then pull down the **Draw** menu and select **Lock**. This will lock your grid so that it cannot be moved or edited.

9. Turn off the Grid Snap option so that you can use the guides you created, and save your grid as a separate file before beginning to draw over it.

DRAWING THE STARS IN THE HEAVENS

Shakespeare called stars the "burning tapers of the sky." Now that you know how to create and draw on grids, you can draw heavenly bodies on them. The variations are infinite. Your grid's lines can be separate from the design, or you can incorporate them into the design. As your comfort with drawing on grids grows, you'll discover a whole new cosmos opening for you.

DRAW FOUR- OR EIGHT-POINTED STARS

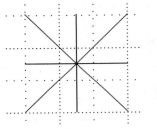
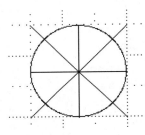
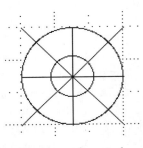

1. To create a grid for drawing four- or eight-pointed stars, first draw a series of intersecting lines.

2. Draw a circle on top to determine the size of your star.

3. Draw another circle inside the first one to define the "core" of the star.

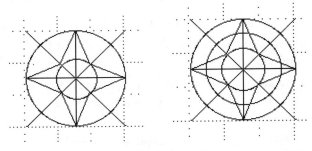
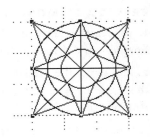

4. Draw lines connecting intersections on your grid to create a star block.

TURN A WEDGE INTO A SHOOTING STAR

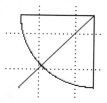

1. To make a shooting star, first draw a quarter-circle.

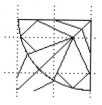

2. Draw lines in the wedge. The lines extending outside the wedge will connect to adjacent blocks.

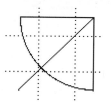

3. Group the wedge, duplicate it, and flip the duplicate to create a half-circle. Group the half-circle, duplicate it, and flip the duplicate to create the full circular block.

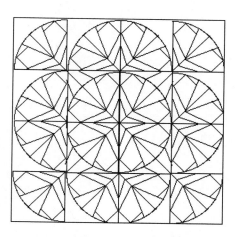

Two layouts created with the same wedge.

CREATE MANDALA STARS FROM PIE PIECES

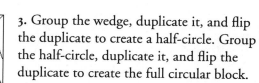

1. To create a mandala star, first draw a quarter-circle and bisecting line.

2. Select the line and shorten it so that it meets the arc of the wedge. Draw lines inside the wedge.

3. Duplicate and flip or rotate the wedge to create the mandala design.

The same wedge used in a different layout, with the mandala blocks laid out on a traditional grid of squares.

DRAWING STARS IN QUILT-PRO

Most of the grid-drawing magic described in this chapter can also be accomplished with Quilt-Pro. Quilt-Pro lets you easily configure a variety of uniquely shaped grids on which you can draw blocks. Head to Chapter 3 for examples.

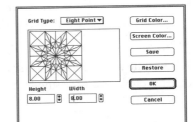

*Set the eight-pointed star grid in Quilt-Pro by pulling down the **Options** menu, clicking **Screen**, and scrolling through the **Grid Type** list.*

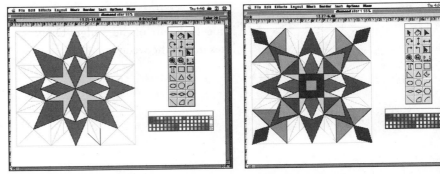

We used the eight-pointed star grid and the Polygon tool to draw this block in Quilt-Pro.

We turned off Grid Snap and overlapped other shapes to create this variation.

CHAPTER 12

MORE MARVELOUS DESIGN IDEAS

Duplication versus replication, working with negative space, binding objects, line magic, and other cool things that software manuals rarely tell you about.

We have a confession. Gloria has this huge filing cabinet. We're talking really huge. Half of it's stuffed with computer-drawn quilt designs; the other half is full of notes on little tricks for drawing quilt designs like Grandma's Flower Garden without ripping up the grass in frustration. When we wanted to write this book, we just pulled everything out of the cabinet and—poof! We had a book. Well, it wasn't that simple. But almost. Here are more design tricks from Gloria's bursting filing cabinet.

GLORIA'S FILING CABINET TRICK #1: USING DUPLICATION

It sounds like a controversy in a sci-fi movie: Do we duplicate or clone the organism? Depending upon your drawing program, the feature may be called cloning, duplicating, or replicating, but, whatever it's called, it's not the same as copying. Duplication is an advanced form of copying that can resize multiple copies, rotate them by specific degrees, and place them on the canvas at regular, predefined intervals.

Why would you want to use duplication? It's great for creating a circle of flowers or more complex drawings like a series of twisted blocks, each bigger than the one next to it. And duplication comes in handy for creating special grids to draw on (as you'll recall from Chapter 11).

To duplicate an object, you select it and then pull up a duplication or transform menu in your drawing software. You can select whether to spiral the copies, place them side by side or above one another, and other things. You can also type in the degrees by which the duplicate is rotated or placed in relation to the original object on the canvas so that your transformation will be more precise.

DUPLICATE OBJECTS IN CORELDRAW

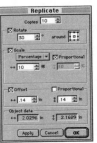

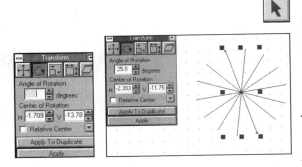

To duplicate an object in CorelDraw, start by selecting the object with the Pick tool. Pop up the Transform Roll-Up in CorelDraw 5 by pulling down the **Effects** menu and selecting **Transform Roll-Up**. To rotate the duplicate, click the rotation button. Type in the angle of rotation and then click **Apply to Duplicate**. [In Corel-Draw 7, pull down the **Arrange** menu, select **Transform**, and slide over to **Rotate**. Type in the angle of rotation, and click **Apply to Duplicate**.]

DUPLICATE OBJECTS IN CANVAS 5.0

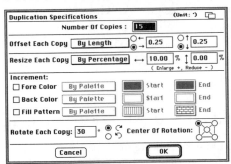

To duplicate an object in Canvas 5.0, first select an object with the Selection Arrow tool. Then pull down the **Edit** menu and select **Replicate** to open the Replicate dialog box. After you make your selections, click **OK**.

DUPLICATE OBJECTS IN CANVAS 3.5

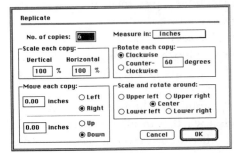

To duplicate an object in Canvas 3.5, first select an object with the Selection Arrow tool. Next go to the **Edit** menu and select **Duplication** to open the Duplication Specifications dialog box. Make your selections and click **OK**.

DUPLICATE OBJECTS IN SUPERPAINT

To duplicate objects in SuperPaint, start in the Draw layer. Select an object with the Selection Arrow. Pull down the **Edit** menu and select **Replicate** to open the Replicate dialog box. Specify the number of copies and how far apart they should be, as well as whether the copies should be scaled or rotated, and click **OK**.

PLAYING WITH THE DUPLICATION TOOL

The following illustrations are just some of the effects you can achieve by using a particular tool in your drawing program and then applying the duplication tool to it.

TOPOLOGICAL DREAMS Using our drawing program's 3-D tool (called the Extrude command in some programs), we drew a box. We duplicated it eight times. Each time it was slightly increased in size and rotated 45 degrees.

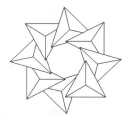

STAR WREATH We started by drawing a single star. We then made eight copies, each rotated 45 degrees toward the upper left of the design.

STAR WREATH II We used the same duplication settings as those used for the first star wreath, but started with a 3-D triangle (tetrahedron).

STAR BLOCKS We applied the same duplication settings used for the star wreaths to a simple nine-patch to get what looks like a Middle Eastern mosaic.

STAR BLOCKS II We overlapped shapes to create this new variation on the Star Blocks design.

RETRO DAISY CHAIN We started by drawing a flower. We drew a line about double the flower's length from the center of the flower and then grouped the flower and line. We replicated the grouped object six times, rotated around the center with a 60-degree clockwise rotation. Then we ungrouped the design and deleted the lines. Voilà! A headdress straight from the sixties.

GLORIA'S FILING CABINET TRICK #2: BINDING OBJECTS TO CREATE NEW ONES

We're not talking about sewing things together with quilt binding, but the concept is close. We're talking about taking a duplicate of one object and binding or attaching it to other objects. You won't find this option in low-cost drawing programs like SuperPaint, but you will find it in high-end Macintosh programs. (Sorry, PC fans, there's nothing quite like it in CorelDraw, but we talk about similar features like "weld" below.)

T * I * P

Remember that after you bind objects, you can ungroup the image and move around elements in it until you're satisfied with them.

BIND OBJECTS IN CANVAS

To create a design using the binding features of Canvas, first create the elements of the design. For example:

1. Using the Multigon tool, select a triangular framed wheel and make an elongated triangle.

2. Duplicate the shape to make eight triangles (seven copies).

3. Select all the shapes . . .

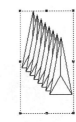

and group them as shown.

4. Use the Oval tool to draw a circle.

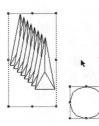

5. In order to bind, you must first select both objects; here, select the circle and the grouped triangles.

6. In Canvas 5.0, pull down the **Effects** menu and select **Bind Group**. In Canvas 3.5, pull down the **Effects** menu, select **Special Effects**, and then select **Bind Group**. The group then binds to the selected shape.

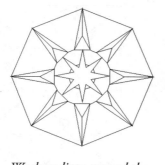

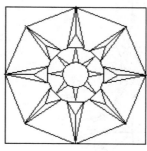

Here the group of triangles is bound to the circle. You can now do all sorts of interesting things to this motif.

We drew lines around the outside and inside edges of the triangles. Then, using the Multigon tool (in Canvas 5.0) or the Star tool (in Canvas 3.5) set to an eight-pointed star outline, we draw a star in the center.

*We selected the star and shuffled it to the back (by choosing **Arrange** from the **Object** menu and selecting **Send to Back**) and scaled the block down in size.*

We took elements from inside the block and duplicated them to create a border.

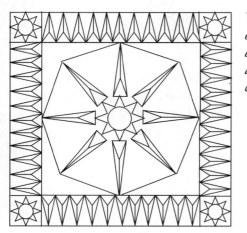

We duplicated the triangle to create one side of a border. We then grouped, duplicated, and rotated the side to form a complete border. We duplicated the central star into each corner.

We distorted the original motif and then duplicated and rotated it.

Back to the original block. This time we just duplicated it into rows.

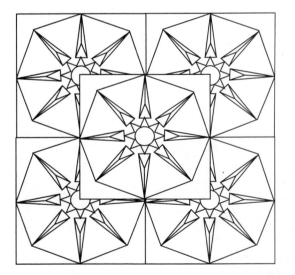

We overlapped the original block and resized it to fit on a base of four blocks.

The original block is in the center. We applied two-point perspective to the duplicated block and flipped it to create a new design.

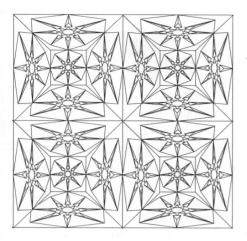

We couldn't resist putting four of these together. Now this would make one stunning quilt!

GLORIA'S FILING CABINET TRICK #3:
USING POSITIVE AND NEGATIVE SPACE TO CREATE NEW DESIGNS

You can create variations in a repeating design by overlapping portions of it. But you can create even more intriguing variations by creating reversals of fill. Different drawing programs provide different features for playing with positive and negative space. Here are tips for our favorite drawing programs.

USE POSITIVE AND NEGATIVE SPACE IN CORELDRAW

CorelDraw offers four tools for playing with the boundaries of shapes and how they're filled: Combine, Weld, Intersection, and Trim. They're all found under the **Arrange** menu. To use them, select your objects with the Pick tool and apply the desired command.

1. Start with two overlapping hearts, each filled with a different shade of gray.

2. Unite the hearts with the **Combine** command. They become one object, with a common fill and a peek-a-boo cutout.

3. Apply the **Weld** command to the hearts. Notice that there's no cutout where the hearts' lines join.

4. Apply the **Intersection** command to the two hearts. The spot where the hearts overlap becomes a separate patch that you can fill with a third color.

5. The hearts remain separate objects that you can pull apart when you use the Intersection command. Their former point of intersection creates a separate path.

6. Use the **Trim** command and, when you separate the hearts, a negative space appears in the spot where they overlapped.

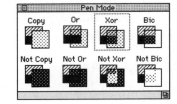

Needless to say, playing with negative and positive space works best when you're using basic shapes like squares and circles rather than identifiable shapes like hearts.

USE POSITIVE AND NEGATIVE SPACE IN CANVAS 3.5

T * I * P

For information on the types of effects you can achieve with other pen modes, see your manual.

To use positive and negative space for overlapping shapes in Canvas 3.5, you first choose the way you want your shapes to combine, and then you draw the shapes. Start by holding the mouse button down on the **Copy** box to open the Pen Mode dialog box. Select the **Xor** setting in the top row. Select a black fill, and then use a tool such as the Rectangle tool to draw overlapping shapes. Any overlapping areas will appear white. When you are finished, display the Pen Mode dialog box again and click **Copy**.

USE POSITIVE AND NEGATIVE SPACE IN SUPERPAINT

Using positive and negative space in SuperPaint works in much the same way as it does in Canvas 3.5. Start in the Draw layer. Click and hold on the **Opaque** button, slide down, and select **Invert**. Then use a tool filled with black to draw overlapping shapes. Return the setting to Opaque when you are done.

Go nuts! Experiment with squares, ovals, and other shapes to see what you come up with.

USE POSITIVE AND NEGATIVE SPACE IN CANVAS 5.0

Trying to accomplish this effect in Canvas 5.0 is not as much fun as it is in Canvas 3.5 or SuperPaint, because you cannot set the effect and then use tools. Instead you need to use a drawing tool to create some shapes first and then select them and apply the effect. First draw two overlapping filled shapes. Then pull down the **Effects** menu and select **Combine**. The Combine Manager appears. Select **Transparency** and type 75 percent in the **Level** box. Then click **Apply**.

The overlapped portion of the squares turns white.

GLORIA'S FILING CABINET TRICK #4:
TO KEEP IT FUN, KEEP IT SIMPLE, AND KEEP IT ASYMMETRICAL

Don't go crazy drawing lines all over your computer screen—a few lines go a long way. Spice things up with asymmetry to give your lines and squares new looks.

Start by drawing a square and a circle filled with black. Combine them in various ways to create some shapes. Keep them simple, and keep your design asymmetrical. Group your block and duplicate it four times.

Rotate and flip the blocks to create new block units.

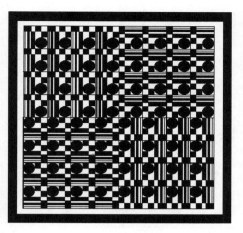

Duplicate the block sets and arrange them. The four-block unit was duplicated into a sixteen-block one. That set was duplicated and rotated. Borders were added to make a complete quilt.

GLORIA'S FILING CABINET TRICK #5: SOMETIMES YOU JUST HAVE TO GET BACK TO THE BASIC LINE

In this book we show you all sorts of snazzy tricks to draw quilt designs. But sometimes all you need is one line. The quilt *Shattered* that appears in the color gallery section of this book began with a design of just a few lines. Chapter 19 gives the pattern for the *Shattered* block and tells how to piece it. Here's how Gloria designed this quilt:

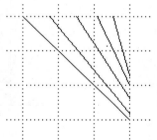

1. She drew a series of lines with the Line tool.

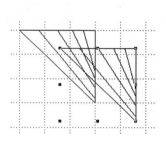

2. She drew two more lines to create a right triangle.

3. She grouped and duplicated the first set of lines.

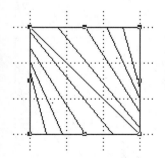

4. She rotated the duplicated block 180 degrees, lined it up to form a square, and grouped it.

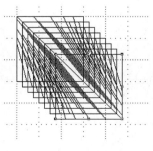

5. She duplicated that block.

6. She spread the blocks out on the screen.

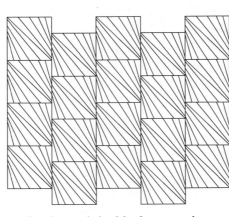

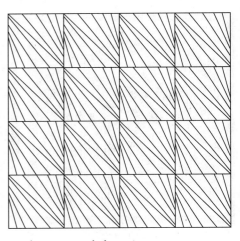

7. She dragged the blocks around to explore different arrangements.

8. She arranged them in rows.

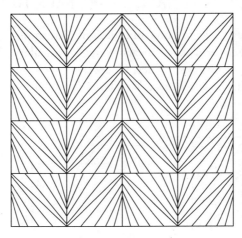

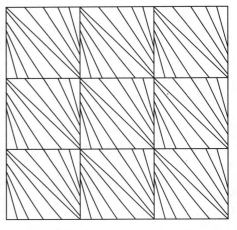

9. She flipped every other row.

10. She deleted some blocks, and created a 3x3 arrangement.

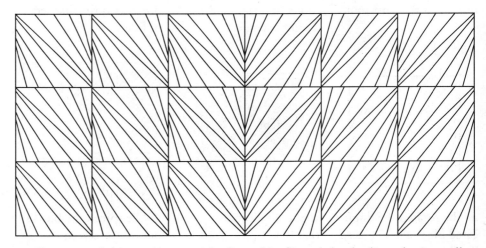

11. She grouped the arrangement, duplicated it, flipped the duplicate horizontally, and dragged it to the right side of the previous arrangement to create a 3x6 set.

12. She grouped the 3x6 set, duplicated it, flipped the duplicate vertically, and dragged it to the bottom of the first set.

13. The two halves change places for another design layout.

14. In another drawing layer, she copied one block with the polygon tool and added value.

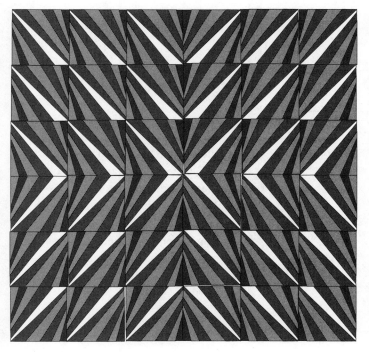

15. She filled the selected layout with value.

See, that wasn't difficult at all!

She paper-pieced the quilt. Here's how she made the pattern:

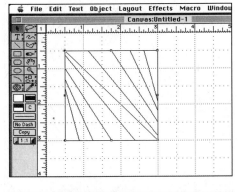

1. She opened the original block.

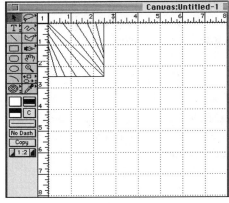
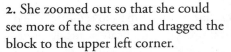

2. She zoomed out so that she could see more of the screen and dragged the block to the upper left corner.

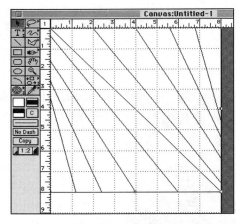

3. She resized the block to 8 inches square.

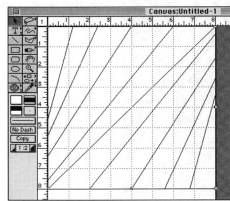

4. She printed the original block on tracing paper. This way you can flip the paper over and use both sides of it. It also lets you place your fabric very accurately. If you decide not to use tracing paper, you'll need to print the reverse of the block as well. Simply select the block, flip it horizontally, and print it.

That's it!

APPLIQUÉ FOR EVERYONE

FEW THINGS ARE AS ARTISTICALLY GRATIFYING AS THE GRACEFUL
PETALS AND SWIRLS OF APPLIQUÉ DESIGNS. LET YOUR COMPUTER
HELP YOU EXPLORE A NEW WORLD IN APPLIQUÉ DESIGN.

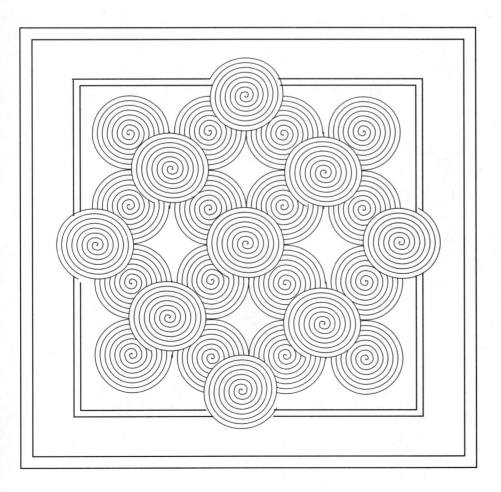

CHAPTER 13

OLD-FASHIONED APPLIQUÉ FROM QUILT DESIGN SOFTWARE

Drawing appliqué and stencil patterns in quilt design software is remarkably easy—when you start with the things that are already drawn for you.

Appliqué patterns are surprisingly easy to draw in programs like Electric Quilt and Quilt-Pro. As soon as you master these programs' techniques for drawing and manipulating curves, you're on your way. You can use them to draw appliqués of flowers, barns, peacocks, and cars. These programs will turn anything you draw with your computer mouse inside a block into an appliqué pattern.

But drawing with a mouse can be awkward. None of the quilt design programs let you use a drawing tablet to do your drawing. And none of them let you import a digitized image—like a photo of your daughter's wedding, a doodle of a pot of begonias, or even a piece of clip art—and turn it into an appliqué pattern. And that's something that a lot of quilters desperately want to do. For this you'll need a high-end drawing program like CorelDraw or Canvas (although SuperPaint for the Mac will also work). You'll want a drawing program that has:

- A "trace" feature that will either automatically trace lines around the areas that you specify in an image or turn the image into a "wireframe."

- Different layers that you can draw on, so that you can place your imported image on one layer and sketch or trace on another layer.

If you're an appliqué addict, you should buy a good drawing program that will let you turn a scanned image into a pattern within minutes and let you resize it too. When you're done, you can print your pattern directly on freezer paper if you wish. (See Chapter 15 for complete directions.)

That said, the appliqué drawing tablets in Electric Quilt and Quilt-Pro are remarkably easy to use compared with the drawing tools of high-end drawing programs. Their manuals are also excellent sources of instruction.

THE PAINLESS APPLIQUÉ 12-STEP PROGRAM

Every one of life's traumas seems to have a 12-step coping and recovery program. We'd like to introduce you to our 12-step program for creating appliqué. Yes, designing appliqué can be a pain, even in the most cooperative of quilt design software. No matter how you struggle, your daisies wilt like cow-pies, your rose-entwined gates smear like tire tracks in the mud. Did the pioneers have it this hard when they stitched quilts by candlelight? Probably not, but they didn't have computers, either. Or little boys wheedling, "Ma, can you make me a quilt with a bunch of spaceships on it?"

Here are our tips to speed your mastery of the appliqué drawing features in quilt design programs. Specific hints and revelations about designing appliqué in Electric Quilt and Quilt-Pro follow.

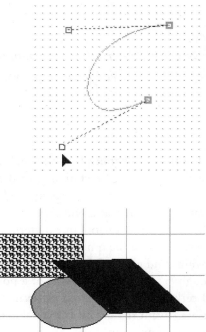

1. TURN OFF SNAP-TO-GRID. It's easier to position naturalistic shapes like leaves and petals if their lines and points are not being pulled toward grid lines. But turn on the grid if you want to see it, and use it to line up leaves and petals symmetrically. If you can't turn off snap-to-grid, make the grid squares large if you want to draw a highly detailed design. Make the grid squares small if you want a highly symmetrical design.

2. FORGET THE LINE TOOL. You're going to do most of your drawing with the Bezier curve tool, which will let you draw smooth and symmetrical curves. The line tool will give you nothing but scraggly lines. Once you get the hang of pulling on the levers and handles that the Bezier tool pops up around a curve, using it is not as hard as you may think. But you will need to practice.

3. RECTANGLES AND OVALS ARE YOUR FRIENDS. Remember that your appliqué patches must be drawn as closed patches—surrounded by one unbroken line. The easiest way to draw such a closed patch is with the rectangle and oval tools.

4. KEEP YOUR SHAPES SIMPLE. If you want to draw fantastical, detailed objects, buy a high-end drawing program. The easiest way to draw appliqué patterns is to draw one simple shape, like a leaf or petal, and then duplicate and mirror it to produce a more complex design.

No

Yes

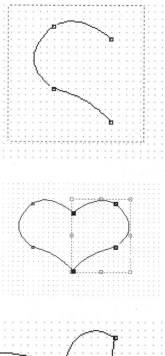

5. DRAW HALF YOUR SHAPE OR LINE AND THEN COPY AND MIRROR IT. Don't sweat trying to draw a complete heart or petal. Remember that in appliqué symmetry is king. Draw half a leaf, petal, or heart. Duplicate it, then mirror the duplicate, and paste the two halves together.

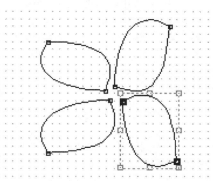

6. DON'T DRAW EVERYTHING FROM SCRATCH. Start your flower by drawing a single petal. Make a half-dozen copies and push them around. Resize and reshape them if you wish. Then do the same thing with a single leaf. Copy all the foliage. Rearrange it.

7. BE A JOINER. The shapes you draw with the Bezier or line tool must be drawn as closed objects for your quilt design software to recognize them as patches. To make the line a closed object, you'll sometimes need to join the nodes at the end of the lines. You can see if a patch is closed by trying to fill it with color. If it won't fill, it's not closed.

8. HANG OUT WITH NODES. When you draw curves with the Bezier tool, you'll see strange little black lumps on its curves and at the ends of the lines. These are nodes. Sometimes they're called handles. By moving these lumps you can change the shape of the curve. You can also add and delete nodes to effect other transformations to the curve. Spend time learning how to do this in your quilt design software. Nodes work differently in every program.

9. LEARN TO LAYER. For years the perennial fashion advice in *Cosmo* was "Layer it!" (Layer what? Socks? Wigs?) Your quilt design software lets you layer appliqué patches just like you'd layer fabric patches. To do so, you first select the patch you want to put on top of or behind another and then use the **Send to Front** or **Send to Back** command. (In Electric Quilt these commands are hidden in the Color menu—you don't have to worry about how appliqué patches are layered until you start coloring them.)

10. BECOME A GROUPIE. The quickest way to create lovely, symmetrical appliqué patterns is to draw a small part of the design, group its patches together, duplicate them, and rotate them. Even if all you're drawing is one small flower, grouping portions of the flower together and then duplicating them can speed your drawing. To group patches, select them by drawing a rubber-band box around them and then choosing the **Group** command. Electric Quilt lacks a **Group** command per se, but you can still select areas of your design and copy them as a group.

11. LEARN FROM OTHERS' BLOCKS. Take a look at the appliqué patterns that come with your quilt design software. Look at how they're drawn—how their nodes are joined and how their patches are formed. See if you can mentally retrace the steps the artist took to draw each one.

12. PLAGIARIZE WHENEVER POSSIBLE. This is possibly your most important rule for survival. Take an appliqué block from your quilt design software's library and change it slightly by transforming some of its patches—stretching their lines, bending their curves. If you don't feel comfortable drawing your own appliqué pattern yet, erase everything in the block except for a few shapes like a couple of flowers and leaves. Duplicate and resize those patches and pull them around to create new designs. Or cut and paste pieces from one quilt block into another.

Electric Quilt offers the most powerful set of appliqué drawing tools of the quilt design programs. It's the only quilt design software that lets you layer appliqué designs on a block. But, while its Bezier Pencil tool is especially easy to use, its appliqué features can be befuddling at times—and it has its testy moments. Here are some hints to get you over the hurdles.

QUICK-START TIPS AND TRICKS FOR DRAWING APPLIQUÉ DESIGNS IN ELECTRIC QUILT

BEGINNING A NEW APPLIQUÉ DRAWING

To begin drawing a new appliqué design, pull down the **Draw** menu and select **Appliqué**. Once you've done some drawing, be sure to click **Keep** to store your drawing in the Sketchbook. Clicking **Erase** will erase the entire drawing (but if you clicked Keep previously, a copy of any joined patches can be found in your Sketchbook).

To start a new drawing, click the **Keep** button to save your drawing in the Sketchbook, then click **Erase** to clear the drawing pad.

EDITING APPLIQUÉ BLOCKS FROM ELECTRIC QUILT'S LIBRARY

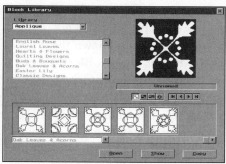

1. Pull down the **Library** menu and select **Block Library**. Select a block from Electric Quilt's appliqué library. Click **Copy** to put it in your Sketchbook. Click the X in the upper right corner to close the dialog box, then pull down the **Draw** menu and select **Sketchbook**.

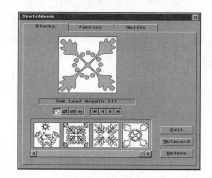

2. Click on the **Blocks** tab. Select the block you want to edit by clicking on it in the display box at the bottom of the Sketchbook window. The block will appear in the color view at the top of the window. Click **Edit**.

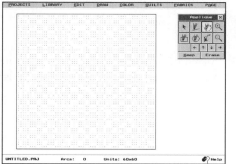

3. The appliqué drawing board pops up with the block in it.

CUTTING AND PASTING PATCHES FROM ELECTRIC QUILT'S APPLIQUÉ LIBRARY

One way to create appliqué patterns is to cut and paste patches from blocks in Electric Quilt's appliqué library that have already been drafted for you. Cutting and pasting in Electric Quilt isn't exactly intuitive, but it can be done. Here are the steps you need to follow:

1. Start with a blank appliqué drawing board. To get it, pull down the **Draw** menu and select **Applique**.

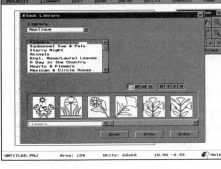

2. Select the block in Electric Quilt's appliqué library that you want to cut and paste patches from. To get to the appliqué library, pull down the **Library** menu, click on **Block Library**, and scroll to **Applique**. Copy the block you want into your Sketchbook by clicking on the block to select it and then clicking **Copy**.

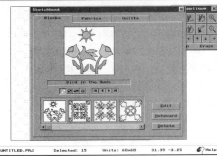

3. Close the block library and then head to your Sketchbook by pressing **F8**. Select the block you want to copy pieces from and click **Edit**.

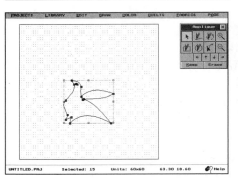

4. The selected block will pop up in Electric Quilt's appliqué drawing board. Click on the Pointer tool, and use it to select the patch or patches that you wish to copy. Press **CTRL-C**, or pull down the **Edit** menu and select **Copy**.

5. Click **Erase** to clear the appliqué drawing board. Press **CTRL-V** to paste in the selected patch, or, from the **Edit** menu, select **Paste**. You can also load a different appliqué pattern into the appliqué drawing board and paste the patch into that. Click **Keep** to save the block in your Sketchbook.

You can now open up another appliqué block and cut and paste patches from it into your saved appliqué block. Be sure to click **Keep** after each new patch is pasted into the block.

SHUFFLING PATCHES IN ELECTRIC QUILT

As you're drawing, Electric Quilt displays the patches as transparent. It's not until you head to the coloring toolbox to color the patches that Electric Quilt shows you how they're layered.

To change how patches are layered in your appliqué drawing, pull down the **Color** menu and select **Toolbox**. Click the **Back** and **Next** buttons at the bottom of the Color toolbox to flip through the blocks stored in your Sketchbook to find one with overlapping layers.

To change the order of patches in the block, select the Pointer tool. Click on the outline of the patch you want to change so that its lines turn to dashed turquoise lines. Pull down the **Color** menu again and choose **Send to Front** or **Send to Back**.

JOINING CURVES INTO PATCHES IN ELECTRIC QUILT

Electric Quilt automatically joins lines that you draw one after another. But if you draw by copying the lines and then flipping them or moving them together, you'll need to join them manually. To do this, click on the Bezier Shape tool and then double-click on the nodes you wish to join. If they're sitting one on top of the other, the **Edit Node** menu will appear, and you simply click **Join**. But it doesn't always work. What's going wrong? Joining lines is trying at times. Here are some tips:

- To find out if two line nodes need to be joined, right-click on the node. A status message will appear on the bottom of the screen. It will tell you if the patch is "closed" or "open."

- Use the Zoom-In tool to make sure the handles at the ends of a line align.

- To join nodes that are aligned, you sometimes need to move both nodes slightly. Once you join them you can always move them back. The Join command seems to appear more consistently if you've just moved the node with your mouse.

T * I * P

To configure Electric Quit so that you can place appliqué blocks on top of pieced blocks, pull down the Quilts menu and select Layers. Place a check next to Add Layers. The Layers command is dimmed unless you have chosen New Quilt from the Quilts menu and selected a layout. For more information on working with Electric Quilt's layers, see the next section.

THREE APPLIQUÉ EDITING MENUS YOU SHOULD REMEMBER

Find your way around these three menus, and you'll be on your way to becoming an appliqué drawing pro in Electric Quilt.

THE APPLIQUÉ DRAWING TOOLS

Whenever you select **Appliqué** from the **Draw** menu you'll get the Appliqué toolbox and the special appliqué drawing board.

 Use the Pointer tool to select lines, patches, and portions of your design to edit them, clone them, or flip them around. Hint: Always click on the object's line to select it.

Use the Line tool to draw straight lines.

Use the Rectangle tool to draw square and rectangular patches.

Use the Oval tool to draw oval and circular patches.

 Use the Bezier Shape tool to lengthen or shorten lines, as well as to edit Bezier curves.

The dreaded Bezier Pencil tool. Use it to draw curves.

 Use the Zoom-In tool to zoom in on a portion of your design.

Use the Zoom-Out tool to view your design from a distance.

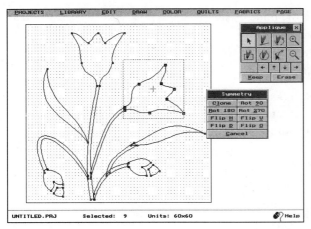

THE SYMMETRY MENU

 To pop up the **Symmetry** menu, click on the Pointer tool and then double-click on the line or patch you want to change. This will simultaneously select that part of your drawing and bring up the menu. Click on its buttons to duplicate (clone), flip, or rotate portions of your design.

THE EDIT NODE MENU

 Select the Bezier Shape tool and then double-click on the node or the spot on the line that you wish to edit. This menu pops up. Use it to add and delete nodes to the curve, break lines apart, join lines to form patches, and smooth the curve. The edit will occur at the spot where you originally clicked. You can use it on both curves and straight lines. You will need to activate this menu frequently to join line ends to make appliqué patches.

Double-click on a line and then click the **Add** button. Electric Quilt will add a node to the spot you double-clicked. You can use the new node to reshape the line.

Double-click on a node and then click the **Delete** button. Electric Quilt will delete the node. You can use this to make a triangular area of your drawing straight.

Double-click on a node and then click the **Break** button to break the line into two parts.

Double-click on two nodes that are one on top of the other and then click the **Join** button, and Electric Quilt will join them into one node. You will need to use this to unite your individual appliqué lines into patches.

Double-click on a curved line and then click the **toLine** button, and the curved line will become a straight line.

Double-click on a straight line and then click the **toCurve** button, and the straight line will turn into a curved one that you can edit with the Bezier Shape tool.

When you join two nodes and click the **Corner** button, you can move the handles on each side of the corner independently.

When you join two nodes and click the **Smooth** button, the handles radiating from the joined node form a straight line, but one side can be longer than the other, which allows you to make your patch asymmetrical.

When you join two nodes and click the **Cusp** button, the handles radiating from the joined node are one on top of the other. You can pull them to form a needlelike point.

When you join two nodes and click the Symm button, the handles radiating from the joined node form a straight line of equal length on each side of the node.

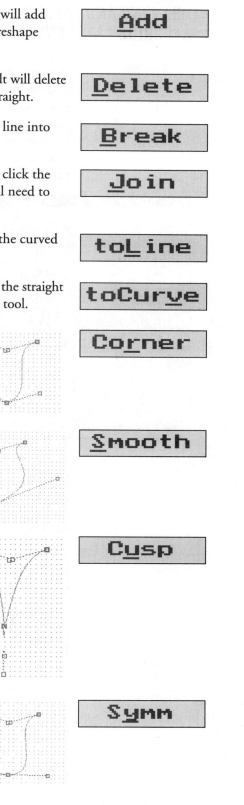

DRAWING AND LAYERING STENCILS AND APPLIQUÉ PATTERNS IN ELECTRIC QUILT

You can create your own quilting stencil patterns in Electric Quilt by drawing them on the appliqué drawing board and saving them as block patterns. You'll also find a selection of stencil patterns in Electric Quilt's block library—or you can use any blocks from the library as stencil designs. Lay them out on the screen just as you would ordinary blocks in a quilt. Electric Quilt offers a layering feature that lets you lay stencil patterns on top of your quilt design, select the thread color if you wish, and move and resize the patterns. Then you can print the patterns on paper to transfer to your quilt top. Here are some tips:

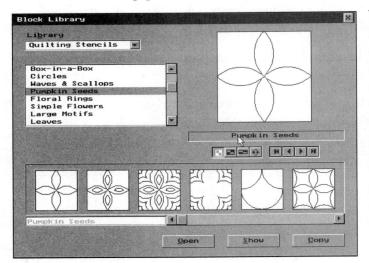

You can use any block design in Electric Quilt's block library as a stencil pattern, particularly the appliqué designs, but there are some specially designed stencil patterns that you should consider first. To get to the stencils, pull down the **Library** menu and select **Block Library**. Under Library, scroll to **Quilting Stencils**. When you find a design you like, select it and click the **Copy** button to add it to your project's Sketchbook.

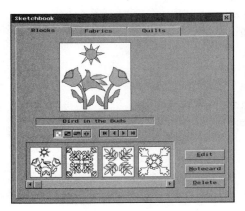

Press **F8** to open your project Sketchbook and sift through the blocks (including the ones you plan to use as stencil patterns) in it. Click the **Blocks** tab to see the blocks you've chosen. If you'd like to redraw any part of a block, select the block and then click **Edit**.

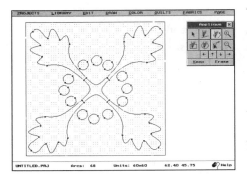

This drawing board appears when you select a block in your project's Sketchbook and click **Edit**. If the block is an appliqué design, you'll get the appliqué drawing board and tools; if it's pieced, you'll get the EasyDraw tools. You can change any of the block's lines; just be sure to click **Keep** to save it in your Sketchbook.

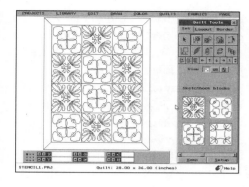

You can lay out your stencil designs just as you would lay out a quilt. Pull down the **Quilts** menu and choose **Toolbox** to display the Quilt toolbox, then pull down the **Quilts** menu again and select **New Quilt**. Specify a layout and click **OK**. Click the **Layout** tab to set up your quilt layout dimensions. You can set the size and number of blocks to be the same as those in the quilt top for which you're designing the stencil, or you can create a layout of different-sized blocks that will complement the design of your quilt top. If a selected quilt block appears colored in the Quilt toolbox, click on it several times until you get its outline version. Be sure to click the **Keep** button to save the stencil design and add it to the Quilts section of your Sketchbook.

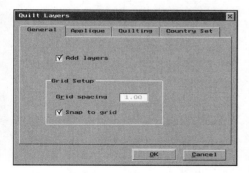

Experiment with different-sized blocks in which to place your stencil patterns by clicking the **Layout** tab in the **Quilt** toolbox. Here the sashing is widened until it becomes more like a series of narrow blocks. For fun, try some unconventional-sized sashes. You can also give your quilt layout multiple borders.

You can also lay out your stencils right on top of your quilt design by activating Electric Quilt's nifty layering feature. To activate the layering feature, pull down the **Quilts** menu and select **Layers**. In the dialog box that appears, check **Add Layers**. This will give your quilt three layers: the pieced foundation layer, a quilting layer, and an appliqué layer. Click the **Quilting** tab to set the thread color. Keep in mind that you must specify the basic layout of your quilt (dimensions, how many blocks, etc.) before you can start layering. On the **Quilting** tab, you can also specify whether you'd like your stencil blocks laid out in a diamond, rectangular, or square pattern. On the **General** tab, you can activate snap-to-grid so that your designs snap to the underlying grid of the quilt pattern. The **Country Set** feature is neat. It lets you lay out your designs in any size block or shape you want. To use it, you must first specify Country Set in the layout box that appears when you choose **New Quilt**.

 To move between the pieced and stencil layers of your quilt, click on the scroll button in the Quilt toolbox. Layer 1 is the pieced layer, layer 2 is the optional appliqué layer, and layer 3 is the stencil layer.

To place your stencil designs on the quilt, go to layer 3, then click on the Set tool. Click on the block or stencil pattern in your sketchbook or the toolbox that you wish to put on your quilt, and then click somewhere on your quilt layout. Click multiple times to place multiple copies of the block on the quilt.

To move and resize a block in your layout, click on the Adjust tool, and then click on your block. Handles appear around the block (they may be dim and hard to see). Drag the top left corner of the stencil to the spot on the quilt where you want to place that corner of your stencil. Release the mouse button. Move the cursor to the bottom right corner of the block, and drag the corner to the right, left, up, or down to resize the block.

 To delete a stencil block, click on it with the Pointer tool and then click **Delete**.

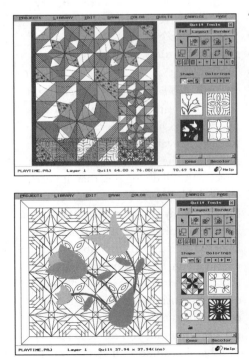

The stencil patterns laid out on this quilt top may be hard to see, but it's clear how easy it is to create complex and beautiful stencil patterns using different patterns from Electric Quilt's library.

You can use the same technique for laying out stencils on a quilt top to layer an appliqué pattern over a pieced quilt top. The difference is that you'd use layer 2 for your appliqués. Here's a tip: When arranging appliqué on top of a pieced top, select the colored version of the appliqué block, either by coloring it yourself or by clicking on the block displayed in your Quilt toolbox. That way Electric Quilt will remove any background from the block when you lay it on your pieced background.

Print your stencil patterns by selecting the Pointer tool and clicking on the block you want to print. Then pull down the **Projects** menu and select **Print**. The Print Block dialog box will appear. If instead you see the Print Quilt dialog box, it means that you didn't select a block before choosing Print. In the **Print Block** dialog box, click the **Scale Drawing** tab and select **Quilting Stencil** to print a stencil. Then click **Print**.

QUICK-START TIPS AND TRICKS FOR DRAWING APPLIQUÉ DESIGNS IN QUILT-PRO

Quilt-Pro's use of Windows' graphical interface makes drawing appliqué designs fairly easy in some respects, but its tool selection is limited compared to that of Electric Quilt. For instance, there's no way to skew the shape of an appliqué patch. Grouping and ungrouping pieces and moving them can also test one's patience. But it's much easier in Quilt-Pro to cut and paste patches between blocks than it is in Electric Quilt. That means you can easily assemble appliqué designs by raiding Quilt-Pro's block library for predrawn patches—a terrifically fun thing to do.

HOW TO SET UP THE APPLIQUÉ DRAWING PAD

You draw appliqué patches on the same grids you use for pieced blocks. Pull down the **File** menu and select **New** to begin drawing a new block.

In the **Options** menu, remove the check beside **Grid Snap** if you plan to draw naturalistic shapes or any other pieces that you don't wish to snap to the grid.

Also in the **Options** menu select **Screen** to open the dialog box to set up your grid. We like the **Solid** setting with a **Size** of 0.125, which will give you eight squares per inch. This is a nice size to use to line up your patches. Click **OK** to activate the new settings. Back at Quilt-Pro's main screen, pull down the **Zoom** menu (the **View** menu on the Macintosh) and select **Fit to Screen** or **Reduce** to get a nice working area.

If you're adventurous and experienced, set up a circular grid to help you line up a design with a block of four quadrants. Choose **Screen** from the **Options** menu, and set the grid type to **Circular**. Set **Radials** to 8. Set the **Size**, which is the space between the rings, and the number of **Rings** so that the circular graph is larger than your planned block size. (For example, for an 8-inch block, you could set Rings to 2 and Size to 4.) Pull down the **Options** menu and select **Grid Snap** so that your design will line up with the grid. Use **Fit to Screen** to see your entire block.

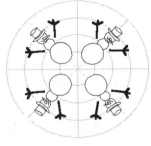

We cut these merry snowmen from an appliqué block in Quilt-Pro's library and arranged them around the circular grid. After cutting the snowman from the original block, we selected its pieces by drawing a rubber-band box around it, grouped them so that the patches wouldn't separate, and then duplicated the snowman.

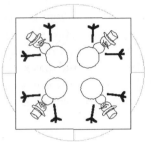

*To complete the block we used the Square tool to draw a square around the snowmen, using the grid to align the square properly. Then we selected the square and used the **Send to Back** command to place it behind our snowmen.*

EDITING APPLIQUÉ BLOCKS FROM QUILT-PRO'S LIBRARY

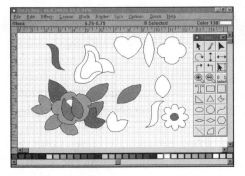

The easiest way to start drawing appliqué designs in Quilt-Pro is to take portions of images from appliqué blocks in Quilt-Pro's appliqué library and move, resize, and reshape them. In fact, there's a collection of appliqué patches designed specifically for that purpose. Pull down the **Block** menu and select **Open**. Select the **Blocks Library** and the **Appliqué** subdirectory or folder. The file you want is Common Appliqué Shapes, also called BLK30020.BLK on the PC.

You can use the predrawn appliqué patches to create an infinite number of designs. Resize the pieces, flip them around, and duplicate them, or place a smaller version of a patch inside a larger patch. Here are some tips for working with appliqué patches:

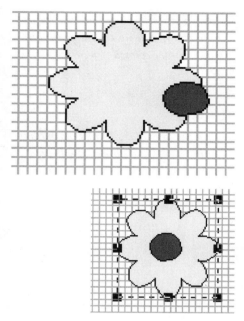

You don't want this to happen. You need to select the pieces and group them into one piece.

- To keep the patch's parts from scattering when you move them around, start by drawing a rubber-band box around the whole thing with the Select tool. Then pull down the **Effects** menu and select **Group**.

- To edit a patch, start by clicking on the patch's outline with the Select tool so that black handles appear around it.

- To move the patch, place the cursor inside the selected patch, hold the mouse button down so that the cursor becomes a hand, and drag the patch where you want it.

- To resize the patch, position the cursor over one of the side handles so that the cursor changes to a pointing finger. Hold the mouse button down and drag the handle to resize the patch. To resize the patch without distorting it, hold down the **SHIFT** key while dragging a handle.

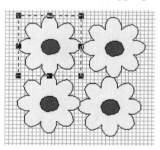

- To duplicate the patch, press **CTRL-D** (**COMMAND-D** on a Mac).

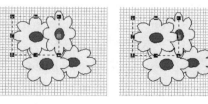

- To place one patch on top of or behind another, select the patch you want to move with the Select tool. Pull down the **Effects** menu and select **Bring to Front** or **Send to Back**.

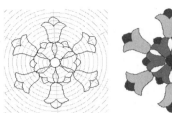

We turned off Grid Snap but used the circular grid to line up the tulips in this design. Then we colored it with different shades of gray.

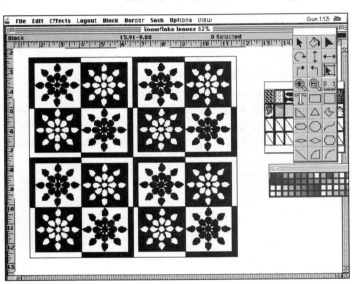

We took the Snowflake Leaves block from Quilt-Pro's appliqué library, duplicated it, and colored it with alternating black and white blocks.

CUTTING AND PASTING ELEMENTS BETWEEN BLOCKS

Another easy way to design appliqué blocks is to take patches from blocks that are already drawn and combine them. Start by pulling down the **Block** menu and selecting **Open**. Search through the appliqué library to find a block with patches that you want. Select it and click **OK** to open it. Use the Select tool to draw a rubber-band box around the pieces you want and then drag them to your drawing screen. When you're finished with the block from the library, you can delete it from your drawing screen by selecting it and pressing **DELETE**.

1. For this design, we selected a pansy from a design in Quilt-Pro's library and duplicated it.

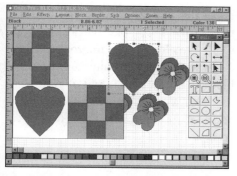

2. Then we opened another block from Quilt-Pro's library, dragged its selected object (a heart) to the drawing screen, selected the block, and deleted it.

COMPUTER APPLIQUÉ TIP

When you create a new block, save it. Then open it as a new file or document, reduce it, duplicate it, and start brainstorming. Add elements from other blocks in the software's block library and so on.

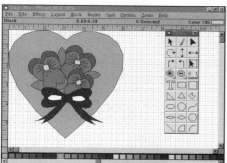

3. We resized the heart and resized and flipped the pansies. We took leaves and a bow from other appliqué blocks in Quilt-Pro's library, resized them, and added them to the design. As we worked, we made frequent use of the **Bring to Front** and **Send to Back** commands in the **Effects** menu.

T * I * P

*Group your patches to ensure that they don't scatter. Select them with the Select tool, draw a box around them, pull down the **Effects** menu, and select Group. You'll probably want to ungroup them before coloring or printing them.*

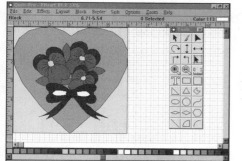

4. We completed the block by selecting the Square tool and drawing a block around the design. We selected the square and placed it behind the heart and pansies with the **Send to Back** command.

Who says a computer can't design quilts as good as Grandma?

QUILT-PRO APPLIQUÉ TIP

Be sure to look at Quilt-Pro's stencil library for appliqué ideas.

1. For this design, we took a portion of the Mariner's Compass block from Quilt-Pro's library and ungrouped it. Then we copied the Tulips and Leaves block to the work area and ungrouped that too. We took the tulip motif and added eight duplications of it to the compass block.

2. To complete the block, we placed a tulip cluster in the central area and moved the circle to the top.

3. We duplicated the block four times and darkened the central tulip cluster to emphasize it.

4. We added borders and played with the values a bit more.

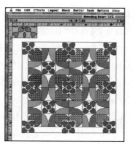

We joined elements from an appliqué block to the Bleeding Heart block to create this layout.

DRAWING APPLIQUÉ PATTERNS FROM SCRATCH IN QUILT-PRO

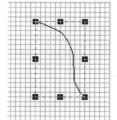

DON'T BE AFRAID OF THE BEZIER MONSTER. The easiest tool to use to draw curved lines, like the outlines of leaves and petals, is the Bezier Curve tool. To draw with it, click on the tool to select it, then position the cursor where you want to start drawing. Hold the mouse button down as you drag the mouse to the second point of the curve. Release the mouse button, press it again, and hold it down as you draw to the third point in your curve. Release it at the third point, press it again, and hold it down as you draw to the fourth point. Release the mouse button when you're done and the line will draw itself.

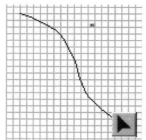

USE THE SELECTION MARQUEE AND THE CORNER TOOLS TO RESHAPE CURVED LINES. One way to reshape curves and arcs in Quilt-Pro on the PC is to click on the line with the Select tool and then pull on the black handles to stretch or distort the line.

Another way to reshape lines is to select the Edit tool, right-click on the line, and then pull on the black control handles to reshape the curve. On a Macintosh, select the Reshape tool, hold down the **OPTION** key, and click on either end of the curve. The black control handles will appear. Pull on a handle to reshape the curve.

CONQUER THE ARC. The Arc tool is easy to use, as long as you put aside logic. To draw with it, select the tool by clicking on it. Think of your arc-to-be as part of a circle, and position the cursor at the center of that circle. Hold the mouse button down while dragging the mouse to the spot where you want the right-hand side of the arc to start. Release the mouse button, then hold it down again as you drag the mouse to the left. Release the mouse button when you reach the point where you want the arc to end.

T * I * P

Use the Bezier Curve tool to draw leaves and petals in one continuous line.

JOINING TIP

If your lines don't meet, Quilt-Pro will draw a straight line to join the lines. This can be good or bad, depending upon how far apart the lines are.

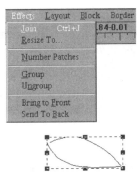

DON'T FORGET TO JOIN LINES INTO PATCHES. To turn two or more lines into a patch, you need to join them. This is easier in Quilt-Pro than in other drawing or quilt design programs. To do so, choose the Select tool and draw a rubber-band box around the lines to select them all. Press **CTRL-J** (**COMMAND-J** on a Mac), or pull down the **Effects** menu and choose **Join**.

As you join patches, fill them with color or fabric so that you can see which parts of your drawing are complete patches.

DRAW ONE SHAPE OR LINE AND DUPLICATE IT TO DEATH. The secret to easy appliqué is to draw one or two shapes and duplicate them, group them, and then duplicate the group. In Quilt-Pro, click on the Select tool, draw a rubber-band box around the patch or group of patches, and press **CTRL-D** (**COMMAND-D** on a Mac) to duplicate them, or pull down the **Effects** menu and select **Group** to group them. Or click on one of the transform buttons in Quilt-Pro's toolbox to flip the patches or rotate them.

Can you identify which button in the Quilt-Pro toolbox will perform what transformation to your selected patch? Here's a hint: The buttons in the second and third rows turn the patch or selected group of patches in the direction of the button's arrow.

Use the Oval tool instead of the Circle tool. Quilt-Pro's Circle tool is a bit unintuitive. It's easier to draw circles—and ovals—with the Oval tool.

Use the Zoom-In tool to position pieces precisely and align the ends of lines.

FLOWER-MAKING TIP

Use the Bezier Curve tool to draw one side of the flower's stem. Then select it and press CTRL-D or COMMAND-D on a Mac to duplicate it. Move the duplicate next to the original to form a stem.

DON'T PANIC, UNDO IT!

If you make a mess of your appliqué design while drawing, don't fret. Pull down the Edit menu and select Undo. Selecting Undo repeatedly will take you back step by step to earlier versions of your drawing.

GROUP, GROUP, GROUP

We can't say it often enough. Group patches and then duplicate the groups. Move them and resize them to make new patterns. This works especially well for drawing foliage.

Even a very simple block can create a beautiful design. All the leaves in this holly design are the same. Keeping all or most of the patches in an appliqué block the same makes sewing easier than having to cut out and arrange many pieces of slightly different sizes and shapes.

MOVING SELECTED OBJECTS IS SOMETIMES HARD IN QUILT-PRO

Sometimes it's hard to move selected objects to the area of your block where you want them. No matter how hard you "pull" with the mouse, Quilt-Pro mulishly refuses to move them. Why? It's a glitch. But you can work around this problem by making multiple copies of an object. Move one copy of the object to a different quadrant of your screen, then copy it again, and move that copy in the direction that you want.

GROUPING AND UNGROUPING OBJECTS MAY BE DIFFICULT IN QUILT-PRO

Sometimes when you select a collection of objects, like leaves and flowers, and attempt to group them, Quilt-Pro groups only portions of the design. When you move the grouped objects, some of the pieces scatter or, worse, mysteriously disappear.

To help combat this, be sure you're selecting the objects correctly. Click on the Select tool and draw a rubber-band box around the objects you wish to group. Make sure the black handles appear around the outside edge of your objects, not inside the collection of objects. Then pull down the **Effects** menu and select **Group**.

Unfortunately, even when you select and group objects correctly, some of the patches may not be grouped. This is painfully obvious when you try to select all the patches in a complete block—Quilt-Pro often leaves out a few on the left edge of the design. The solution to this is to pull down the **Edit** menu and choose **Select All** to select everything on the screen when appropriate.

NOTE

Save your drawing frequently. That way, if Quilt-Pro ungroups patches, scattering them hither and yon, you can revert to a previously saved version of the block.

DRAWING AND LAYING OUT STENCIL PATTERNS IN QUILT-PRO

There are three steps to designing stencil patterns in Quilt-Pro: First, design the stencil, either by drawing it yourself, taking a design from Quilt-Pro's stencil library, or taking pieces from different stencil designs and rearranging and sizing them. Next, experiment by placing portions of the stencil on your quilt block to see how they look. Finally, size your stencil to fit the dimensions of your quilt design and print it. Here are tricks we have discovered that speed the designing of stencils in Quilt-Pro.

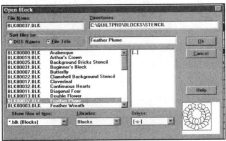

1. To draw a stencil pattern, start by opening some stencil blocks. Pull down the **Block** menu and select **Open**. Click your way to the stencil collection. Quilt-Pro includes a large selection of stencils from the Stencil Company that you can size and lay out on your quilt top. They include both block-based patterns and all-over designs like the clamshell.

2. Remove the white block in back of the stencil by clicking on it with the Select tool and pressing the **DELETE** key. To prevent the stencil's lines from fluttering about as you attempt to move and resize it, group all the lines in the block by pulling down the **Edit** menu and choosing **Select All** or pressing **CTRL-A** (**COMMAND-A** on a Mac). Now group it by pulling down the **Effects** menu and selecting **Group**. Or, if you wish to pull apart individual pieces from the stencil pattern—the leaves, say—and move and resize them, select only the portion of the stencil you want to play with, and group that.

3. Once you have a selection of stencil pieces on your screen that you wish to play with (don't worry about making them the proper size—you can resize them later), open your quilt block by pulling down the **Block** menu and selecting **Open**.

4. Before you become more involved with your stencils and block, you should group the block so its patches don't go fluttering across the screen. First, color the block with colors that you'll be able to see your stencils against. Next, select the block by drawing a rubber-band box around it with the Select tool. Pull down the **Effects** menu and select **Group**. Make the block its final size.

5. Now pull pieces of your stencil patterns onto the block, resize them, transform them, and pull them around until they look good. If you can't see your stencil patterns when you pull them onto the block, pull down the **Effects** menu and select **Bring to Front** to shuffle the stencil in front of the block.

T * I * P

You can also use Quilt-Pro's drawing tools to draw stencil designs right on your block.

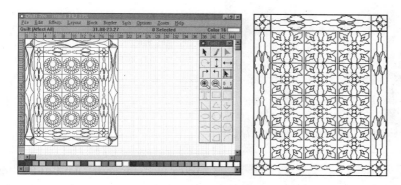

Now try laying out your stencil designs on a quilt layout to see the overall look.

1. Pull down the **Layout** menu and click on **Quilt**. In the tabbed dialog box that appears, set the dimensions of your planned quilt top.

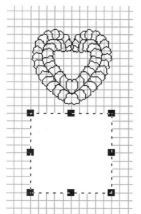

2. To remove the background square from the stencil pattern before you lay it on your quilt, open the stencil you want to use. Drag it to the side of your layout and ungroup it. Carefully select the background box and drag it away from the stencil, being careful not to separate any of the stencil's lines.

IMPORTANT!

Don't duplicate a stencil pattern on the actual quilt layout, because sometimes the stencil accidentally ungroups during duplication, and you could end up with a mess of lines all over your quilt layout.

3. Once you've separated the stencil from its background, regroup it. If necessary, duplicate the stencil in your work area before dragging it to the quilt layout.

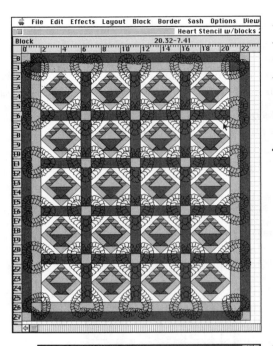

Here's our quilt layout with heart-shaped stencils on top of it. Notice how we changed the direction on some of the stencils and reduced the corners. We did this right on the quilt layout. But first we duplicated the stencil off to the side of the layout and made sure that it was a grouped object before dragging it on top of our layout.

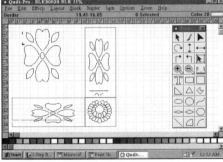

You can draw your own border stencils in Quilt-Pro by pulling down the **Border** menu and selecting **Design**. In the dialog box that appears, choose the dimensions of your stencil design. Specify relatively small ones—you can always resize the design later.

A BEVY OF BORDERS

To get to Quilt-Pro's library of border stencil patterns, pull down the Border menu and select Open.

Draw your own stencil designs or cut and paste pieces of stencil patterns from Quilt-Pro's library by pulling down the **Block** menu and selecting **Open** and then selecting stencil patterns to use. Remember to remove the white square behind stencil patterns. Also remember to select the stencil design and group it before you move it or resize it.

You may want to regroup a portion of a stencil design before transforming it. Remember to save your design frequently as you work.

Actually, we think it's easier to use stencil designs from Quilt-Pro's library rather than futz around designing your own.

*To print a stencil pattern, select it with the Select tool, pull down the **File** menu, and select **Print**. In the dialog box that appears, select **Actual Size**, or specify the size you want the stencil to be. Choose **Selected Objects Only** and click **OK**.*

CHAPTER 14

MARVELOUS AND PAINLESS WAYS TO DRAW APPLIQUÉ AND STENCIL PATTERNS

Use some unusual drawing tools to draw the Garden of Eden—and make a stencil for it!

Stylized flowers. Graceful leaves. Curling tendrils and vines. The gardens of appliqué are what the poet Andrew Marvell might have had in mind when he rhapsodized about idealized paradisiacal gardens where flowers and trees conspire to "weave the garlands of repose."

Getting a computer to make the lines flow like the petals raining in Marvell's garden is not always easy. You need to get the mouse to stop wiggling lines all over the screen. To do this, you need to use something called the Bezier tool, which sounds like, and sometimes acts like, an eighteenth-century torture machine. You need to struggle with the oval tool to draw luscious fruits like the kind Marvell described in that immortal line "stumbling on melons . . . I fall on grass."

Or do you?

We'll show you a few nifty tricks that will rid you of the headaches of trying to draw natural outlines with a mouse and drawing program. We'll show you how to make flowers pop up like springtime daisies. Then we'll show you how to turn those buds and whorls into stencil patterns. Once you get everything working, and the blossoms begin curling over your screen, you'll join the ecstatic Marvell in rejoicing, "What wondrous life is this I lead!"

These might have been flowers that Marvell trampled in his barefoot, prehippie ecstasy. All the flowers—and even the feet—in this appliqué pattern come from CorelDraw's symbol library.

FIRST, YOU NEED TO LEARN TO SHUFFLE

You remember the shuffle. It was that dance everyone was jigging to sometime between the bunny hop and the macarena. If you haven't already noticed, your drawing program places overlapping objects on its canvas one on top of another. It's like what happens when you arrange fabric appliqué pieces on a muslin block. Some pieces overlap; some hide under others. In order to pick up some pieces, you need to move the ones on top.

Your computer is nowhere near as good as you are at arranging teeny fabric petals on top of one another. It requires your gentle touch. That's why you need to learn how to make your computer shuffle. You need to learn how to rearrange the pieces, and pull out the bottom pieces and put them on top.

Your drawing program thinks of objects that you place on the screen as layered one on top of another. You can change this order, taking, say, the black bunny from the top of the stack and putting it behind the gray bunny.

You do this by selecting the object so that black handles appear around it and activating the drawing program's arrange feature.

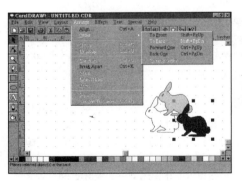

To shuffle in CorelDraw, pull down the Arrange menu and slide down to Order. A series of ordering choices appears in a pop-up menu. You can also click the To Front button or the To Back button in CorelDraw 5.

TIPS FOR SHUFFLING

Usually the newest item drawn or placed on your drawing area is the one on top of the stack.

In some drawing programs, to select an item that is not colored or filled, you need to click on its outlines. This is true in SuperPaint and in CorelDraw 5, for example, but not in CorelDraw 7. Similarly, when you want to move an unfilled item, hold the mouse button down while the cursor is pointed at its outline. Don't try to select it or move it when the cursor is pointing toward the object's unfilled interior.

To shuffle in Canvas, pull down the **Object** menu, select **Arrange**, and slide over to select **Bring to Front, Send to Back, Shuffle Up,** or **Shuffle Down.** Shuffling an item up or down moves it one level.

To shuffle in SuperPaint, pull down the **Draw** menu and choose either **Send to Back** or **Bring to Front.**

JUDY & GLORIA'S GRAB BAG OF AMAZING TOOLS FOR DRAWING APPLIQUÉ AND STENCILS

Every drawing program has a grab bag of tools that can make a quilter's life easier. The problem is finding them and figuring them out. For instance, there's the

"Allgon" tool that's everywhere in the Mac world. (Wasn't Allgon that kitchen cleanser that was found to cause warts?) There's the Contour Roll-Up thingie in CorelDraw that masquerades as a quilting stencil maker. There's the alley-oop tool in Windows 95 that will dunk a basketball in the middle of any drawing of fruit. (We were only joking about that last one.)

Get a cup of coffee, sit back, and join us in an unorthodox foray into the World of Wacky Appliqué Drawing Tools. We'll tell you about the unusual tools we've found in drawing programs that do amazing and useful, if sometimes peculiar, things. We'll also show you a few time-saving techniques.

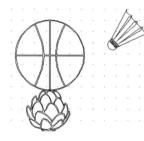

An artichoke victim of the Windows 95 alley-oop drawing tool.

NOTE

If your drawing program isn't among the ones that we use as illustrations, don't stalk off muttering "I'll show them! I'll figure out my own Bezier!" Many, if not most, of the phenomena we describe in this chapter are available in other drawing programs.

USING CORELDRAW TO CREATE APPLIQUÉ AND STENCIL PATTERNS

USE THE CORELDRAW SYMBOLS ROLL-UP

There's something wondrous hiding in the CorelDraw 7 Tools menu, or the Special menu in CorelDraw 5. It's called the Symbols Roll-Up—a mini-collection of clip art, including stars, symbols, and outlines of plants, people, and trees. They're black-and-white drawings with simple outlines that make them ideal for appliqué or stencil patterns.

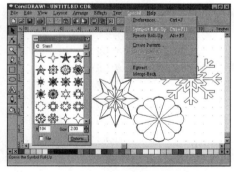

Pull down the **Tools** menu in CorelDraw 7 or the **Special** menu in CorelDraw 5. Select **Symbols Roll-Up** (in CorelDraw 5) or **Symbols** (in CorelDraw 7). You can also just click the star icon in the ribbon bar at the top of the window. You can fish through this roll-up—via its scroll bar and pull-down menu—to find all sorts of goodies: stars, flowers, trees, furniture, borders, outlines of people, holiday stuff like wreaths and stockings, and even sports stuff like footballs and hockey sticks. To put them in your drawing window, click on them and drag them to your drawing area.

USE THE CORELDRAW ERASER TOOL

FINALLY! SOMETHING TO MAKE THE LIVES OF CORELLIANS EASIER! CorelDraw 7 includes a new tool called the eraser. "An eraser?!" you cry. "Finally!" Actually, it's not that kind of eraser. It erases a portion of a closed object, or patch, and forms one or more new closed objects. This is an especially nifty tool for creating appliqué patches. It is in the flyout menu that appears when you hold the mouse button down on the Shape tool. Select the Pick tool and click on your drawing to select it. Then click on the Eraser tool. As you rub the Eraser tool over portions of your closed object, CorelDraw makes new closed objects.

SPECIAL CORELDRAW 7 WARNING

Many of the nifty things found in the symbol library in older versions of CorelDraw have been moved to the clip art CD-ROM. This is a bummer because it takes longer to sift through than the symbol library. But in some ways it's a good thing because there are more good images. To get to these goodies, stick the clip art CD-ROM disk in the drive, pull down the Tools menu, and click on Clipart.

THE TUTORIAL YOU'VE BEEN WAITING FOR!
HOW TO DRAW HEARTS AND TULIPS

JUDY & GLORIA'S BIG BEZIER TIP: THINK SYMMETRY!

Ever since you noticed that one side of your head was capable of having a good hair day while the other side was suffering a bad hair day, you've known that the world was an intrinsically asymmetrical place. But if you think back to the Marvell allusions that opened this chapter, you'll recall that we tried to make the point that appliqué often depicts an idealized world—a perfect world where petals are symmetrical and bouquets are never lopsided. This symmetrical perfection is achieved by drawing only half of any shape—half a heart, half a leaf—then selecting it, duplicating it, and flipping the duplicate around. Making a design as symmetrical as possible can hide many sins.

Admit it. The first thing you did after ripping the shrink-wrap off that $300 drawing program was try to draw a heart. But it looked worse than something your four-year-old would cart home from daycare. So you attempted a tulip. But it showed even less artistic promise than your four-year-old's attempt at the same.

You were probably trying to draw with the Freehand tool. Instead, you should have been plying the Bezier tool, which draws curves. Check out Chapter 5 for our directions on how to wield this often bedeviling device.

Here are some special tutorials and hints for drawing appliqué and stencil patterns with the Bezier tool. Follow them and you'll be like that giddy hair conditioner devotee in the commercial, who gushes, "I control my hair now, my hair doesn't control me!" Just replace "hair" with "Bezier," but don't say it too loudly or people with think something's wrong with your expectations of lingerie.

HOW TO DRAW A HEART

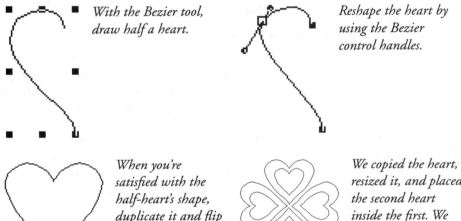

With the Bezier tool, draw half a heart.

Reshape the heart by using the Bezier control handles.

When you're satisfied with the half-heart's shape, duplicate it and flip the duplicate. Then group the two halves and save it.

We copied the heart, resized it, and placed the second heart inside the first. We grouped this new heart and then copied and rotated it.

With dashed lines our heart would make a nice quilting pattern and is ready to pop into a newsletter or printed pattern.

HOW TO DRAW A TULIP

Draw half a tulip with the Bezier tool.

Reshape it by using the Bezier control handles.

Once you are satisfied with your half-tulip, duplicate it, flip the duplicate, and drag it into place to form the tulip's base.

Draw half the tulip tip with the Bezier tool. Reshape it with the control handles. Duplicate it, flip the duplicate, and drag it into place to finish the tulip. When you're finished with your drawing, group it and save it.

MORE BEZIER DRAWING TIPS

- *Turn the grids on, so that you can accurately place starting and ending points of objects. But don't turn on snap-to-grid.*
- *Make the drawing larger than it needs to be so you can see what you're doing. When it's done, you can reduce it.*
- *Add or delete Bezier nodes or control points when needed.*
- *Keep your drawing simple.*
- *When you're finished, select the drawing and change its solid lines into dashed lines with the drawing program's pen fill tool. We tell how to do this later in the chapter.*

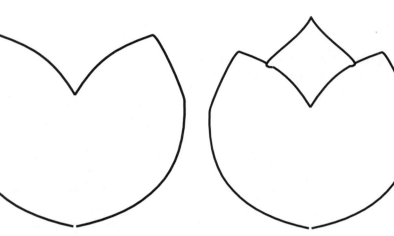

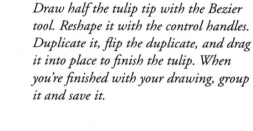

For another kind of tulip, draw and refine half of a central tulip petal with the Bezier tool. Duplicate it, flip the duplicate, and drag it into place. When you're finished with your drawing, group it and save it.

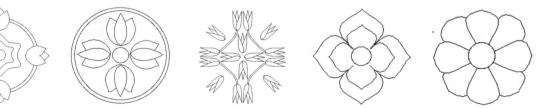

We created these floral designs with the Bezier and Oval tools.

USE THE ERASER TOOL TO MAKE PEACE SIGNS INTO ROSEBUDS

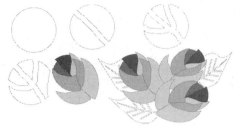

To use the Eraser tool to draw roses, we started by drawing a circle. Using the Eraser tool, we broke it into a jagged peace sign. Plying the eraser further, we erased more of the peace sign so that its segments looked like petals. Then we grouped them, duplicated the group several times, resized a few of them, mirrored others, shifted them around, and—presto! A small bunch of roses. The leaves are from Corel's clip art library.

USE RESIZE, MOVE, AND UNGROUP TO REFINE YOUR APPLIQUÉ PATTERN

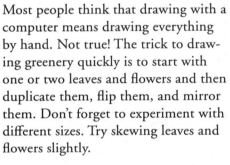

Most people think that drawing with a computer means drawing everything by hand. Not true! The trick to drawing greenery quickly is to start with one or two leaves and flowers and then duplicate them, flip them, and mirror them. Don't forget to experiment with different sizes. Try skewing leaves and flowers slightly.

Notice how we've made our spray of roses a little more realistic looking by resizing a few of the leaves and flowers. Remember that no two flowers or leaves are the same.

You can use grouping, duplication, and mirroring to create elegant effects with just a few pieces of art. For instance, to separate a single leaf from a piece of clip art, so that you can duplicate it, resize it, and move it, select the art with the Pick tool. Pull down the **Arrange** menu and select **Ungroup**. Similarly, group elements of your design, like flowers and leaves, as you work. Duplicate them, resize them, and shuffle them around for unique effects.

USE CORELDRAW'S TILE OPTION
TO CREATE QUILTING STENCIL DESIGNS

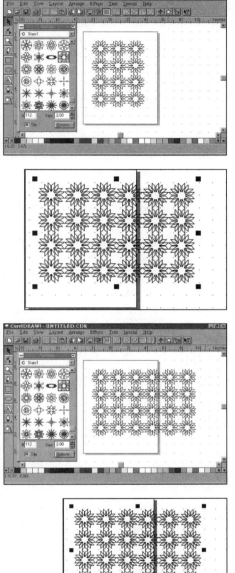

Before you drag a symbol to your drawing area, click on the **Tile** box in the Symbols Roll-Up to tile the symbol over the drawing page. You can also use the **Symbols Roll-Up** to specify the size that the symbol will be on your drawing area.

Once you've tiled a symbol, such as a star, over the page, use the Pick tool to 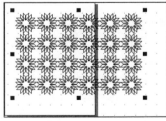 select it. Then pull down the **Arrange** menu and select **Group**. This will make all those little stars into a single cosmic entity, which you can then copy and move around without scattering the stars.

To copy your group of tiled stars, select them again, pull down the **Edit** menu, and select **Copy**. Use **Paste** to add a second set of stars on top of the first. Then select it and move it off to the side, being careful not to accidentally resize it.

Select and group both sets of stars to make an even larger galaxy.

To make your stars into a stencil, save the arrangement as a file (name it something like STENCIL.CDR so you remember what it is).

TRY OUT YOUR STENCIL ON A QUILT DESIGN

1. To see how your stencil will look on a particular quilt design, open your stencil's file and cut and paste it into another drawing file containing a quilt design.

2. To move your stencil, make sure all the elements of your stencil are grouped. Select the Pick tool. Use it to point at one of the stencil's lines and, holding the mouse button down, jiggle the mouse slightly until an **X**-marks-the-spot symbol appears, then drag it over your quilt design.

3. To shuffle the stencil on top of the quilt, if necessary, select the Pick tool, click on one of the stencil's lines to select it, then pull down the **Arrange** menu and select **Order**.

4. You can also use the **Layers Roll-Up** to place or draw your stencil on top of your quilt design. Or you can put your stencil design on one drawing layer and your quilt design on another. That way, you can print them separately, and you can easily move and change elements without accidentally mucking up the other design. If you're drawing your stencil from scratch, drawing it on one layer while the quilt design rests below on another layer is the easiest way to go. See Chapters 5 and 15 for directions on using CorelDraw's layer feature.

5. Use the Outline tool to make your stencil a different color than your quilt design. You can make your stencil's lines red, green, or another color to stand out on top of your quilt design. You can also make its lines fatter. First, click on the stencil's lines with the Pick tool to select it. Click on the Outline tool to bring up the Outline flyout. As you can see, this gives you buttons that will fatten the lines of your stencil as well as add outlines, borders, and whatnot to your design. Click on the pen icon in this flyout, and the Outline Pen dialog box will pop up. Here you can change the selected lines' color and shape.

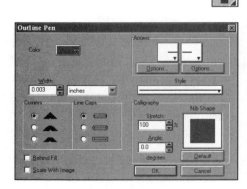

USE THE CONTOUR ROLL-UP TO CREATE PERFECT STENCIL PATTERNS

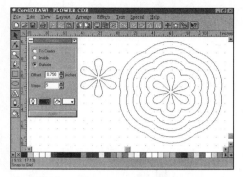

You can use the Contour Roll-Up to create a stencil for any drawing. In Corel-Draw 7, you'll find it on the **Effects** menu, and it's in the **Special** menu in earlier versions. You can set the distance between your stencil lines by specifying the number of inches in the **Offset** box. **Steps** is where you set the number of sewing lines you want surrounding your design. Click **Outside** so that the lines are outside, not inside, the drawing. Select the white fill from the box next to the paint can. The daisy shown on the left is the design we started with.

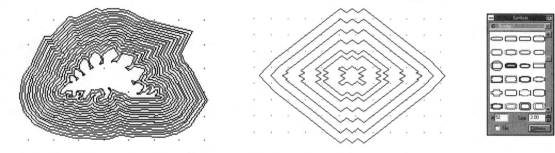

The border collections found in CorelDraw's clip art and symbols library make especially good stencil patterns.

USE THE SPIRAL TOOL TO DRAW
REVERSE APPLIQUÉ PATTERNS AND STENCIL DESIGNS

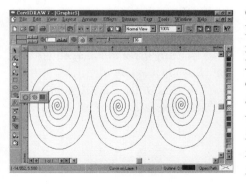

CorelDraw 7 offers a Spiral tool (on the Polygon flyout) that is living proof that PC drawing programs are becoming more like their Mac counterparts. Use it to create quilting stencil designs. When the Spiral tool is selected, buttons appear in the Property Bar at the top of the drawing window that you can use to set the number of spirals and the mathematical nature of the spiral.

USING CANVAS TO CREATE APPLIQUÉ AND STENCIL PATTERNS

DRAW SPIRALS WITH CANVAS 5.0

1. To draw a spiral with Canvas 5.0, first click on the Selection Arrow tool. Press and hold the mouse button down on the Oval tool to bring up the Oval toolbar. Slide the cursor over to select the Spiral tool and release the mouse button.

2. Double-click on the Spiral tool to bring up its dialog box. Type the number of spirals you want and click **OK**.

3. Position the crosshairs where you want to begin your spiral. Press and hold down the mouse button, and drag diagonally to create the shape. Release the mouse button to complete.

We repeated and flipped the spiral to create this motif. Duplicate it again, and the guidelines for a reverse appliqué border begin to emerge.

DRAW SPIRALS WITH CANVAS 3.5

1. To draw a spiral with Canvas 3.5, first click on the Selection Arrow tool. Press and hold the mouse button down on the Concentric Circles tool to bring up the Objects toolbar. Slide the cursor over to select the Spiral tool, and release the mouse button.

2. Double-click on the Spiral tool to bring up the Spiral Manager. Type in the number of spirals you want, and click **OK**.

3. Position the crosshairs where you want to begin your spiral. Press and hold down the mouse button, and drag diagonally to create the shape. Release the mouse button to complete.

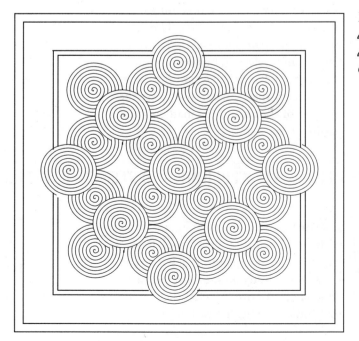

You can easily make this design with any drawing program that has spiral and line tools. It would look great as Celtic or reverse appliqué on a border.

USE THE MULTIGON TOOL TO DRAW FLOWERS, STARS, AND CELTIC DESIGNS

You can draw multisided objects with ease with the Multigon tool in Canvas for the Mac. Unfortunately, there's no similar tool in CorelDraw.

DRAWING WITH THE MULTIGON TOOL IN CANVAS 5.0

1. To use the Multigon tool in Canvas 5.0, first click on the Selection Arrow tool. Press and hold the mouse button down on the Dimensioning tool to bring up the **Objects** toolbar. Slide the cursor over to select the **Multigon** tool, and release the mouse button.

2. Double-click on the Multigon tool to bring up its manager. By selecting options in this dialog box, you can create all types of shapes. Click on the **Style** bar to select **Frame, Framed Star, Spoke, Star, Star Outline,** or **Wheel.** Indicate how many points you want, whether the points should be smooth, and the angle at which the sides meet. Drag the slider bar to change the interior area of stars, framed stars, and star outlines. (Anything you create is displayed in the preview box, so you know just what you're going to get. We set the Style to Wheel, specified 8 sides, and selected Smooth.) Click **OK** when you're done.

3. Position the crosshairs on your document where you want to begin your shape. Press and hold down the mouse button, and drag to create the shape. Release the mouse button to complete.

4. By adding a center circle, we made a flower.

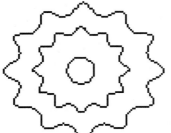

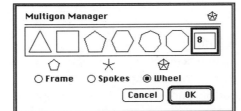

All these designs started with the Multigon tool. We also used the Oval tool and the Curve tool to draw the leaves.

DRAWING WITH THE MULTIGON TOOL IN CANVAS 3.5

1. To use the Multigon tool in Canvas 3.5, first click the Selection Arrow tool. Press and hold the mouse button down on the Concentric Circles tool to bring up the **Objects** toolbar. Slide the cursor over to select the **Multigon** tool, and release the mouse button.

2. Double-click on the Multigon tool to bring up its manager. Here you can select options to create all types of shapes. (We selected a wheel shape with 8 sides.) Click **OK** when you're done.

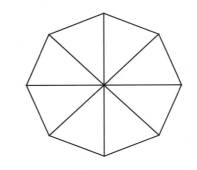

3. Position the crosshairs on your document where you want to begin your shape. Press and hold down the mouse button, and drag to create the shape. Release the mouse button to complete.

MAKE A WHEEL INTO A FLOWER

This does not look like a flower shape for appliqué, does it? But we'll show you how to make it into one with a few clicks of your mouse. Here's how.

1. Click on the Selection Arrow tool. Then click to select the shape. Black handles appear around it to indicate that it's selected.

2. Now pull down the **Object** menu, select **Curves**, and slide over to select **Smooth**. That's it! You now have a beginning of a beautiful flower shape.

SMOOTH A STAR INTO A MICHIGAN ROSE

1. To make a star with Canvas 3.5, bring up the **Objects** toolbar and slide to select the **Star** tool.

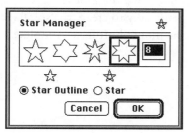

2. Double-click on the Star tool to bring up its manager. Select the options to create the star shape you want, and click **OK**. We specified 8 sides and selected the Star Outline option.

3. Position the crosshairs on your document where you want to begin drawing. Press and hold down the mouse button, and drag diagonally to create the shape. Release the mouse button to complete.

4. To make a Michigan Rose out of your star, click the Selection Arrow tool, then click to select the star. Black handles will appear around it to indicate that it's selected.

5. Pull down the **Object** menu, select **Curves**, and slide over to select **Smooth**. You now have the beginning of a floral shape.

By duplicating this shape a few times, scaling it down, and then adding a circle, you can create a Michigan Rose motif.

USING SUPERPAINT TO CREATE APPLIQUÉ AND STENCIL PATTERNS

DRAW SPIRALS WITH SUPERPAINT

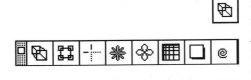

1. To draw a spiral in SuperPaint, start in the Draw layer. Click the Selection Arrow, then press and hold the mouse button down on the 3-D Box tool. When the Draw and Paint Plug-In Tools palette appears, slide over to select the **Spiral** tool and release the mouse button.

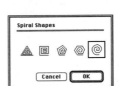

2. Double-click on the Spiral tool to bring up its dialog box. Click on the shape you want for the spiral (we've selected the circular shape), and then click **OK**.

3. Position the crosshairs where you want to begin your spiral. Press and hold down the mouse button, and drag diagonally to create the spiral. Release the mouse button to complete.

MODIFYING A SPIRAL

If you press the **COMMAND** key while drawing a spiral, SuperPaint will create spokes within the spiral.

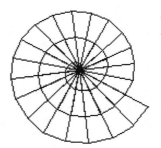

*Hold the **COMMAND** key down while drawing a spiral to create spokes within the spiral.*

You can control the spacing of the spiral's lines. To do so, type on the keyboard's number pad a number between 1 and 9 after selecting the Spiral tool but before using it. When you type 1 you get the tightest spiral.

Spiral created with tight spacing.

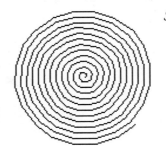

USE THE FLOWER TOOL IN SUPERPAINT

SuperPaint actually has a tool for drawing flowers. Here's how to use it.

1. Display the Draw and Paint Plug-In Tools palette by holding the mouse button down on the 3-D Box tool.

2. Double-click on the Flower tool to bring up its dialog box. By dragging the sliders, you can change the number, width, and smoothness of the petals. You can even include a center. A preview box lets you see what you're creating. After you select your settings, click **OK**.

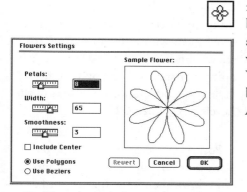

....

T * I * P

If your flower is all black, set your fill to white.

_____

DESIGN TIP

You can ungroup the flower created by the tool and then take a petal and stretch it into leaf shapes.

3. Position the crosshairs where you want to begin your flower. Press and hold down the mouse button, and drag diagonally to create the shape. Release the mouse button to complete.

The flower shape, complete with center.

All these designs started with the Flower tool. The leaves were created by stretching an ungrouped flower petal and rotating it into position. The Freehand tool was used for stems, and the Rectangle tool was used to create the boxes.

USE THE ALLGON TOOL IN SUPERPAINT

The Allgon tool is another tool you'll want to experiment with. Here's how to use it.

1. Display the Draw and Paint Plug-In Tools palette by holding the mouse button down on the 3-D Box tool.

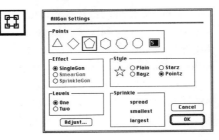

2. Double-click on the Allgon tool to bring up its dialog box. You'll want to experiment with different settings to see what it inspires. (We selected a five-pointed shape, clicked Pointz in the Style box, and specified one level in the Levels box.) Click **OK**.

3. Position the crosshairs where you want to begin your shape. Press and hold down the mouse button, and drag to create the shape. Release the mouse button to complete.

Double-click on the Allgon tool to go back to its dialog box. This time set the **Levels** to **Two**. Now create the shape and watch an exciting design emerge.

Created with the Allgon tool set at Level Two.

HOW TO GIVE YOUR DESIGN DASHED LINES

Some drawing programs will convert any design into dashed lines. Dashed lines are perfect for creating a quilting stencil. A wider pen width helps make your stencil easier to see and use.

DRAW DASHED LINES IN CORELDRAW

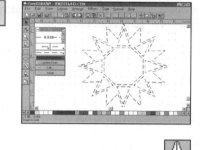

1. To make an object's lines dashed, first select the object with the Pick tool.

2. Position the cursor over the Outline tool, and hold the mouse button down so that the Outline flyout appears.

3. Click on the pen icon in the flyout; the **Outline Pen** dialog box appears. Under **Width**, type **0.30** inch. Click on the arrow in the box under **Style**. A box with a sampling of dashed line styles should appear. Select one.

4. Click **Apply**. If all systems are working, your pattern should be transformed to a thick dashed line.

DRAW DASHED LINES IN CANVAS 5.0

Canvas 5.0 will dash the line of any drawing tool. This is ideal for drawing quilting patterns or for converting a solid-line design into a dashed line for quilting.

1. Click the Selection Arrow tool.

2. Press and hold the mouse button down on the **Strokes** tool, and slide the cursor to select the **Dash** tab. Select a dashed line from the Dash Manager, and release the mouse button. (See your manual for how to customize dashes.)

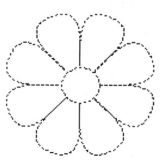

3. Draw any shape you wish, and the lines will be dashed. For example, here we selected the Multigon tool and created a flower, as described earlier. Instead of a solid line, the line is dashed.

T * I * P

When you have finished making dashed lines, remember to select the line width you like to work in from the Pen Manager. Our preference is 0.75.

The Pen Manager can be customized. See your manual.

You can also take a design you've already created and change it to dashed lines, as follows:

1. First click on the Selection Arrow tool.

2. Place the arrow inside the design, and click to select it. Black handles will appear around the shape, indicating that it's selected.

3. Select the **Strokes** tool, slide to select the **Dash** tab, and select a dashed line from the Dash Manager. Release the mouse button.

Let's make the dashes thicker.

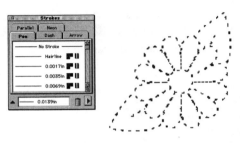

1. Select the design with the Selection Arrow tool.

2. Select the **Strokes** tool, slide the cursor to select the **Pen** tab, and then choose a thicker line width from the Pen Manager. Release the mouse button. The dashes of the motif are now thicker.

DRAW DASHED LINES IN CANVAS 3.5

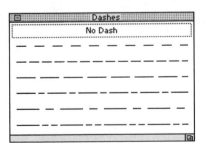

1. To draw dashed lines in Canvas 3.5, first click on the Selection Arrow tool. Press and hold down the mouse button on the **No Dash** icon in the toolbar to display the **Dash** palette. Slide the cursor to select a dashed line, and release the mouse button.

2. Draw any shape you wish, and the lines will be dashed. For example, we selected the Star tool (using the outline option) and drew a star. We duplicated it, scaled the duplication down 50 percent, and moved it inside the first image to create a double star. Instead of a solid line, the line is dashed.

A double star using a dashed line.

You can also take a design you've already created and change it to dashed lines, as follows:

1. Click the Selection Arrow tool. Place the arrow inside the design and click to select it. Black handles will appear around the shape, indicating that it's selected.

2. Press and hold down the mouse button on the **No Dash** icon to bring up the **Dash** palette. Slide to select a dashed line, and release the mouse button.

Let's make the dashes thicker.

1. Select the design with the Selection Arrow tool.

2. Press and hold the mouse button down on the **Pen Size** icon in the toolbar to display the Pen Size palette. Slide to select a thicker width, and release the mouse button. The dashes are now thicker.

Quilting design with a wider pen width.

T * I * P

When you are finished making dashed lines, remember to select No Dash to create a solid line and return your pen width to its normal setting.

T * I * P

The pen size can be customized. See your manual.

DRAW DASHED LINES IN SUPERPAINT

Oh no! In SuperPaint, only lines drawn with the line tools can be made into dashed lines. Well, the program *is* only $50.

To dash your line before creating it, pull down the **Options** menu, select **Dashes**, slide over to select **Dashed**, and release the mouse button.

To dash your line after creating it, use the Selection Arrow to select the line.

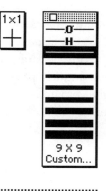

Pull down the **Options** menu, select **Dashes**, slide over to select **Dashed**, and release the mouse button.

To create a thicker line, press and hold down the mouse button on the **Line Width** button, located in the **Line & Fill** palette above your document page. Slide to select a wider line width from the Line Widths display. Release the mouse button. You can also customize the line width. See your manual.

PRINTING STENCIL AND APPLIQUÉ PATTERNS

T * I * P

When you import an appliqué design from Quilt-Pro or Electric Quilt into a drawing program, one of the first things you'll need to do is ungroup the drawing so that you can manipulate and redraw different parts of the drawing if you wish.

SCAN YOUR PRELIMINARY HAND SKETCH AND REFINE IT IN YOUR DRAWING PROGRAM

Computer artists often begin their designs with a handmade sketch. They scan it and import it into the drawing program, where they continue working with the image and the design. If you have access to a scanner, you'll want to do the same. When you have a quilt block sketch you like, scan it as a black-and-white line image, save it, and then import it into your drawing program. Using the rectangle tool, and holding down the CTRL key on a PC, the SHIFT key on a Mac, draw a box the size that you'd like your quilt block to be. Select your drawing and resize it to fit into your quilt block.

If your drawing program lets you draw on different layers, save the sketch and box on one layer, and then move to a different layer to begin drawing. Be sure to activate snap-to-grid. With your drawing program's line tool, draw over the ragged lines of your sketch. This will allow you to quickly give it geometric veracity. (See Chapter 15 for tips on drawing on different layers.)

To make drawing easier, at some point you may want to make your drawing line a different color to stand out on top of the black-and-white sketch. Later in your drafting, you'll probably also want to make the drawing layer containing your original sketch invisible, so that you can continue to work with the geometric elements on the upper layer, undistracted by the sketch below.

Your stencil or appliqué pattern looks great on top of your quilt design. You've sized it to the dimensions you want. How do you get it from the computer to your fabric? You have several options:

- Print it on regular paper. Use traditional transfer methods like transfer paper or a light box to trace it onto your quilt.

- Print it on the back of embroidery transfer paper. Trace over the design with a pencil to transfer it to your fabric.

- If it's an appliqué design, print it directly on freezer paper or paper-backed fusible web. Print it on the nonshiny side of the freezer paper. You'll probably need to experiment to see if this works with your printer. The paper may be too curly to feed through your printer.

- Use an old dot-matrix printer to print the pattern on freezer paper. This gives the design a serrated edge that makes it easy to cut or tear out.

- Heirloom Stitches (262 Shadowood Lane, S.E., Warren, OH, 44484) sells template plastic that can be printed in a laser printer. It's very inexpensive.

- Print the design on plastic transparencies. Use a mat knife to cut out appliqué templates, or cut the stencil design so that you can trace it on fabric. Again, you'll need to experiment to see if you can feed transparency plastic through your printer.

Okay, we cheated. We took this appliqué pattern from the block library in Quilt-Pro. We told you we like to do things the simplest way possible. If you'd rather not try to wring hearts and flowers from your drawing program, give yourself a break: buy one of the quilt design programs. Then see Chapter 13 on designing appliqué with these programs.

You can use any of the appliqué patterns in Quilt-Pro in any Windows drawing or graphic design program simply by cutting and pasting a design from one program to the other. You will need to resize it once it gets into the drawing program, because it will probably appear on the canvas as a minuscule blob. You can also use the appliqué patterns in Electric Quilt with any drawing program by exporting a pattern to a file and then using your drawing program's import feature to import it. It will import it into the drawing program as a bitmap, which means that you'll need to trace over it in order to be able to work with the design's lines and to color it, resize it, and so on.

CHAPTER 15

HOW TO TURN PHOTOS, DRAWINGS, AND OTHER ART INTO APPLIQUÉ DESIGNS

Your computer can make it easy to turn a favorite family photo or rough sketch into a beautiful appliqué pattern.

Although you can use quilt design programs like Electric Quilt to draw appliqué blocks, as described in Chapter 13, these programs suffer a great limitation: They won't let you use a photo or drawing as the basis for an appliqué design. To do that, you need to use a drawing program like CorelDraw or Canvas.

In this chapter we will assume that you have taken our advice and have bought a suitable drawing program and are ready to get started turning that underwater snapshot of your nephew Andrew swimming like a frog into some serious appliqué.

First, here are some things you need to know about turning different kinds of art into appliqué patterns.

- A SKETCH. Throughout this book we've been telling you that it's sometimes a good idea to start a quilt design by making rough hand sketches. That's true of appliqué patterns too. If you have access to a scanner, you can scan your sketch as black-and-white art and import it into your drawing program. You can refine the sketch by drawing on top of it, either on the same layer or on a different one, just as a professional computer artist might. If you have a drawing tablet, you can place the sketch on it and trace on top of it with the pen.

- CLIP ART. Clip art is found on CD-ROMS and in clip-art books. You are generally free to use it in your own artwork without worrying about infringing on someone's copyright, but sometimes you do need to obtain permission for specific uses, especially commercial ones. (See Appendix A, "The Quilter's Guide to Computer Graphics," for a discussion of clip art and other art copyright issues.) Most clip art is black-and-white drawings. It is very easy to turn into appliqué patterns—in many instances all you need to do is scan it, import it into your drawing program, resize it, and you're ready to go.

- A PHOTOGRAPH. Photos are a bit harder to create appliqué patterns from, but not as hard as you might think. The difficulty of the procedure depends upon how elaborate you want your pattern to be.

QUICK! BUY THIS!

The most remarkable book ever written on turning photos into appliqué patterns is Charlotte Warr Andersen's Faces & Places (Lafayette, CA: C&T Publishing, 1995). The photo-inspired quilts in this book are breathtaking, and Andersen's methods— from her recommendations on how to snap proper photos of models (she takes lots of them) to how to do needle-turn appliqué—directly relate to the methods you use with a computer. We love this book and think you will too.

You can approach photo appliqué in two ways. You can turn a photo into a very simple appliqué pattern with few or no facial features in the photo's subjects. For this you would choose a photo depicting some kind of action, like your subject riding a bicycle or diving into a pool. Or you can create a more elaborate appliqué pattern with complex facial details, coloring, and shading—the kind of sophisticated appliqué portraits that Charlotte Warr Andersen is famous for. This kind of appliqué portrait is obviously going to take a great investment of time—both to make the original pattern and to sew it, so think about that before tackling this kind of project.

The photos you use needn't be in color. In fact, black-and-white photos often work better than color ones when you will be transforming their lines and shadows into appliqué patterns inside a computer. Choose a photo with good contrast, well-lit faces, and, most important of all, no shadows.

STEPS FOR TURNING A PHOTOGRAPH OR OTHER ART INTO AN APPLIQUÉ PATTERN

Here are the basic steps you'd follow to turn a photo or other piece of art into an appliqué pattern. The exact steps will differ depending upon the art, your drawing program, and how much you want to do inside the computer versus how much you'd prefer to do with pencil and paper instead. And remember, we always recommend using pencil and paper when it's easier than using the computer.

JUDY & GLORIA'S RULE #1 OF COMPUTER APPLIQUÉ

The difficulty of transforming a photo—or any art, for that matter—into an appliqué pattern is roughly proportional to how difficult that appliqué pattern will be to sew. In other words, Difficulty in the computer = Difficulty to hand-sew.

Be careful that you don't create an appliqué pattern with your computer that is so complex it will take you three blue moons to sew.

JUDY & GLORIA'S RULE #2 OF COMPUTER APPLIQUÉ

Whether the basis of your appliqué pattern is a photo or a sketch, you may find that the only step in the appliqué process in which you want to use the computer is to resize the art. That's okay. In fact, doing so may be the easiest route you can take to create an appliqué pattern. To do this, scan your drawing or photo, import it into your drawing program, and enlarge it to the size you want your appliqué pattern to be. Then print it. With a pencil, trace over the enlarged art with tracing paper to make your appliqué pattern—just like Grandma would. This technique is generally faster than fooling around with the computer's drawing tools to draw appliqué lines—which invariably come out jagged anyway when you draw them with a mouse.

BEGIN BY SCANNING THE ART

The first step in creating an appliqué pattern is getting your art inside the computer as a graphics file. If you downloaded the art from the Internet, it's probably already in a form that you can use. If the art is a photo or sketch, you'll need to scan it. Here's how:

I. Prep the image. If it's a sketch, erase stray pencil lines. If it's not flat, press it between books. If the photo is glossy, dim the light around the scanner or lower the scanner's contrast dial. Also, if the photo is glossy or on textured paper, place a clear matte plastic film over it.

WHAT SHOULD YOU DO IF YOU DON'T HAVE A SCANNER?

Not everyone can afford the luxury of having a scanner attached to their computer. If you don't have one, here are some alternatives:

- If your computer has a fax modem, fax the art from the fax machine at a copy store (for about $2) or from an office to your computer. Use your fax software to save the resulting electronic fax as a graphics file.

- Take your art to a copy shop or service bureau to have it scanned. A copy shop will charge you from $9 to $35 (gasp!) to scan it once, and you can't scan it again and again until you get a scan that's just right. A service bureau is generally much cheaper. Be sure to bring your own diskette, because they'll charge you extra for that.

- Rent a scanner from a copy shop or service bureau. You'll find service bureaus in big cities. Look in the phone book under "Printers/Service Bureaus." If you

2. Scan the image at a resolution of 200 dots per inch or lower. Scanning at higher resolutions will give you a humongous graphics file that may cause your drawing software to choke or slow down, and you'll end up with lots more detail than you'll need. The resolution setting either is found on a dial on the scanner (if it's a handheld scanner) or, in the case of flatbed scanners, is made with the scanner's software. Scan only the area of the photo that you want to make into a pattern. (Remember, you want to make that graphics file as small as possible, because small is easier to work with than big.) Don't scan with bright light pouring into the scanner's window; that will wash out the picture's details and cause streaking. If the photo's contrast is weak, turn up the scanner's contrast dial slightly.

3. If your scanner scans with a red light, it may have a hard time interpreting the reds in the photo, causing them to appear washed out in your scan. If the scanner has a green light, it may have a hard time seeing greens. Try putting a sheet of transparent yellow plastic over your artwork, or experiment by turning up the scanner's contrast dial. If scans created with a handheld scanner suffer from shade variations between strips, you need to calibrate the scanner. Check the scanner's manual for directions. Most scanners sold today use either a fluorescent bulb or a "cold-cathode" bulb, which generates less heat and produces light that is whiter than that produced by a fluorescent bulb.

4. If you're scanning a photograph, scan both a color and a gray-scale version. (Use your scanner's software to make the choice.) Depending upon the picture, a gray-scale image may prove easier than a color one to work with in your drawing program. Experiment with both.

5. Crop the file so that the picture displays just the details you want. You may also want to use your scanner's software, or a picture processing program like Paint Shop Pro, to sharpen the image and to despeckle it if it's black and white or gray-scale. If your picture is in color, turn up the brightness on some of the colors for more contrast. Use the zoom and eraser features of the software to erase any errant black spots, also known as scanning artifacts.

WARNING!
BE CAREFUL OF COPYRIGHT

When creating applique patterns, it's always best to use your own sketches or photos. Even when you transform someone else's image—no matter how slightly—that person still owns the copyright on it, and you need to obtain permission to use it. Appendix A, "The Quilter's Guide to Computer Graphics," discusses copyright. But the rule of thumb is that if you didn't draw it or photograph it, you must obtain permission before turning someone else's art into a pattern or quilt.

live in a small town, you may have a hard time finding one. Call a graphics design firm to see if they can rent you a scanner or point you in the right direction. The cost will vary depending upon what you rent and for how long.

• Have your photos developed to a CD or diskette. If you have a CD-ROM drive (an up-to-date, multisession, double-speed one; an older drive won't work), you can have your negatives, slides, or undeveloped photos turned into digital files for $0.65 to $1.35 each by a photo processing firm. One such firm is Advanced Digital Imaging (112 E. Olive St., Fort Collins, CO 80524; 800/888-3686). Or take your undeveloped negatives to a film developer and have them developed to a diskette. The cost is about $12 for a roll of 24 negatives. One company that does this is Seattle Film Works (1260 16th Ave. W., Seattle, WA 98119; 800/445-3348).

6. Erase any portion of the picture that you don't want in your appliqué pattern. For instance, you might erase the entire background of a photo so that only people remain in the picture.

7. If the image is a color one, save it as an 8-bit file. That will give you a digital picture with fewer colors than a 24-bit file (15,999,744 fewer colors, to be precise), but the file will be much smaller, and the fewer colors will be easier to work with in your drawing program. The 8-bit choice is one that's made in the scanner's software or in your image processing software.

8. Save the file as a bitmap (.BMP), if that's what your drawing program prefers to import (it will if you're running Windows). TIFF files will give you the best color retention, but they can be huge, occupying lots of disk space and computer memory. Files of this size can be difficult to work with. A suitable alternative that produces smaller files is the PCX format, or the PICT one if you have a Mac. These file formats are also preferred if your image is black and white.

IMPORT THE ART INTO YOUR DRAWING PROGRAM OR ITS TRACING SOFTWARE

The next steps to transform that picture of your prized peonies into an appliqué pattern will depend upon the art and how elaborate you want your appliqué to be. Basically, you will import the digitized image into your drawing program or its separate tracing software if you're using a program like CorelDraw (that would be CorelTrace). You do so by choosing **Import** from the **File** menu and then specifying the graphic file type (.BMP, .PCX, etc.). If you're using a Mac, choose either **Open** or **Place** from the **File** menu and select your file.

You could also use the drawing program's cut and paste facility, cutting the image from one program, like your scanner's software, and pasting it into the drawing program. But depending upon your drawing program, this can hog memory, so you're better off using the more efficient Import feature.

If you intend to trace the art, either with your mouse, with the drawing program's auto-trace feature, or with a drawing pen if you have one, don't worry about resizing the drawing to its finished size until the end. For now, merely resize it so that it's easy to work with on your computer screen.

USE AUTO-TRACE TO TRACE AN APPLIQUÉ PATTERN

Most drawing programs give you several different ways to trace a piece of art. You can do it manually with your mouse or drawing pen. There may be an "auto-trace" feature that will trace the entire drawing for you automatically, in the blink of an eye, outlining colors and shadows in the drawing or photo. There may also be some kind of semiautomatic trace feature that allows you to specify segments or areas of a drawing for the program to trace. The semiautomatic trace can create a trace that's more precise than the one generated by the auto-trace feature—it also gives you more control over the tracing process. But using it can be slow and laborious.

Neither of the automatic methods will produce a trace that's "appliqué ready" for anything but a simple black-and-white silhouette (see the descriptions later of the creation of the Nancy Drew silhouettes). If your art is a photograph, the most you can hope for is a correct delineation of some of its forms and shadows. If the art is a color pen-and-ink drawing, like a sketch of a flower from a seed catalog, you may have better luck, but you'll still need to edit some of the lines to make the trace less fussy.

T * I * P

One problem with auto-trace features in drawing programs is that they often don't trace an image as precisely as you'd like, even if the art is black-and-white clip art. Now, logic would tell you that such clip art would be the simplest of all to trace, because the lines are definite and there are no shadows to contend with. But often drawing programs don't trace as precisely as they might.

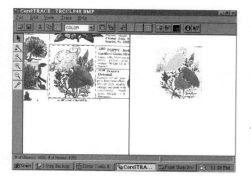

Here is a scan of a picture of poppies taken from a seed catalog. We scanned it directly into CorelDraw's tracing program, CorelTrace. Then we drew a box around the area we wanted to trace. The "trace" of the poppies is on the right. As you can see, it traced nicely, creating the basic color shapes.

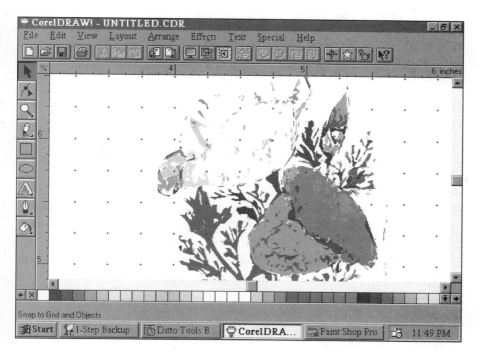

Here the poppy "trace" that was created in CorelTrace is imported into CorelDraw.

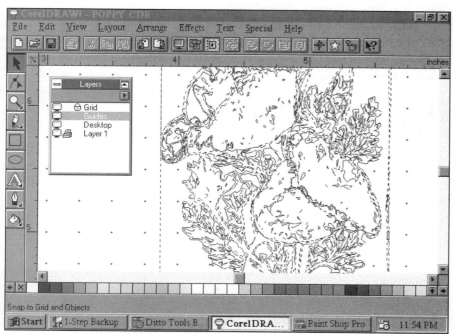

We turned the poppy trace into guidelines in CorelDraw by moving it to the Guides layer (see Chapter 6 for how to do this). It's almost "appliqué ready." The final step is to resize it and print it.

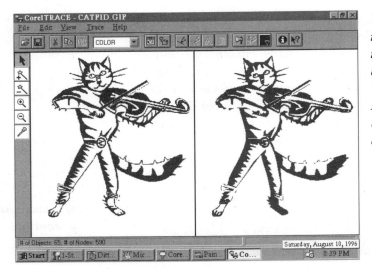

The original clip-art image is on the left; the "trace" produced by CorelTrace is on the right. Notice that the details have not been copied precisely, even though the "precision" settings have been activated. For instance, the cat's zigzag stripes have been turned into curves, and one of the cat's feet is now black.

You can make the tracing more precise by using settings such as the curve precision and line precision settings in CorelTrace. Still, no matter how you futz, your auto-trace will not necessarily come out as a copy of your original art. Also, even the most nicely traced lines don't always translate easily into appliqué pieces. You'll still need to edit and delete lines you don't like. You may find that for the final stage of appliqué pattern creation—drawing the fabric pieces—it will be easier to revert to pencil and tracing paper than to try to draw the individual fabric pieces on the computer screen.

With some art, like that of the clip-art cat shown on this page, you may be better off skipping the tracing completely and instead simply importing the clip art into your drawing program, resizing it, and then printing it.

*In CorelTrace, set the curve precision and line precision settings to **Very Good** so that your trace comes out as accurate as possible. But even with these settings, you may not get a perfect copy of your original art.*

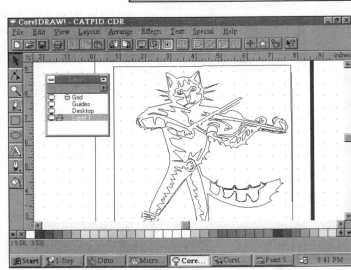

When our trace of the cat fiddler is imported into CorelDraw and the wireframe view is turned on, it's an appliqué pattern all right, but more details of the drawing have been washed out. For instance, those stylized zigzag stripes in the legs of the original cat picture became kind of craggy in our trace. If you're a perfectionist, you might want to skip the tracing step and simply import the original clip art picture into your drawing program, resize it to the size you want your appliqué pattern to be, and then print it and trace over the printout with tracing paper the old-fashioned way.

1. Remembering Nancy Drew. *Judy Heim, Madison, WI, 1997.*

Judy created the center appliqué by scanning an image from the front pages of a Nancy Drew book from the '30s and turning it into an appliqué pattern in CorelDraw. She used sun printing to create the blue-and-white silhouette blocks and Canon Fabric Sheets to print color covers from the books on muslin. The "pages" were created by scanning pages from old books in the series, then printing them on muslin with a laser printer. They are slightly padded for a three-dimensional look. See Chapters 15, 17, and 18 for more information.

2. *Detail,*
   Remembering Nancy Drew.

Judy scanned the front page of an old Nancy Drew book, turned it into a black-and-white image, then printed it on a transparency—which she used to sun print this image. See Chapter 18 for more information.

3. *Detail,*
   Remembering Nancy Drew.

Judy created the pattern for this large appliqué in the center of the quilt by scanning the front page of a Nancy Drew book, then using the auto-trace feature in CorelDraw to turn it into a line image. She enlarged this to the size she wanted, then printed it across multiple sheets and taped it together. She used needle-turn appliqué to render it in cloth. See Chapter 15 for directions on using your computer to create appliqué patterns.

4. *Detail,*
   Remembering Nancy Drew.

Judy printed scans of covers from Nancy Drew books of the '50s and '60s on Canon Fabric Sheets.

5. *Detail,* Remembering Nancy Drew.

Lower portion of quilt, showing sun-printed blocks and muslin blocks printed in a laser printer. Note how in the sun-printed blocks Judy flipped the transparencies to create mirror images. See Chapter 17 for directions on how to print fabric using different kinds of computer printers.

6. *Hand-sketch of Ann Johnston's draft of* Merry-go-round 2. *Johnston began her design of* Merry-go-round 2 *by sketching a horse that looked like it was leaping out of its carousel.*

7. *Color printout of Johnston's design draft of* Merry-go-round 2. *As Johnston worked with images in her computer, she printed them in color on graph paper to scale. She also printed them on plain paper, cut out parts of her design, and played with different arrangements.*

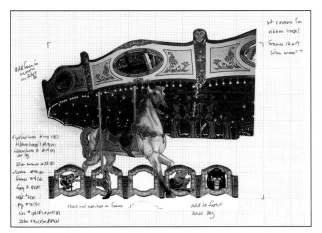

8. *Johnston says that deciding where to place the quilting lines was difficult. "The stitches impact the photograph so much because they're hard lines. I matched threads very carefully from a large selection of colors of fine cotton thread."*

9. *The zebra and frog are based on photos that Johnston took of a merry-go-round in Portland,* OR. *"I picked my favorite animals, ones that I remembered as a kid, and animals that looked like they had personality." She jokes, "It's all a blur now, but I have stopped having Photoshop dreams."*

10. Merry-go-round 2. *Ann Johnston, Lake Oswego, OR, 1996.*

Johnston started her quilt by taking two hundred photos of carousel horses at amusement parks around the country. She played with the images in Adobe Photoshop and printed them on fabric with an inkjet printer.

11. A Father's Life. *Sharyn Craig, El Cajon, CA, 1996.*

Craig scanned photos of her father while growing up. She cropped and colored them with the software that came with her scanner and printed them on fabric to serve as the center of the pieced blocks.

Reprinted with the express written consent of Canon Computer Systems, Inc. All rights reserved.

Canon and BJ are registered trademarks of Canon Inc. Bubble Jet is a trademark of Canon Inc.

12. Autumn in New England.
Judy Mathieson,
Woodland Hills, CA, 1996.

Mathieson used variations of a traditional Attic Windows block enhanced with autumnal images taken from a CD-ROM of pictures. She printed blocks of different sizes on Canon Fabric Sheets.

13. Canon Gardens.
Sharyn Craig,
El Cajon, CA, 1996.

Craig took pictures of flowers from a graphic arts CD-ROM to enhance what is otherwise a very traditionally constructed quilt.

16. These pillows, created with Canon Fabric Sheets, use images of old Christmas postcards Judy downloaded from CompuServe. See Chapter 16 for more information on obtaining images for printing on fabric.

14 & 15. Judy created these sun-printed blocks from scans of photos from the family photo album. Use your computer and simple graphics software to crop and spruce up your own image, then turn it into a negative. Print the negative on a transparency with either your computer printer or a photocopier. See Chapter 18 for information.

17 & 18. Gloria scanned this photo, then, using the exact same settings, she printed the image using two different printers. The results are noticeably different. Colors can be brightened or adjusted using your software. See Chapter 17 for more information.

19. Gloria created this set of color photo transfer pillows using inkjet T-shirt transfer paper. The pillow on the right is of her mom's parents on their wedding day in 1917.

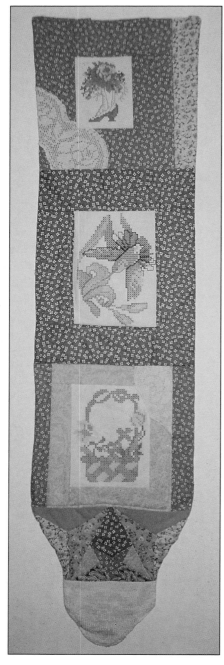

21 (left) & 22 (right). Details, Cross-Stitcher's Favorite Things.

Giant cross-stitch charts were created in Cross-Stitch Designer (software that you can download from the Internet!), then printed on special T-shirt transfer sheets in an inkjet printer. The "T-shirt transfers" were then ironed on muslin. See Chapter 17 for instructions.

20. Cross-Stitcher's Favorite Things. *Judy Heim, Madison, WI, 1997.*

This charming little wall quilt is patched with 1930s reproduction fabrics, old bits of crocheted lace, and giant cross-stitch charts.

23. *Judy created this lovely pillow by scanning a photo from the family album and printing it with an inkjet on one of the Canon Fabric Sheets.*

24. Detail, Cross-Stitcher's Crazy Quilt (*left*).

Judy created giant cross-stitch charts by downloading clip art from the Internet and importing the images into cross-stitch design software. The charts were printed on muslin in a laser printer. She stitched giant cross-stitches on the blocks for embellishment.

25. Cross-Stitcher's Crazy Quilt (*below*).
Judy Heim, Madison, WI, 1997.

This whimsical quilt combines patchwork and appliqué with giant cross-stitch charts created by printing on muslin in a laser printer.

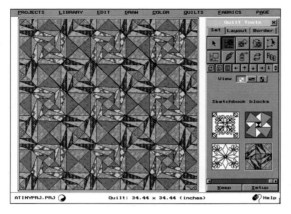

26. *We took a nothing-special quilt design and applied the Andy Warhol color palette in Electric Quilt.*

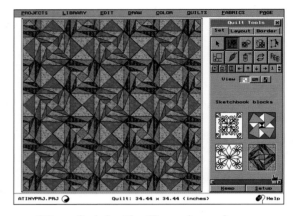

27. *We applied the Alex Katz color to the same design.*

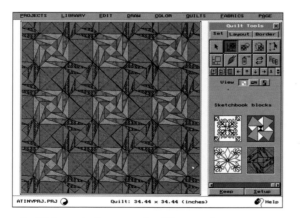

28. *This variation uses the Giotto palette.*

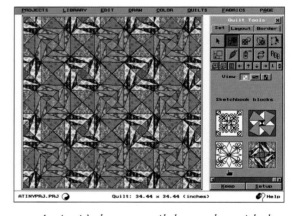

29. *Again, it's the same quilt layout, but with the Vermeer palette.*

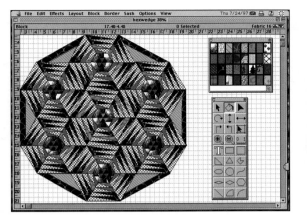

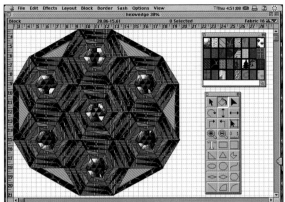

30. *This hexagon layout was created in Quilt-Pro. See Chapter 3 for information on how we made the hexagon block.*

31. *Simply changing the background color gives the layout a whole new look.*

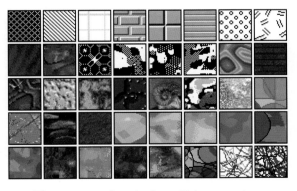

32. *The texture palette in SuperPaint contains some nice fabric-like fills. We added some of our own fills into the palette by scanning fabric or creating fabric-like patterns. See Chapter 16 on how to do both.*

33. *Using our textures palette, we created the Ohio Star layout.*

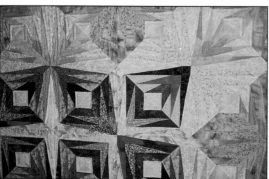

34. Awakenings (*above*).
Gloria Hansen, Hightstown, NJ, © 1992.

Gloria created this design on graph paper. It then was drawn into an old version of Canvas. The block was flipped to create a four-way unit, and the unit was repeated to create the overall design. It's machine-pieced and hand-quilted. See Chapter 19 for information on how to create this block.

35. *Detail,* Awakenings (*left*).

36. *Detail,* Heat Wave (*above*).

37. Heat Wave (*right*).
Gloria Hansen, Hightstown, NJ, © 1993.

Gloria first created the block for this quilt using Canvas. The block was flipped and duplicated to create the central area. After the first border was added, Gloria extended the lines in the exterior blocks to create the appliquéd section. Gloria dyed, airbrushed, or painted all but two of the fabrics in this quilt. It's machine-pieced and hand-quilted. See Chapter 19 for information on how to create this block.

38. Save the Green.
Gloria Hansen, Hightstown, NJ, © 1993.

Using the same block as Heat Wave, *Gloria created this layout for a Hoffman Challenge. She made all of the fabrics in the quilt except for the Hoffman Challenge fabric. It's machine-pieced and hand-quilted.*

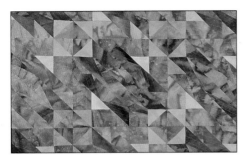

39. *Detail,* Directions (*above*).

40. Directions (*right*).
Gloria Hansen, Hightstown, NJ, © *1995.*

Gloria created this block and layout using Canvas 3.5. Although she selected a straight repeat of the block, many interesting layouts are possible by turning the block in different directions. Gloria wanted a no-focal-point, low-contrast look, and achieved it by painting all of the fabrics in the quilt. It's machine-pieced and hand-quilted. See Chapter 19 for information on how to create this block.

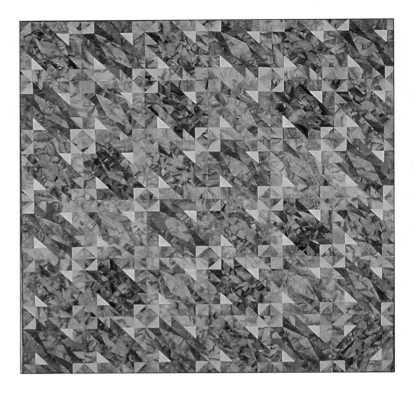

41. *Detail,* Dancing Shadows (*above*).

42. Dancing Shadows (*right*).
Gloria Hansen, Hightstown, NJ, © *1995.*

Gloria created this block and layout for the GEnie Online Quilters' "Road Less Traveled" exhibit using SuperPaint. The layout uses a repeat of the same block, but the corner blocks are made larger. The triangle shapes that make up the block were printed onto tracing paper for paper piecing. It's machine-pieced and hand-quilted and uses many fabrics that Gloria painted or dyed. See Chapter 19 for information on how to create this block.

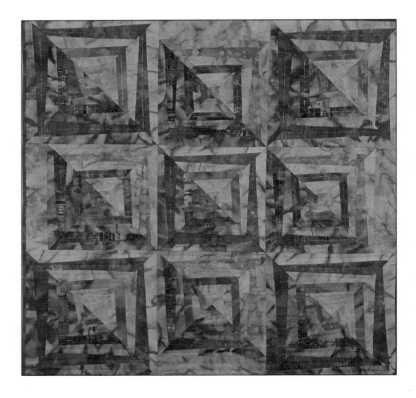

43. *Detail*, Petals of Hope (*above*).

44. Petals of Hope (*right*).
Gloria Hansen, Hightstown, NJ, © 1996.

Using Canvas 3.5, Gloria created this block and layout. It's machine-pieced and hand-quilted and uses many fabrics that Gloria created. See Chapter 19 for information on how to create this block.

45. *Detail*, Shattered (*above*).

46. Shattered (*right*).
Gloria Hansen, Hightstown, NJ, © 1996.

Gloria created this block and layout using Canvas 3.5. It's machine pieced and hand-quilted and uses many fabrics that Gloria created. See Chapter 19 for a step-by-step of how this quilt was created.

47. Breaking Free (*above*).
Gloria Hansen, Hightstown, NJ, © 1994.

Starting with the Awakenings *block, Gloria changed some lines to create a new block. She created a four-block unit made up of two different-sized square blocks and two elongated blocks. This unit was then grouped and duplicated creating the central area. Borders were added. It's machine pieced and hand quilted and uses many fabrics that Gloria painted, airbrushed, or dyed. See Chapter 19 for information on how to create this block.*

48. *Detail,* Breaking Free (*left*).

MANUALLY TRACE THE ART WITH DRAWING TABLET PEN OR MOUSE

To trace an image with your mouse or drawing tablet pen, you first import the art into your drawing program. If your drawing program allows you to draw on different layers, place the image on one layer and then trace over it on another layer, using a line color like red that's easy to see.

If you don't enjoy the luxury of owning a drawing tablet and are constricted to drawing with a mouse, this can be a long and laborious process. You're better off simply resizing the image, printing it—across multiple sheets if necessary—and tracing over it with pencil and tracing paper to create your appliqué pieces.

Tracing the image manually, either with your drawing program or with an old-fashioned pencil, is the preferred route if you're working with a photograph. Tracing by hand will allow you to create your appliqué pieces by tracing over the shadows.

An easy way to get a picture inside the computer is to place the photo on your drawing table and trace it with the tablet's pen.

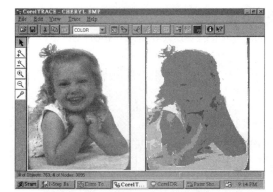

Some photographs, such as the one shown here, don't trace well in CorelTrace. As you can see, the trace, shown on the right, is pretty useless. Sometimes you can get a better trace by scanning a color photo with the gray-scale setting of your scanner. When you do this, though, you lose a lot of the photo's highlights. Skin tone especially appears washed out.

A better technique for this kind of photo is to import it as a color bitmap image directly into your drawing program, as shown here. Enlarge it to a size that you can easily work with, then "lock" the drawing on one drawing layer. Move to a different drawing layer, and with the pencil or freehand tool—and using a color that you can easily see—trace over the lines of the photo to make appliqué patches. This is where having a drawing tablet helps. Another strategy is to enlarge the photo to the size of the final appliqué and then print it. Tape the pages together if the picture runs across multiple pages, and trace over them with tracing paper and a pencil.

RESIZE THE IMAGE, CREATE THE FINAL PATTERN, AND PRINT IT

Once you've finished tracing the art and airbrushing it or whatever in the drawing program, resize it to the dimensions you want your appliqué pattern to be by turning on the on-screen rulers. You can "stretch" the art by selecting it and pulling the "handles" that appear around the art. But a better way to resize it is to invoke the program's scaling feature. With this feature you can increase the size of your art by a percentage like 200, and you won't distort the image by stretching it.

If the drawing is large, you can print it out across multiple sheets by selecting your drawing program's "tiling" option from its print settings menu.

If you like, you can print your design directly on freezer paper for freezer paper appliqué. (This is most easily done on a dot-matrix printer, since freezer paper curls. Also, inkjet and laser printer inks don't hold very well on freezer paper.) Cut the paper into 8½-by-11-inch sheets. Feed it through the printer so that it prints on the dull side of the paper. You can then cut out your appliqué pieces from the freezer paper, iron them onto your fabric, and cut the appliqué pieces from the fabric with a ⅛-inch seam allowance around the freezer paper.

DRAWING APPLIQUÉ DESIGNS WITH A DRAWING TABLET

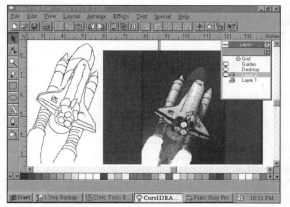

On the right is a photo of the space shuttle that was downloaded from NASA's Web site on the Internet. On the left is a trace drawn by hand with a Wacom drawing tablet and pen. The photo was imported into CorelDraw and placed on one drawing layer. We used to the Wacom pen and tablet to manually trace the photo on another drawing layer. It might have been easier to print the photo, place it on top of the Wacom tablet, and use the pen to trace on top of that. Easiest of all would have been to simply resize the photo as desired, print it across multiple sheets, and then, using tracing paper, trace an appliqué pattern on top of it. But we like to do things the hard way!

Drawing appliqué patterns with a drawing tablet is a lot of fun. Whether you import a scanned photo into your drawing software to trace it, or place the photo on top of the drawing tablet and trace over it that way, drawing tablets provide a quick way to draw appliqué patterns with naturalistic lines (as opposed to the perfectly smooth curves we taught you to draw with the Bezier tool in Chapter 14). Here are some tricks:

- Be sure to turn off snap-to-grid in your drawing software, as well as snap-to-object and snap-to-guides if those are activated.

- Use the pencil or freehand tool if your drawing program requires you to select a tool. These will be easier to draw with than the Bezier tool.

- Use your drawing program's line smoothing feature to work the kinks out of your lines.

- If your drawing program lets you set the width of your drawing lines, increase the width slightly so that you can see it better as you draw.

- If you import a drawing or scanned photo into your drawing program with the intent of drawing on top of it, import it as a gray-scale image. You'll be able to see its lines better as you draw.

- Place your scan on one drawing layer and trace on another layer, if your drawing program supports layers. Be sure to "lock" the scan into place so that it and your drawing lines don't accidentally separate as you draw.

- Trace the image in the size you feel most comfortable working with. Drawing is usually most comfortable when the entire image is displayed on the screen. Use the zoom tool to zoom in on portions as you draw. Don't bother resizing your trace until it's time to print your pattern.

- When you're ready to print, print only the layer on which you drew. You want to print just your hand-drawn lines, not the photo beneath it.

- If your computer is an old one, be aware that underpowered computers sometimes have a hard time keeping up with the speed of the drawing pen. You'll have to slow your drawing down so that your computer can keep up.

- If you place your photo on top of the drawing tablet to trace it, be aware that some tablets have an electrostatic switch that will hold your photo in place electrostatically as you trace it. That switch is located on either the top or the side of the tablet.

- Yes, you can simultaneously sketch with your mouse and your drawing tablet pen. When you get the hang of it, this is a very quick and effective way to draw.

- Don't let cats—or children—scurry over the drawing tablet as you sketch!

TURNING SIMPLE BLACK-AND-WHITE ART INTO AN APPLIQUÉ PATTERN

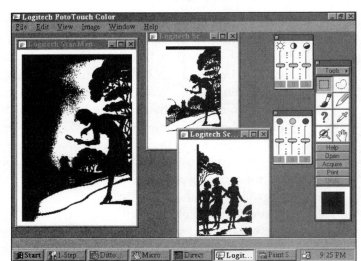

A simple black-and-white image, like a silhouette, is the easiest kind of art to turn into an appliqué pattern. For the Nancy Drew quilt, shown in the color gallery, Judy scanned silhouettes of the "girl detective" from the inside covers of Nancy Drew books from the 1930s. They were scanned as black-and-white line drawings. Judy didn't have to do much to prep the scanned images except to despeckle them and crop them in the scanner's software.

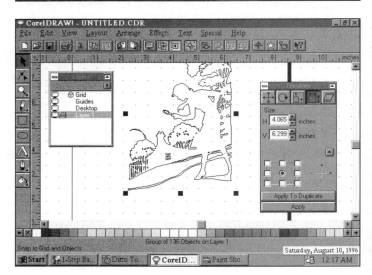

After tracing the scans in CorelTrace, Judy imported them into CorelDraw and displayed them in wireframe view (pull down the **View** menu and put a check beside **Wireframe**) to get a better sense of what the appliqué pattern would look like. Judy enlarged Nancy Drew's silhouette with the **Transform Roll-Up**. The silhouette ballooned to be larger than the paper, but that didn't matter; she just used the tiling option when printing it. To print just the lines of the pattern, and not the darkened silhouette, Judy moved Nancy to the Guides layer, and from the Layers Manager (Layers Roll-Up in CorelDraw 5) specified that only the Guides layer be printed. When she first tried to print the pattern, she got non-sensical error messages, and only blank sheets spewed from the printer. Judy resized the pattern to be just a couple of inches smaller, and it printed nicely. When the pages were taped together, she resketched a couple of the lines (like the shoe) that looked askew. The appliqué pattern was traced onto muslin with embroidery transfer paper. The entire process of creating the appliqué pattern—from scanning the image to tracing it, resizing it, and printing it—took less than 20 minutes. Amazing!

1. Jane Austen was a quilter. She used Regency period chintzes to stitch together beautiful bed quilts while writing *Pride and Prejudice*. From Jane's Web site (**http://uts.cc.utexas. edu/~churchh/janeinfo.html**), Judy captured her regal silhouette. (Click the right mouse button in Windows 95 to pop up a menu to save a Web page image.)

2. Unfortunately, when Judy enlarged Jane's silhouette to the size that she wanted our applique pattern to be, it appeared lumpy. She could have used the drawing tools in graphics software like Paint Shop Pro to smooth it out, but why go to the trouble when something like that is easier to draw by hand?

3. Her next step was to print the image at the size she wanted the final pattern to be. Judy used Paint Shop Pro to do this, but you can use any graphics or drawing program. Somewhere on the **File** menu you'll find a print or page setup option. You can use it to specify the size at which you want your image to print and how you want it centered on the paper. If you print the image larger than a single sheet of paper, you'll need to specify the print tiling option so that it will print over multiple sheets. Select the **Print Preview** command to see exactly how the image will print out.

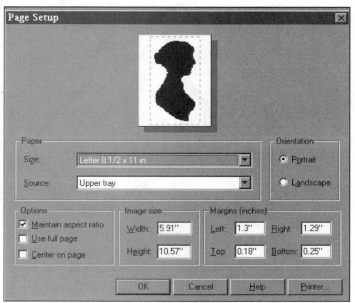

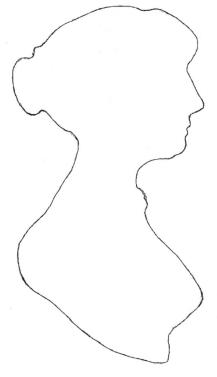

4. Judy printed on paper Jane's silhouette to the size she wanted, lumps and all.

5. Then she traced over it with another sheet of paper, smoothing out the lumps.

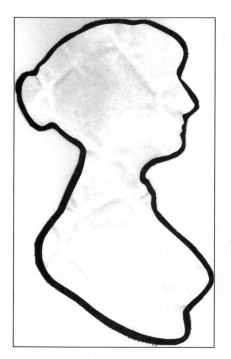

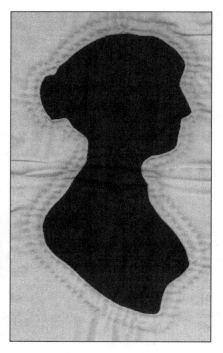

6. She cut out the paper appliqué pattern and pasted it onto fabric, then cut the fabric with a ¼-inch seam.

7. Judy hand-appliquéd Jane's silhouette onto fabric, cutting the back of the fabric and removing the paper when she was done sewing.

TURNING A PHOTOGRAPH INTO AN APPLIQUÉ PATTERN

1. Start by scanning your photo or drawing and prepping it in your scanner's software or your photo or image software. Crop the picture. Sharpen it to brighten it up. Despeckle it if it's a line drawing, or if it looks like a swarm of flies is hovering over it—those are scanner "artifacts." Brighten some of the color levels if any of the colors look washed out. Use the zoom

tool to zoom in and, with the eraser tool, erase any remaining artifacts (the blotches). Also erase any unnecessary background elements. Save it as a .BMP or .PCX file for the best color retention if you're using a PC, or as a .PICT file if you're using a Mac.

2. Once your scanned photo is ready, you have two choices for how to proceed. You can import the image into your drawing program. You'd place the image on one drawing layer and then trace over it on another layer, either manually, with your mouse or drawing tablet pen, or by using the program's auto-trace feature. If you have CorelDraw, you're better off importing it into CorelTrace, a separate program that comes packaged with CorelDraw. Select the color setting, even if the photo is a black-and-white one, for better shadow interpretation. Trace it

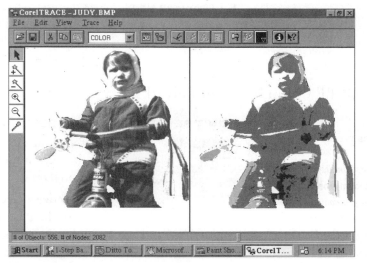

with the default settings—in other words, don't turn on any of the fancy options. Once the image appears in traced form, select **Save Trace**. The file will be saved with the same name as the original .BMP file, but with an .EPS extension.

3. Open CorelDraw and import the traced image. CorelTrace will have stored it with an .EPS file extension and in a directory called TRACE, using the same "first" name on the file as the original file name. If you can't find it, use Windows' Find File feature to locate it. Select the image and size it so that you can work with it easily on the screen. If you put it into wireframe view (select **View** and place a check beside **Wireframe**), you'll be able to see the image's lines.

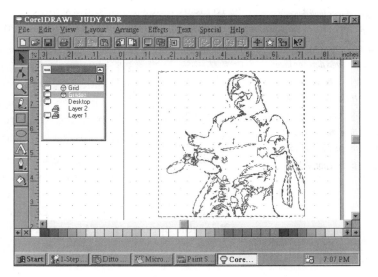

Once you have a traced image, you have several options for how to proceed to create your appliqué pattern:

- You can move the image to the Guides layer. Turn on the snap-to-guidelines feature; turn off snap-to-grid. Lock the **Guides** layer. Now move to a drawing layer, such as layer 1. Using the freehand tool, trace on top of the guides. Keep the original photograph close at hand so that you can refer to it as you draw. Use the zoom tool to zoom in on sections of the drawing to better see the lines you're drawing. Make sure your appliqué pieces are complete patches. Start by drawing the bottom appliqué layers. End by drawing the top appliqué layers. To see what your appliqué looks like, make the guidelines invisible. When you're done, resize the drawing to the size you want.

- You can move the image to a different drawing layer (layer 2) and turn off wireframe view, so that you see the color components of the trace instead of the skeletal lines. Use the freehand tool to draw on top of those with a contrasting color.

- Or you can simply resize the image to the size you want your appliqué pattern to be and then print it. Tape the sheets together if the image runs across multiple pages, and trace your appliqué pieces with tracing paper and pencil.

MORE CORELDRAW APPLIQUÉ TIPS

DRAWING ON LAYERS IS LIKE DRAWING ON TRACING PAPER

Working with a drawing program's layers is like drawing on tracing paper. You may need only one sheet to draw on. But when you want to want to retrace the design or trace particular segments, you find yourself using multiple sheets. Drawing on a computer is analogous. A high-end drawing program will give you multiple layers, or sheets, to draw on. (An exception is the SuperPaint program we recommend for the Mac. SuperPaint gives you just one drawing layer, plus a layer to paint on.) As you work, you can make some sheets invisible or have them all visible. You can remove layers or move objects from one layer to another. You can print one layer or all of the layers. You can even dim one layer so that you see only a shadow of it through the other layers. There are lots of tricks you can do with layers, especially when creating appliqué patterns. That's why you should spend time learning how to move between and create different layers in your drawing program. The tips in this section will get you started.

DON'T BE INTIMIDATED BY CORELDRAW'S LAYERS

- To see the Layers Roll-Up, press **CTRL-F3**, or pull down the **Layout** menu and select **Layer Manager** (in CorelDraw 7) or **Layers Roll-Up** (in CorelDraw 5).

- To move a piece of art to a different layer, select it with the Pick tool by either clicking on it or dragging a rubber-band box around it. Head to the **Layers Roll-Up** and click the right-pointing arrow in the top right corner. A flyout menu will appear. Click **Move To**, and with the fat arrow that appears, click **Guides**.

- To move to a different layer and draw on it, simply highlight it and click on it in the **Layers Roll-Up**.

- To create a new layer to draw on, click on the right-pointing arrow in the **Layers Roll-Up** and select **New** in the flyout menu.

- To make a layer invisible, in CorelDraw 7, simply click to dim the eye icon in  the **Layers Roll-Up** next to the layer that you want to hide. In CorelDraw 5, select the layer in the **Layers Roll-Up**, then click the right-pointing arrow, and select **Edit** from the flyout menu. Remove the check from the **Visible** option in the Edit Layers dialog box, and click **OK**.

- Similarly, to print only the Guides layer, in CorelDraw 7's **Layers Roll-Up** click the printer icon next to the **Guides** layer to darken it, and click to dim the printer icon for all other layers. In CorelDraw 5's **Layers Roll-Up**, click the right-pointing arrow and select **Edit** from the flyout menu. Check the **Printable** option for the **Guides** layer, and uncheck it for all the other layers.

ANOTHER WAY TO TRACE IN CORELDRAW

You can auto-trace within CorelDraw, but it's not as precise as tracing with CorelTrace. (Older versions of CorelDraw also tend to use up a lot of memory and crash the PC if your trace is complex.)

1. First you need to import a bitmap image (.BMP) into CorelDraw. You do so by pulling down the **File** menu and selecting **Import**. If the picture appears as a tiny blob on your screen, use your mouse to drag one of its corner handles to enlarge it. Select the Freehand tool.

2. Click to the left of any dark area you wish to trace. CorelDraw will do its best to trace it (but sometimes that's not good enough). So that you can better see what you're doing, in CorelDraw 7, pull down the **View** menu and select **Wireframe**. In CorelDraw 5, click on **Bitmaps** on the **View** menu, and turn **Visible** on and off so that you can see how your image is tracing. Bitmaps can also be fairly easy to trace by hand with your mouse.

3. Be sure not to move either the bitmap image or its tracing until you're done tracing. When you're finished, select and delete the bitmap. With the Pick tool, draw a rubber-band box around your tracing lines, then pull down the **Arrange** menu and select **Combine** to group those lines into a whole.

In CorelDraw 7, double-click on the Freehand or Bezier tool to pop up this dialog box, where you can set the accuracy of manually traced curves. Generally, the default is fine and you don't need to mess with this. But it's always helpful to know where this setting can be made if you need to twiddle.

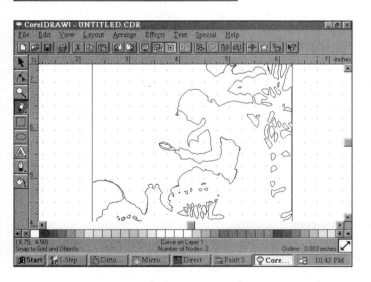

Tracing Nancy Drew with the auto-trace feature in CorelDraw proved far too time-consuming. It also kept crashing the PC.

MORE CANVAS APPLIQUÉ TRICKS

QUICK TIPS FOR DRAWING ON CANVAS'S LAYERS

- When you create a drawing in Canvas, it is automatically placed on Layer One. You'll find the Layer palette icon in the bottom left corner of the Canvas document .

- To create a new layer in Canvas 3.5, hold the mouse button down on the Layer palette icon and slide up to **Layer Specs**. (Or press **COMMAND-B**, or choose **Layer Specs** from the **Layout** menu.) Click **New Layer** in the Layer Specifications dialog box. Canvas will highlight the new name. You may want to name the new layer something obvious so that you'll know what the layer contains. You can make any layer gray or give it a color. You can also delete a layer by selecting it and clicking **Delete Layer** in the Layer Specifications dialog box.

- To create a new layer in Canvas 5.0, press **COMMAND-B**, or select **Layers** from the **Layout** menu and slide over to **Layer Info**. In the Layer Info dialog box, click **New** to add a new layer; rename it if you like. To delete a layer, select it and click **Delete**.

- To draw on a particular layer in Canvas 3.5, hold the mouse button down on the Layer palette icon and slide up to select the layer name. In both Canvas 3.5 and 5.0, you can also move between layers by selecting **Layers** from the **Layout** menu and sliding over to select the name of the layer you want.

- If your drawing has many layers and becomes large, you can save layers individually. In Canvas 3.5, select **Save Layer As** from the **File** menu. In Canvas 5.0, choose **Save As** from the **File** menu and click **Save Layers**. Click the **Layers** button, and then choose the layer or layers to save.

- To print a single layer in Canvas 3.5, select **Print Special** from the **File** menu and slide over to select **Layer**. The Choose Layers To Print dialog box will appear, and you can select which layer you want to print. In Canvas 5.0, print a single layer by choosing **Print** from the **File** menu. From the pull-down box next to **Print**, choose **Layers**. Click the **Layers** button, and select the layer or layers to print.

WHEN TO OPEN AND WHEN TO PLACE IN CANVAS

As you probably already know, to open a document in any Macintosh program, you pull down the **File** menu and select **Open**. A dialog box appears, and you find the file you want to open. But you'll also notice a **Place** command on the **File** menu. We're often asked what command should be used when. Here's an easy way to determine which to use:

- Use **Open** to import a file (such as a scanned image) into a new illustration.

- Use **Place** to import a file into a current Canvas document, meaning a document already containing other images. When you select the document in the dialog box, a "place pointer" appears. Use your mouse to position the place pointer on your document where you want the image to appear. Press and hold the mouse button down, and drag the place pointer to create a boundary box the size you want the image to be. Then release the mouse button, and the image appears.

File	
New...	⌘N
Open...	⌘O
Close	⌘W
Place...	⌘⌥P
Save	⌘S
Save As...	⌘⌥S
Revert	
Preferences...	
Page Setup...	
Print...	⌘P
1 Mustang1.pict	
2 blue	
Quit	⌘Q

TRACING PICTURES WITH CANVAS'S AUTO TRACE FEATURE

We'll illustrate auto-tracing in Canvas with a picture of Gloria's dog, Mustang. To get the image shown here, we adjusted the brightness and contrast of the scanned image, erased the background, and saved it as a PICT file.

The original scanned image of Mustang saved as a PICT file.

USE AUTO TRACE IN CANVAS 3.5

Here's how to auto-trace a scanned image in Canvas 3.5:

1. Open the PICT file containing the scanned image.

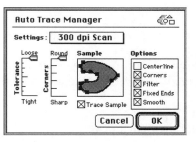

2. Pull down the **Edit** menu, select **Managers**, and slide over to **Auto Trace**. The Auto Trace Manager opens. We find the best results with the **Tolerance** set to **Loose**, the **Corners** set to **Round**, and the **Corners**, **Filter**, **Fixed Ends**, and **Smooth** options checked. Click **OK**.

3. Use the Selection Arrow to select the image you want to auto-trace. Then pull down the **Effects** menu, select **Auto Trace To**, and slide over to **Polygon**. A traced image is drawn.

4. Select the image and drag it away from the original scan.

T * I * P

See Chapter 6 for how-tos on working with layers in Canvas.

T * I * P

Try selecting Bezier Curve and Smooth Polygon instead of Polygon for different effects.

T * I * P

Prior to auto-tracing, remove as much of the background as you can so that you trace only the image you want.

NOTE

Auto Trace is not available for color images in Canvas. They must be gray-scale or black and white.

Here we placed a MacPaint file of Mustang into Canvas 3.5 in a small size. This condensed the image and made it very black. We auto-traced it, getting a line silhouette.

USE AUTO-TRACE IN CANVAS 5.0

When we tried to open the same PICT file of Mustang in Canvas 5.0, the Auto Trace command was grayed, and we were unable to use it. Unable to get a response from Deneba's technical support, we turned to the excellent shareware program called Graphic Converter (see Chapter 2 for information on how to obtain this must-have program) to convert the scan to a different file format. We used it to open the PICT file and convert it to a MacPaint file. Canvas 5.0 opened the MacPaint file with no problem and allowed us to auto-trace it. Here's how you can do the same:

1. Open the file containing the scanned image.

2. Use the Selection Arrow tool to select the image you want to auto-trace.

3. Pull down the **Image** menu and select **Auto Trace**. A dialog box will appear. By varying the settings, you can alter the final auto-trace. Make your selections and click **OK**. A traced image is drawn.

4. Select the image and drag it away from the original scan.

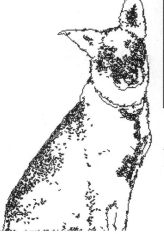

This trace was made with the Auto Trace Manager set to smooth curves, with loose and round settings.

This trace was made with the Auto Trace Manager set to Polygons, with settings midway between loose and tight and midway between round and sharp.

T * I * P

Try saving your scan in different formats for different effects. A MacPaint file will give a very grainy appearance, but, as demonstrated here, it can create the basis for some interesting auto-traces.

Here the Auto Trace Manager was set to Smooth Curves with tight and sharp settings.

For this trace, the Auto Trace Manager was set to Smooth Curves, with settings midway between loose and tight and midway between round and sharp.

ADOBE STREAMLINE QUICKLY TURNS GRAPHICS INTO APPLIQUÉ PATTERNS

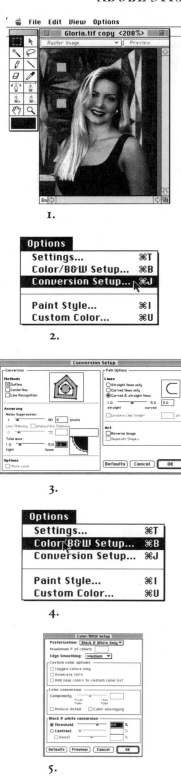

1.

2.

3.

4.

5.

As you can see in this chapter, using the auto-trace features in high-end drawing programs can be tricky. They don't always trace pictures as precisely as you'd like. You also usually need to turn bitmap pictures (you know, GIFs and BMPs) into vector drawings before you trace.

And what if you don't have one of those pricey high-end drawing programs?

Adobe Streamline, available for both PCs and Macs, offers a fast and painless way to trace a bitmap and turn it into an appliqué pattern. The program's street price of about $140 makes it a nice alternative to a costly drawing program.

What's more, Streamline's tracing features are more sophisticated than those of drawing programs like Canvas. It gives you more control over tracing options and in general produces traces that are easier to turn into appliqué patterns than the traces produced in drawing programs.

Here's how Gloria turned a photo into an appliqué self-portrait:

1. You can scan an image directly into Streamline or import it. Gloria started with a photo of herself standing in front of one of her quilts. The photo was stored in TIFF format, which provides the best line and color retention.

2. She pulled down the **Options** menu and selected **Conversion Setup**.

3. In the Conversion Setup dialog box, she selected the **Outline** method (which traces an outline of every element in the image), tightened up the tolerance, and clicked **OK**. The tighter the tolerance, the more exact the line to the original image (with more anchor points). A loose tolerance creates a smooth, nonjagged edge with fewer anchor points. This is one place where you can experiment to get different effects. In some instances, a looser tolerance may produce a more workable line; in others, a tighter tolerance may be better. But all the settings in the Conversion Setup box produce variations in the overall look.

4. She pulled down the **Options** menu again and selected **Color/B&W Setup**.

5. She set **Posterization** to Black & White Only, **Edge Smoothing** to Medium, and the **Black & White Conversion Threshold** to 69%. This is another place where you can experiment to get different effects. The Posterization setting, when set to Black & White Only, will break the image down into only black and white. Edge Smoothing sharpens fuzzy edges; here a setting of Medium gave the best result. The Conversion Threshold lets you specify as a percentage the gray level above which Streamline will convert a pixel to black. In other words, everything above a certain gray-scale level will be black, and everything below it will be white. Using a setting of 69% created a good balance of black and white areas.

6. Still in the dialog box, Gloria clicked **Preview** to see what the image would look like with the settings she had chosen. You can continue adjusting the options (in this case, the Edge Smoothing and the Black & White Conversion Threshold) and previewing the image until it is just what you are after, clicking **OK** when you are finished. As you can see, this already looks as though it would make a pretty good appliqué pattern.

7. To convert the picture to a vector drawing, Gloria headed to the **File** menu and selected **Convert**. The resulting image appeared as it had in the Preview box.

8. She held the mouse button down on the **Preview** box above the image and then selected **Artwork** to display the lines of the image.

9. Streamline converted the photo into a line drawing that she could edit. Changing a line involves simply clicking on the line to select it and then using the editing tools.

10. To return to the original image to try other settings, Gloria held the mouse button down on the **Converted Art** box above the image and then selected **Raster Image**. Raster is another word for bitmap. Selecting it displays the original bitmap image that you started with. Remember to save your work if you come up with something you like.

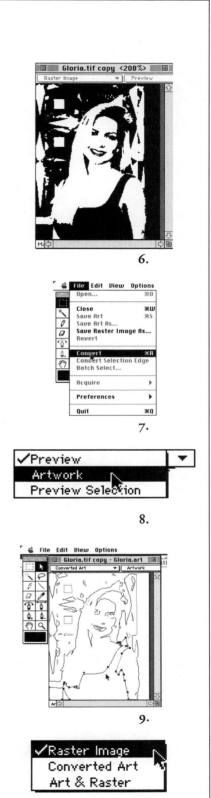

6.

7.

8.

9.

10.

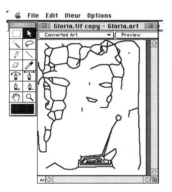

Here the Centerline setting was selected in the Conversion Setup dialog box. By varying the line thinning, different effects were achieved. Centerline works only on black-and-white images and gives the resulting images a consistent line weight by locating the center of each line and creating a path for it. Line thinning is how thin or thick the line is. The thinner the line, the more pixels get "shaved off."

The Centerline and Outline settings were selected in the Conversion Setup dialog box for this effect.

The image at left is shown in the Artwork view.

V

FABRIC AND PRINTERS

WANT TO PUT FABRIC IN YOUR QUILT DESIGN OR PRINT ON FABRIC
WITH YOUR COMPUTER PRINTER? IN THIS SECTION YOU'LL LEARN THE
SECRETS OF THE FABRIC-COMPUTER CONNECTION.

CHAPTER 16

PUTTING FABRIC IN YOUR COMPUTER

How to scan fabrics from your stash, and what to do with them once you get them into your computer.

It elicits gasps at quilt shows. Fabric scanned with a handheld scanner magically appears on a computer screen. Just a few clicks of the mouse, and the fabric colors the patches of a quilt.

It's inevitable: Once you start coloring quilt block patches, you'll want to fill them with something resembling fabric. After all, you didn't pay $500 for that Diamond Viper video card and hi-res Sony Trinitron color monitor just so your significant other could watch ESPN in a desktop window.

There are many ways to put fabric on your computer screen. You can:

- Use the fabric designs in quilt design software to fill blocks with color. Some quilt software makers sell disks with scans of popular fabric lines sold in stores. You can use them to color quilts designed with their programs. In some cases you can use them with other programs too. You can buy disks like this for Quilt-Pro and QuiltSoft (from Quilter's Design Studio).

- Scan real fabric with a handheld or flatbed scanner, import the resulting graphics file into your drawing program, and then turn it into a fill pattern.

- Use your drawing program's fill patterns to color and fill the blocks with a design.

- Create your own digital fabric fills, either by editing your drawing program's fill patterns (changing the color, scale, etc.) or by drawing your own fabric designs in a painting or drawing program and then turning them into fill patterns.

- Buy a pricey graphic artist's CD-ROM containing predesigned fabric-like fills. Or buy special software that will let you design beautiful patterns to use as fills. One popular program is Adobe's TextureMaker for the Mac for $199 (800/628-2320 or **http://www.adobe.com/**). We think such products are overkill for the average quilter.

- Snip out teeny pieces of fabric and glue them to your computer screen.

Okay, we were only kidding about that last method, but we'll talk about the other methods in this chapter, including how best to work with the fill tools in drawing programs to create fabric patterns, how to scan real fabric and use the scans in a quilt design, how to get the most out of your handheld or flatbed scanner when scanning textiles, and how to create your own personal digital fabric library to use for your designs.

JUDY & GLORIA'S RADICAL IDEAS

We think that scanning real fabric to put in quilt designs on your computer screen is less useful than it may appear at quilt shows. The colors are never the same on a computer screen as they are on the bolt, and the scale of fabric prints doesn't translate well to a computer screen, where everything is so small.

We think that the best way to design a quilt on a computer is to work with black, white, and values of gray, not with color. See Chapter 10, "Exploring Shadow, Shade, and Color," to see what we mean. In other words, there's no substitute for laying the fabric all over the floor. Still, some quilters love these fabric disks, and their publishers tell us they sell bunches. That's not surprising—they are irresistibly fun to use!

HOW TO SCAN REAL FABRICS TO PUT IN YOUR QUILT DESIGNS

Even though we don't think it's all that useful, we know you're still dying to take that fabric from your closet and display it on your computer screen. And it is lots of fun to organize different fabrics in blocks on your screen. Here's what you need to do:

1. IRON THE FABRIC. Don't laugh. Do you want wrinkles all over your computer screen?

2. SET YOUR SCANNER'S RESOLUTION TO A LOW SETTING, LIKE 100 DPI, TO KEEP THE IMAGE SMALL. (You can also reduce a scan's resolution through the scanner's software.) Keep the resulting image file as small as possible so that it's easy to work with— ideally smaller than 100KB.

3. SCAN A SMALL PORTION OF THE FABRIC. Don't scan an entire repeat of a design, because you'll never be able to scale it correctly on your screen.

4. USING YOUR SCANNER'S SOFTWARE OR YOUR DRAWING OR GRAPHICS SOFTWARE, CROP OR CUT OUT A SMALL AREA OF YOUR SCANNED IMAGE. Look for the square-shaped tool with the broken outline (the cropping tool) in your graphics software. You may need to cut and paste it into a new file.

5. ONCE YOU'VE SCANNED THE FABRIC, BRIGHTEN UP ITS TONE (TONE CONTROL) AND ADJUST THE COLOR (COLOR BALANCE) WITH YOUR SCANNING SOFTWARE OR WITH THE PHOTO TOUCHUP FEATURE, IF YOUR DRAWING PROGRAM HAS ONE. Sometimes fabric on the computer screen looks washed out, especially if a bright light was shining in the area when the fabric was scanned.

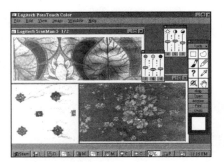

Here we've scanned an assortment of fabrics that we should have ironed first. Once you scan a fabric, you need to brighten up its colors and possibly adjust its color balance.

6. IF YOUR SCANNED FABRIC APPEARS ON THE SCREEN WITH DISCOLORED WAVES OR SHADOWS, YOU MAY NEED TO CALIBRATE YOUR SCANNER (see "How to Get the Most from Your Scanner" below). These "moiré" patterns also occur if you enlarge or reduce the scale of your scan. To get rid of them, try rescanning the fabric at 100 percent scale.

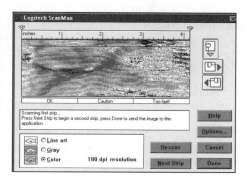

We scanned a lovely hand-painted pastel fabric, but it appeared as grainy moiré. Too much light in the vicinity of the scanner and an improper scale setting were to blame.

7. SAVE THE SCAN IN THE FILE FORMAT USED BY YOUR QUILT SOFTWARE OR IN A FORMAT THAT'S EASY TO IMPORT INTO YOUR DRAWING SOFTWARE. For instance, the format to use for Quilt-Pro is the BMP format. The BMP file format is the best one to use for importing into drawing programs too, but BMP files are three times larger than the same image stored in PCX format. Beware of the TIFF format: A TIFF file is about five times larger than a comparable PCX image. For most Macintosh programs, stick with the PICT format. For a detailed discussion of graphics formats, see Appendix A.

8. IF YOUR SOFTWARE ASKS IF YOU'D LIKE TO SAVE THE FILE IN 16 MILLION COLORS, DON'T DO IT! Save it as an 8-bit or a 256-color file to keep it to a reasonable size.

9. TO USE THE IMAGE AS A FILL PATTERN, IMPORT IT INTO YOUR QUILT DESIGN SOFTWARE OR DRAWING PROGRAM ACCORDING TO THE PROGRAM'S DIRECTIONS. You can import scanned fabrics into Quilt-Pro and Quilter's Design Studio (see the directions given later). Electric Quilt and BlockBase don't permit you to import scanned fabrics, but they come with enough digital fabrics to keep you busy.

Thanks to Quilt-Pro Systems for many of these tips!

REMEMBER

Like quilt patterns, fabric designs are copyrighted. You can scan them to incorporate into your own work, for your own private use, but it is illegal to reproduce them in patterns, books, or photocopies, or to put them on the Internet without the owner's permission. If you want to do any of these things, contact the fabric's manufacturer first and ask for permission.

HOW TO GET THE MOST FROM YOUR SCANNER

- Be sure to calibrate your scanner. Check its manual for directions.

- If your scanned fabric looks discolored, try adjusting the scanner's contrast.

- Avoid scanning near a bright light or in direct sunlight. The resulting image may appear washed out, discolored, or streaky.

- Your scanner's light may distort the color of an image. If it does, try placing a yellow plastic sheet over your fabric.

- When using a handheld scanner, scan slowly and with a steady hand. Get a scanner tray to keep the sweep of your scanner even, or drag your scanner along the edge of a ruler.

- Try placing a plastic sheet on top of the scanner to avoid scratching the glass when scanning something bumpy.

T * I * P

The Logitech Web site (http://www.logitech.com/) offers great technical advice to owners of Logitech scanners.

IF YOU DON'T HAVE A SCANNER . . .

If you don't have a scanner, there are ways to beg or borrow one. Obviously, the first place to look is at a meeting of your local quilting guild—surely someone owns a scanner. If not, try calling a print shop; many rent scanners by the day or hour. Or you can take your fabric to a copy shop to be scanned for about $9 to $35 per scan. (Pricey, eh?) Be sure to bring your own diskette (they charge extra for those)—and the directions for how you'd like your image scanned and saved.

USING AND MAKING FABRIC DESIGNS IN ELECTRIC QUILT

JUDY & GLORIA'S QUICK FABRIC PALETTE CREATION TIP

All image-editing programs (the software that came with your scanner) and drawing programs let you adjust the brightness/contrast, hue saturation, and color balance of images. Scan in a single fabric print, and create an entire palette of prints from the same image by adjusting these options. Turn purple into lavender or yellow into green and save each of the variations in a different file. Within minutes and with just one scan you can create an entire range of colors.

One of the fundamental differences between Electric Quilt and Quilt-Pro is that the former includes digitized versions of over 3,000 fabric prints. You'll find print libraries of commercial fabrics from famous designers like Nancy Crow and VIP Color Works—fabrics that you can actually buy in the store (they even include the bolt numbers you'll find in the store); a library of historical prints, containing collections like "'50s Fall Housedress," "1890 Pineapple Plaids," and "'40s Sherbet Prints"; and a contemporary library with hundreds of modern fabrics.

Electric Quilt also includes a huge range of color libraries, including hundreds of historically researched color palettes like half-mourning prints, dyes and double-pinks, 1890s sateens, and a palette mixed especially to reproduce Baltimore album quilts. (Remember, Electric Quilt's author, Penny McMorris, is a leading quilt historian.) You can select from Amish palettes, palettes built around the preferred colors of particular artists like Cézanne or Warhol, or the colors of Nancy Crow or S. Barrington Dyes. You can also mix your own colors to simulate dyes you're using or to create a value range (see our discussion in Chapter 10).

The one thing Electric Quilt doesn't do that Quilt-Pro does is let you incorporate scanned fabrics into your designs (an insignificant limitation, given all the colors and choices available to you). However, Electric Quilt does let you create your own fabric designs with easy-to-use drawing tools and a grid. Its color and fabric possibilities are truly unlimited.

DESIGN YOUR OWN FABRICS IN ELECTRIC QUILT

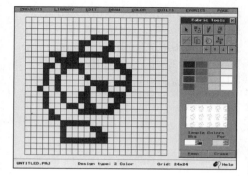

1. Pull down the **Fabrics** menu and select **Toolbox**. Also on the **Fabrics** menu, select **Two-Color** to draw a two-color fabric or **Multicolor** for more colors. Draw your design on the grid. Click with the On/Off tool to color individual boxes in the grid, or use one of the drawing tools to draw lines and shapes. Keep your drawing as simple as possible: A few boxes. A couple of swervy lines.

NOTE

You cannot use the fabric collections in Electric Quilt's or BlockBase's databases with other quilt design programs, or with drawing programs for that matter, since the fabrics are stored in a proprietary file format.

2. Change the foreground and background colors by selecting **Fgr** and **Bkg**, respectively, and scrolling through the colors. You can see the fabric pattern as it materializes in the box above the sample colors. You'll be amazed at how Electric Quilt will work it into a fabric pattern. Click the **Keep** button to add the fabric to your Sketchbook (where all the parts of a current quilt project are stored).

By adding more boxes, or pixels, to the grid (change it in the **Fabrics** menu), you can create larger, more complex designs. The drawing board's tools let you make multiple copies of a portion of the design and rotate, flip, and mirror them.

USE YOUR NEW FABRIC TO FILL QUILT PATCHES

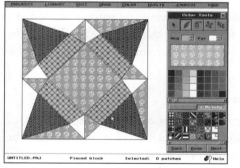

1. To color a quilt block that's been stored in your Sketchbook, pull down the **Color** menu and select **Toolbox**.

2. Click on your fabric (use the scroll bar to find it if you can't see it) or on a solid color.

3. Click on the Spraycan tool to fill multiple patches with the fabric or color. Click on the Paintbrush tool to fill a single patch.

4. Change a selected fabric's color by clicking the **Prints** button and then clicking on a solid color. The colors in the **Bkg** and **Fgr** box will change. You can also use the scroll bars beside those boxes to change the fabric's color yourself.

5. When you're satisfied with the block's coloring and fabrics, click the **Keep** button to add it to your Sketchbook.

You should create numerous different colorings of each block in your Sketchbook so that you have a lot of choices to play with when you lay out your quilt. You can scroll through your different saved versions of the block by clicking the **Next** and **Back** buttons in the Color toolbox.

EXPERIMENT WITH DIFFERENT BLOCK COLORINGS

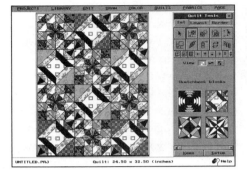

1. To lay out the blocks that you've filled with fabric, pull down the **Quilts** menu and select **Toolbox**. Then choose **New Quilt** from the **Quilts** menu, select a layout, and click **OK**.

2. Click on the **Set** tab. At first all the blocks stored in your Sketchbook will appear in black and white. Click repeatedly on the block to see the different colorings you've saved.

3. Click on the colored block of your choice and then click on the spot in your quilt outline where you want to place it.

4. To place a solid-colored square in your quilt, click on the **Plain Block** tool, click on the fabric and color, and then click on the spot on your quilt where you want a solid block.

Even after a quilt is laid out, it's not too late to change colors and fabrics. To recolor an individual patch, click on the Paintbrush tool, click on the color or fabric you want, and then click on the patch you want to recolor. Use the Spraycan tool to recolor all patches in a block that have the same coloring. Click on the Spraycan tool, and then click on a patch to select all patches in the block with the same coloring. You can then click on the fabric or color you want to use to recolor those patches.

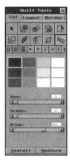

MIX YOUR OWN COLORS WITH THE RGB TOOL

Click on the RGB tool in the Quilt toolbox to mix your own colors. RGB stands for red/green/blue. You can change any color into any other color by changing the amounts of red, green, or blue that it contains. Click on the color chip you want to change, and move the slides on the bars to change the color. Keep in mind that if you've used this color elsewhere in your quilt design, all of its occurrences will change to the new color you create.

CHOOSE FROM BAZILLIONS OF FABRICS IN ELECTRIC QUILT

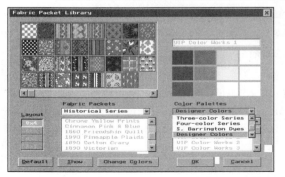

Electric Quilt's fabrics come in fabric selections called "packets." Pull down the **Library** menu and select **Fabric Packets** to display the collections of fabrics. Think of them as digital fabric medleys. When you install one in your Sketchbook, it replaces the fabrics currently in the Sketchbook. You can choose from a wide range of historical, contemporary, and designer packets. To display one, click on its name and then on **Show**. You can change its color palette too (the palettes are listed on the right). To do so, choose a palette, click on **Change Colors**, and the fabrics' colors will change. Click **OK** to add it to your Sketchbook.

FIND MORE FABRICS IN THE FABRIC LIBRARIES

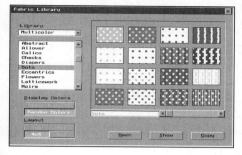

Still more fabrics are available individually in Electric Quilt's fabric libraries. Pull down the **Library** menu and select **Fabric Library** to see the basic fabric collections, which run the gamut from "diaper" prints to dots, eccentrics, and flowers. They will be displayed in the color palette that's currently installed in your Sketchbook. Click on any fabric you like, and then click on **Copy** to add it to your Sketchbook. The fabric libraries differ from the fabric packets just described in that you add fabrics from the library one at a time to your Sketchbook, whereas choosing a fabric packet adds all of the fabrics in that packet to the Sketchbook at once.

ADD PIZZAZZ WITH THE COLOR LIBRARY

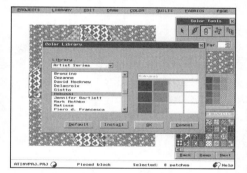

Electric Quilt also features a number of palettes of coordinated colors. Pull down the **Library** menu and select **Color Library** to view all of the color palettes in the Color Library. You can choose from a wide range of color palettes, from historical ones to the favorite colors of well-known artists. Select the library you like and then click **Install** to replace the color palette currently in your library. (If you're like us, that will be the default one.) All of your block and fabric colorings will be replaced by different colors of comparable value (remember our discussion in Chapter 10 on value?). You can give your quilt a whole new color with one click of the button simply by swapping in a new color palette.

USING AND MAKING FABRIC DESIGNS IN QUILT-PRO

Quilt-Pro lets you import fabric designs that you've scanned or drawn in a drawing program. You can also buy from Quilt-Pro disks of scanned images of leading fabric lines. When you buy Quilt-Pro, it comes with some fabric designs built in. Although these aren't real fabrics—they're designs drawn in a drawing program— their wide variety of florals, geometrics, stripes, and plaids makes them wonderful tools for coloring quilts, and you can change their colors to suit your whim.

HOW TO IMPORT IMAGES THAT YOU DRAW OR SCAN TO MAKE FABRICS IN QUILT-PRO

1. Once you've scanned and cropped the fabric design, save it as a BMP file, or as a PICT file on the Mac. Copy it to one of Quilt-Pro's fabric directories, but be sure you don't give it the name of a fabric already in the directory. The main fabric directory is \QUILTPRO\FABRICS, or the Fabrics folder on the Mac. It contains subdirectories for different fabric types like florals, novelty prints, and geometrics. You can copy it to any of these directories or subfolders.

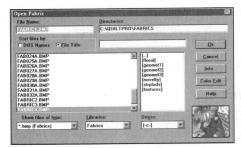

2. Head to Quilt-Pro's Fabric Palette. If it's not on your main Quilt-Pro screen, pull down the **Options** menu and choose **Show Fabrics**. Position your mouse cursor over the fabric that you wish to replace with your new fabric. Then click the right mouse button (double-click on a Macintosh) to bring up the Open Fabric dialog box.

3. In the Open Fabric dialog box, scroll through the list of file names and select the name of your scanned fabric. Click **OK** on the PC (**Open** on the Mac) to add it to the palette. On a PC, you can also change the colors in your scanned fabric by clicking the **Color Edit** button in the Open Fabric dialog box. This brings up the Fabric Palette Editor. The Mac version does not have a Fabric Palette Editor. Instead, you can simply open the PICT file in any graphic program (such as SuperPaint), change the colors, and save it as a new PICT file.

4. In the Fabric Palette Editor on the PC, you can change any color in your scanned fabric by clicking on the color in the fabric sample. A frame will appear around the corresponding color in the Fabric Palette. To specify a new color, click on the color of your choice in the Color Palette at the bottom of the dialog box. Click **OK** when you are done.

5. Color your block with your scanned fabrics by clicking on the Paint tool (the paintbrush icon on the PC, the bucket icon on the Mac), selecting the fabric in the palette, and then clicking on a patch.

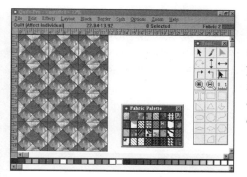

6. As you can see, because of how tightly patterns are scaled down on a computer screen, this isn't exactly how your quilt would look if you used the fabrics you scanned to create it, but it does give you some idea of the play of color in the resulting quilt.

7. Pull down the **File** menu and select **Save Fabric Palette**. Quilt-Pro will prompt you to type a name with an .FPL suffix. The next time you load your quilt layout or block design you will also need to load its fabric palette. Otherwise, Quilt-Pro will color the design with the default fabric palette—the one that's loaded at the time.

USE THE FABRIC LIBRARIES IN QUILT-PRO

Quilt-Pro comes with lots of digitally designed fabrics, from jazzy geometrics to muted calicos. You can use them as they are or change their colors. One thing that's not apparent about the program is that these fabrics are stored in different libraries. To use them, you must open the library, add the fabric you want to use to the Fabric Palette on the main Quilt-Pro screen, and then save the Fabric Palette with a new name. To use that selection of fabrics again, or to open a quilt block or design colored with those fabrics, you must open that particular fabric palette.

1. To change the fabrics in the Fabric Palette, position your cursor over a fabric and click the right mouse button (double-click it on a Mac). The Open Fabric dialog box opens.

2. Scroll through the directories to find fabrics you like. Click on the name of a fabric to see a sample displayed in the lower right of the dialog box (on the right side of the dialog box on the Mac). To add a displayed fabric to your palette, click **OK** on the PC, **Open** on the Mac.

REMEMBER

When you open a saved quilt, open its fabric palette too so that the blocks will appear with the fabrics you used to color them. If you don't, Quilt-Pro will display the quilt with fabrics you did not intend. To open a fabric palette, pull down the File menu and select Open Fabric Palette.

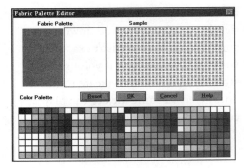

3. To change a fabric's colors, click the **Color Edit** button in the Open Fabric dialog box, and proceed as described in step 5 of the previous section.

4. When you've finished adding new fabrics to your palette, save the new palette by pulling down the **File** menu and selecting **Save Fabric Palette**.

USE SUPERPAINT TO CREATE COMPUTER-GENERATED FABRIC FILLS FOR USE IN QUILT-PRO

If you're using the Macintosh version of Quilt-Pro, here's how to create fabric fills with SuperPaint that you can use to color blocks in Quilt-Pro.

1. First create a new folder on your hard drive called Fabrics, and then launch SuperPaint.

Turn to the color gallery to see some examples of scanned fabrics and fabric fills created in SuperPaint, including a quilt laid out in Quilt-Pro.

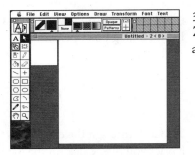

2. Click on the paintbrush icon to go to the Paint layer of the program. Pull down the **File** menu and select **Document Info**. In the dialog box that appears, set the width and height to 1 inch and click **OK**. This will create a small document on your screen.

3. Pull down the **View** menu and select **Zoom In**. This will magnify the page and make it easier to work with.

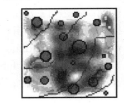

4. Select a texture from the Textures palette, pull down the **Paint** menu, and select **Fill**. The entire 1-by-1-inch document will fill with the selected texture. Or use the paint tools to create your own texture. Overlap shapes, layer colors—be creative.

5. When the document is complete, pull down the **File** menu and select **Save**. Select the **Fabrics** folder (the one you made earlier) and give your fabric a unique name, something to jog your memory, like Green/Yellow Swirl. Click the **Save As** button and select **PICT** from the text box next to it. Then click **Save**.

For a PICT file to work correctly in Quilt-Pro, the entire document must be filled with the image, which is why we're using such a small document. The document can be any size you want, but keep in mind that a 1-by-1-inch PICT file is approximately 18KB, while an 8½-by-11-inch PICT file is approximately 400KB.

T * I * P

Move your fabric file into Quilt-Pro's Fabrics folder for faster access.

One fabric fill with four different effects applied to it.

To vary the effects in one fabric-like fill, select the entire document (press **COMMAND-A**) and pull down the **Paint** menu. Then select **Invert**, **Splatter**, **Trace Edges**, **Lighten**, **Darken**, and so on. You'll see why it's important to keep the files small—they add up fast!

USING AND CREATING DIGITAL FABRIC FILLS IN DRAWING PROGRAMS

Drawing programs are supposed to be the most versatile at letting you fill your designs with undulating waves of purple and other weave-like confections. But they're not as easy to use as quilt design software in this regard. True, they give you more ideas for fill patterns, and they let you import all kinds of computer graphics with which you can fill quilt patches. But importing scanned fabrics into them is sometimes a pain, and creating fabric-like fills is often an ordeal you may want to skip. Worse, working with fills as you design quilts in drawing software is cumbersome. (See our tutorials on working with values in Chapter 10 to learn a better way.) But it can be done, and here's how.

USING SCANNED FABRICS AND CREATING FABRIC-LIKE COLOR FILLS IN CORELDRAW

If the people who designed CorelDraw ran a fast-food joint, it wouldn't be the kind of place where you could just walk in and order the chicken. You'd have to choose from all kinds of chicken: crispy, light-crispy, tender-crispy, extra-crispy, cardiovascularly safe crispy, boiled, char-broiled, and breaded. Then, to go along with it, you'd have to choose from corn bread, oatmeal bread, white bread, wheat bread, rye bread, potato sticks, potato curls, potato salad, coleslaw, baked beans, and on and on. A similarly overwhelming bounty of choices confronts you when you want to create patterns and colors to fill quilt blocks in CorelDraw. Of your many options, the most noteworthy are these:

- Import scanned fabric and turn it into fill patterns
- Riffle through CorelDraw's texture and pattern libraries, where you'll find many textures to put in your designs
- Draw your own full-color patterns to use as fills

Which do we prefer? We skip the whole fiasco and use Electric Quilt, or lay the fabric on the floor. But if you insist on doing it, here's how.

TURN SCANNED FABRIC INTO FABRIC FILLS IN CORELDRAW

1. You can scan your fabric directly into CorelDraw 7 or, in earlier versions, into Corel's Photo-Paint, a photo touchup, paint-like program. In CorelDraw 7, pull down the **File** menu and select **Acquire from CorelScan**. In earlier versions, pop into Photo-Paint, pull down its **File** menu, select **Acquire Image**, slide over to **Select Source**, select your scanner, and then click **Acquire**.

2. Once you scan the fabric, you need to boost its brightness a good bit, since it will appear dark. In CorelDraw 7, pull down the **Effects** menu and choose **Color Adjustment**. In earlier versions, choose **Color** from the **Effects** menu in Photo-Paint.

3. Save the file in BMP format to get the best color value and to keep it small. Be sure to save it in a subdirectory where you can find it later. (We like \COREL\CUSTOM.) Give it a name that will make it stand out from other files, like FAB_NAME.

4. Open the scanned fabric in CorelDraw by pulling down the **File** menu, selecting **Import**, and then double-clicking the name of the scanned fabric file.

5. To make your fabric scan into a fill pattern in CorelDraw 7, pull down the **Tools** menu, select **Create**, and then slide over to **Pattern**. In CorelDraw 5, pull down the **Special** menu and select **Create Pattern**.

6. Click the **Full Color** button and then click **OK**. Large crosshairs appear. Drag the mouse, holding the button down, to select a very small square. We like to make it perfectly square because Corel is going to tile it, and the fabric pattern will appear less distorted that way. Click **OK** in the dialog box that appears.

7. CorelDraw will prompt you for a name with a .PAT extension. Again, we like to preface it with the word "fabric" or "fab" so that we know it's a fabric scan. Click **OK** after you've typed the pattern name.

8. To load your fill pattern into a quilt block, click on the Fill tool. From the fly-out menu (in CorelDraw 7 and in CorelDraw 5), click on the Pattern Fill icon in CorelDraw 7 or the Full Color Pattern icon in Corel Draw 5. In CorelDraw 7, click **Full Color** in the dialog box that appears.

9. Click **Load**. Then click on the name of your pattern (FABRIC.PAT, for instance), and click **Import** in CorelDraw 7, **OK** in CorelDraw 5. Click **OK** again in the Pattern dialog box. This will place your pattern on the Fill palette, and it will also fill any shape that is selected with the pattern.

10. To use your pattern, click on the Fill tool and then click on the icon that opens the Special Fill Roll-Up in CorelDraw 7 or the Fill Roll-Up in CorelDraw 5. In CorelDraw 7, select **Special Fill** under Attributes.

11. Click on the Pattern icon in CorelDraw 7, and then select **Full Color** from the drop-down list box. In CorelDraw 5, simply click on the Full Color Pattern icon.

JUDY & GLORIA'S ADVICE FOR FABRIC SCANNING SANITY

We prefer to scan fabric into the software that came with our scanners rather than scanning directly into drawing programs—it's just a lot simpler. We save the fabric as a BMP or PICT file and then hop into our drawing program and turn the scan into a pattern fill, beginning with step 4 here.

REMEMBER

Be sure that Full Color is checked, or this is not going to work.

Fill tool icon.

CorelDraw 7 fly-out menu.

CorelDraw 5 fly-out menu.

Pattern Fill icon.   Full Color Pattern fill icon.

12. Click on the arrow on the sample pattern to display the Fill palette. Scroll until you find the pattern you created, and click to select it (double-click in CorelDraw 5). Using the Pick tool, select the patches to which you want to apply the pattern, and then click **Apply**.

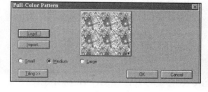
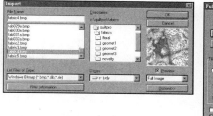
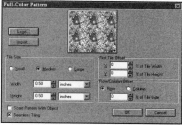

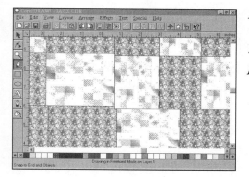

Adding fabric to your quilt designs in CorelDraw isn't all that helpful. The screen is small, the prints aren't scaled properly, and it's just a hassle.

USE THE FILL ROLL-UP LIBRARY TO FILL YOUR QUILTS WITH CLOUDS AND BUBBLES

Probably more useful than the ability to paint quilt blocks with fabrics in CorelDraw is the variety of fill patterns and colors you'll find in CorelDraw's Fill Roll-Up (it's called the Special Fill Roll-Up in CorelDraw 7, but we'll just refer to it as the Fill Roll-Up here for the sake of simplicity). There are two-color patterns, full-color patterns, textures like clouds and bubbles, and fountain fills that fill your patches with gradations of color.

These patterns are bolder and more vibrant than any scanned fabric you can import. You can edit them and change their colors. Here's a brief tour.

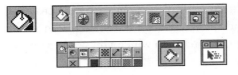

To get to the Fill Roll-Up, click on the Fill tool. From the flyout menu (in CorelDraw 7 and in CorelDraw 5), click on the Fill Roll-Up icon (in CorelDraw 7 and in CorelDraw 5).

The Fill Roll-Up has many personalities. Click on the Fill tool. From the flyout menu in CorelDraw 7, click on the Fill Color icon. This is the Fill Roll-Up's color wheel persona. You can select solid colors and mix new colors here. To get this color-mixing box in CorelDraw 5, simply click on the color wheel button in the Fill Roll-Up, and then click **Edit**.

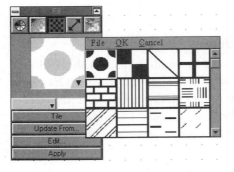

When you click on the buttons at the top of the Fill Roll-Up, you get dialog boxes that let you play with different kinds of patterns. This is the two-color pattern box. In CorelDraw 7, click on the Pattern icon and select **2-color** from the drop-down list box. In CorelDraw 5, simply click on the Two-Color Pattern icon. Then click on the downward-pointing arrow on the crazy-looking design and you'll be able to choose from more two-color patterns. You can also change their colors. These are great patterns to use as fills for quilt designs. Click **Edit** to change the pattern or to create your own pattern.

The Texture Fill box is where you find things that look like hand-dyed fabric.

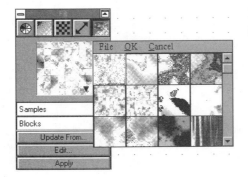

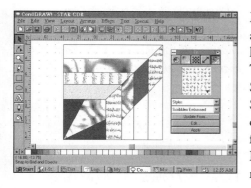

Most of the texture fills look tie-dyed and modernistic. They have names like Cosmic Clouds and Bubble Land. The only calico-like texture is in the Styles texture library under the name Scribbles Embossed. You can change its colors to create a palette of small-print fabrics. (CorelDraw 7 users: The Special Fill Roll-Up does not show texture names, only samples. To see the names, click on the Fill tool and then click on the Texture Fill icon in the fly-out menu. This brings up the Texture Fills dialog box.)

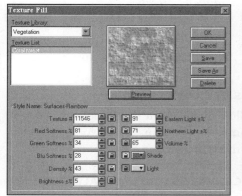

The Texture Fill dialog box in CorelDraw 7.

The Texture Fill dialog box in CorelDraw 5.

You can alter the color, brightness, and other graphic values of the textures in Corel's texture library to make infinite variations. Click **Edit** in the Fill Roll-Up to reach the dialog box to do it.

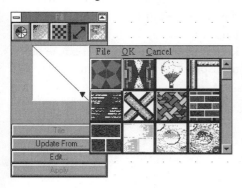

There are full-color patterns as well as textures. Yes, it's confusing, but it's good to know where to go if you want to fill a quilt with Jules Verne's balloons. In CorelDraw 7's Fill Roll-Up, click on the pattern icon and then select Full Color from the list box. In CorelDraw 5, click on the Full Color Pattern icon in the Fill Roll-Up. Click on the downward-pointing arrow on the design to see a library of more patterns.

CORELDRAW SUPER-QUILTER COLORING TIP

When you're coloring a quilt block, it can be a pain to have to fish around in CorelDraw's texture libraries to find a particular texture that you previously used to fill a patch. You want to fill a new patch with the same texture, but how do you get back to *it? Easy. Select the patch to be filled, then click the Eyedropper tool in CorelDraw 7, or click the Update From button in earlier versions. A fat arrow appears. Move it to the patch whose texture you want to load, and click on the patch. Its texture will appear in the roll-up. Now click Apply.*

DESIGN TIP

Because they hog memory, color patterns can really slow down your drawing program and video display. So fight the urge to use them until the very end of the design process—when you've finished drawing your quilt block and its patches, or when you've already laid out your quilt design.

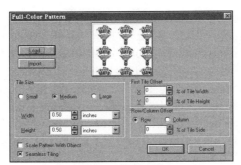

*This dialog box, which lets you change any of CorelDraw's full-color patterns, appears when you click on the **Edit** button beneath the pattern.*

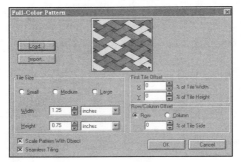

You can tell CorelDraw how to tile your patterns. To get an idea of what the pattern would look like in a real quilt, you can scale the pattern to the quilt block and set it to its "real world" width and height.

USING SCANNED FABRICS AND CREATING FABRIC-LIKE COLOR FILLS IN CANVAS 5.0

To scan directly into Canvas 5.0, first follow the excellent instructions in the program's manual to install a Photoshop-compatible plug-in. When you've got your scan, follow these instructions to import the scan into Canvas 5.0.

IMPORT A SCANNED FABRIC INTO THE CANVAS 5.0 TEXTURES PALETTE

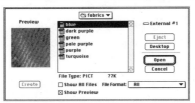

1. To import a scan into Canvas 5.0, begin by pulling down the **File** menu and selecting **Open**. In the directory, find and select the fabric that you would like to add. Then click **Open**. The fabric appears on your document.

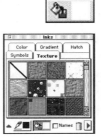

2. Press and hold the mouse button down on the **Fill Inks** button. Drag the palette box away from the toolbox to keep it open. Click on the **Texture** tab to display the Texture palette.

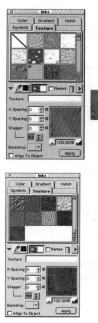

3. Click on the small triangle on the lower left edge of the palette to open the Texture palette manager. Drag the fabric square to the preview box. The fabric square will fill the box.

4. To add your fabric to the Texture palette, drag it from the preview box to the Texture palette. The fabric is now displayed as a new texture at the bottom of the palette.

5. Click on the small triangle to close the Texture palette manager. Use the fabric fill as you would any other fill: Just click on it to fill a selected shape.

ADD YOUR FABRIC SCAN TO THE TEXTURE PALETTE

1. To save any added fabric scans to the default Texture palette, first click on the arrow to the right of the trash can in the Inks palette and select **Save Texture Inks.** Click to open the **Color Inks** folder, if it is not already open. Type **Textures** in the **Save Canvas Palette As** box.

2. A dialog box will ask if you want to replace the existing Textures file. Click **Replace.** You have now saved the entire set, including your fabric scan, as your default Texture palette.

You may decide to work in a particular palette of fabrics and need to scan them into your computer to use as fills. This range of fabrics can be saved under a unique name and be available for loading into Canvas 5.0 on command. Again, we advocate working with values and doing this away from your computer. But this is something to consider if you are doing a commission piece and want to print out a color rendering of a proposed quilt.

T * I * P

- *You can delete any unwanted texture by selecting the texture in the Texture palette and dragging it to the trash can on the Inks palette (not the trash can on your desktop).*

- *Remember to keep the scanned image small. If the file contains more than 30KB, save a smaller portion of it.*

T * I * P

If you erase any of the palettes included with Canvas, just reload what you need from the program disks.

CANVAS 3.5 USERS

If you want to use scans for fills, you'll need to purchase an add-on module (contact http://www. deneba.com for more information). We suggest you upgrade to Canvas 5.0 instead or, if you don't have a PowerPC Macintosh, buy SuperPaint or Deneba artWorks.

DON'T REDRAW—CUSTOMIZE

You can customize a current fill to create a new one. For example, draw a square with a selected fill pattern, such as hatch lines. Next do something to the pattern-filled square, like add lines, circles, or teeny squares. Then add it to your palette.

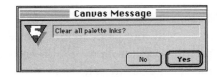

1. To save a range of fabrics to use for special projects, open the Inks palette, click on the Texture tab, and click the downward-pointing arrow to display the palette manager, as described earlier. To the right of the trash can is an arrow pointing to the right. Click on the arrow and select **Clear Palette Inks**. A warning box appears asking if you really want to do this. It may seem frightening to clear all the palette inks, but we'll show you how to get them back. So click **Yes**. The Texture palette is now empty.

2. Following the directions given earlier on importing a scanned fabric, insert each of the fabrics that you want to include in the Texture palette.

3. When you've added all the fabrics you need, click on the arrow to the right of the trash can in the Inks palette box and select **Save Texture Inks**. In the **Save Texture Inks** dialog box, type a new name in the **Save Canvas Palette As** box. Do not use the name of an existing palette—if you do, you will erase that palette.

Whenever you want to load a particular fabric set, open the Inks palette and click on the **Texture** tab. Click on the arrow to the right of the trash can in the palette box and select **Load Texture Inks**. Then click to select the name of the set you want to load, and click **Open**. That's it!

To restore your default textures, choose **Load Texture Inks** and select the palette named **Textures**.

USING SCANNED FABRICS AND CREATING FABRIC-LIKE COLOR FILLS IN SUPERPAINT

ADD FABRIC SCANS TO SUPERPAINT'S TEXTURES PALETTE

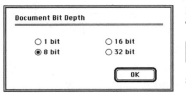

1. To add fabric scans to SuperPaint's Textures palette, go to the Draw layer by clicking on the compass icon. Pull down the **File** menu and select **Open**. In the directory, find and select the fabric that you want to add. The **Document Bit Depth** box opens. Select **8 bit** and click **OK**. The fabric will appear on your screen.

2. Click the fabric with the Selection Arrow tool.

3. Pull down the **File** menu and select **Selection to Texture**. A dialog box opens, indicating that you are inside the **My Textures** folder.

4. Type a name for the fabric scan in the **Save Texture As** box. Click **Save**. You can use the fill as you would any other texture.

CREATE FABRIC-LIKE PATTERNS WITH SUPERPAINT

1. To create stunning fabric-like patterns with SuperPaint, go to the Paint layer by clicking on the paintbrush icon in the upper left corner of your screen.

2. Select a texture or a solid color and a tool such as the Airbrush tool and start doodling on your screen.

3. Continue overlapping colors until you have something interesting.

4. Use the Rectangle Selection tool to select a portion of the painted area.

5. Pull down the **File** menu and select **Selection to Texture**. In the dialog box that appears type a name for your new texture and click **Save**.

Your newly created fabric-like pattern is now in the Textures palette. To use it, go back to the Draw layer by clicking on the compass icon in the upper left corner of your screen, and start drawing.

CHAPTER 17

HOW TO USE YOUR COMPUTER TO
PRINT PHOTOS AND OTHER ART ON FABRIC

You can use your computer to print on fabric, but do you really want to? Here's what you should know before you try.

We've all seen it, and we want to do it. We want to make one of those sweet and glorious remembrance quilts pastiched with pictures of Grandma in her wedding dress and grandpa with his farm hoe. We've heard about quilters printing photos right on fabric fed through their computer printers. Does that work? And how about all those special papers that are popping up in computer stores that let you create iron-on transfers with your computer printer? Do they work? Will these high-tech toys transfer photos to fabric as crisply as those $1.25 "magic transfer" sheets you find in quilt catalogs?

We decided to find out.

We purchased some of those special fabric sheets that you can print in inkjet printers. We purchased a number of different brands of papers that let you create iron-on T-shirt transfers with your computer printer. We also purchased an assortment of photo transfer papers from quilt catalogs, the kind that do not use a computer at all, but that you use with a color copier.

We used all these products to transfer a pastiche of photos and computer drawings to different types of muslin. Afterward, we put the fabric transfers through the washer and dryer multiple times to test color-fastness.

We also fed fabric directly through inkjet and laser printers. We treated the resulting printed fabric with some of the many different recipes for making computer ink permanent that are floating around the Internet. We also tried some of our own recipes, using dye-setting chemicals commonly found at art stores.

We discovered some pretty fascinating things about these techniques and products. Some are useful, some less so. All have limitations. What's more, the cost and complexity of some of the techniques make those $1.25 "magic transfer" sheets in quilt catalogs a comparative bargain.

THINGS TO KNOW ABOUT PRINTING PICTURES WITH ANY PRINTER

What appears on your computer screen won't necessarily appear on your fabric if you feed it through the printer. That's true of both laser and inkjet printers. There are several reasons why the color or black-and-white picture that looks so pretty on your screen may look disappointing when it's printed.

- The printer's low resolution may make the picture look grainy. Printers print by placing a certain number of dots per inch on a sheet of paper. Low-cost inkjet printers often have a relatively low resolution (not many dots per inch and the dots are fatter). Most of the popular Canon bubblejet printers that are sold with craft software for under $200 print at only 360 dpi on fabric or other treated sheets. Slightly better inkjets that print at 720 dpi retail for $300 to $400. Better still are inkjets that print at 1,400 dpi and retail for $300 to $460. High-end desktop publishing printers have a much higher resolution and thus print sharper pictures.

- The picture's low resolution may make it look grainy when it's enlarged. The outlines of your picture may look smooth on your screen, but when you print it, the picture looks like blocks of color or gray stacked on top of each other. That's because when the printer magnifies the image's pixels to make them fit the dimensions that you specify, the number of dots per inch doesn't increase, the dots just get bigger and clunkier. To make the picture look better, you should print it smaller or rescan it at a higher resolution.

- The printer may not always interpret colors correctly. Computer monitors create colors by emitting light, while printers create colors by placing ink on paper that reflects light. Monitors often create colors that printers can't print, and a certain amount of intelligence is required on the part of the printer to interpret the monitor's colors. The printer needs to translate that pale sepia in your photograph, using the limited number of golds in its palette. Needless to say, printers don't always interpret colors perfectly, but some do a much better job than others. Some printers come with software that lets you preview the way pictures will print and correct the colors. Some programs like Corel Photo-Paint include color correction and calibration features, but these features aren't perfect and they're tricky to use. Some artists use a color target from a photo store to match colors between their digital image and printout. None of the solutions to mismatched colors is simple.

All that said, it's important to understand the limitations of your printer before embarking on any project. If you know that the photos of that Hawaiian sunset you scanned are going to print a garish orange, or that the soft sepia tones of that antique sketch will turn into a grainy yellow haze when printed, you may need to investigate alternatives for printing images on fabric. We talk about some of these later in the chapter.

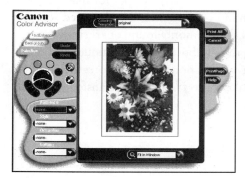

Canon printers include color correction software that lets you preview your pictures before you print them, but it rarely gives you an accurate view of what your picture will actually look like when printed. Adjusting colors with it is tricky too. Use graphics processing software instead.

She sallied forth to scold them into harmony and plenty.

If your printer prints at a low resolution, a picture may look like it's made of tiles when it's enlarged and printed. Similarly, if the picture itself is a low-resolution one, it will look like tiles when it's enlarged and printed. The solution is to tell the printer to print the picture smaller.

FEEDING FABRIC THROUGH COMPUTER PRINTERS

You hear about it all the time: quilters feeding muslin ironed onto freezer paper through their laser or inkjet printers.

Is it safe? Yes, perfectly. It won't harm the printer. The printer's heat is localized enough that it won't melt the plastic-coated paper backing onto the roller. (Although if you head to a copy store and ask them to run muslin through their expensive laser printers, the employees will probably freak. People who work at copy shops tend not to be as adventurous with technology as quilters.)

Canon sells fabric sheets that you can print on in Canon inkjet printers (they work in other inkjet printers too, but Canon won't guarantee it). The fabric is lightly starched and adhered to a plastic sheet similar to a transparency. After you print your photo or other image on the fabric, you peel off the plastic backing and then rinse the fabric and slosh it around in a chemical bath to fix the ink.

Is the fabric treated with anything special to help it hold ink? We think it is, based on some of our tests and on the fact that the water-soluble ink doesn't bleed off the fabric when it's rinsed prior to the chemical bath. Sources at Canon tell us that the fabric is specially treated, but what it's treated with is a trade secret. Other sources at Canon, however, insist that the fabric isn't treated at all. The trade secret is the kind of muslin that's used to make these fabric sheets. Canon apparently did extensive research into the thread count, the type of cotton, and the tightness of the weave that will hold ink the best. The good news is that the fabric they use for these sheets is commonly available.

We talk more about Canon Fabric Sheets later in this chapter, and also reveal our money-saving home-brew recipe for pretreating fabric and mixing up a chemical bath similar to that used to set ink in the Canon sheets.

HISTORICAL NOTE

Many workplace laser printers have been sacrificed by quilters on the Internet to test fabric printing recipes. So far there have been no reported fatalities among the printers. In fact, an internal newsletter at Hewlett-Packard reportedly told employees how to feed fabric through the company's laser printers.

JUDY & GLORIA'S TIPS FOR
PREPARING FABRIC TO FEED THROUGH PRINTERS

1. Buy 100 percent cotton muslin with a high thread count, mercerized white cotton, or cotton broadcloth. Other fabrics, like polyester or silk, won't work. The cotton fabric should be crisp, thin, tightly woven, and as smooth as possible. Ideally, you want fabric that's heavier than a bed sheet but thinner than duck cloth. Avoid anything nubby or "hairy," since you'll be able to print the crispest images on smooth fabric. As Canon found, the type of fabric, its weave, and its thread count can make a big difference in how well it holds ink. Some quilters do not prewash fabric before printing on it, but we're uncomfortable with the uncertainty that that injects in our lives.

2. Buy high-quality freezer paper, like Reynolds. Cheap freezer paper separates from the fabric. It also sometimes doesn't ride through the printer as well as more substantial paper. Reynolds has a nice thick plastic coating that doesn't separate from the fabric.

3. Theoretically, you cut a piece of freezer paper 8½ by 11 inches—letterhead size—and iron it on a piece of muslin the same size. But we like to do things quickly and we know you do too, and you should have lots of these sheets handy to experiment with. So . . .

4. Unroll about two yards of freezer paper. With a ruler and a couple of sheets of letterhead, trace about a dozen 8½-by-11-inch segments with a pencil on the paper.

5. Iron a yard or two of muslin, and then iron the marked freezer paper onto the fabric. Cut out your letter-sized pieces with scissors or a rotary cutter, and then iron each paper-backed fabric sheet again, on both front and back, to make it extra flat.

You can feed these sheets through both inkjet and laser printers just as you would a normal sheet of paper. But before you print, always print test images on regular paper. If you're using a color inkjet, to save ink in those pricey color ink cartridges, print test images in black and white to get the image's size right and then print one in color to check the colors.

Once you've printed on your fabric sheet, you need to make the image permanent. How you do that will depend on your printer.

PREPARING A PHOTO OR OTHER ART FOR PRINTING ON FABRIC

Whether you plan to print your picture directly on fabric or to turn it into a negative for sun printing or blueprinting as we describe in the next chapter, you'll first need to get your art into the computer and prep it in a graphics program.

We talk about scanning art in Chapter 15 and provide tips for working with scanners. But here are some special considerations for getting a picture ready for printing on fabric:

- If you're going to print a photo, select one with no shadows. The faces should be well-lit, especially the eyes. If it's a color photo, the colors should be sharp.

- If you're using an old drawing, keep in mind that sometimes a gray-scale scan of a black-and-white drawing will look better than a scan with the line drawing setting. Similarly, if it's an old black-and-white photo, sometimes a color scan will look better than one done with the gray setting.

- If you plan to print a photo on a laser or inkjet printer with a resolution of 360 to 1,400 dots per inch (dpi), you should scan the photo at 120 to 180 dpi for the best results. A picture scanned at a higher resolution will be unwieldy in size (in other words, it will use so much computer memory that it will be hard or impossible to work with), will eat disk space, and slow down your graphics software. And you won't get any better resolution in exchange when you print it. Now, that assumes you'll be printing the photo in its original size. You'll need to scan the photo at a higher resolution if you plan to enlarge it, especially if it's a color photo. If you enlarge a photo with your graphics software, the computer will "fill it in," guessing the color the extra pixels should be. Your picture can end up looking muddy. So don't leave things to the computer's guesswork. If you plan to enlarge your picture to twice its original size, and you'd normally scan it at 150 dpi to print it in its original size, scan it at twice the resolution (300 dpi) to print in the larger size. Likewise, if you plan to print your picture at half its original size, scan it at half the resolution (75 dpi).

- If your picture is a line drawing, scan it at the same resolution that your printer produces. For instance, if you're printing on a 360 dpi printer, scan line drawings at 360 dpi. Otherwise the pictures will print with jagged lines. If you plan to enlarge the picture, scan it at a proportionally higher resolution as discussed above.

- Scan only as much of the image as you want. Remember, you ideally want to keep that image as small as possible so it's easy to work with. If your scanner has a prescan feature, select the area you want to scan with the selection marquee.

- Ideally you should save the scan as a TIFF. With this format you can alter the picture's color balance or grays, as well as resize it without distorting the halftone screen, which is the pattern of dots your computer uses to print the picture. The PCX file format and the PICT format on the Mac are acceptable alternatives for color pictures. See Appendix A, "The Quilter's Guide to Computer Graphics," for more on file formats.

Always save your original scan to one file and subsequent tweaks of the image to other files. That way, if you screw up the picture, you can always go back to the original scan.

- Use your scanning software or a graphics program like Paint Shop Pro or LView to spruce up the picture. If it's black-and-white line art, load the paint-brush tool with white (or black) and click on errant blemishes to erase them. Adjust the width of the paintbrush to match the size and extent of blemishes.

- Adjust the picture's colors to brighten them up if you like, or boost the picture's contrast and brightness. The latter is especially true if the picture is a gray one, but it can also make a line drawing less apt to print dark or be marred by gray streaks. Boost the brightness by about 15 percent and the contrast by 10 percent. If your graphics software includes a "sharpen" command, use it to sharpen the highlights of a dark photograph.

- Most scanned pictures need to be sharpened, regardless of the resolution at which you scanned them. Use the sharpening feature in your graphics software to do this.

- If you're going to print your fabric in an inkjet printer, use the color saturation adjustment in your graphics software to deepen the image's color intensity. Since

TAKE HEED!

In previous chapters we've told you to scan art at lower resolutions—100 dpi for fabric that you plan to use in your quilt designs or clip art that you want to make into appliqué designs. If you plan to put a picture on the Internet, you also need to scan it at a low resolution, so it won't take Net surfers a long time to download. But images you print on fabric are a different matter: You want the detail that a high-resolution scan will give you. However, if your PC has less than 16MB RAM, a high-resolution scan can sometimes crash your graphics software when you crop and manipulate the image, because the file size is so large (depending, of course, on the software). If that happens, experiment by scanning at lower resolutions to create smaller files.

USE SPECIAL CARE WHEN ADJUSTING COLORS IF YOU'LL BE PRINTING ON T-SHIRT TRANSFER PAPER

If you're going to print your image on T-shirt transfer paper, note that colors printed on that paper tend to turn out darker and more acid. Sometimes they're more garish. Images often lose their coloring subtleties. This is probably because the ink is being absorbed into a glue-like material. You'll want to sharpen the image and boost its brightness, but you need to use special care when adjusting the colors. Frankly, sometimes images that print well on fabric print too dark and gaudy when turned into a T-shirt transfer.

fabric soaks up more ink than paper does, an image's colors will appear lighter when printed on fabric. We got the best results by increasing cyan, magenta, and yellow by 25 percent and boosting the saturation by about 25 percent.

- If you're going to print a gray-scale image, boost its darkness by about 25 to 30 percent.

- Crop your image tightly, cutting out any unnecessary portions. If it's a photo, use the oval or circular crop to cut it like an old-fashioned framed photo.

- Run a test print on paper to check colors and determine the size you want the picture to be. If the picture prints grainy, try printing it at its true size, rather than expanding it to the size of the paper. If the picture prints dark, try going back to your graphics software and boosting its contrast and brightness.

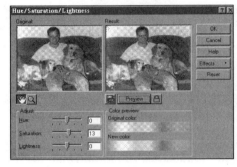

When printing an image on fabric, boost the color saturation of the picture so that the printer dumps more color into the absorbent cotton. The Photo-Paint module in CorelDraw is great for preparing photos for printing on fabric.

If you have a scanner, the software that came with it is probably perfectly adequate for sprucing up photos and other art for printing on fabric. Slider bars in Logitech's scanner software make it easy to boost contrast, brightness, and color levels in a photo.

These scans of drawings from an old Nancy Drew novel were printed on freezer paper–backed muslin with a laser printer. The grayed-out print on the left is the original scan. The crisper-lined print on the right is the same image with the brightness increased by 15 percent and the contrast increased by 10 percent. These adjustments were made in the scanner's software after the picture was scanned.

A detail from Judy's Nancy Drew quilt.

Judy's mom made many copies of this photo of herself in her high school's darkroom to send to the boys during World War II. (Notice the airman's wings on her jacket. She had several versions of this photo, with a different pin in each, to send to different branches of the armed forces.) On the left is the darkened, partially faded, splotched original. On the right is a digitized version that was touched up in Corel Photo-Paint. We turned up the contrast and brightness, rubbed out the holes in the photo with the Paint tool, and smeared a little bright paint around the hair to make it stand out. It's now ready to e-mail to a new generation of beaus—or to print on fabric.

Adobe's Photoshop, available for both PCs and Macs, is the ultimate program for working with photos. It was the program used by the makers of the magnificent Canon quilts shown in the gallery section of this book and discussed later in this chapter. You can use this program to do anything you want to a photo, including reduce graininess, add texture, change colors, and airbrush. You can even work on different drawing layers. The program is costly (around $500), and frankly we think that for most quilters Paint Shop Pro or LView are perfectly adequate.

KNOW YOUR PAGE LAYOUT RIGHTS!

Every graphics and drawing program contains a dialog box in which you can specify how you want your picture printed on the page. You can tell the software what size to print it, how to position it on the page, and whether to print it to fill the whole page. Unfortunately, this dialog box is often well hidden. You have to fish around clicking **Option** and **Page Setup** buttons, either in the **File** menu or in the dialog box that appears when you go to print something.

This is the Page Setup dialog box in Paint Shop Pro. When you click on Maintain Aspect Ratio, the printer will print the picture to the size you specify, keeping the proportions (width to height) the same as in the original. (Type in just the width that you want the printed picture to be, and the software will calculate the corresponding height.)

HOW TO PRINT ON FABRIC WITH LASER PRINTERS

Printing freezer paper–backed muslin sheets in a single-color laser printer is as easy as feeding in sheets of paper. You just have to know what side the printer prints on, because some lasers flip pages around as they print.

Once your sheet is printed, make the image permanent by spraying it with Krylon Workable Fixitif #1306, which gives the powdery laser ink a plastic coat. Use three coats, letting it dry between coats. Some quilters on Prodigy discovered through painstaking tests that that's what works the best.

Here are some tips:

- Always do a test print on paper to make sure your image looks right and is the proper size.

- Put a new toner cartridge in your printer for the crispest images.

- Clean the roller in your printer between printing sheets of fabric. Ink sometimes builds up on the roller and smears across subsequent printings. After printing a sheet, print a couple sheets of paper with your printer's test pattern to get rid of any extra splotched ink.

- If you have problems with ink smearing on your images, general darkening of your fabric while an image is being printed, or images that are too light, try adjusting your printer's darkness dial, if it has one. If the picture is still gray or too dark, go back to your graphics software and boost the image's contrast and brightness.

- If your picture looks grainy, print it smaller for better resolution. Or rescan it at a higher resolution.

- If you spot any ink splotches or errant specks of black on your printed fabric, dampen the corner of a towel and carefully rub them off. Remember that until you spray the fabric with fixative, the image can rub off or run in water because the ink is a powdery substance that can easily wash away.

- When you spray fixative on your image, don't spray it too heavily or the image will run.

- Be careful with that fixative. The fumes are potent—and flammable. Spray it outdoors or with the windows wide open. Do not spray near flames, a gas water heater, or a furnace. Hang your fabric sheets on a portable laundry rack to dry.

WHY DO PRINTERS SOMETIMES CHOKE WHEN YOU TELL THEM TO PRINT BIG PICTURES?

You scan your godchild's tap-dance recital photos at the highest resolution possible. While the resulting graphics file is huge, it poses no problem for your 64MB super-Pentium. You can brighten it up and crop it in your graphics software without a hitch. But when you send it to the printer, the computer kicks back an out-of-memory error message. Or the printer prints only the top half of the picture. What's wrong?

If you have a laser printer, the printer may not have enough memory to print a picture so large. For instance, if your printer contains only 1MB RAM, and the picture's file is 1.5MB, the printer will print only the first 1MB of the picture. "But

• After your fabric sheet has dried, peel off the paper backing and wash the fabric in a washing machine set on gentle, with a tablespoon of Orvus quilt soap. One quilter we know who participates in quilt block swaps on the Internet laments, "I always know when there's a laser-printed quilt block in my mailbox because the envelope reeks of fixative!" You can get rid of the fixative smell by washing the fabric. Washing is also the only way to find out if your image has been sprayed with enough fixative to make it permanent.

NOTE

See the chart "Caring for Computer-Printed Fabrics" near the end of this chapter for advice on laundering your laser-printed images.

HOW TO PRINT ON FABRIC WITH INKJET PRINTERS

Color inkjet printers are amazing appliances. For under $200 you can print images of near photo quality. They have drawbacks, some of which we've already mentioned. Their resolution isn't always good, and their interpretation of colors can sometimes be garish.

But perhaps the biggest problem with inkjets is that their color ink cartridges are so expensive—from $25 to $40 each. If you're printing on fabric, you may get as few as 25 full-color 8½-by-11-inch pictures from one cartridge—fewer if the pictures you're printing are dark. Ouch! Factor in your test prints, the prints wasted by glitches, and the $3 per sheet or so you may pay for specially treated fabric sheets or T-shirt transfers and that becomes a pretty expensive proposition. So before you plan a big project with images printed on fabric, think twice about the cost and investigate alternative methods. (Read our interviews with the Canon quilters later in this chapter if you're still not convinced that putting together a quilt with inkjet-printed fabric can be costly.)

IS ONE BRAND OR MODEL OF INKJET PRINTER BETTER THAN ANOTHER FOR PRINTING ON FABRIC?

Rumors circulate the Internet incessantly extolling the virtues of one brand or model of printer over another. While there are slight variations in the inks among the many brands of printers, we've found that in general the inks are pretty similar and can be made permanent on fabric in much the same fashion.

A SMART ALTERNATIVE TO PRINTING PHOTOS ON FABRIC WITH A COMPUTER PRINTER

We love those "magic transfer" sheets that you can buy in quilt catalogs like Keepsake Quilting (800/865-9458) and Dharma Trading Company (800/542-5227). You feed these specially treated sheets through a color photocopier. You use the copier's zoom and mirror features to enlarge your photo or other art and flip it around, just as you would in a computer. Once the photo's printed, you cut out the individual transfers and iron them on your fabric. It's that simple.

These sheets run from $1.25 to $3 each (shop around!). Color photocopying at a copy store costs $1 to $1.75 per sheet. As you can see, if you plan to make a remem-

WARNING!

The color cartridges for inkjet printers are expensive. They run from $25 to $40 each. If you're printing on fabric, you'll get only about 25 full-color 8 1/2- by-11-inch pictures printed with one cartridge. If you're planning a family remembrance quilt with lots of photos transferred to fabric, you're better off investigating other methods of printing them on the fabric—like those "magic transfer" sheets you can buy in quilting catalogs.

wait a minute," you say. "I was trying to print a GIF graphics file that was only 1MB in size, and the printer wouldn't do it." That's because GIF files are compressed. The printer must uncompress them to print them, and when it does it runs out of memory. The solution: Buy more memory for your printer. A laser printer needs at least 3MB to print efficiently. The extra memory is cheap enough. It will cost only about $60 to add a couple of megabytes.

If it's an inkjet printer that chokes, you need to buy it a bidirectional cable, which will allow the computer and printer to carry on a semi-intelligent conversation in which the computer sends the printer the file piece by piece, and when the printer gets done printing each piece, it asks for more.

brance quilt with 25 or more family photos reproduced on fabric, that's a far cheaper route than using the computer to print on fabric. And it's less messy and far more foolproof! Plus, the image resolution and the color interpretation are going to be sharper than what you'll get by printing on fabric with your home computer. In fact, it's going to be much, *much* better!

The color fastness of these transfers in the washing machine is also superior to that of any of the computer fabric-printing methods we discuss in this chapter, including the T-shirt transfers. Amazing, huh? These sheets have a thin, glue-like surface that picks up the color photocopier's ink. Both glue and ink are heat-set into the fabric when you iron the picture onto the fabric. The resulting fabric picture does have a slightly rubbery feel—don't expect to hand-quilt through it—but it's not as heavy a rubber as the glue-like coating you get with computer-generated T-shirt transfers.

If you're thinking of making a remembrance quilt with magic transfer sheets, arm yourself with one of the many excellent books that tell you all the tricks. We like *Family Keepsake Quilts* by Vivian Howell Ritter (Wheatridge, CO: Leman Publications, 1991); and *Creating Scrapbook Quilts* by Ami Sims (Flint, MI: Mallery Press, 1993).

So that's our bottom line. We generally like these "magic transfer" sheets better than any of the computer printing methods, especially for remembrance quilts. We think that you'll find them an easier and cheaper alternative too.

NOTE

Some copy store chains, like Kinko's, will not permit you to feed "magic transfer" sheets into their copy machines because they're afraid they'll melt. But the sheets are safe, and some copy stores will let you use them. When you take these sheets to a copy shop, always take extras with you, and ask the technicians to check which side of sheets the machine prints on before you start copying.

THREE WAYS TO PUT COMPUTER PICTURES ON FABRIC WITH INKJET PRINTERS

All that said, it is fun to print a picture on fabric occasionally. You can see in the color gallery section of this book some of the pillows and quilts we made by printing on fabric with inkjet printers. There are three basic ways you can take that scanned photo of grandma and grandpa and put it on fabric. Each of these techniques is discussed in the sections that follow.

1. You can buy special Canon Fabric Sheets. You feed these legal-sized, plastic-backed sheets of muslin directly into your Canon bubblejet printer. After the

PRINTER TIP

To prevent your color inkjet cartridge from drying out and to extend its life, always remove it from the printer when you're finished using it and store it in the airtight cartridge box that came with the printer, if it has one. Or seal it in a zipper-lock plastic bag. Sometimes you can rejuvenate dried out cartridges by wetting a paper towel with warm water and gently soaking the nozzles to loosen and remove the dried ink. Be careful not to rub the nozzles, which may damage them; simply soak the ink off.

PRINT YOUR OWN QUILT LABELS

You don't need high-powered graphics software to create your own custom quilt labels and print them on fabric using any of the techniques described in this chapter. All you need is a word-processing program like Microsoft Word, a few clip-art borders, and perhaps some clip art. Start by importing a border (you'll find them in your word processor's or drawing program's clip-art library). Make it the size you want your labels to be, import a drawing or two, and add some fancy text (experiment with the word processor's fonts to see which one strikes your fancy). If you have a color printer, fill your design with color or shading, and voilá! Now all you need to do is print your labels on fabric. If you have a black-and-white printer, use permanent markers to add some color to the labels.

sheet is printed, you pull off the plastic and soak the fabric in a chemical bath. These sheets are expensive—about $3 each—but they work wonderfully, they're colorfast, and they're foolproof. Canon doesn't guarantee they'll work with other brands of printers, but if you have an inkjet, they're worth trying. We found that the photos printed on these sheets came out looking sharper than those printed with any of our home-brew fabric-printing methods. Only the "magic transfer" sheets that work with color copiers produce sharper, more vibrant photos on fabric. To order Canon Fabric Sheets, head to **http://www.canon.com/** on the Web.

2. You can print on freezer paper–backed muslin and set the ink with some combination of fabric fixatives. Several recipes for doing this are floating around the Internet—we tried them all. We also tested all sorts of dye-setting solutions and even clear silk-screening ink to set the ink. Which technique works best for you will depend upon the type of ink used by your printer. You'll find Judy & Gloria's Secret Home-Brew Recipe for Printing on Fabric with an Inkjet Printer on page 268.

3. You can buy T-shirt transfers that work with inkjets. This is specially coated paper that you print your design on with a color inkjet printer. You iron it on your T-shirt or other fabric just like any other T-shirt transfer. It creates a heavy, rubbery image on the fabric. These T-shirt transfers don't produce transfers of as high a quality as the ones you buy in a craft store, such as Daisy Kingdom transfers. And they're certainly nowhere near as good as the T-shirt transfers a T-shirt store can create for you. You can only iron them on cotton and cotton/poly fabrics. They're also expensive—from $1.50 to $3 a sheet (shop around!). The ones we tested also tended to flake in the laundry after just a couple washings. But kids love using these computer T-shirt transfers. And heck, we think they're fun too. They're not just for T-shirts either. You can use them to stitch up a fun, quick quilt—like our *Cross-Stitcher's Favorite Things* quilt at the end of this chapter. They're also great for making special pillows with family photos. See our chart on page 272 for information on which printer manufacturers sell them. Then read our tips below on how best to use them.

CANON FABRIC SHEETS

We love the Canon Fabric Sheets, designed for Canon's bubblejet printers, and think that you will too, even though they're pricey at $3 each. They are 9½ by 14 inches, white, and 100 percent cotton. (No natural muslin-colored sheets are available.) The fabric is backed with acetate film for easy feeding through the printer. After you print a photo or other image on the fabric, you peel off the acetate film, rinse out any excess ink, and soak the fabric in a bath of powdered fixative for 40 minutes. That powder is dicyandiamide cationic resin with sodium carbonate, or soda ash, which sets fiber-reactive dyes. It's a safe substance but a bit caustic, so you may want to wear gloves and a breathing mask since it's fine and easily airborne.

The colors in a printed fabric sheet are a little less intense than they'd appear when printed on paper, but overall the color hold of these sheets is excellent. Because the fabric itself is treated (we think, although some at Canon claim otherwise), you get much better color than by printing on ordinary muslin. And the colors don't fade with repeated washings.

Always do a test print on paper first so that you don't accidentally ruin one of these pricey sheets. Set up your inkjet to print on coated paper, or use the fabric sheet setting if it has one. Set it for manual feed.

JUDY & GLORIA'S SECRET HOME-BREW RECIPE FOR PRINTING ON FABRIC WITH AN INKJET PRINTER

Recipes for making inkjet ink permanent when it's printed on fabric are popular on the Internet. About a year before this book was published, we started testing them. We soon found that none worked as well as we liked. When we laundered photos and other art printed on fabric, they bled and faded.

So we decided to invent our own recipe. Ten months, $500 in chemicals, 150 square feet of freezer paper, 75 yards of cotton fabric, and a mountain of inkjet cartridges later, we cried "Eureka!" simultaneously on the phone.

We tested the recipe below with both Epson and Canon printers. From what we've been able to learn, the color ink used in most inkjet printers is similar enough that this recipe will work with fabric printed in any inkjet. The ink is what's known as "fiber reactive"—it bonds with the fibers of the fabric. But because it's water soluble, it will bleed when wet, so it must be set with some sort of dye-setting fixative.

What about black ink cartridges? Black ink cartridges for some inkjet printers, like the Lexmarks, are advertised as being water resistant. Water resistant they may be, but they're still ink. The images they print are prone to bleeding, and they must also be set with chemicals to be made permanent. (Although some quilters on the Internet claim that they've been able to make permanent images printed on fabric with black water-resistant ink simply by ironing the back of the fabric, we haven't been able to get that to work with our printers.)

We've found that our recipe works for images printed with black inkjet ink as well as with color ink.

Our recipe has six basic steps: Pretreat the fabric, iron the fabric onto freezer paper, print it in the inkjet printer, let the fabric sit for a specified period, soak the fabric in fixative, and launder the fabric to test color-fastness.

INGREDIENTS

FABRIC   The best fabric to print in an inkjet is tightly woven cotton similar to bed sheeting in its crisp smoothness but heavier in weight. Think of home dec fabric. One hundred percent cotton holds ink the best. Silk won't work at all. Since silk has little absorbency, the ink will run before it even gets out of the printer, and it will be difficult to make permanent later.

FIXATIVE   The fixatives listed below are available from Dharma Trading Company (800/542-5227). They can also be found at art supply stores. You will need either the Pro Retayne fixative or soda ash for pretreating the fabric, and you will also need the Deka fixative for treating the fabric after you've printed it.

Pro Retayne Dye Fixative A fiber-reactive dye fixative from Pro Chemical & Dye, Inc., PO Box 14, Somerset, MA 02726.

Soda ash A fine white powder used to set dyes. Sold in big bags that are specially measured to be a lifetime supply.

Deka Series L Textile Dye Fixative Another dye fixative, from Decart, Inc., PO Box 309, Morrisville, VT 05661.

INSTRUCTIONS

1. **PRETREAT THE FABRIC.** Wearing rubber gloves and, if using soda ash, a dust mask or respirator, prepare a bath of about a gallon of hot water and ½ cup Pro Retayne or 9 tablespoons soda ash. Mix it up well. Make sure the soda ash is dissolved.

Dunk the fabric in and let it soak for about an hour. After the hour's up, remove the fabric, squeeze it out (don't rinse it), and let it dry. (You can dry the soda ash–soaked fabric in a dryer, but it may leave white crystals on the inside of the dryer.)

2. **IRON THE FABRIC ONTO FREEZER PAPER.** Once the fabric's dry, iron it to freezer paper, as instructed earlier in the section "Judy & Gloria's Tips for Preparing Fabric to Feed through Printers." The hot iron may cause brown scorching on fabric treated with soda ash, but the scorch marks will wash off.

3. **PRINT THE FABRIC.** Set your inkjet to print on its fabric sheet setting, if it has one. If it doesn't, use the coated paper or envelope setting. Set your printer's software to the "vivid" setting if it has one. The "transparency" setting also works well. The "photo-realistic" one usually doesn't deposit enough ink for our purposes. Set the printer for manual feed. If your printer has a paper adjust lever, set it to +.

Print your fabric sheet as you would a sheet of paper.

4. **LET THE PRINTED FABRIC SIT.** With the freezer paper still on, set your printed fabric aside for at least 24 hours. This will give the ink time to cure. (Be careful not to splatter any water drops on it, since inkjet ink smears easily.)

5. **SOAK THE FABRIC IN FIXATIVE.** Once the fabric has set, carefully peel off the freezer paper backing.

Pour 1 ounce, or 2 tablespoons, Deka Series L Textile Dye Fixative into about ½ gallon of warm water. Mix it up well, and plunge your printed fabric in it. *Be careful not to splatter water drops on the fabric before dunking it in the fixative!* Soak it for at least an hour, possibly longer, depending on the fabric. *Don't rinse the printed fabric first!* Agitate it every once in a while to prevent streaking of the image. You can soak numerous pieces of printed fabric simultaneously.

After the hour's up, take the fabric out, rinse it, and let it dry.

6. **LAUNDER THE FABRIC TO TEST COLOR-FASTNESS.** Machine-launder the printed fabric with Orvus soap to test its color-fastness. If the image fades, print another one, and this time soak the fabric in Deka L for a bit longer.

See the chart "Caring for Computer-Printed Fabrics" later in this chapter for more advice on washing and caring for your inkjet-printed fabric.

T * I * P

Don't dump your mixed solutions. We used the same batch of soda ash water for more than a month!

T * I * P

Make sure you have lots and lots of extra fabric sheets backed with freezer paper because, as they say, glitches happen. It's easy to use up a dozen sheets trying to get one good print.

T * I * P

For more advice and inspiration about all the different ways you can print on fabric with high-tech tools like copy machines, get a copy of Jean Laury's book Imagery on Fabric *(Lafayette, CA: C&T Publishing, 1992).*

YOU CAN ALSO USE SILK-SCREENING INK TO MAKE INKJET INK PERMANENT

Another way to make inkjet ink permanent is to paint the printed fabric with a thin coat of colorless silk-screening ink and then heat-set it with an iron. This works best on small images, since the process of painting the silk-screening ink can cause the inkjet ink to smear.

Our favorite ink is Deka-Print Colorless Textile Screening Ink, available for about $7 for an 8-ounce bottle. Don't dilute it when you use it. Use a large, soft brush to paint it on your image to avoid streaking. Let it dry and then iron it on the back for several minutes, using the cotton setting and pressing down hard with the iron.

Since this can be a potentially messy process, and one fraught with problems, try Judy & Gloria's Recipe first.

COMPUTER T-SHIRT TRANSFERS FOR INKJET PRINTERS

Convinced that in the typical household the individual with the most compelling interest in creating T-shirt transfers with the computer is likely to be the ten-year-old son (or his equivalent), we gave several packs of T-shirt transfer paper and an iron to the husband of one of the authors. We instructed him to scan family photos into the computer and then iron them onto shirts.

A short time later we found him brandishing a smoking iron over the kitchen counter. His brow was wrinkled in despair. "I don't understand these directions!" he huffed.

Indeed, the instructions for these T-shirt transfer sheets often challenge both the computer-savvy and the craft-erudite. They usually fail to mention that you need to use some sort of image processing or graphics program to crop, resize, and then mirror your picture once it's inside the computer. They don't always tell you how to set up the printer properly. And they almost invariably fail to tell you how to iron the transfer onto the T-shirt or other fabric to get the best results.

In the case of certain computer T-shirt transfer sheets, the fact that their directions tell you to iron on a nonporous, nonwood surface like a Formica countertop, with only a pillowcase and the T-shirt separating your hot iron from the counter, are alarming. Okay, they're not so alarming if you're the one doing the ironing, but they are if kids or other less careful members of your household are the ones wielding the iron.

The bottom line is that you need to supervise kids (and husbands) when you give them these transfers.

Here are some tips and caveats for using these sheets, plus some things that their makers fail to tell you.

IMPORTANT THINGS TO KNOW ABOUT T-SHIRT TRANSFER SHEETS

- T-shirt transfer sheets work with color inkjet printers, but not with laser or dot-matrix printers.

- T-shirt transfer sheets imprint fabric with heavy, rubbery images that are difficult, if not impossible, to sew through by hand. Some describe them as plasticizing fabric. They're great for creating novelty quilts for kids (you know, a blanket with a dozen images of outer space downloaded from NASA's Web site or something like that). But for a softer quilt with a more elegant look, you'll want to use Canon Fabric Sheets or print directly on muslin with an inkjet printer.

- You can iron these transfers onto smooth cotton and cotton-poly blend fabrics, but other fabrics won't work. Synthetics like rayon will melt under the iron's high heat. Silk and nubby fabrics like wools are out of the question. Even cotton with a high polyester content may be unsuitable.

- These transfers look best when ironed onto white or off-white fabric. If you iron them onto colored fabric, be aware that the fabric's color may show through the transfer, tinting your transfer with its color.

- Some quilters have complained that their irons aren't hot enough to transfer these T-shirt transfers to fabric properly. To test different brands of T-shirt transfer sheets for this book, we used an old iron from the 1950s. It weighed a ton but was capable of scorching temperatures, and it worked like a charm. But most irons today are light and don't get that hot. Some quilters have resorted to borrowing the commercial presses at T-shirt shops to transfer these sheets to fabric; a few have even purchased commercial presses. (By the way, we've spotted those big old irons from the 1950s lined up by the dozens on shelves at church consignment shops. Estate sales are another place to look for them.)

- A picture printed on paper may look garish or too dark when turned into a T-shirt transfer. Subtleties in the image may disappear. Yellows and oranges may have an acid look.

- Although there's much talk about which brands of inkjet printers print T-shirt transfers the best, the ink in most of these printers is similar. You'll get pretty much the same results whatever brand of T-shirt transfer paper you put in your printer. (We tried a variety of brands, including Epson, Canon, and some from the fabric art supply company Dharma Trading. We tried them in various brands of inkjet printers, even some they were not designed for. We got pretty much the same results no matter what printer or brand of paper we used.)

TIPS FOR TRANSFERRING IMAGES

- Use a graphics program like Paint Shop Pro to crop your picture or design and spruce it up according to the directions earlier in this chapter. You may want to brighten the colors a bit. You'll need to mirror the design too (in other words, flip it around so that when you iron it on your shirt it doesn't appear backward). Print a test on paper before feeding a T-shirt transfer sheet into the computer. Make sure it fits on the page properly.

- Some printers offer a T-shirt transfer paper setting. (If your printer does, you'll find it in the printer's Setup dialog box, which is usually accessible from the File menu of whatever application you're using.) This setting deposits extra ink on the page. Another option is to set your printer to print on a transparency—that setting also puts more ink on the page.

- If you are not using the latest printer driver from Epson and are experiencing ink smearing with your transfers, choose **Advance** from the **Print** menu and then select **Coarse Dithering** and the **Photo-realistic** color setting. Or go to **http://www.epson.com** to download the latest printer driver.

- Once you print your design, trim away any excess transfer paper around it. If you don't, it will leave a gluey film around the design when you iron it on your T-shirt or other fabric.

- Pour any water out of your steam iron before you begin ironing.

- You'll get the best results by ironing your transfer on a hard surface, like a kitchen counter or board. If you use a board, cover it with a towel and at least two pillowcases, so that the brown of the board doesn't stain the fabric. Cover your Formica counter with at least two pillowcases. Use old cotton pillowcases that you can discard if they are damaged. A poly-blend pillowcase may melt or char under the high heat and pressure of your iron.

- Press down hard on the iron as you move it slowly from side to side over the back of the transfer. Move the iron at a steady pace to distribute the heat evenly; if your ironing motions are chaotic, your T-shirt transfer will end up looking blotchy.

REMEMBER: HEAT AND PRESSURE ARE YOUR FRIENDS

Computer T-shirt transfers do crumble and crack in the wash, even when they're applied to the shirt or other fabric properly. Their makers maintain that the only reason they crumble is because the consumer did not iron them properly to the shirt. That's not always the case. We tested a bunch of these transfers using a weighty, industrial-hot iron. The transfers still cracked in the wash. But we found that the more heat and pressure you can apply when ironing the transfer to the fabric, the more permanent the image will be. The transferred image will look better too. The moral: When you're ironing that transfer onto your fabric, press down hard. Stand on a stool if you must in order to put all your weight on it. And use the hottest iron you can find. If you have a lightweight, cheapo iron that doesn't get terribly hot, borrow a better one from a friend.

YOU DON'T HAVE TO PRINT T-SHIRT TRANSFERS EXCLUSIVELY ON T-SHIRTS

You can use T-shirt transfers to make pillows, purses, even quilts. T-shirt transfers print photos and other designs with more vibrancy of color than you'll get from fabric transfer sheets or other forms of printing computer pictures on fabric. The difference is that T-shirt transfers print their designs by placing a rubbery, gluey substance on the fabric rather than dying it. One of the Cross-Stitcher's Favorite Things quilts pictured in the gallery section of this book was created with T-shirt transfers.

- Your iron has a "sweet spot" just like a tennis racket does. That's the point just above the center where the most heat is generated. As you iron, frequently move that sweet spot around the edge of the transfer. You need to apply extra heat and pressure to seal the edge of your transfer to the fabric. That will help keep it from flaking in the wash.

- The paper should pull off the shirt easily when the transfer is fully cooked. If it doesn't, or if there are any spots where the paper sticks when you try to pull it off, apply more heat and pressure.

- Pull the paper off the fabric slowly and evenly to keep the fabric from distorting. Once the paper has been removed, quickly lay your fabric flat to cool.

- Never iron the top of your T-shirt transfer. To avoid cracking or crumbling of the transfer, wash it in cool water. Avoid putting it in a hot dryer.

WHERE TO ORDER T-SHIRT TRANSFER AND FABRIC SHEETS

If your printer isn't listed in the table below, call its manufacturer and ask if it sells fabric or T-shirt transfer sheets for your model of printer. These sheets are popular, and more and more printer makers are selling them. In fact, most of these sheets are manufactured by the same company with slight modifications for different printers. The sheets retail for around $15 for a pack of ten. Canon Fabric Sheets run about $30 for a pack of ten.

COMPANY	ORDERING	PRODUCT	COMPATIBILITY	SIZE
ALPS	800/950-2577 http://www.alps.com/	T-shirt transfer paper	Alps MD color printers; Alps printers use dry ink and these papers may not work with wet inkjet printers	8½" x 11"
DHARMA TRADING COMPANY	800/542-5227 http://www.dharmatrading.com	T-shirt transfer paper	Works with "almost any" inkjet printer, according to Dharma.	8½" x 11"
CANON	800/423-2366 http://www.canon.com (you can order the sheets online)	Canon Fabric Sheets	Work with BJC 70, 600, 4000, and 600 series color bubble-jets. Also work with Apple Color StyleWriter printers.	9½" x 14" white fabric
CANON	800/423-2366 http://www.canon.com	T-shirt transfer paper	Works with BJC 4000 and 600 series bubblejets. Also works with Apple Color Style Writer printers.	8½" x 11"
EPSON	800/873-7766 http://www.epson.com/	T-shirt transfer paper	Works with Stylus Color 500, 800, II, II 50, & Pro models.	8½ x 11", 13" x 19" available for Stylus Pro XL & Stylus 150.
HANES	800/Hanes2U	T-shirt transfer paper	Works with Canon inkjet printers.	8½" x 11"
LEXMARK	800/438-2468 http://www.lexmark.com/	T-shirt transfer paper	Works with Lexmark, Canon, Epson, and Hewlett-Packard inkjet printers; check Web site for complete compatibility list.	8½" x 11"

*Visit Hanes on the Internet (**http://www.hanes2u.com/**) to find out just about anything you'd ever want to know about embellishing T-shirts, from marblizing or beading them to creating computer T-shirt transfers. The site offers lots of information about digitizing images to create fabric transfers. You can also download free software for making T-shirt-designs. Epson also offers downloadable T-shirt designs on its site at **http://www.epson.com/**.*

JUDY & GLORIA'S IRREVERENT OPINION ABOUT T-SHIRT TRANSFER SHEETS

Which do we prefer using: those cute preprinted T-shirt transfers that you can buy in craft stores (you know, the bunnies, bears, ducks, and bouquets) or the computer-printed T-shirt transfers? We like the ones you can buy in craft stores. They're generally cuter than what you can create on a computer. They're easier to use than the computer stuff. They're cheaper (usually under $3, often on sale for $1 each). And the final, ironed-on image is thicker and more enduring than the ones created with the computer T-shirt transfer sheets.

CARING FOR COMPUTER-PRINTED FABRICS

Fabrics printed in a computer printer or embossed with a computer-printed T-shirt design require special care to preserve their colors. Images printed on fabric with an inkjet printer are most indestructible when the ink is properly set into the fabric. You can make your computer-printed fabrics last for generations by following these care tips:

TYPE OF FABRIC TRANSFER	HOW TO WASH & DRY	HOW TO IRON	OTHER CARE TIPS
Fabric Printed in an Inkjet Printer (including Canon Fabric Sheets)	Machine wash in cool water. (Hand washing is preferable.) To preserve color, avoid strong detergents; use Orvus quilt soap instead. Avoid bleach. Line drying is preferable, but tumble drying is acceptable.	Iron with iron set to "cotton." It's okay to iron on both sides of printed fabric transfer since inkjet printer ink bonds with the fabric's fibers when properly set. The image is fairly indestructible.	Avoid direct sunlight to prevent fading. Consider treating fabric with Scotchguard, stain removal may be tricky. Test any stain removal products on sample swatches of similarly printed fabric before using them on your quilt.
Fabric Printed in a Laser Printer	Hand wash in cool water with Orvus quilt soap. Avoid bleach. Line dry. Drying in a dryer may damage image by melting Krylon fixative coating.	Do *not* place iron on top of printed image; image may smear. If you "set" image by spraying on Krylon fixative according to the directions in this chapter, you placed a thin plastic-like coating on top of the laser printer powder. That coating can melt under an iron. Iron on the back of the fabric with the iron set to a cool setting.	Avoid direct sunlight. Images printed on fabric with a laser printer are far more fragile than those printed with inkjet ink. Any rough treatment can destroy the image.
Fabric with Computer-Printed Iron-On T-Shirt Transfer	Machine wash in cool water with mild detergent. (Hand washing is preferable.) Avoid bleach. Line drying is preferable. Use permanent press setting if drying in a dryer.	Do *not* place hot iron on top of the transfer because the iron will melt the rubbery transfer. Iron the back of the fabric with a cool iron.	Transfers will crack with multiple machine washings. They will melt on contact with any heat source.
Sun-Printed or Blueprinted Fabric (as described in Chapter 18)	Hand wash in cool water with small amount of mild soap, like Orvus. Too much soap will fade image. Avoid strong powdered detergents with phosphates, baking soda, or bleaches, such as Tide and Arm & Hammer. Rinse thoroughly. Line dry.	Iron on the back of the printed fabric; the blue or other colored dye may transfer to the iron and streak over lighter portions of the design. Water spots may mar a print, especially on newly printed fabric. Steam iron only on the back of the fabric.	Handle gently. Avoid direct sunlight to prevent fading. Test any stain removal products on sample swatches of similarly printed fabric before using on your quilt.

HEAVENLY QUILTS THAT CAME FROM INKJET PRINTERS

Canon Computer commissioned three well-known quilters to design quilts with fabric printed in computer printers. The quilts they created are breathtaking. You can see them in the gallery section of this book.

"When I tell people that the fabric in my quilt was printed in a computer printer, they hardly believe it," says Ann Johnston. Johnston was one of three quilters Canon Computer commissioned to create quilts with Canon printers and Canon Fabric Sheets.

Canon gave the quilters PCs, printers, scanners, piles of graphics software, and cases full of color inkjet cartridges and Canon Fabric Sheets. The women set to work pairing old-fashioned piecing with computer-generated imagery, printing photos and clip art on fabric, and stitching the printed pieces into lush, imaginative scenes or evocative traditional designs.

For all the quilters, the greatest challenge of the project was learning how to use their computer tools to create the images they envisioned. Here's how a few talented women made some extraordinary quilts with their computers, and the things they learned along the way.

ANN JOHNSTON AND MERRY-GO-ROUND 2

Ann Johnston has always loved carousel horses. They've served as a subject for her quilts in the past, and it was such a quilt, in which she painted horses leaping out of a silk border, that inspired Canon to hire her.

Ann started her quilt *Merry-Go-Round 2* by envisioning carousel horses in different angles and poses. In her treks around the country, she snapped countless rolls of film of merry-go-rounds at amusement parks, focusing on features she liked in particular horses.

Once she had a collection of about 200 photos, which she disparages as "bad amateur shots," she had them transferred to a Kodak Photo CD at a copy shop (for about 60 cents per shot) in a range of five resolutions, and began planning her design.

"I went through the photos and picked out horses I liked and angles I liked," says Johnston. "Then I sketched on graph paper where I wanted the horses and played with different compositions of pillars and fences. I also played with different arrangements of lighting."

Using Adobe Photoshop, she viewed the photos in their lowest resolution so that the images would be easy to work with in her 32MB RAM PC. She began carving out pieces of photos that she liked. "For instance, I'd delete the pole and paint in the rest of the horse's face. I didn't worry about colors or resolution at that point. I was only concerned with composition."

Photoshop lets you manipulate images on different layers like a drawing program does, and Johnston used this feature extensively, shifting horses and background and foreground elements around. "I could point to the horse in front and move it to the back. That was the most fun. The options were endless."

She also edited features of the horses themselves. "If you look at the animals on merry-go-rounds, their faces are exaggerated and they look alarmed," says Johnston. For instance, one merry-go-round horses' nostrils were flared and his eye was glazed as if he were frightened and running away from something. She softened the nostrils and turned the eye so that it was looking forward.

She printed the horses and other elements of her carousel on blue-lined graph paper designed for use with photocopiers, choosing the paper because its blue lines won't pick up inkjet ink. (You can see preliminary sketches and a graphed version of the design in the gallery section of this book.) She ended up with a small-scale version of her quilt on a single sheet of paper. She used this to calculate the final size of the quilt, creating resolutions of her images that would print at the proper size on the Canon Fabric Sheets.

She ended up with about 20 individual graphics files containing various components of the quilt. She never actually created a single computer image of the quilt as a whole, because her 32MB RAM computer did not have enough memory to allow her to easily work with such a big file.

Once her quilt's design was in final form, she printed parts of the horses on Canon Fabric Sheets with an inkjet printer. She'd print a forelock, a nose, a neck, a tail. Once she had a suitable image printed on a fabric sheet—and it often took many, many tries to get the coloring right—she ironed fusible web to the back of the Canon Fabric Sheet, then cut the pieces from the fabric. (Johnston says she tried seven different types of web to get the right feel and hold that she wanted in the fabric.) As she cut pieces from the fabric, she stuck them to her workroom wall, assembling the horses like a large jigsaw puzzle.

Canon had given her a case of the fabric sheets, and she went through most of it trying to print images that looked just right. "Glitchy things would happen, like the inkjet's cartridge would run out halfway through printing a sheet," says Johnston. "I printed about a hundred sheets just experimenting with different Photoshop filters and color adjustments, trying to get the colors I wanted. I had to learn how to adjust colors from screen to fabric, since what appears on the screen doesn't appear the same on the fabric. Colors look so much lighter when they're printed on fabric because fabric is more porous than paper. I struggled and struggled with that. At one point I tried printing over a fabric sheet twice to get the color intensity I wanted, but the image still didn't appear dark enough."

Dark colors proved the most problematic. Johnston found that blacks had to be specified as 100 percent black in Photoshop in order to appear their darkest when printed on fabric. She became a pro at learning to adjust colors in Photoshop to get them looking right on the fabric.

Once Johnston printed and fused together all the pieces of her horses, she moved them around her workroom wall with other elements of her picture, just as she had moved images around her computer screen.

She printed the background for her carousel in rectangles, making sure that none of the corners met so that the seams were less apparent. She turned a work-table into a giant ironing board on which she fused the horses and other carousel figures like the pig and zebra to the background.

Johnston basted the quilt and then free-motion machine-quilted it, covering some of the edges of the horses with glitter. She also glued on rhinestones, on the carousel's lights, for example. "By the time you've put fabric in your computer, you're liberalized enough to glue rhinestones on your quilt," laughs Johnston.

"I think everybody would love to do this kind of thing," she says, "but it's an expensive proposition." She adds, "Personally, though, I can't wait to do another one."

JUDY MATHIESON AND AUTUMN IN NEW ENGLAND

Judy Mathieson's modernistic quilt *Autumn in New England* is built around variations of the traditional Attic Windows quilt block but with photos of colorful autumn foliage "floated" inside each one.

Her husband, Jack, a retired software manager, started the design by drawing the blocks' windows on a computer screen. Judy chose fall images from a Corel CD-ROM of photos. Using Photoshop, her husband manipulated the images to fit the window spaces, pruning them, resizing them, and erasing portions. "A lot of it was me watching over his shoulder, saying, 'Yes, yes,' and 'No, no,'" says Mathieson.

The wood print that makes up the windows in the quilt is clip art from another graphic arts CD-ROM.

Once the blocks were designed, the Mathiesons printed them on paper to check resolution and sizing. Some of the Attic Windows were big, spanning four sheets of paper, while others were smaller, fitting onto a single sheet. This play of block size is at the heart of the quilt's design.

Once the Attic Windows blocks looked the way she wanted them, Mathieson printed them on fabric.

The process was quick, says Mathieson. It took about a month to print the fabric and sew the quilt once its images were in final form in the computer. What took time was learning how to use the software to get the images right.

SHARYN CRAIG AND A FATHER'S LIFE AND CANON GARDENS

Talk to Sharyn Craig and you wouldn't think there's anything extraordinary about the exquisite quilts she created with Canon Fabric Sheets and an inkjet printer. The quilts are traditional in their block-based designs; their visual power comes from the flowers and photos she manipulated in a computer and printed on fabric.

MAC USERS:
DON'T TOSS OUT THAT OLD IMAGEWRITER II.
IT PRINTS ON FABRIC!

You find them at computer flea markets. Sometimes they pop up in newspaper classifieds. Apple no longer makes its color ImageWriter II dot-matrix printer, and that's a shame because the ink it prints with is waterproof. You can use these antique printers to print directly on freezer paper–backed muslin, and you don't have to treat the fabric with anything to make the image permanent.

Fortunately, you can still buy color ribbons for ImageWriter printers. However, the printer driver that currently ships with Macintoshes allows the ImageWriter to recognize only eight colors. Microspot USA sells a replacement driver called MacPalette II for $69. It lets the printer recognize 250,000 colors and 65 shades of gray. It also doubles the printer's dots per inch from 72 to 144. While 144 dpi isn't great by today's standards, and printed photos look grainy, the quality of other printed images is darn good!

So if you spot one of those dinosaurs at a flea market for $10, snap it up! You can buy the MacPalette II driver from Microspot USA, Inc., 2380 Saratoga-Sunnyvale Rd., Suite 6, Saratoga, CA 95070, 800/622-7568, **http://www.microspot.com**

For *A Father's Life,* Craig scanned pictures of her father as he was growing up. Using the software that came with her scanner, she cropped and sized the pictures and then printed each as a 6-inch square image on Canon Fabric Sheets. She chose a traditional pieced block called Snow Crystal, replacing the center square with her photo squares.

Canon Gardens is a similar design, but it is created with fabric printed with botanical images taken from a CD-ROM. Craig played with the colors in the flower pictures, resized the pictures when she was done, and printed them on Canon Fabric Sheets.

Craig says she enjoyed sewing the Canon Fabric Sheets. The sheets have a much higher thread count than muslin and are more like decorator fabrics in their weight and crispness. "The piecing I did was very intricate, and I expected to have problems, but I didn't," says Craig. She found that using a very sharp needle helped. She also found that once the quilts were pieced and quilted with their batting they looked much softer than she had expected, considering the fabric's crispness. She is particularly enthusiastic in her recommendation of these sheets for use in making quilt labels.

Craig recommends that anyone who uses these sheets treat their finished quilt with Scotchguard fabric protector. (All the quilts that Canon commissioned were treated with Scotchguard protector.) She also advises quilters to be especially careful not to drip water on printed sheets before fixing the sheets in their chemical bath; since inkjet ink is water soluble, the smallest drop of water will leave a blemish.

CROSS-STITCHER'S FAVORITE THINGS QUILT

"I wouldn't mind printing giant cross-stitch charts on muslin and making them into a quilt," said Pat Papoure, a quilter on CompuServe. What a great idea! Here are directions to do just that.

I. GET SOME CROSS-STITCH DESIGN SOFTWARE. Many shareware cross-stitch programs are available for downloading from the Internet and commercial online services. The best spot to find them is on Kathleen M. Dyer's cross-stitch Web page at **http://www.wco.com/~kdyer/xstitch.html**

For PCs, our favorite is Pattern Maker from HobbyWare, PO Box 501996, Indianapolis, IN 46250; 317/595-0565; e-mail 71543.1504@compuserve.com. (Pattern Maker comes packaged with some of the Canon bubblejet printers.)

For Macs, call EduCorp at 800/843-9497 and ask for their $20 program called Cross Stitch Design. Or visit **http://www.ilsoft.co.uk/** to find information on X-Stitch Designer Gold, a commercial program available from England for $79.99. There's also a Photoshop plug-in tool that creates cross-stitch patterns. You can download it from **ftp://ftp.asi.com/pub/photoshop/filters-mac/**.

2. EXPERIMENT WITH PRINTING CHARTS ON PAPER. Try printing some cross-stitch charts to see how they look. Note how many squares print in the width and length of the page. Will the program let you print actual cross-stitches, or only patterns with symbols? If only symbols, which are the darkest?

CONSIDER TREATING COMPUTER-PRINTED FABRIC WITH SCOTCHGUARD

The Canon quilts pictured in the gallery section of this book were all treated with Scotchguard fabric protector. You can buy aerosol cans of Scotchguard at fabric stores for about $7 a can. While treatment with Scotchguard can ward off stains, it gives fabric a plastic feel. If your quilt is destined for a bed and not a wall, you may want to take your chances and skip the Scotchguard. Although fabric printed in an inkjet printer doesn't stain any easier than normal fabric, stains can be tricky to remove because of the delicate coloring of, say, a photo printed on fabric. In other words, it's probably not a good idea to rub a toothbrush full of liquid detergent, baking soda, or other stain removal product over fabric that was printed in an inkjet. Scotchguard is a superb treatment for quilt labels.

3. MAKE, SCAN, OR DOWNLOAD SMALL BLACK-AND-WHITE CLIP ART IMAGES. Look for very small, very simple black-and-white pictures. Flower buds work well. So do small cartoons. Not all clip-art will work, so find lots of little pictures to play with.

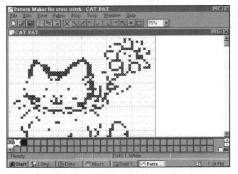

4. PREP THE IMAGE. In a graphics program like Paint Shop Pro, crop the pictures tightly. Remove any scanning artifacts (little black dots). Find out what file format your cross-stitch program will import, and convert your clip-art pictures to that format. (All you usually need to do is simply save them in the new format.)

5. MAKE THE ART INTO A STITCH CHART BY USING THE CROSS-STITCH SOFTWARE'S IMAGE IMPORT FEATURE. Import your little pictures into the cross-stitch software by using its image import feature or by cutting and pasting. Select **Preserve aspect ratio** if you want to keep the image's original dimensions (in other words, if you don't want it stretched or smooshed.)

- We like to create charts of about 50 or 60 squares wide. That gives you a bit of selvage around the edges for sewing. Also, images that are reduced to charts smaller than that are often illegible.

- If the cross-stitch software offers a Print Preview feature, you can see what the chart looks like before you print it out. You may have to add or delete some stitches to make the design visible.

- Not all clip art will look good once it's imported into a chart.

6. PRINT YOUR CHART ON MUSLIN. Once your cross-stitch chart looks the way you want it to, print it on muslin backed with freezer paper or on a Canon Fabric Sheet. But first print some tests on paper. You may need to make the symbols or stitches darker.

7. EMBROIDER, THEN SEW INTO A QUILT. Once your cross-stitch charts are printed fabric blocks and you've gone through whatever steps are necessary to make the ink permanent, embroider some highlights on your charts with silk ribbon or six strands of embroidery floss. When you're done, sew your squares into a crazy quilt.

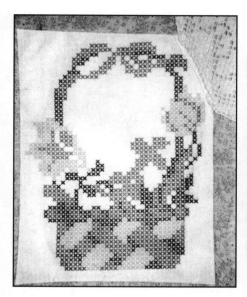

At the top left is a detail of Judy's Cross-Stitcher's Crazy Quilt. *Judy printed this chart on muslin with a laser printer and embellished it with giant cross-stitches. At the top right and at the bottom are details of Judy's* Cross-Stitcher's Favorite Things *quilt. Judy printed these giant cross-stitch images using T-shirt transfer sheets in an inkjet printer. The "transfers" were then ironed onto muslin. To see both quilts, turn to the color gallery of this book.*

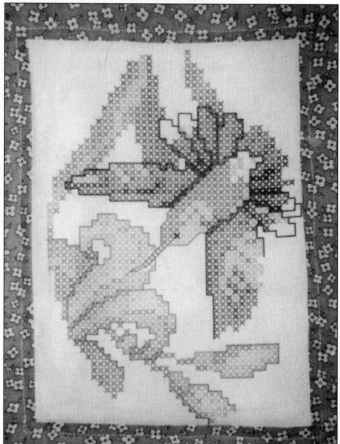

CHAPTER 18

USE YOUR PRINTER TO CREATE STENCILS AND NEGATIVES FOR FABRIC PAINTING, SUN PRINTING, AND BLUEPRINTING

One of the easiest (and most fun) things you can do with your printer is to make transparencies for painting and sun printing.

You've probably seen those sun-printing or blueprinting (sometimes referred to as cyanotype) kits that pop up occasionally in quilting catalogs. They include specially treated fabric that you lay in the sun. On top of the fabric you place a photographic negative or things like leaves and buttons to mask the sun's rays. You set an egg timer for 15 or 20 minutes. When the time is up, you bring your fabric into the house and rinse it to reveal a beautiful "sun-printed" pattern. If you used a negative your photo appears etched in the fabric as if a photographer had printed it there.

These kits are great fun, and if you've never tried them, you owe it to yourself to buy one. Like a cruise through the Panama Canal, they're the sort of thing everyone should do at least once.

If you protest, "But what can I use for sun printing except those same old maple leaves that everyone else uses?" or, "It's too expensive to have a photo shop make negatives of all my old photos so that I can blueprint them," wait until you see what we have in store for you.

You can use your computer to make some marvelous transparencies for sun printing. You can also use your computer to print negatives of old photos for blueprinting. And you can use some of these techniques to create stencils for fabric painting.

So quick, get yourself a sun-printing kit and a box of photocopier transparency sheets. The fun is about to begin.

WHERE TO BUY THIS STUFF

The best place to look for sun-printing books and kits is the Dharma Trading Company catalog (800/542-5227). You'll find sun-printing kits with fabric colors as wide-ranging as white, fuchsia, and turquoise. The kits may include about 20 quilt

**THE MOST IMPORTANT
BOOK YOU CAN BUY**

*A book worth its weight in mercerized cotton is
Barbara Hewitt's* Blueprints on Fabric: Innovative
Uses for Cyanotype *(Loveland, CO: Interweave
Press, 1995). It includes directions for "do-it-
yourself" fabric blueprinting and lots of inspiration.*

block–sized squares of fabric. They usually run under $20. We've also seen these kits
in quilt catalogs like Quilts & Other Comforts (800/881-6624) but only sporadically.

You can buy transparency sheets (they are meant to be used in overhead projec-
tors) at any office supply or copy store. We like the ones with the paper along one
edge because they feed into copy machines nicely. Be sure to cut the paper edge
off before you sun print though, or it will be branded into your fabric along with
your design.

CREATING TRANSPARENCIES

TRANSPARENCY TIP

*You can buy special transparency paper for
inkjet printers that doesn't smudge when you
print on it. Look for it in office supply stores and
computer catalogs. Apple Computer even sells
it (http://www.apple.com/).*

In a nutshell, you're going to use your computer to make transparencies. You'll
print a design or photo negative on the transparency and then lay the transparency
on your specially treated sun-printing fabric. The sun will beam down on them,
causing a chemical reaction in the exposed areas of the fabric (where the transparency is still clear), and that's how you'll get your print.

Some quilters print designs directly on transparencies with a laser or inkjet
printer. We don't think that's a good idea because the images smear unless you use
transparency sheets especially designed for inkjet printers. You want sharp images.
A better tactic is to print your design or negative on a white sheet of paper, take
that paper to a black-and-white copy machine, and use the copy machine to copy
the image onto a clear acetate sheet. That's what you'll use to do the sun printing.

Transparencies of a young Judy and Judy's mom . . .

. . . created these positive images when sun printed on fabric.

CREATE A PHOTO NEGATIVE TRANSPARENCY

Now that we're clear on the best way to print a transparency, let's talk about what to print on it. In the previous chapter we talked about the best way to scan photos and how to crop them, size them, and touch them up in a graphics program. To make your photos into negatives, you add one more step: You tell your graphics software to turn the image into a negative image. If it's a color picture, first convert it to a gray-scale image. Then turn the gray-scale image into a negative. Save the negative image, print it on paper, take the paper to a copy machine, and copy it onto a transparency. That's it. Place the transparency on your treated fabric, expose it to the sun, and your photo will be "developed" into the fabric.

T * I * P

You may want to boost your negative's contrast to get a better print. You'll need to experiment with the contrast in your graphics or image-editing software.

Use your graphics software to change a scanned photo into a negative image of itself. Print it on paper in the size that you want it to be on your quilt block. Then copy it to a transparency with a photocopy machine.

JUDY & GLORIA'S BLUEPRINT PHOTO TIP

We can't emphasize it enough: Be sure to choose photos in which there are no shadows and in which the eyes are well delineated. Otherwise, your photo's subjects will look as though they have charcoal briquettes for eyes. You may also need to brighten the photo up a bit in your graphics software to make the clearest negative.

We used the shareware graphics program LView to turn our scanned photo of a bunch of flowers into a negative. Since it was a color photo, we first turned it into a gray-scale image.

We boosted the contrast of the negative slightly to create a negative with sharper lines.

CREATE TRANSPARENCIES OF OTHER IMAGES FOR SUN PRINTING

Photos are the most fun to sun print on fabric, but you can use your computer to create lots of other images that will print equally well.

Raid your graphic or word-processing software's clip-art library for pictures and shapes. Select simple shapes like stars and boxes. Fill them with black-and-white patterns or fountain fills to create gradations of shading. Duplicate them, tile them, and resize them. Thicken their lines to make heavier images if you like. Print them on paper and then photocopy them onto transparencies.

This is a scan of an illustration in a Nancy Drew book from the 1930s. We used the paintbrush tool to erase the black spots that came from scanning it, and then we cropped it, sized it, and printed it as a transparency.

Your drawing program can be a source of endless inspiration for creating whimsical designs to sun print.

On the left is a transparency and on the right one of the sun prints used for the Nancy Drew quilt shown in the color gallery.

PRINT STENCILS FOR FABRIC PAINTING

Now that you've got the hang of creating transparencies for sun printing, why not use the same techniques for creating stencils for fabric painting, airbrushing, or even stippling with permanent markers? Print simple clip art or scanned designs on paper, use a copy machine to copy them onto a transparency, and then use a mat knife to cut the design into a stencil. When you think of all the images you can find as clip art—outlines of dinosaurs, crocodiles, palm trees, stars, and even basic shapes like circles or squares—the possibilities for fabric painting are endless.

Sample transparencies.

VI

PATTERNS

HERE'S A SPECIAL TREAT—PATTERNS FOR MANY OF THE QUILTS
DISCUSSED IN THIS BOOK!

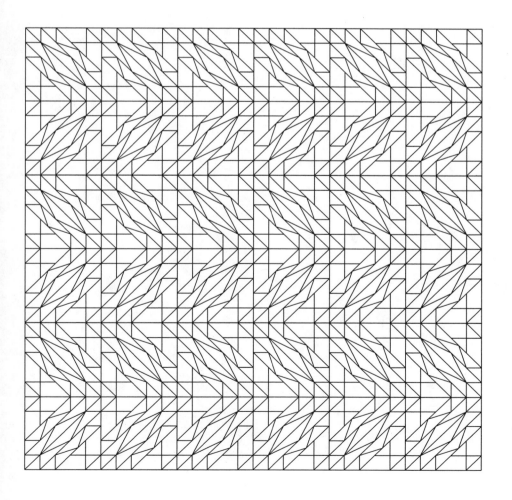

CHAPTER 19

GLORIA'S GALLERY: PATTERNS FOR MANY OF THE QUILT DESIGNS IN THIS BOOK

As we mentioned earlier, one of the authors of this book is an accomplished artist who designs exquisite quilts with her drawing software, while the other churns out endless Drunkard's Path blocks with quilt design software. We'll let you ponder which is which. Meanwhile, in this chapter you'll find patterns for some of the quilts used as examples in this book. You'll find full-color pictures of these quilts in the gallery section of the book.

You can use these patterns for your own personal use. Draw them in your favorite quilt design or drawing program to change their size. Add or subtract lines, or change straight lines to curves. Combine different kinds and sizes of blocks. Your quilt or drawing software will let you do all these things. You'll be amazed at the number of beautiful variations you can create.

We've also included the actual line drawing for each quilt as it's pictured in its color photo, in case you'd like to make one exactly like it.

Some of these blocks can be made with the flip-and-sew paper-piecing technique. Others require that you use traditional templates. We've noted the method used for each block.

To draw accurate templates, use a fine-tipped permanent marker to trace the *sewing*, or *seam line* of each shape on clear template plastic. Write on the template any registration marks and the template number. Carefully cut the plastic on the sewing line. When you trace the piece on the fabric, the line you will be drawing is the sewing line rather than the cutting line. This will let you sew patches together with more precision. (This is how they teach girls in Europe to sew.) When you cut out your fabric patches, cut ¼ inch away from the sewing line. Now match and pin the sewing lines and sew.

GLORIA'S PRECISION TEMPLATE-MAKING TIP

For making certain blocks, you just can't beat old-fashioned templates. This is particularly true for blocks containing odd-shaped patches.

GLORIA'S ROTARY CUTTING TIP

I like tracing my templates onto precut fabric strips. It speeds up the cutting considerably. With your rotary cutter, slice strips of fabric wide enough to fit both your template and its seam allowance. Trace as many patches as you need. Then cut between the patches using scissors or your rotary cutter and a plastic ruler.

GLORIA'S PAPER-PIECING TIPS

Paper piecing helps me sew blocks that lie flat with their patches lined up perfectly. It also helps ensure that my quilts don't end up as finalists in Ami Simm's "Worst Quilt in the World" contest! Here are some good things to remember:

• Always use high-quality tracing paper in your computer printer. With good paper you can see both sides of your design, which will help you piece the fabric accurately.

• Leave the paper on the blocks until your quilt top is complete. If your quilt is large, you should especially strive to leave the paper on the outside border blocks. When the top is complete, machine-baste 4- to 8-inch fabric strips around the edge of the quilt top before removing the paper. This will help keep the quilt's edges from crinkling or distorting. And the extra fabric will make quilting the outside edges of the quilt easier.

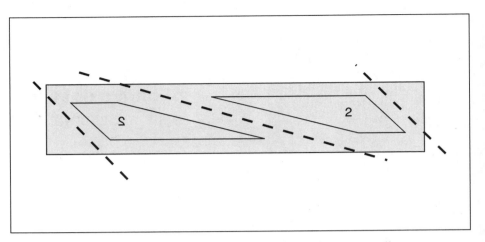

A fabric strip wide enough to include both the template and its seam allowance.

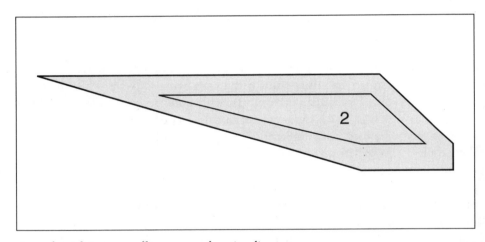

A patch with its seam allowance and sewing line.

AWAKENINGS

You can use templates to make this block, or you can paper-piece it.

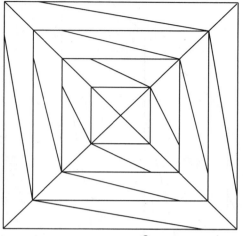

The Awakenings *block.*

©1992 GLORIA HANSEN

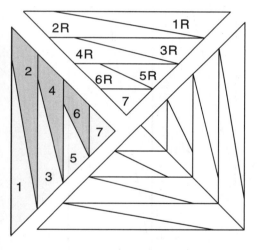

The piecing order to construct the block.

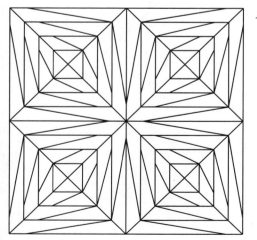

A 4-block unit.

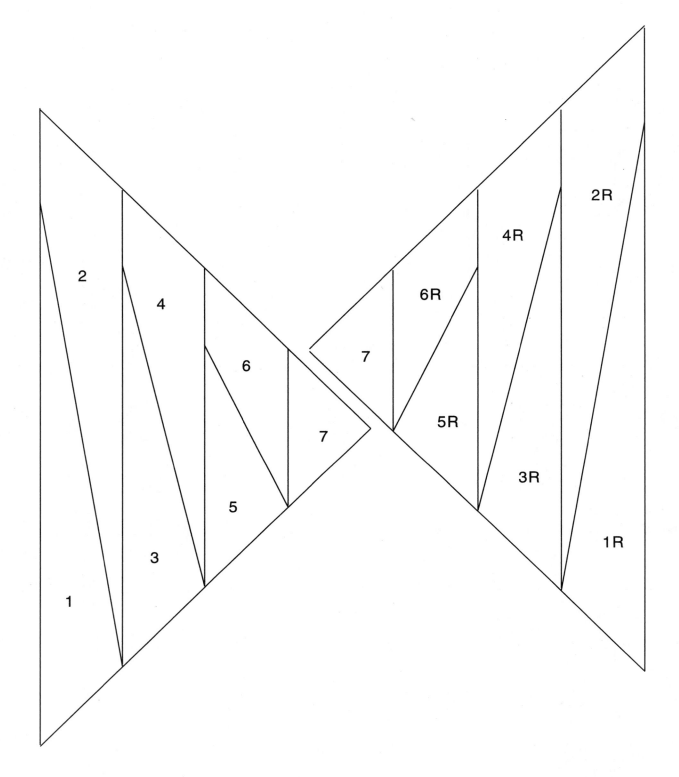

The 7-inch Awakenings *pattern with numbering for paper piecing.*

A 36-block (or 9-unit) layout. The layout for the quilt pictured in the color gallery.

BREAKING FREE

The block in *Breaking Free* is a variation of the one used to make *Awakenings*. It was made using templates but could also be paper-pieced in sections. This quilt uses different shapes and sizes of the same basic block.

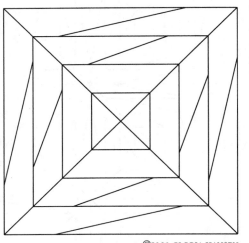

©1992 GLORIA HANSEN

The *Breaking Free* block.

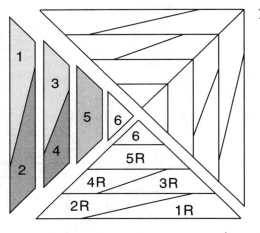
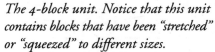

The piecing order to construct the block.

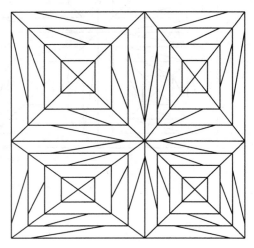

The 4-block unit. Notice that this unit contains blocks that have been "stretched" or "squeezed" to different sizes.

©1994 GLORIA HANSEN

The layout for the quilt pictured in the gallery section of the book.

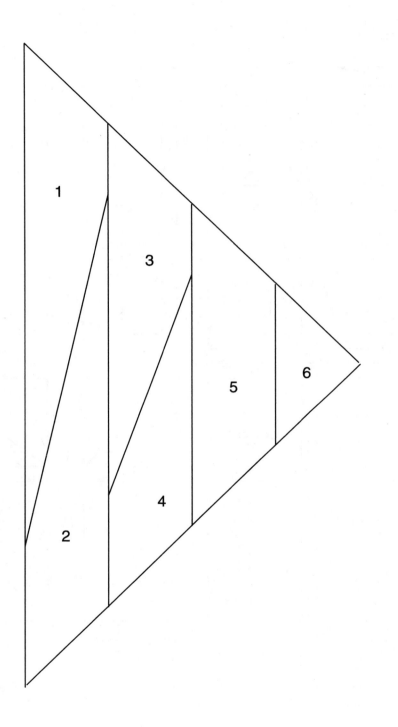

A quarter of the 7-inch Breaking Free *pattern with numbering for paper piecing.*

HEAT WAVE

The *Heat Wave* block uses seven templates, plus some strip piecing.

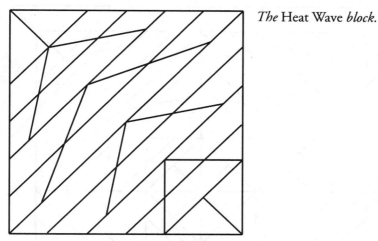

The Heat Wave *block.*

©1992 GLORIA HANSEN

The piecing order to construct the block.

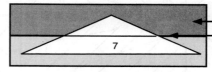

Using two strips of fabric sewn together, line up the seam to the template's center line to cut out the center triangular patches.

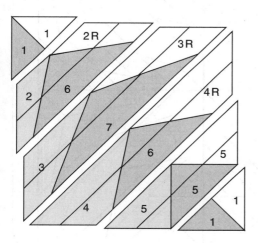

A 4-block unit.

The layout used for the Save the Green *quilt pictured in the gallery section of the book.*

The layout used for the Heat Wave *quilt pictured in the gallery section of the book.*

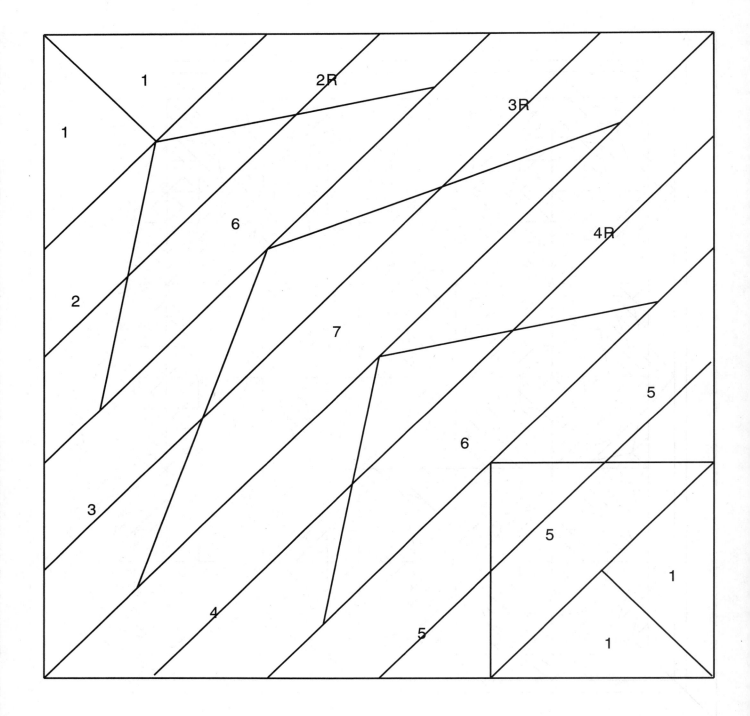

The 7-inch Heat Wave *pattern.*

DIRECTIONS

This block uses six templates, five of which are also used in reverse. We suggest placing registration marks on your templates and on your sewing line. Match the marks while sewing.

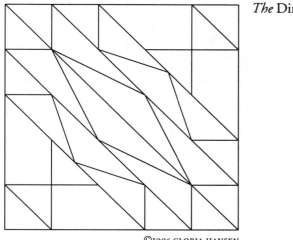

The Directions *block.*

©1995 GLORIA HANSEN

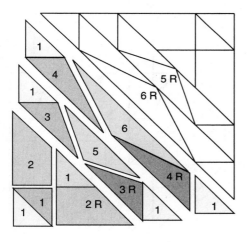

The piecing order to construct the block.

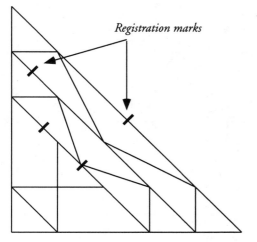

Registration marks.

Registration marks

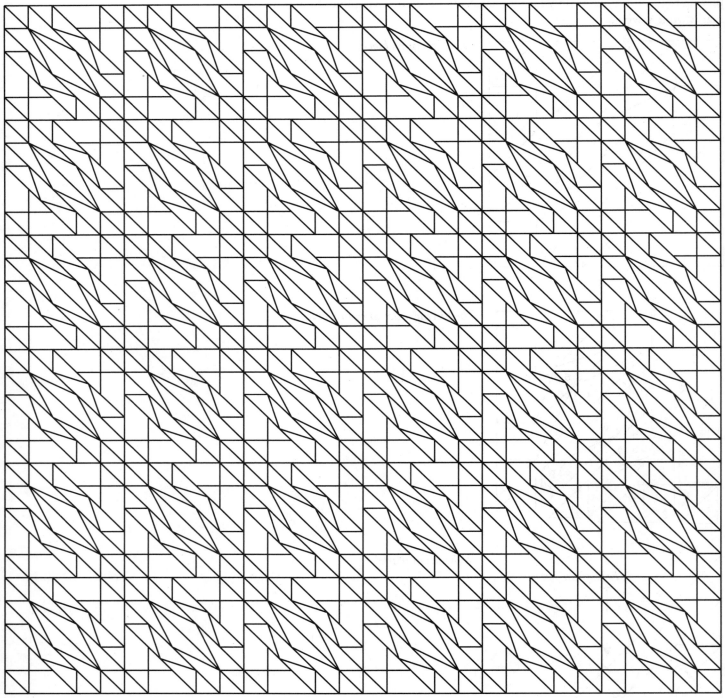

The layout used for the Directions *quilt pictured in the gallery section of the book.*

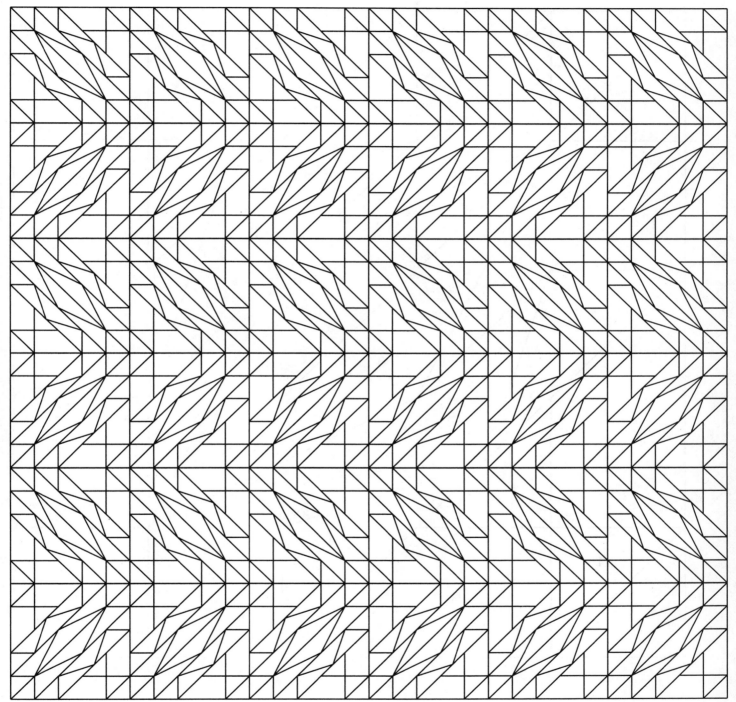

To create visual movement, lay out the blocks with alternating rows.

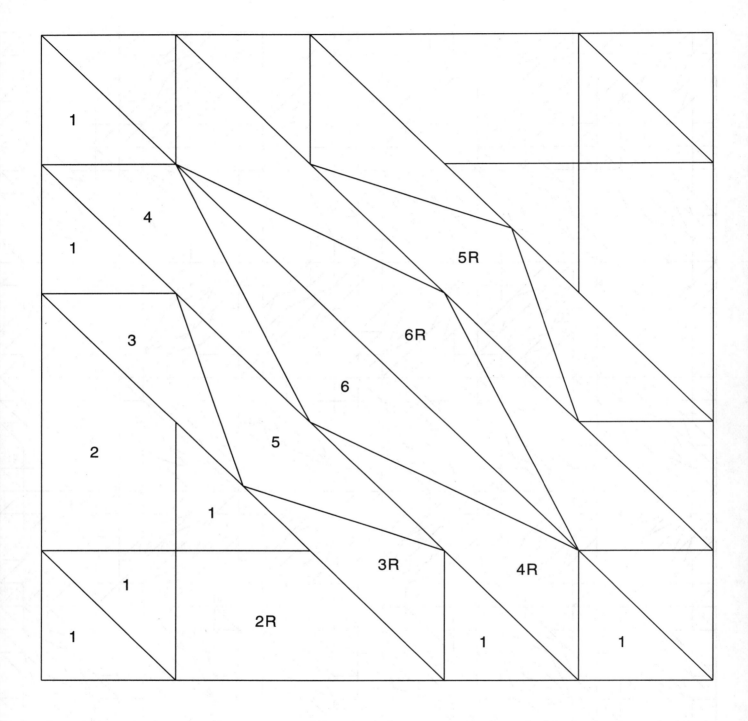

The 7-inch Directions *pattern.*

DANCING SHADOWS

This block is easiest to make with paper piecing. Each quarter of the block is rotated 90 degrees. The original *Dancing Shadows* quilt contains five small blocks and four large blocks, with strips added to the outside edges of the small blocks to square off the design.

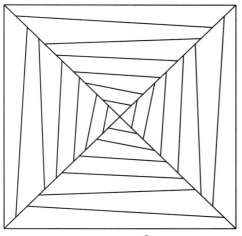

©1995 GLORIA HANSEN

The Dancing Shadows *block.*

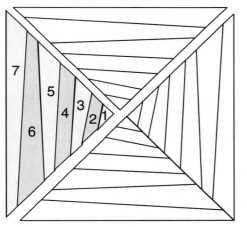

The piecing order to construct the block.

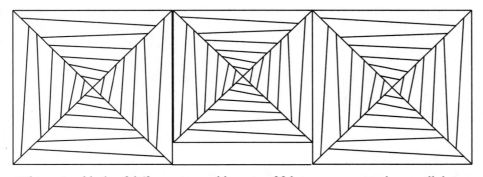

When using blocks of different sizes, add a strip of fabric to square up the overall design.

A layout using nine blocks of the same size.

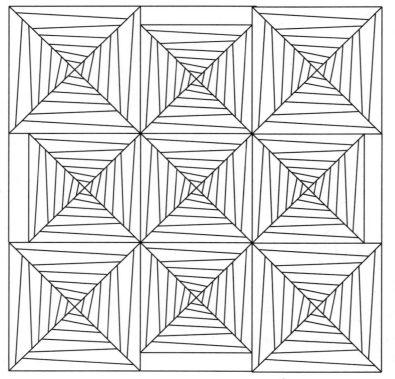

The layout for the quilt pictured in the gallery section of the book.

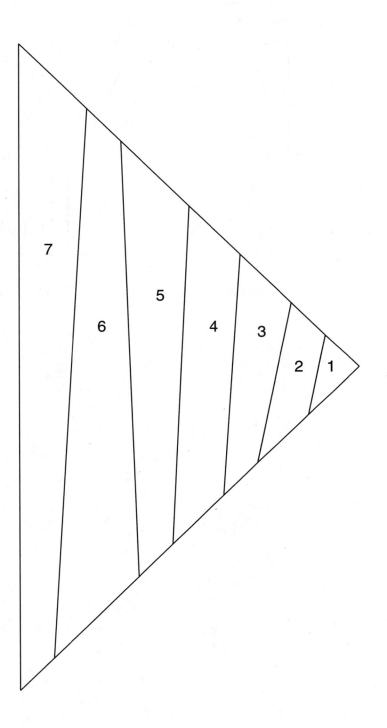

A quarter of the 7-inch Dancing Shadows *pattern with numbering for paper piecing.*

SHATTERED

The *Shattered* block works best when paper-pieced. Remember that you'll need to make some mirror-image blocks. We've included both patterns here.

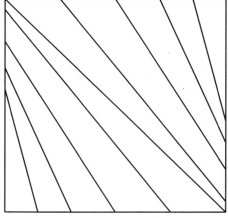

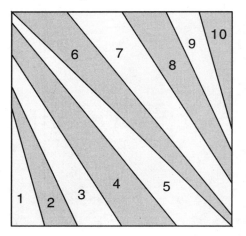

©1996 GLORIA HANSEN

The Shattered *block.*   *The piecing order to construct the block.*

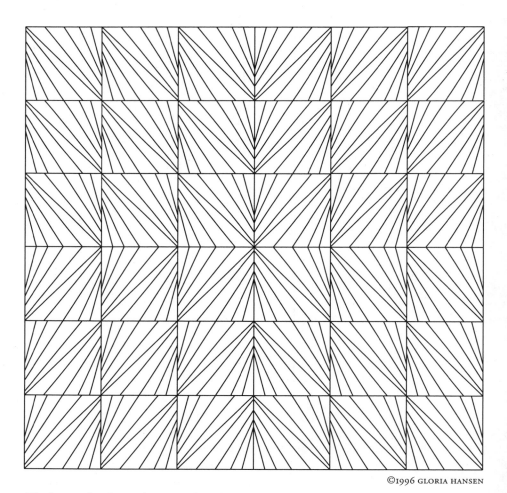

©1996 GLORIA HANSEN

The layout for the quilt pictured in the gallery section of the book.

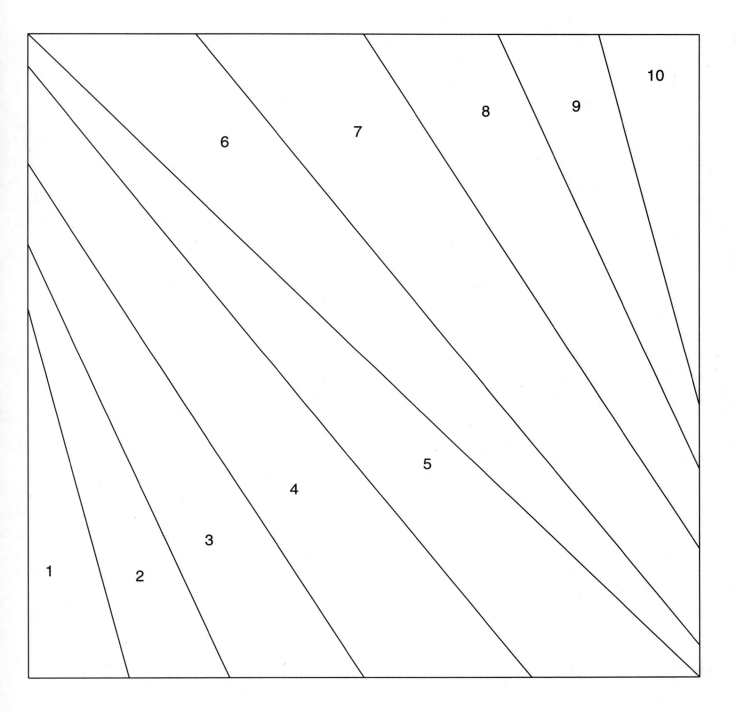

The 7-inch Shattered *pattern with numbering for paper piecing.*

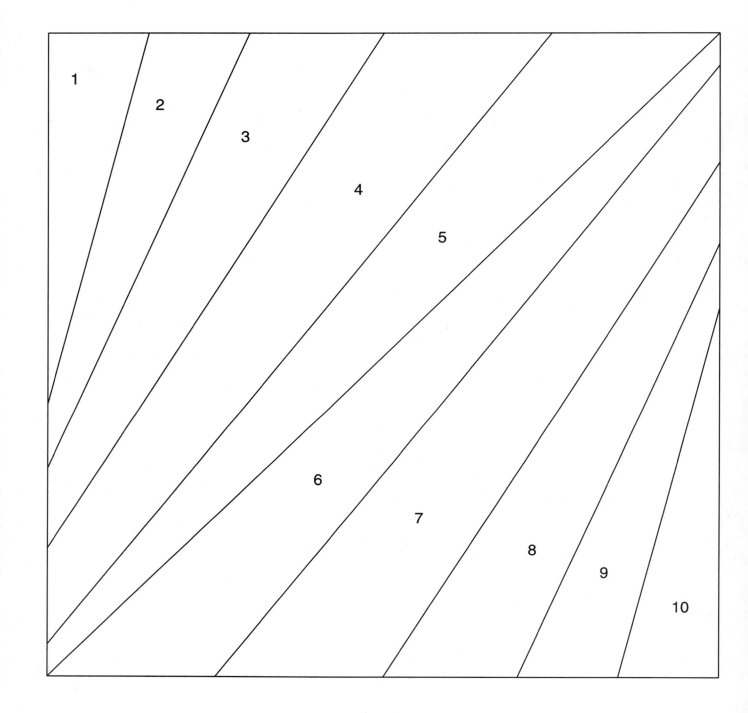

The mirror-image 7-inch Shattered *pattern with numbering for paper piecing.*

PETALS OF HOPE

The *Petals of Hope* block can be pieced with patches cut with templates, but it's easiest to paper-piece it in sections.

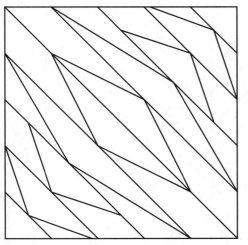

©1996 GLORIA HANSEN

The Petals of Hope *block.*

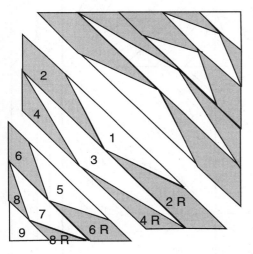

The piecing order to construct the block. (The block can be paper-pieced this way.)

The 4-block unit.

The layout for the Petals of Hope *quilt pictured in the gallery section of the book.*

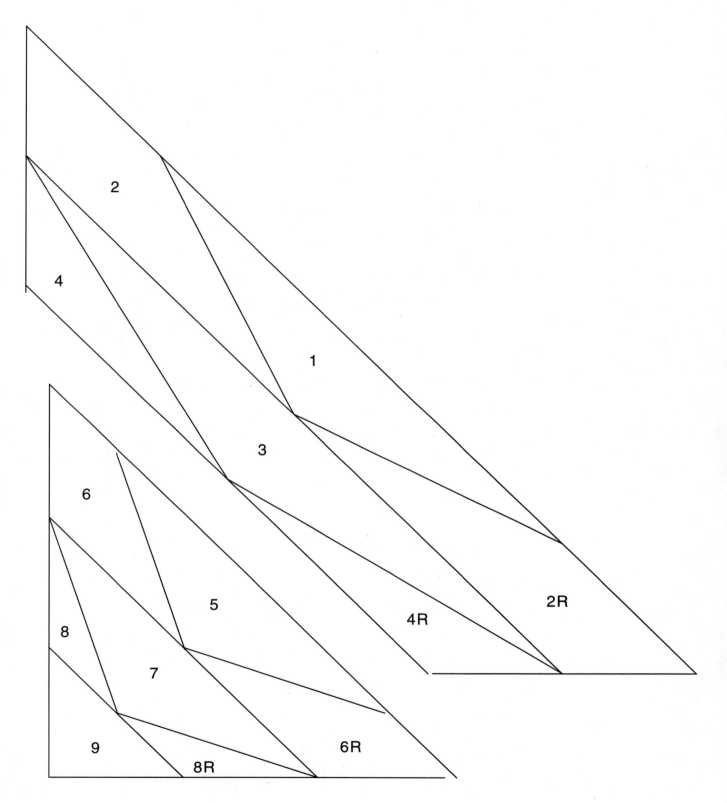

The 7-inch Petals of Hope *pattern.*

VII

CYBERSPACE AND MORE

GET ONLINE, TOUR THE INTERNET, FIND SOME GOOD BOOKS, GET HELP
WITH COMPUTER GRAPHICS, AND MORE IN THE PAGES THAT FOLLOW.

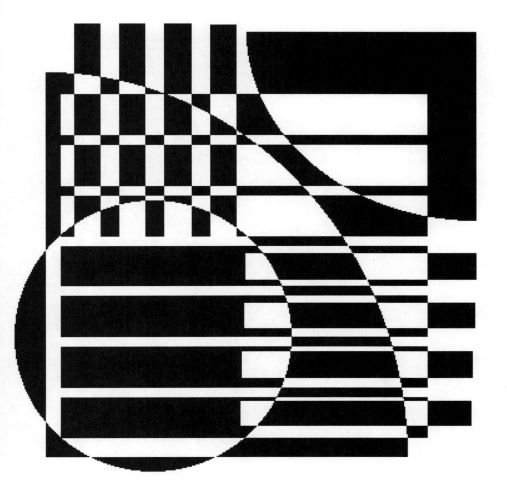

A QUILTER'S GUIDE TO CYBERSPACE

What is the Internet? Why should you care? An irreverent look at what cyberspace offers quilters.

If someone had predicted ten years ago that the Internet—that vast tangled web of links between university and corporate research computers—would become an integral part of the American quilting scene, they would have been accused of having snarled bobbins for brains.

You can hear disbelievers scoffing, "We are sewing calico squares together, not designing spaceships!" Some still do. The fact is that the Internet is a marvelous way for like-minded souls to share thoughts and inspirations across the vast distances of continents.

A woman in Georgia runs out of a pink fabric that she's using for the border of a quilt. She writes an e-mail message lamenting that her local quilting store no longer carries it, and the next day a quilter in Ontario mails her a piece of it. A quilter in Minneapolis traveling to New York asks for fabric store recommendations. She is deluged with e-mail from New York quilters offering to go shopping with her. A dollmaker in Baltimore sends an e-mail request for handmade dolls for a children's cancer hospital and receives so many that she and other dollmakers around the country have to organize a search for hospitals that need toys.

In fact, the two authors of this book became pals after meeting via e-mail.

Face it, sewing is a solitary pursuit, and in an age when quilting bees are the stuff of grandma's memories and sewing machines are more often spotted at garage sales than in family rooms, it's a treat to have a few good friends with whom to share one of your passions.

That's why tens of thousands of quilters flock to the Net. Each night quilters around the world sit down at their computers, often after spouse and children are asleep, and tap out e-mail messages to each other. Like quilters around a quilting frame, they gossip, bicker, tell stories about their lives, make friends, share quilting tips, swap fabric and notions, and celebrate the victories and soothe the hurts in one another's lives. They even mail quilt blocks around the country to assemble quilts in a cyberage equivalent of the old-fashioned quilting bee.

Our grandmothers might have said that the best thing about quilting was being able to share in others' lives while helping them assemble something of beauty. The fact that we cyberage quilters are separated by oceans and mountains is irrelevant. Words and the immediacy of electronic communication bring us together.

Has the Internet changed quilting? Only in the sense that it has increased the quilter's access to information, products, and ideas. One of the things that every quilter who has ventured into cyberspace marvels at is how the camaraderie of others has inspired them to try things they never dreamed they were capable of doing.

The Internet has injected new slang into the quilting world. A UFO is an "unfinished object," while a DH is a "dear husband." It also has its own rules of deportment. For instance, talking about UFOs (for "unfinished objects") is strictly forbidden in some niches of quilting cyberspace. Once that subject is broached, e-mail flies as quilters everywhere tap descriptions of their unfinished craft projects, like laundry lists of unresolved problems. Talking about one's cat may also be taboo. Once a public e-mail string drifts into the land of cats who riffle through sewing baskets, quilting is forgotten as everyone eagerly describes how Miss Kitty unwound an entire spool of elastic thread in her frolicking last night.

Like a thimble or sewing pins, the Internet is a tool. Like any other tool, its purpose is to help us accomplish our goals. Its advantage is that it helps us talk and learn more quickly than we otherwise would in our isolated lives.

It's an amusing irony that the original intent of the Net was to help the military-industrial-scientific complex communicate to build a better arsenal. The military computer makers who originally built and financed it could have never dreamed that in a little over 20 years their private communication network would become a party line for peaceful (mostly), artistic people writing to each other about the creation of things that bring hope and comfort. So come join the party online!

If you do nothing else with your computer quilting-wise, you *must* jump into cyberspace.

WHAT IS THE INTERNET?

We could have written a whole book about the Internet, and others (many others) have. But all we could spare was a chapter—just enough to touch on the highlights. If you find that you need more, a good place to start is Needlecrafter's Computer Companion (No Starch Press, 800/420-7240), which devotes twelve chapters to the Internet and online services. Another good source is Dr. Bob's Painless Guide to the Internet & Amazing Things You Can Do with E-mail, by Bob Rankin (No Starch Press, 800/420-7240). A quick browse through your bookstore or library will undoubtedly turn up numerous other introductory books. Use this chapter as a guide to what's out there, and don't hesitate to jump in. Everyone on the Net was a beginner at one time.

The Internet is like that big tangle of thread in your sewing basket. Tens of thousands of businesses, universities, and government agencies are entangled electronically, their computers linked by convoluted, crab-like telephone connections that stretch around the globe, to places as far away as Sri Lanka or as near as down the block. Created to keep military contractors and researchers in touch, the Internet grew until it linked most universities and many businesses around the world. Then ordinary people started wanting access to it. Today anyone with a computer modem can tap in. Does anyone control the Internet? Not really.

WHAT IS THE WEB?

The Web is the graphical portion of the Internet, the Net for short. Think of it as the billboard portion of the information highway. You tap into the Web just as you tap into the Internet. The only difference is that you use special software so that the Internet's pictures appear on your screen. The Web is where you can view other quilters' quilts and visit quilting stores.

HOW DO I GET ON THE INTERNET?

BIG ONLINE SERVICES

One way to get on the Net is to go through an online service like America Online, CompuServe, or Microsoft Network. By tapping into such a service, you can read news and sports scores and join in public discussions on soul-edifying topics like dirt-biking. Or more worthwhile ones like quilting (use the keyword "quilting").

You can tap into the Internet from any of these services, but they can be pricey, as can their access to the Net. Still, if you're new to computers, these services are a great way to get started. You can always trade up (down?) to cheaper Internet-only access services later.

INTERNET SERVICE PROVIDERS

In addition to the commercial online services, you can get on the Net through Internet service providers, or ISPs. These low-cost services let you access the Internet by dialing a local number. They usually charge about $20 per month. Is there one in your community? Try calling your local newspapers and TV stations and asking which Internet service they subscribe to. Often local media are pretty shrewd shoppers for Internet access.

The downside of ISPs is that they pretty much leave you to your own devices in logging on to their service and then navigating your way onto the Internet. Big commercial online services like America Online give you the software; all you need to do is install it and feed it your credit card number. That's why you should try them first if you're new online.

JUDY & GLORIA'S INTERNET SURVIVAL TIP #1

If you stumble upon CD-ROMs offering free Internet access (we won't reveal the names of the companies distributing these, but you'll know them if you see them), avoid them! Don't install any free-Internet-anything in your computer unless it comes from America Online or CompuServe. There's a lot of free-bie Internet gunk out there that can truly turn your computer into an "unfinished object."

WHAT KIND OF COMPUTER DO I NEED?

You can access the Internet with any computer that has a modem either attached or inside it—even a junker you find tossed out on the curb. (See "How to Become a Net-Surfing Quilting Nerd with Grandma's Computer" later in this chapter.) But to enjoy the wild graphics of the Web, you'll need at least a 486 PC or a Macintosh with System 7.5 and at least 8MB RAM (16MB for a PowerPC). Or a lot of patience.

WHAT ABOUT SOFTWARE?

If you install software for America Online, CompuServe, or Microsoft Network, you pretty much have all the software you need to surf the Net, assuming you use their connections.

If you subscribe to an Internet service provider, you'll need a special dialing program that will call up the Internet service and forge the special Internet network connection that your computer needs. In the PC world it's called a "winsock" or Windows socket. A popular one is Trumpet.

In the Mac world, there are a few small programs you'll need to connect to your Internet service provider. One is Open Transport TCP/IP, a control panel that allows your Mac to communicate with your server. The other is a PPP extension, which is a utility that dials the phone number and makes that special Internet connection. Both are included with System 7.5 or later. Often your ISP will supply them to you or will provide you with the information you need to properly configure these panels. If you don't have the latest version of these programs, you can download them from Apple's support Web site (**http://www.support.apple.com**). Look for Config FreePPP, our favorite dial-up utility.

You'll also need a browser. A browser lets you peruse the graphics of the Web, hopping from site to site by clicking on pictures. Newer browsers also let you send and read mail.

The most popular browser is Netscape Navigator, which you can download from the Internet for free (**http://www.netscape.com/**). Equally popular is Microsoft's Internet Explorer, which is also available for free (**http://www.microsoft.com/**). Mac users should check out Cyberdog from Apple (**http://www.cyberdog.apple.com/**). This browser lets you view text, movies, pictures, and sounds without the need for helper applications.

Other useful programs speed the gathering of e-mail and the retrieval of software. But a browser is all you need to get started.

When you've got everything working, hit the BrowserWatch Web site at **http://www.browserwatch.iworld.com/** to find more information on using your browser, as well as audio and video utilities.

HOW DO I MEET OTHER QUILTERS IN CYBERSPACE?

There are a couple of ways to make cyberfriends. You can join a commercial online service, or you can tap into the Internet, or you can do both.

COMMERCIAL ONLINE SERVICES

All the commercial services host large parties of quilters, as well as other needlefolk, who log on each night to exchange tips and gossip. These include the big services like America Online, CompuServe, Prodigy, and Microsoft Network. But other, smaller services, like Delphi, are equally popular with quilters because they're often cheaper and you don't need a state-of-the-art computer to log on.

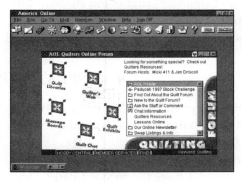

Meet other quilters on America Online by using the keyword "quilting."

You'll find a huge quilting discussion area, plus libraries of software and advice, on CompuServe. Use the "go" word "quilting."

*Delphi has always been a popular spot for quilters. You can access it with any old computer (and we do mean old) by dialing it up through normal telephone lines. Or you can tap into Delphi through the Internet. Type **http://www.delphi.com/quilting** into your browser. The forum is hosted by Judy Smith.*

INTERNET MAILING LISTS

A mailing list is like a chain letter. One person sends e-mail to a particular computer that then forwards it to a list of subscribers who have told this computer that they want to receive copies of the e-mail sent to it. Mailing list subscriptions are usually free. There are thousands of mailing lists, and there may be hundreds or even thousands of people subscribed to any mailing list. When readers respond to a message that they receive from the mailing list, their response is broadcast to everyone on the list.

There are about 75 to 100 mailing lists on the Internet devoted to needlecraft topics. Many are for quilters. Each has a distinctive personality, depending on the participants and the person who manages the list. The most popular (and famous) is Quilt-Net. At last count it had almost 1,000 members and was not accepting new subscribers. Our favorite is Judy Smith's QuiltArt, which hosts hundreds of quilters. You'll find sign-up directions in the "Quilter's Internet Yellow Pages."

One of the best things about mailing lists is that an e-mail address is all you need to participate in them. And depending on how you've set up your e-mail account, you can retrieve your e-mail almost anywhere: at work, at school, or even through a public library or Internet cafe. You also don't need a snazzy computer to participate, since mailing list messages are text-only.

USENET NEWSGROUPS

Usenet is a collection of tens of thousands of message subjects and messages related to those subjects. Usenet newsgroups are groups of messages on a similar topic. They are similar to the message forums on commercial online services, but they are more freewheeling since no one supervises them. There are several newsgroups devoted to quilting. You can read and participate in them through the Internet feature of any online service, through Web sites that offer access to these newsgroups, or through a local Internet service. Discussion in the quilting-related newsgroups is more restrained than in the mailing lists, and less chatty. Some consider them icy.

JUDY & GLORIA'S INTERNET SURVIVAL TIP #2

Join a large quilting mailing list like QuiltArt and your e-mail box will be flooded with mail in no time. Keep things under control by subscribing to the digest version of the list. That means that one big e-mail message will be sent to you once or twice a day, and it will contain all the messages posted in the mailing list that day. Not all mailing lists offer digest versions, but if the list you subscribe to does, you can get information on it from the list's Web page or from the list itself.

HOW TO FIND MORE QUILT- AND CRAFT-RELATED MAILING LIST DISCUSSIONS

*There are numerous Internet directories of mailing list discussions. Our favorite is Liszt (**http://www.liszt.com/**). Another good one is Tile.Net/Lists (**http://tile.net/lists/**). You can also read some of the Usenet craft newsgroups in mailing list fashion (good for those who have only e-mail access to the Internet). To find out more, head to **http://www.cis.ohio-state.edu/hypertext/faq/usenet/mail/news-gateways/part1/faq.html**.*

WEB SITES WITH MESSAGE FORUMS

Some Web sites offer forums resembling bulletin boards, in which visitors can participate in discussions. These aren't as popular with quilters as mailing lists, but their appeal is growing. Not all Web sites host message forums, but a few do. You tap into a Web site with your browser and read and respond to messages from other Net surfers. The Web pages that host these message forums typically offer a small selection of topics and messages.

INTERNET RELAY CHAT (IRC)

Internet relay chat (IRC) has served as the butt of countless gags in TV sitcoms. Most people think of it as the Internet equivalent of a 900 sex-chat phone number, but there are lots of family-oriented Internet chat channels, several of which are devoted to quilting. To join in, you first locate the chat channel and find out what software you need to join in. In the case of most quilting chats, the chat channel is located on a Web page that you can tap into with your Web browser. The Web page will tell you what software to use, where to get it, and how to install it.

You can chat with other quilters in real time at #QuiltChat. Start by heading to http://www.kathkwilts.com. You'll find excellent directions on how to download and install the necessary Internet relay software. (For the PC, that would be mIRC, available at http://www. mirc.co.uk.) You use the software with your browser. Once it's installed, you log back on to the Web site and start chatting.

At a designated day and time, you tap into a specific Internet telnet channel or chat Web site. You converse with other quilters live, by typing one- or two-line messages. The conversation rolls over the screen like dialogue in a play script. Some quilt chat lines have played host to famous quilters, staging "interviews" in which quilters around the country type questions to them and they type back their replies.

HOW DO I FIND MY WAY AROUND?

Cyberspace is not nearly as confusing a place as the people who sell Internet searching software and books might have you believe. Once you find your way to a couple of Web sites that you enjoy, it's easy to click your way to similar sites through links on those pages. We've highlighted some spots in the "Quilter's Internet Yellow Pages" that will start you on your way to all the fabulous quilting sites and finds on the Net.

Wandering around the Internet is like exploring a new city. All it takes is your feet and a couple of turns and you're on your way to an adventure. But on the Web, your feet never hurt and you never get winded. If you get lost, all you have to do is click on your browser's Back button to take you back to the site you just came from, or pull down the list of sites you've visited previously and click on one to go back to it.

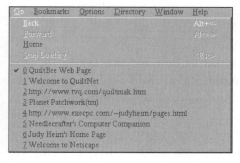

In your browser you'll find a drop-down list of the sites you've visited in your Internet travels.

JUDY & GLORIA'S INTERNET SURVIVAL TIP #4

Do cryptic error messages like "DNS Lookup Failure" make you cry? For an explanation, head to one of the big Web searchers like Excite! at http://www. excite.com/. Type the error message into the search box and specify your request as a "concept" search if you are given such a choice. Chances are good that the searcher will come up with a Web site that offers an explanation of the error.

HOW CAN I FIND QUILTERS I KNOW ONLINE?

Maybe you know a name but not the person's e-mail address. Maybe you're looking for a quilting friend who has moved to a different city. There are e-mail directories on the Internet with millions of addresses. They don't contain the e-mail addresses of everyone on the Net, but chances are good you'll find who you're looking for. Here are a few big ones:

Four11: **http://www.Four11.com/**

NetFind: **http://www.nova.edu/Inter-Links/netfind.html**

Switchboard: **http://www.switchboard.com**

HOW CAN I FIND QUILT PATTERNS AND ADVICE IN CYBERSPACE?

While there are only a few patterns to be found in cyberspace, there are plenty of FAQs, or "frequently asked questions" files, to be had. FAQs are compilations of questions that quilters frequently ask on the Net—like "How can I machine-quilt with metallic thread?" or "How can I restore my grandma's treadle sewing machine?"—and the answers that other quilters have given over the years. There are dozens of quilting FAQs on the Internet, and their number seems to increase monthly. There are FAQs on appliqué, paper piecing, fabric, and making remembrance quilts.

Some of the FAQs are affiliated with specific Usenet quilting newsgroups; others with mailing lists. Some have been compiled by companies about their products, while others were written by enthusiasts of particular topics.

The best way to find these FAQs is to visit some of the major quilting sites, like Sue Traudt's Quilting Pages at **http://quilt.com/MainQuiltingPage.html**. We've listed many of the most popular FAQs in the "Quilter's Internet Yellow Pages."

IS THERE QUILTING SOFTWARE OUT THERE? HOW CAN I DOWNLOAD IT?

Several makers of quilt design software offer downloadable versions of their software at their Web sites. We've listed them in Chapter 2 and also in the "Quilter's Internet Yellow Pages." Some of this software is distributed as shareware, which means that if you try it and like it, you are expected to send in a small registration fee. You are on your honor to do so if you use the program regularly. Other software is available in stripped-down or limited demo versions—when you pay, you get the full product. Demos of Quilt-Pro are available on the Internet.

To download software or to see if a company is offering any for downloading, head to the company's Web site, follow the directions, and click on the links or buttons where the Web page tells you to. Your browser does the rest.

Some software is also available for downloading from FTP sites (FTP stands for "file transfer protocol"). FTP sites are computers that store large file collections for easy downloading from the Internet. You can use FTP software (special software that usually comes with your suite of Internet software) to download the file. Or you can simply type—in the spot where you'd type a normal Web address—the FTP address of the software's location and then click your way to the proper directory.

For instance, to download the demo version of Nina Antze's PC Quilt for the Mac, type the location of this FTP server in Europe: **ftp.luth.se**. Then click your way to the appropriate directory on the server, in this case **/pub/mac/demo**. (These servers and directories often change, so sometimes you need to do a bit of fishing through the directories to find what you're looking for.)

Finally, you can also find craft software to download in the software libraries on America Online (head to the software library for your type of computer) and CompuServe (use the "go" word "crafts."). But company Web sites are really the best places to look first.

T * l * P

Always head to the "pub" directory on an FTP site. That's the public directory, the one where most software for public consumption is stored.

JUDY & GLORIA'S INTERNET SURVIVAL TIP #5

If you're looking for a specific company, try typing its name into your browser as a URL—prefixed by www. and suffixed by .com. For instance, if you want to find the home of Corel Corp., the makers of CorelDraw, type http://www.corel.com/.

JUDY & GLORIA'S INTERNET SURVIVAL TIP #6

If you're looking for a shareware program or a program demo and can't find the maker's Web page, head to C/Net's shareware library at http://www.shareware.com.

You can download the demo version of Nina Antze's PC Quilt for the Mac from this software site in Europe.

HOW CAN I DISPLAY MY QUILTS IN CYBERSPACE?

You can display your quilts by setting up your own personal Web site. Creating a Web site is much simpler than it appears. (Why do you think there are so many Web page consultants out there?) You can use the latest versions of Netscape's Communicator and Microsoft's Internet Explorer browsers to quickly generate a simple Web page with their "wizards." Or, you can use your word processor or special Web page creation software to write the text that you want to appear on your Web page. If you're using your word processor, you format it by typing in some simple codes that are a lot like word-processing formatting (if you remember those early word processors), like <P> to specify a paragraph break, or <HI> for a level-one heading. These codes are called HTML (hypertext markup language) coding. If you're using specialized software, you'll probably be able to click on a few buttons to style your Web page the way you like it.

You can include graphics on your Web page too by entering the names of the graphics files in your HTML code. When you're done typing your HTML code in your word processor, you save the file in Text Only format (meaning without your word processor's own formatting codes) and give it a file name that ends with the suffix **.HTM** or **.HTML** so that a Web browser will recognize and interpret it.

You'd write a file like this for each "page" you want on your Web site.

When you're done creating all of the pages for your Web site, you upload them (using FTP or your Web browser), along with any graphics that they require, to your private directory on your Internet service or commercial online service. (Not all Internet services let you post Web pages, but most do.) Often your Internet service will give you a subdirectory named www, and that's where the files go. CompuServe, America Online, and Prodigy also let users create private Web pages in this fashion on their services.

T * I * P

Good Internet services will give you directions for finding your private directory and will tell you how to upload files to it. They'll also tell you the necessary commands to make this subdirectory "public" so that others can read it—an important step.

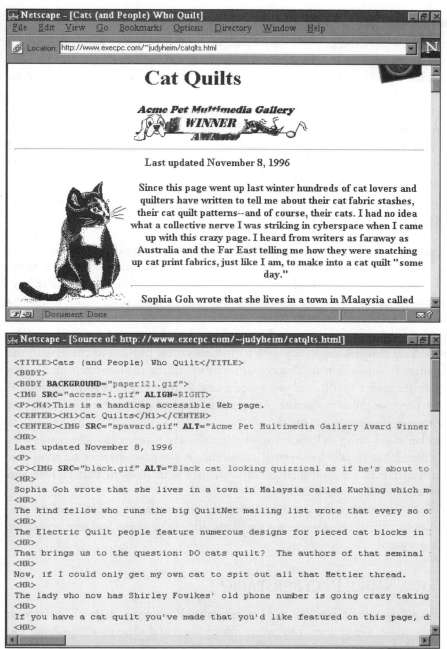

JUDY & GLORIA'S BUDDING CYBER-HACKER TIP

Our favorite book for painlessly learning the rudiments of Web page publishing is Laura LeMay's Teach Yourself Web Publishing with HTML in a Week *(Indianapolis: Sams, 1995). There are lots of little "page creation" programs you can download from the Internet, like HotDog (http://www.sausage.com/), that will generate a Web page for you, prompting you for the elements you want, but we think these are cumbersome to use. Web page coding is so easy, it's good to learn a bit of basic HTML coding yourself and create your Web page in your word processor.*

*The HTML coding for most Web pages is very simple. You can take a look at the coding for any page by selecting the **Document Source** command in your Web browser—it's usually found in the **View** or **File** menu. This is a good way to see how pages you admire are assembled.*

The URL for your page will probably be a combination of the name of your Internet service, the name of your private subdirectory on it, and the name of your HTML file. For instance, say your Internet service is named Monkeys Abroad. Your private directory on it is named maryb, the World Wide Web subdirectory is WWW, and you've uploaded into that directory an HTML file named mypage.html. Therefore, the URL would be **http://www.monkeys_abroad.com/ ~maryb/mypage. html.**

T * I * P

URLs are often case-sensitive.

WHERE CAN I GET GRAPHICS FOR MY WEB PAGE?

Where do you get the graphics to include on your Web page? Be careful not to include graphics that are copyrighted by someone else. (See Appendix A, "The Quilter's Guide to Computer Graphics," for guidance.) You can scan your own photos, create graphics in your drawing program, or buy CD-ROMs full of Web-ready (and royalty-free) art that you can use on your site.

Save your graphics in GIF format, and be sure to keep the files small so that they don't take others too long to download. Of course, you can get fancy and add things like CGI and Java scripts, but all you really need to know to create a lovely page are a few simple HTML commands.

IS IT SAFE TO BUY THINGS ON THE INTERNET?

How safe it is to buy things on the Internet depends on whom you're buying from. There are many respectable retailers on the Internet, but there are also some whose practices are dubious. The best rule of thumb is to know whom you're buying from. But even that's not always a guarantee of safety, since many scammers use multiple fake user IDs to vouch for the character of the scam artist.

If you don't know whom you're buying from, look for a toll-free number and a street address that you can verify with a business yellow pages, and check with the local Better Business Bureau. Place your order by calling the toll-free number (it's always faster than e-mail). And use a credit card so that you have some recourse if you don't receive the merchandise. Also, make your first orders small so that if you get burned it won't hurt too much.

Another good thing to look for is whether the site is linked to other quilt sites on the Net. If the retailer has burned a customer in the past, chances are good that the customer may have notified other Web sites with links to that retailer and asked them to remove their links.

With all that said, we've purchased everything from fabric to hard-to-find patterns, books, and even antiques on the Web, and we've never had any problems. Knock on wood.

HOW DO I SET UP MY OWN STORE IN CYBERSPACE?

If you're a store owner, you first need to ask yourself what you hope to accomplish by going online. Do you want to gather information and ideas about quilting? Do you want to hobnob with quilters? Do you want to search out information about setting up and running a small business? Or do you want to create a high-tech mail-order business? All are excellent reasons to get on the Internet.

There are some very profitable mail-order businesses on the Internet. They're successful because their products appeal to a niche market of enthusiasts and often are difficult to obtain elsewhere. For example, we have a friend named George who sells mineral samples to rock collectors through a very modest Web site he set up on CompuServe. One may not think there would be much of a market for rocks, but the business has become so successful that George has given up his other jobs, including his software company and computer consultancy.

At the same time, we know of countless other Internet-based mail-order businesses, including craft ones, that are no more than hobbies for their proprietors. Being on the Internet doesn't guarantee success.

Still, there are tremendous advantages to putting a mail-order business on the Internet. For starters, all you need to spend is $20 per month on an Internet service and Web page and you can market products to a well-defined niche. No need to spend lots of money on mass mailings and ads. In fact, we know of one mail-order company that discontinued mass-mailing catalogs and running magazine ads because its Web site was attracting more new customers for very little money.

Here are more tips:

- It's not necessary to hire an expensive Web consultant to design your Web site. Sit down with a book on basic HTML coding one afternoon, and you can have your own Web site by the evening. You don't need an elaborate site either. You just need good products and good customer service. Remember our friend George and his simple Web page on CompuServe. We know of other successful mail-order business run from bare-bones Web pages on America Online.

- Be credit card friendly. Few people ever get around to mailing in those checks. List a toll-free ordering number and street address on your site. You should also consider shopping around for an Internet service that offers what's called a secure server—that's a network server through which hackers can't "eavesdrop" on credit card numbers. If you don't have a storefront, the credit card companies may want to see all these things before they give you permission to accept credit card orders.

- Include full-color pictures of all your products. It's amazing how many people try to sell things on the Net without bothering to show pictures of their products. Make your pictures small so that they don't take forever to download, but when surfers click on them they should be able to view a magnification. Buy one of those cheap digital cameras that let you snap a picture and pop it right into your computer. Include in your Web page catalog a thorough description of the product, including its dimensions. People love to read lots and lots of ad copy before buying anything.

- Make customer service your top priority. Remember, your best customers are going to be repeat customers. Ship orders within 24 hours. Answer all e-mail within 24 hours too. Put your business's name, e-mail address, URL, toll-free number, and ordering address at the end of all your e-mail correspondence. Often, when Net surfers write to businesses they encounter on the Web, by the time an answer arrives, they've forgotten both the name of the business and its Web site.

- Include more than a catalog on your Web site. Offer features that quilters will want to read regularly, and they may be inspired to bookmark your site or link their Web site to yours. Quilters should have more reasons to visit your Web site regularly than just buying things.

- Offer to exchange links with other similar businesses on the Web, even if they're competitors. There are many retail niches on the Net in which retailers make a concerted effort to exchange links with related mail-order businesses. Vintage clothing dealers, for instance, are avid "cross-linkers." Quilt stores and mail-order houses tend not to be so cooperative. In fact, we often hear from vendors who request that we include on our Web site a link to their Web home, but they grow surly if we ask them to reciprocate. Exchanging links benefits everyone because it makes everyone's business easier to find. It's analogous to opening a store in a craft mall. Would you rather set up shop next to other craft stores, or ten miles down on Highway J with only a Tasty Dee-Lite Chicken for a neighbor?

HOW TO BECOME A NET-SURFING QUILTING NERD WITH GRANDMA'S COMPUTER

You use Grandma's sewing machine, so why not use grandma's computer to get on the Internet? Yes, you can burn rubber on the info-highway even with that old Tandy or Apple I. You may not be able to see the whimsical graphics of the Web with it, but you'll still be able to exchange e-mail, tap into conversations with other quilters, and even download software and search for information.

To get on the Internet quickly and easily and get all the graphics, you'll need at least a 386 PC with 4MB RAM, VGA graphics, and Windows 3.1 running in enhanced mode. You should also have at least a 14.4Kbps modem, or your connections will creep. These are the bare-bones requirements for using one of the leading Web browsers like Netscape Navigator or Internet Explorer, or for using America Online, CompuServe, or Prodigy to tap into the Net.

If your PC is a 386 or older and it's running DOS, you can still get on the Web and see some pictures. But you won't get as many graphics or get them as quickly as you would with a newer PC running Windows.

Older PCs are great if all you want to do is use the Internet for e-mail. If all you have is Internet e-mail, you can still participate in Internet quilt mailing list discussions, read Usenet discussions, and even search and download software and information off Web pages. For directions on how to do it, get yourself a copy of *Dr. Bob's Painless Guide to the Internet & Amazing Things You Can Do with E-mail* by Bob Rankin (San Francisco: No Starch Press, 1996, 800/420-7240, $12.95).

If you use an older PC, you'll use an old-fashioned modem program like Procomm Plus to dial your Internet service. You'll log on just as you would to a computer bulletin board. Once logged on, you'll type Internet commands to download files from other computers (FTP), travel to other computers (telnet), retrieve e-mail, and read Usenet messages. This is how computer users surfed the Net for decades before Web browsers were invented, and, in fact, this is how the author of one popular quilt design program still prefers to travel the Net. You can also use PCs as old as the 286 to tap into CompuServe, Delphi, and Prodigy with their software.

There are a number of DOS-based Web browsers that you can download from the Internet. One popular one is the $50 shareware program Minuet by the

University of Minnesota (**http://www.cesnet.cz/pub/gopher/minnesota/minuet/** or **ftp://minuet.micro.umn.edu/pub/minuet/latest/minuarc.exe**). Minuet will run on any PC-compatible computer with 512KB RAM, DOS 2.1, and a hard disk. Its Web browser is text-based, but it will display GIF and JPEG files on a 386 PC with VGA or better graphics (though the images won't be clickable). It also offers e-mail, Gopher, telnet, FTP, and Usenet news. It will run only with a SLIP connection, while most Internet services use PPP these days. You can use it with a PPP connection, but it won't be smooth sailing.

DOSLynx is a text-based Web browser that will work on almost any PC as old as an 8086 with 512KB RAM, DOS 3.0 or later, and a monochrome monitor. It will work with both SLIP and PPP connections, but you'll need to download an appropriate driver for the type of connection you have (**ftp://ftp2.cc.ukans.edu/pub/WWW/DosLynx/support/**). You'll also need to download a dialer, or else use a modem program to call your Internet service and learn the commands to put it into SLIP or PPP mode. After that, you exit the dialing program, load the SLIP or PPP driver, and fire up DOSLynx. You can download it for free from **http://www.lynx.browser.org/**.

Net-Tamer is a $35 shareware program (**http://www.people.delphi.com/davidcolston/**) that automates access to the Web for folks with PCs as old as a 286 XT with a Hercules graphics card. It offers e-mail, FTP, telnet, and Web browsing. It will display graphics only on a 386 or better PC. It supports only PPP connections.

Two other intriguing browsers for antique PCs come from the other side of the ocean. SPIN is a Dutch browser that will display graphics on a 386 or better PC with SVGA (**http://www.saturnus.nl/spin/engels/index.html**). Arachne is a graphical DOS browser from Czechoslovakia (**http://www.naf.cz/arachne/**).

Other Internet utilities like mail and FTP programs are available in DOS versions for old PCs. To find them and to get more information on accessing the Net with a clunker, head to "The DOS User's Guide to the Internet" (**http://www.palms.4kz.com.au/dos.html**), run by Nigel Gorry in Queensland, Australia.

What if grandma's old computer is a Mac? A Mac Plus running System 7.1 with 4 MB of RAM will get you on the Internet. But it will be painfully slow, and the color graphics will dither to black and white. But an old 68020-based system, like an LC, running System 7.1 with 8MB of RAM, will have no problem. You'll even be able to enjoy graphics and sound.

Here's one fast way to connect to the Internet with an older Mac. First, purchase a fast modem. Connect it to your computer and load America Online 2.7 (AOL 3.0 doesn't work well on older Macs) and its Web browser software. It will add everything you need into your system and configure it to get you up and running.

Otherwise, for an older system you'll need to install MacTCP and PPP utilities to connect to an Internet provider. If your Internet provider doesn't give you the necessary software, head to your nearest bookstore. For $29.95 you can purchase *The Internet Starter Kit for Macintosh* by Adam C. Engst (Indianapolis: Hayden Books, 1996). The book contains a floppy disk with the necessary extensions and some useful programs and utilities.

JUDY & GLORIA'S INTERNET SURVIVAL TIP #8

Keep your browser up to date. Some Web graphics may appear fuzzy or discolored if your browser is a dinosaur. Another good reason to use the latest version of your browser is that makers are always adding new security features that make shopping and banking on the Internet more secure. Versions of Netscape prior to 4.01 contain a bug that allows Web site owners to read the contents of the hard disk of anyone logged on to their site. That's true of both PC and Mac versions. Similarly, old Windows 95 versions of Microsoft's Internet Explorer (including the version used with America Online software) suffer a similar security leak. Use version 3.02 or later.

YOU CAN DO ANYTHING WITH E-MAIL

Have a clunker of a computer, and all you can use it for is to pick up and send e-mail? Don't let that stop you from enjoying the Internet. Subscribing to Internet quilt-related mailing lists is the first thing you should do. You'll meet lots of friends and have many good conversations that way. But you can also use e-mail to search for software, retrieve FAQs (frequently asked questions) about quilting, and even get the text off Web pages.

GET "FREQUENTLY ASKED QUESTION" FILES FROM USENET NEWSGROUPS

Send a message to a FAQ server like **mail-server@rtfm.mit.edu**. The message should contain this line:

> **send usenet/news.answers/crafts**

This will garner you a list of all the FAQ files related to the craft discussion groups on Usenet. Some examples are the Cross-Stitch FAQ and the Textiles ones. Find the ones that interest you, and send another e-mail message like

> **send usenet/news.answers/crafts/textiles**

The above message will get you the textile FAQ.

SNARE TEXT (INCLUDING FAQS) FROM WEB PAGES

Send a message to a Web mail server like **agora@info.lanic.utexas.edu**, telling it the URL you want. In the message you'd type

> **send http://www.planetpatchwork.com/**

This message will get you the text from Planet Patchwork's main Web page.

THE QUILTER'S GUIDE TO COMPUTER GRAPHICS

What's a pixel? What's bit depth? In which file format should you save pictures? Here are the explanations you need to make sense of it all.

While using your printer or graphics software, you've probably run across some terms that didn't make sense. What does "dot pitch" mean? What's "24-bit color" and why should you care? You probably also have questions about whether and how you can use art that you find on the Internet—or in quilt programs in your quilts. This appendix addresses a grab bag of questions that you may have while using your computer to design quilts.

WHAT YOU NEED TO KNOW ABOUT USING OTHERS' ART IN YOUR QUILTS

Some quilters are passionate about it: They refuse to use in their quilts any image that they did not render, any photo they did not snap. They even regard using clip art as cheating. They want every element in their quilt to be original. Others borrow liberally from clip art books, images on the Internet, and, alas, even other people's quilts.

It's become so easy to scan a picture and pop it into a quilt design or iron it on a T-shirt that many never stop to consider that *most of the art out there is owned by someone.*

They own it thanks to something called *copyright.* (Trademark is similar, except that it's the symbol that identifies a product or business.) Even if there's no copyright symbol on the picture you download or the greeting card you're contemplating scanning, that image is owned by someone. And before you use it in your quilt (or on your Web page), you darn well better find out who owns that image and ask permission to use it.

In fact, you may want to give serious thought to not using in your quilts any image that you did not personally create. One of the quilts in the color gallery section of this book was created with copyrighted images that the owner, Simon &

Schuster, hesitated to license for use in a quilt. The troubles that arose caused us to swear off using any copyrighted images in our quilts ever again.

THE NANCY DREW QUILT: A CAUTIONARY TALE

Judy's always been a big Nancy Drew fan, and thought that pictures from the books published in the '30s through '50s would make an ideal theme for a quilt. She had seen art work such as paintings that used images from the early editions of the girls' novels, and didn't think there would be any problem in obtaining the owner, Simon & Schuster's permission to use illustrations in a quilt.

She contacted Simon & Schuster and was told that once she determined which images she wanted to use, she should mail the company copies of the images along with a request to reproduce them. Since she's the type of quilter who never knows what's going to appear in her quilt until it's done, she proceeded to assemble her quilt. Armed with a stack of about a hundred antique Nancy Drew books from her own collection and from friends', she scanned dozens of images and experimented with different ways of printing them on fabric. Once she determined which illustrations she wanted to use, she photocopied them and wrote to request permission.

Several months passed. By the time Judy heard from Simon & Schuster she had finished the quilt. At first, Simon & Schuster refused to grant her permission to use any of the Nancy Drew illustrations. They would not tell her why.

Anxious phone calls, faxes, and e-mails ensued. At one point, while pleading her case before a Simon & Schuster representative, Judy pointed out that a series of well-known oil paintings made use of similar Nancy Drew images. "That's fine art," the woman countered. "The rules are different for quilts."

Eventually, Simon & Schuster reconsidered. The company offered to license Judy the images for $150. But the license was heavy with restrictions. The quilt can appear only in this book. Judy cannot publish patterns for it. She can't use the quilt to publicize the book. She can't display it on the Web. When a quilt magazine asked to run a picture of the quilt, Simon & Schuster forbid it. When Judy asked if she could enter the quilt for consideration to appear in a public-television documentary on quilting, Simon & Schuster responded that it would require an extra licensing fee "beyond your budget."

When snapshots of the quilt were passed around privately among Nancy Drew fans, several asked to buy the quilt, but the terms of the licensing agreement forbid even that.

Judy says she has vowed never again to use copyrighted images in a quilt. "I can't believe how stupid I was using these illlustrations without considering that there might be restrictions on how I could use the quilt," she says. "I've learned my lesson."

RULES TO REMEMBER BEFORE USING COPYRIGHTED MATERIAL

Even images that you may think you are free to use in your quilt are probably owned by someone else. An author who wanted to reproduce magazine ads from decades past in a book about vintage clothing spent a maddening year tracking down obscure fashion designers, photographers, and long-gone ad agencies to obtain permissions. She even found herself arguing with the estates of long-deceased models, their heirs demanding licensing fees.

Here are some simple rules to spare you from grief:

- Before using any image in your quilt, find out who owns it and ask their permission. The owner may not be easy to track in this digital age in which pirated art floods the Internet. But if you're in doubt as to where an image originated, don't use it. Even clip art images are not necessarily free for the using. (See "What Is Clip Art?")

- Even if you manipulate someone else's image or pattern in your computer—enlarge it, change its colors, shift its lines slightly, draw a daisy on it—someone else still owns the copyright, and you need to ask permission to use their art.

- What about the quilt block libraries in quilting software like Electric Quilt, QuiltSoft, and Quilt-Pro? The respective manufacturers own the quilt block, border, and stencil patterns found in those programs. It's illegal to republish any of those patterns, even if they're resized or distorted. You can, however, sell or publish any pattern you draw from scratch in quilt software.

- Consider sticking to using your own drawings and photographs (assuming you have the permission of the people in the pictures!). That way you'll have no restrictions on what you may do with your quilt or its pattern. And you'll avoid the red tape of obtaining permission.

WHEN IS AN IMAGE IN THE PUBLIC DOMAIN?

Copyright law is always changing. When an image's copyright runs out and it falls into the public domain—in other words, becomes free for others to use—depends upon many factors, including what copyright laws were in effect when the image was created, whether the author is deceased (and if so, for how long) and other confusing things. (As Mark Twain said, "When copyright laws were written all the fools were invited.") Unless an image is over a hundred years old you should always assume that someone owns it and obtain permission to use it.

WARNING!

Most quilters think that obtaining permission to use a copyrighted image in their quilt is a simple matter of writing the owner and asking permission. But it's not always so easy. Big corporations don't like to give permission for their trademarks and copyrighted images to appear in "Sally's 1997 Summer Vacation Remembrance Quilt, Poughkeepsie," even if it's only going to be hung on the family room wall. Red tape often ensues. Should you get permission, it may come with qualifications. You may be forbidden to let a quilt magazine run a picture of your quilt or even to exhibit it at the state fair.

WHAT IS CLIP ART? WHAT DO I NEED TO KNOW ABOUT USING IT IN MY QUILTS?

"Clip art" is a catch-all term for canned art or photos that other artists can use. Today it's "clip media" in hip-speak.

You can find clip art just about everywhere: in big libraries on the Internet (see our "Quilter's Internet Yellow Pages" for locations), in your word processing software, for sale on CD-ROMs, or in those Dover clip art books that pervade art stores. You can even buy craft-related clip art books and computer disks from quilt catalogs these days.

Whether and how you can use clip art in your own work is another matter. Every clip art collection comes with some sort of license specifying the terms under which you can use the art. You may be free to use the clip art for personal use, but you may need to buy a special license to use it for a commercial purpose.

For instance, lots of craft book publishers like to make liberal use of clip art in their books, but they need to be careful about where that clip art originates. They usually need to pay the originator a special fee to use it in their books. If the clip art is part of a collection—in a drawing program or on a CD-ROM, for example—the publisher may need to track down the original artist and obtain permission to use it commercially.

Here's another example: NASA has on its Internet site a huge library of photos (**http://www.hq.nasa.gov/office/pao/Library/photo.html**). NASA gives Web surfers permission to download pictures of, say, the moon or the space shuttle and use them for personal purposes, but it asks that people refrain from posting photos of astronauts on their own Web pages, as that might constitute a violation of the astronaut's privacy.

The Internet has brought to the fore other clip art/copyright issues. Lots of clip art collections on the Net include pirated images, although some make efforts to keep stolen art out. For instance, you'll find lots of cartoons in clip art collections on the Net—especially of Disney characters. These circulate in violation of the owners' copyrights. Before you could use these *in any fashion,* you would need to obtain permission from whomever owns the drawing.

The bottom line is that you should

- Be certain of the source of any clip art that you use. Be skeptical of art downloaded from the Internet, unless you've downloaded it from the artist's site (with the artist's permission).

- If you buy a clip art book or CD-ROM, familiarize yourself with the terms under which you can use the art. It may be free for personal use, but commercial use may require special permission and an extra fee.

- Always ask permission before using any art in your work, even if the intended quilt or quilt label is for your own use and you don't plan to sell or show it. Write or call the originator of the clip art collection to verify that the art came from them and that you can use it.

- Always be courteous to other artists, and respect their rights of ownership. That may be how they earn their living, and heck, artists rarely earn a lot. If they refuse to give you permission to use their art, or if they ask a fee, respect that request.

TYPES OF ART THAT YOU NEED TO HAVE PERMISSION TO USE

TYPE OF ART OR IMAGE	WHY YOU MUST ASK PERMISSION
Art from other quilters' Web pages	Please, please don't snatch any kind of art—quilt blocks, graphics, even funny signatures—from others' Web pages to use on your own Web page. Or to use in a quilt. Even if no copyright notice appears anywhere on the image or the page, the owner still holds the copyright on the page and its contents.
Art from other peoples' quilts and patterns	Other quilters' quilts and patterns are copyrighted just as books are. You should never use art from someone else's quilt or copy even a portion of another's pattern without asking the artist's or publisher's permission first.
Logos of companies, sports teams, products, or charities; comic strip characters or faces or images of celebrities (celebrities can also include "things" like the Star Trek *Enterprise* or the Batmobile)	They're trademarked—someone owns the image and has the right to determine how others can use it.
Art and photos from books, magazines, company brochures, greeting cards, newspapers, comic strips, and CD-ROMs, even if you alter them	They're copyrighted. That means someone owns the image as well as the right to determine how others use it. Even if there's no copyright notice on the image, it still may be copyrighted.
Single frames or animation sequences from movies, TV, radio, CD-ROMs, or rented or purchased videos, even if you edit or alter them	They're copyrighted. Even if, as the husband of one of the authors argued in defense of his use of TV clips from football games on his Web page, "The pictures fly through the air, so they must be free." They're not; they're still copyrighted. (He and some of his Internet football pals received letters from the NFL's law firm shortly after that.)

WHICH GRAPHICS FILE FORMAT SHOULD I USE TO STORE IMAGES?

The graphics file format you use will depend on how you plan to use your picture. It will also depend upon your software's needs and proclivities. For instance, if your quilt design software imports only PCX graphics, you should save scanned fabric as PCX files.

The best file format for you will also depend upon whether the image is a bitmap (like a scanned photo or a drawing in a paint program like SuperPaint or Corel Photo-Paint) or a vector graphic (a drawing created in a program like Canvas or CorelDraw, or a scanned photo converted to a vector graphic with a tracing feature). Remember, a bitmap, or raster image, is a matrix of dots, while a vector one is made of mathematically defined paths, or lines. Some file formats contain both vector and bitmap elements (although the images saved in these formats don't have to contain both). An example might be a line drawing created in a drawing program that uses a bitmap, such as a scanned photo or texture, as a background. The latter file type is referred to as a metafile and includes Macintosh PICT, Windows WMF, and desktop publishing EPS formats.

SOME DRAWING PROGRAMS STORE YOUR ART IN NATIVE FORMATS

Many drawing programs, and even some quilt design programs, store images that you create in their own special graphics format. CorelDraw, for example, stores drawings in CDR format. In order to use an image you have created in such a program with another application, you must often export it to a file format recognized by the other program. Such exports are not without glitches. A quilt pattern drawn in CorelDraw may end up looking like a stack of straw if you try to export it to a TIFF file. It's important to remember that most of these proprietary graphics formats are vector based. You should always try to export them to another vector graphics format, like WMF or EPS, in order to preserve the lines of your image. Remember too that bitmap drawing programs like Windows Paint and graphics software like Paint Shop Pro won't let you import vector drawings.

PCX

(Bitmap) PCX is the most versatile file format, because almost every graphics program in the world supports it, both on PCs and Macs. It's known as the PC Paintbrush format, after an ancient DOS-based painting program from a company called Zsoft. It stores uncompressed raster images in up to 24-bit color. Quilt programs often let you export designs in PCX format so that you can use them with graphics software and paint-type programs. But when you export a quilt design to a PCX file and then pull it up in another program, you won't be able to move its lines around or redesign it as you could have in the quilt software. You will only be able to "paint" it or erase portions of it.

BMP

(Bitmap) This is the format used by Windows. When you "cut" an image from your screen and "paste" it via the Windows Clipboard, it's saved on the Clipboard as a BMP image. This is actually a "dumbed down" file format (you'll lose a lot in quality) that you should use only for the simplest images containing few colors or

shades. Think of it as the Crayola format. The BMP format was designed for displaying simple images on the Windows screen or storing them on the Windows Clipboard. It was never intended for printed images or sophisticated drawings. Avoid it in quilt designing if you can.

GIF

(Bitmap) Pronounced "jif," as in the name of the peanut butter, the Graphics Interchange Format was designed by CompuServe, which in recent years has claimed a patent to it and has gone so far as to sue software developers who've used it. Still, you see it a lot in images on the Web because early Web browsers displayed it with ease. The format was created to store a lot of graphics information in a very small file. It's good at storing images up to 8 bits (that's gray-scale and 256-color images) and simple animations. GIFs are impractical to use in desktop publishing because you cannot separate the colors to edit them. You'll find GIFs in both the PC and Mac worlds. Use the GIF format for storing artwork with large areas of flat color and line and which you plan to use on a Web page (photos are better stored in JPEG format). Skip it if you're doing quilt design.

JPEG

(Bitmap) The Joint Photographic Experts Group format is becoming standard on the Internet because JPEG supports 24-bit color raster images (allowing millions of colors). Graphics files of so many colors can be huge, but JPEG images are stored in compressed format and then automatically decompressed when loaded into a Web browser. Unfortunately, some data is lost in the decompression process, so the image is not identical to the original. But this is not generally noticeable, since it's usually nonessential pixels that are kicked aside, like those in a large area of a single color. You often see pictures on Web pages stored in both GIF and JPEG format. The GIF picture appears automatically, but if you want to see an enlarged, more detailed version, you can often click on it to see a JPEG format. JPEG is capable of giving you a clearer, richer picture than the GIF format and is better for storing scanned photos and other artwork with subtle color transitions. QuiltSoft uses the JPEG format on its fabric CD-ROMs because of the format's high resolution. JPEG is a good alternative to the TIFF format for photos that you plan to print on fabric or use in designing appliqué patterns because the file size of images stored in this format is smaller.

TIFF

(Bitmap) The Tag Image File Format, developed by Aldus, is the prince of the file formats, because it can handle images of up to 32 bits. It has the best color storage and interpretation abilities and should be your pick whenever you scan a photo, either color or black-and-white. TIFF images are also easier to manipulate than images in other file formats—it's easier to tinker with an image's color balance or grays, or resize it, without distorting things. TIFF format is the standard in the desktop publishing world. TIFF files that you create on one type of computer—say, a Macintosh— look the same on another type of computer, like a PC. The only drawback to the TIFF format is that its high-resolution files can get big—real big— and those monster files can cause some older PCs (and clunkier graphics programs) to choke. Even if you have a lot of memory, their large size can be difficult to work with. Always try to keep your TIFF files as small as possible by scanning and storing

images at a low resolution and cropping them tightly. TIFF isn't supported by any of the quilt programs, and since it's a bitmap format, your drawing program won't store your drawings in it (at least not well). But it's a good format to use when scanning photos for either printing on fabric or turning into an appliqué pattern.

EPS

(Vector and bitmap) You sometimes find clip art on the Internet stored in Encapsulated PostScript format. One of the advantages of this format is that you can edit the clip art, separating its lines and elements. You should use this format for any drawing on a PC or Mac that will be sent to a PostScript printer. Save your vector drawings in this format in your drawing software if you plan to use them in other drawing programs or lay them out with desktop publishing software.

WMF

(Vector and bitmap) Use the Windows Metafile format for all non-PostScript drawings on the PC. Its drawing features are not as sophisticated as those of the EPS format. Unless you're into desktop publishing, WMF is a file format that is irrelevant to most quilters' lives.

PICT

(Vector and bitmap) PICT is the default file format used by the Macintosh. When you "cut" an image from your screen and "paste" it via the Clipboard, it's stored on the Clipboard as a PICT file. Images can contain both vector and bitmap elements. The PICT2 format supports up to 32-bit color. It was designed for the Macintosh, and its colors don't translate well when viewed on PCs.

MACPAINT

(Bitmap) This simple file format originated with the early (but seminal) Macintosh drawing program of the same name from Claris. It supports only small black-and-white images on the Mac.

T * I * P

Images created in a native Mac file format, like PICT, might not look very good when displayed on a PC. Similarly, native PC formats like BMP and PCX may look crummy on a Mac. If you're going to be shuffling art between different computers, store it in a format that looks good on all platforms, like TIFF or JPEG.

QUESTIONS AND ANSWERS ABOUT GRAPHICS AND FILE FORMATS

HOW DO I CONVERT ART FROM ONE GRAPHICS FILE FORMAT TO ANOTHER?

You can use your drawing or graphics program's Export or Save As command to convert art from one file format to another. The import and export features of programs vary tremendously, though, and the translation can result in parts of an image being lost or its colors fading.

File formats also vary in how they store colors and images. If you turn a high-resolution TIFF file into a BMP one, you may end up with a grainy, crudely colored picture.

Similarly, if you convert a vector drawing format like EPS into a bitmapped one like PCX, much is going to be lost in the translation. Ideally, you want to convert vector drawing formats into other vector drawing formats, and bitmaps into bitmap formats.

All that said, there are lots of freeware and shareware programs for converting art from one bitmap format to another. As we've mentioned, one of our favorites is Paint Shop Pro from Jasc, Inc. (800/622-2793 or 612/930-9800). You can download it from the Web at **http://www.jasc.com/**.

A great shareware program for Mac users is Graphic Converter by Lemke Software (e-mail: 100102.1304@compuserve.com). You can download it from C|Net's shareware library at **http://www.shareware.com/**.

Another great program for working with photos is the $30 shareware program LView, from MMedia Research, 1501 E. Hallandale Beach Blvd., #254, Hallandale, FL 33009, e-mail: mmedia@world.std.com. It's available in both Windows and Mac versions, and you can download it from the C|Net shareware library as well.

It's more difficult to convert a bitmap to a vector image, and vice versa. (If you're using CorelDraw, you've probably already discovered this. Take any simple quilt block you draw and convert it to a TIFF file; the resulting image will look speckled, or some of the lines will be lost.) The export features in drawing programs usually let you convert a vector drawing to a bitmap.

Fortunately, none of the things quilters are apt to do with their drawing or graphics programs are likely to require converting images between different formats—save for turning a photo (a bitmap) into an appliqué design (a vector drawing). And the trace feature found in most drawing programs will usually suffice for that.

HOW DO I MOVE QUILT DESIGNS BETWEEN PROGRAMS?

There are two ways to get a quilt design into another program:

USE THE IMPORT FEATURE. You can use this method for any type of graphics file, but it's the only way to move vector drawings, or portions of drawings, between programs.

Save the picture in your first graphics or drawing program. Some programs, like CorelDraw, save images in their own proprietary format, which is often hard, if not impossible, to import into other programs. In such cases, use the Save As or Export command on the File menu when you save your image to save it in the file format that the other program prefers. (As mentioned above, save vector drawings into a vector file format. If you save a vector image or line drawing as a bitmap, the drawing may end up looking grainy, or some of its lines may be lost. And you won't be able to work with its lines, as you could in the original program.)

When you've saved your file, fire up the other program and use its Import feature, usually also found on the File menu, to import the saved picture.

USE THE WINDOWS OR MACINTOSH CLIPBOARD. Although shuffling bitmap images between programs is easy with the Clipboard, it's a far less desirable route than using import/export. The Clipboard uses a simplified file format that will reduce the colors and subtleties of your image. On PCs running Windows, that's the BMP format, and it's the PICT format on the Mac. Also, the Clipboard uses a bitmapped file format, which means that you can't use it for transferring portions of a vector line drawing, such as one created in CorelDraw, into another program without losing the integrity of the drawing and turning it into a bitmap.

To use the Clipboard, select the picture, or a portion of it, using the selection or cropping tool. Use the program's Copy feature, usually found on the Edit menu, to copy it to the Clipboard. Then fire up the other graphics or drawing program and Paste (also found in the Edit menu) the image into place.

JUDY & GLORIA'S COMPUTER GRAPHICS SURVIVAL TIP

Often the same picture will look different in two different graphics programs—lighter in one, darker in another. Or an image that looks beautiful in one program will look messed up in another program. That's because different graphics programs display images in different ways. The proof of the pudding is in how the image ultimately looks in its final form, whether printed or displayed on a Web page. If a picture appears to have some sort of general distortion when displayed, try opening it in another graphics program to see if the distortion persists. Always keep on hand at least two graphics processing programs for this purpose.

WHAT DOES THAT DOTS-PER-INCH STUFF MEAN?

Dots per inch (dpi) is a measure of a printer or scanner's resolution: the higher the dpi, the higher the resolution. A 720-dpi printer will print sharper pictures than a 360-dpi one. And a 200-dpi scan of a picture will be sharper than a 100-dpi one.

Interpolated resolution, like "1200 dpi interpolated," is a phrase you'll see often in descriptions of scanners. Interpolation is a way of telling the computer to increase an image's resolution by adding dots to the image based upon the colors of neighboring dots, so the computer is actually guessing what the image would look like if it were scanned in at a higher resolution. "Optical resolution" is another phrase that you'll often see. Unlike interpolated resolution, optical is the real resolution—the computer doesn't fill in any dots. When choosing a scanner, weigh optical and interpolated resolution against each other. A scanner with 600 dpi optical and 2400 dpi interpolated will give you a better final image than one with 300 dpi optical and 2400 interpolated.

WHAT'S THE BEST RESOLUTION AT WHICH TO SCAN A PICTURE? AND HOW SHOULD I PREPARE AN IMAGE FOR SCANNING?

The answer to this question depends on whether you're scanning fabric for use in a quilt design or a photo to print on fabric, and it depends on your printer too. For more information on this topic, you'll find numerous tutorials on scanning throughout this book (see the index). Also, see Chapter 17 for a discussion of printing photos on fabric, Chapter 16 for information about the best ways to scan fabric for use in quilt designs, and Chapter 15 for details on using scanned photos and other art to create appliqué patterns.

WHY DOES THE SAME IMAGE SCANNED AT DIFFERENT RESOLUTIONS LOOK THE SAME ON MY COMPUTER SCREEN?

Your computer monitor has a different way of interpreting an image's resolution than your printer or scanner. Whereas your computer printer is plopping dots of ink on paper, your monitor creates dots (pixels) on the surface of its screen. So, depending upon the kind of monitor you have, your high-resolution scanned image may look much better when it's printed.

WHY ARE THE COLORS OF MY PRINTED IMAGE DIFFERENT FROM THE ONES I SEE ON MY COMPUTER SCREEN?

See Chapter 17 for an in-depth discussion of this irritating phenomenon.

WHAT IS BIT DEPTH?

Bit depth tells how many bits your computer uses to represent each dot in an image. A black-and-white line drawing has a bit depth of only 1, but a photo-realistic image may have up to 16.7 million colors, or 24 bits. Images like that can really chew up disk space.

Here's a look at the bit depths of different image types.

BLACK-AND-WHITE IMAGES It takes only one bit to define the "colors" of a black-and-white image, so these images have a bit depth of 1.

NOTE

If you're planning on scanning your image at 100 percent size and printing your scan at the same size as the original image, these numbers should be what you're looking for.

PHOTOS:

Printer Resolution	Scanning Resolution
300 dpi	100 dpi
600 dpi	150 dpi
1200 dpi	170 dpi

LINE ART:
Scan at the maximum resolution of your printer.

GRAY-SCALE IMAGES Gray-scale images can have a bit depth of either 4 or 8. A 4-bit gray-scale image has 16 shades of gray. An 8-bit gray-scale image can use 256 shades of gray.

COLOR IMAGES Color images can be 4, 8, 16, or 24 bits. An 8-bit color image has 256 colors. A 16-bit color image has thousands of colors. A 24-bit image has up to 16.7 million colors. (24-bit color is also known as true color or photo-realistic color.) Scanners now boast having bit depths of 30, 36, or even higher. Most software cannot handle anything over 24 bits anyway. Even so, the extra bit depth does capture colors and grays more accurately and helps eliminate "noise" and other problems that may hurt the quality of a scan.

TELL ME MORE ABOUT TOUCHING UP
PHOTOS AND OTHER ART IN GRAPHICS SOFTWARE

Almost every scanned image will need a bit of touch-up before you use it. Our favorite touch-up program is the low-cost shareware program LView, described earlier. The software that comes with scanners also provides most of these options. Here are some of the tools you'll have at your disposal to brighten and brush up pictures. They may have different names in different programs.

SHARPEN The Sharpen feature sharpens the colors and contrast of an image. It accentuates edges and can make a scan crisper. Always apply this as a first step in cleaning up any scanned image, then save your sharpened image to a new file. (That way, if you don't like what it looks like, you can always return to your original scan.)

UNSHARP Many people will be satisfied with the Sharpen command, but if you want to affect just how much sharpening is done, use the Unsharp command. This is a technique that the pros often use. It has three controls areas: amount, threshold, and radius. The amount controls how much sharpening will be done. Threshold is how sensitive the edge is. Most people use a threshold setting of 3 or 4. Radius is tricky. It determines how many pixels from the edge should be lightened or darkened.

SMOOTH The Smooth feature will smooth rough lines or jagged areas of a scan. Use this tool only if you want to create a softer image, or if your picture suffers from the jaggies.

BRIGHTNESS The Brightness setting boosts or reduces the lightness of an image. Scans often create a slightly darkened image. Play with your brightness setting to get the best value. We like to boost the brightness of photos and other images by at least 10 percent. But be careful! Keep in mind, that the entire image is getting lighter by the same amount. This means that an already light pixel will get even lighter or turn white.

LEVELS If your software has a Levels command, use it instead of the Brightness command. Levels allow you to modify the brightness values of selected pixels rather than all pixels.

DESPECKLE Use the Despeckle command on scanned line art and gray-scale images to get rid of fly-like "scanning artifacts."

GRAY-SCALE The Gray-scale option turns a color image into a gray one.

NEGATIVE The Negative command turns the picture into a negative image of itself. If your scan began life as a color photo, it's always a good idea to turn it into a gray-scale image first before turning it into a negative.

GAMMA CORRECTION Use gamma correction to brighten or darken an image. You can adjust the gamma correction for the individual color components of red, green, or blue, or apply it to all the pixels in an image.

INTERACTIVE RGB OR COLOR BALANCE ADJUSTMENT Interactive RGB lets you tweak the basic red, green, and blue components of colors. For instance, a color may be represented as RGB 10, 10, 10. If you up the red portion of the color by 10, the new color will be RGB 20, 10, 10. RGB is a standard for color representation on computer monitors. Electric Quilt lets you mix fabric colors by RGB values.

HUE, SATURATION, AND VALUE ADJUSTMENT Hue is a value that denotes the dominant color—either red, green, or blue. Saturation is the amount of color that's used. Value is a measurement of lightness. Adjust the saturation to tweak the amount of color used in an image. By adjusting its value, you can boost the lightness of the image or darken it. Hue will get rid of color excesses, like too much orange or yellow. You can sharpen up skin tones, for instance, by adding yellow to the reds, lowering the color saturation, and lightening the image.

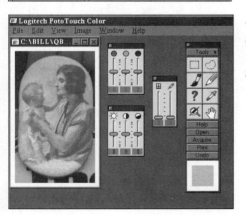

It's always a good idea to sharpen a scanned image to enhance its colors and lines. Save your sharpened image in a new file so that you can always return to your original scan if you don't like the variation you've created.

Some software, like that included with Logitech scanners, gives you lots of slider bars with which to adjust a photo's color and brightness.

This is the original scan.

This is the scan with its brightness boosted 35 percent and its contrast upped 10 percent. Color saturation was boosted 10 percent, and the greens were increased by 8 percent to make the grass sharper in color.

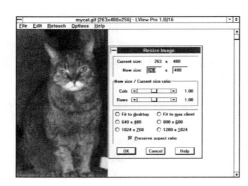

When you resize a picture, be sure to select "Maintain aspect ratio" so that the graphics program will resize the picture proportionally. But remember that any time you enlarge an image, the resulting picture will look grainy, since the computer needed to add extra pixels to it.

BOOKS WE THINK YOU SHOULD BUY

If you're like us, your monthly credit card bill can be divided into two parts: excessive impulse spending at fabric stores and excessive spending at bookstores. Here are some of our favorite books on designing and on using computers in the needle arts.

LEARN MORE ABOUT DESIGNING NEEDLEWORK ON A COMPUTER

Many of these pioneering works on using computers to design needlework are self-published by their authors. That's because, well, most computer book publishers scoff at the idea of using a computer to design quilts or cross-stitch.

The Needlecrafter's Computer Companion: Hundreds of Easy Ways to Use Your Computer for Sewing, Quilting, Cross-Stitch, Knitting, and More!, by Judy Heim (San Francisco: No Starch Press, 1995). ISBN 1-886411-01-8.

   To order, contact No Starch Press at 800/420-7240, **http://www.execpc.com/ ~judyheim/needle.html**

Computer Quilting Made Easy: Quick Reference Guide to 7 Quilting Programs for PC's, by Sharla Hicks (Costa Mesa, CA: Soft Expressions).

Computer Quilting Made Easy: Illustrated Quick Start Reference Guide for Quit-Pro 2, by Sharla Hicks (Costa Mesa, CA: Soft Expressions).

Computer Quilting Made Easy: Illustrated Quick Start Reference for Quilt-Pro for the Mac (version 1), by Sharla Hicks (Costa Mesa, CA: Soft Expressions).

Computer Quilting Made Easy: Illustrated Quick Start Reference Guide for Electric Quilt 3, by Sharla Hicks (Costa Mesa, CA: Soft Expressions).

   To order, contact Soft Expressions at 714/435-0723, **http://www.home. earthlink.net/~mesa1/**, e-mail: **mesa1@earthlink.net**

Digital Fabrics: How to Make Computer Generated Fabrics, by Jan Cabral (Columbus, OH: High-Tech Quilting, 1997).

CorelDraw for Quilters and Fiber Artists, by Jan Cabral (Columbus, OH: High-Tech Quilting, 1997).

To order, contact High-Tech Quilting at 800/865-5255, **http://www.infinet.com/~jan/**, e-mail: **jan@infinet.com**

Software Directory for Fibre Artists, by Lois Larson.

To order, contact West View Designs at 888/222-4034, **http://www.antibe.com/stitchery/directory.html**

The Color Printer Idea Book, by Kay Hall (San Francisco: No Starch Press, 1997).

To order, contact No Starch Press at 800-420-7240, **http://www.nostarch.com**

LEARN MORE ABOUT DESIGN

These are some of our favorite design books. They explore the general principles of artistic design and describe how you can use some of the concepts we talk about in this book, like value and contrast, to effect amazing transformations in your quilt designs.

Basic Visual Concepts and Principles for Artists, Architects, and Designers, by Charles Wallschlaeger and Cynthia Busic-Snyder (Dubuque, IA: William C. Brown Publishers) ISBN 0-697-00651-4.

Design Basics, by David Lauer (New York: Rinehart, Winston, 1990).

Handbook of Regular Patterns: An Introduction to Symmetry in Two Dimensions, by Peter S. Stevens (Cambridge, MA: MIT Press, 1992) ISBN 0-262-69088-8.

Logic and Design in Art, Science, and Mathematics, by Krome Barratt (New York: Design Press, 1994) ISBN 0-8306-4012-6.

Principles of Form and Design, by Wucius Wong (New York: Van Nostrand Reinhold, 1993) ISBN 0-442-01405-8.

The Art of Color, by Johannes Itten (New York: Van Nostrand Reinhold, 1974).

The Magical Effects of Color, by Joen Wolfrom (Lafayette, CA: C&T Publishing, 1992) ISBN 0-914881-53-1.

The Visual Dance: Creating Spectacular Quilts, by Joen Wolfrom (Lafayette, CA: C&T Publishing, 1995) ISBN 0-914881-93-0.

The Quiltmaker's Handbook: A Guide to Design and Construction and *The Second Quiltmaker's Handbook: Creative Approaches to Contemporary Quilt Design*, by Michael James (Englewood Cliffs, NJ: Prentice-Hall, 1996) ISBN 0-13-749408-4 and 0-13-797787-5.

DRAWING PROGRAM MINI-PRIMER

Here's a quick introduction to a few tools and concepts that make drawing programs powerful—but sometimes tricky to master. A drawing program is more than an overpriced Etch-A-Sketch. You can draw on layers. You can align objects like lines and patches to grids and guides. Here's a basic introduction to the concepts.

NODES

Nodes are small boxes that mark the beginning and end of a line. If the line forms a closed object (like a circle), you'll see just one node on it. Nodes also appear at bends in a curve and in the corners of angular shapes.

To change the shape of an object, you move the line's nodes or add or delete nodes. For instance, you might add a node to the middle of a line if you want to bend the line. Or you might delete nodes from a line if you want to smooth the line. (Sometimes it's a good idea to delete nodes from a line if it just has too many of them.) Don't confuse nodes with "handles," which appear around a line or object when you select it.

You'd also add nodes to a line if you wanted to break the line into two lines and move them apart. Depending upon your drawing program, you might place one node on top of the other on the line and then break them apart.

Conversely, to make the path of a line into a closed object, you'd join the nodes at the beginning and ends of its various lines. For instance, say you draw a triangular patch by drawing three lines. In order to make that triangle into a closed patch, you'd need to join the nodes at the ends of each of the lines.

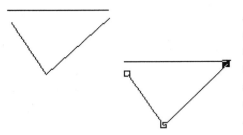

In order to make a scattering of lines into a closed triangular patch, you need to join the nodes at the ends of the lines. This turns your lines into a single path. This is a pain, and something to be avoided. It's easier to draw a square with the Rectangle tool and then delete a node from one of its corners.

*Nodes mark the beginning and end of a line (or closed object). They also mark the curves. To change the shape of an object, you move nodes or add or delete them. CorelDraw has a special pop-up menu for working with nodes. It's called the Node Edit Roll-Up. To get it, you select your drawing with the Pick tool. Then you convert it to curves (choose **Convert to Curves** from the **Arrange** menu). You select the Shape tool and double-click on the node you want to change. The **Node Edit Roll-Up** will pop up. The node will change from transparent to solid black to show you that it's selected.*

DRAWING LAYERS

All high-end drawing programs give you multiple layers to draw on. This is analogous to stacking sheets of tracing paper. Things you draw on bottom layers show through to top layers, but you can always separate the sheets into individual drawings.

You can draft a quilt block or full quilt design on one layer, then trace its patches and templates onto a layer on top of it. That way you can easily color the patches. Or you can separate the templates from each other and give them ¼-inch seam allowances. When it comes time to print, you can print your quilt design on one sheet of paper and your templates on a different sheet just by telling the drawing program to print the layers separately.

Working with layers is also handy for drawing appliqué patterns. You'd import into your drawing program a sketch or photo and place it on one layer. You'd then draw your appliqué design on another layer. We talk more about that in Chapter 15, "How to Turn Photos and Other Art into Appliqué."

You can easily copy things between layers as well as move parts of your drawing from one layer to another. You can also "lock" your layers so that things you draw on one layer don't accidentally become separated from the things on lower layers that you're tracing over. You can make some layers visible and others invisible as you draw. This lets you play with shapes on different layers, moving them around and showing or hiding them.

Some drawing programs have layers with special functions, like a "guide" layer. That's a bottom layer that's essentially locked in place. Objects you place on it serve as guides for drawing on an upper layer.

In some drawing programs the grid has its own layer. You can use just about anything as a grid (a star, diamonds, and so on) by placing it on this layer. You'd then activate snap-to-grid so that patches you draw on an upper layer precisely align to the lines of your unorthodox grid. We talk more about this in Chapter 11, "Good Stars Above! Using Grids to Draw Stars, Suns, and Other Heavenly Bodies."

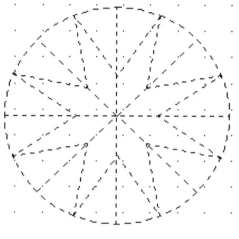

A "grid" needn't be made of squares. Head to Chapter 11 to learn how to use your drawing program's grid layer to create unorthodox quilt block grids.

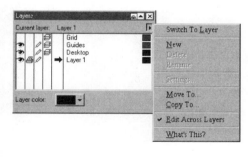

Drawing programs handily provide dialog boxes that you can use to move between your drawing layers—and move things between them. In Corel-Draw 7 it's called the Layer Manager or the Layers Roll-Up. To get it, press CTRL-F3. The layers that are visible are designated with the eye icon.

GUIDES

Guides are drawings that you place on one drawing layer so that you can draw on top of them on another layer. You can make anything into a guide, including quilt block designs and geometric patterns. The guide should be a vector drawing, though, so that the lines you draw will gravitate toward or "snap to" the lines of the guide. In other words, a bitmapped image like that GIF of the UFO you downloaded from the Internet will not make a good guide. A scanned photo will probably not make a good guide either. The advantage of making something into a guide, as opposed to just placing it on a different drawing layer and tracing over it, is that the lines you draw on top of a guide can be made to align precisely with the guide's lines. In order for this alignment to occur, you must activate your drawing program's snap-to-guidelines feature.

SNAP TO . . .

When you want the lines you draw to align with the lines of something else, you activate one or more "Snap to . . ." options. These are:

SNAP TO GRID

We talked about snap-to-grid in Chapter 4. When snap-to-grid is activated, the lines you draw align with those of the invisible grid you have set up, as long as you draw them close enough to the grid's lines. Activate snap-to-grid whenever you do any kind of patch-based quilt designing.

SNAP TO OBJECTS

Say you've drawn two quilt patches and you want to put them together. Activate snap-to-objects so that their lines butt together. Of course, you'll still need to use the Zoom tool to make sure the patches meet properly.

by Christopher Holland

Christopher Holland lives in St. Petersburg, Florida with his wife and two cats. You can get his opinions on just about anything by writing cholland@aol.com, or visiting his Web site at **http://members.aol.com/ stomptokyo.**

Quilters have a blast on the Internet. Where else can you view from the comfort of your family room the quilts of a friend in Maine, then mouse-click your way to Japan to learn about Japanese quilting? A few more mouse-clicks and you're downloading the world's repository of advice on silk embroidery, or chatting with quilters in other lands. The World Wide Web, the graphical portion of the Net, is especially suited to the "quilting frame of mind." It can be simultaneously an artistic medium and an intimate form of personal expression. Like quilts themselves, the Web can be both beautiful and homey at once.

There are tens of thousands of sites on the Internet devoted to quilting including sites for quilt stores, quilt book authors, and individuals. I sifted through thousands of sites and I've listed my favorite ones here—sites that I found to be rich repositories of information about quilting, especially entertaining, or simply inspirational.

I've included in this directory Web sites of artists, quilters, craft magazines, quilt guilds (both cyberspace-based and "land based"), museums, stores, and even sewing machine companies. I've also listed the most popular quilting discussion groups and some sites where you can get information about specific quilting techniques, like appliqué.

I've awarded my favorite sites with ꙮ.

While this directory is a subjective compilation, its entries should not be construed as endorsements of products or ideas promoted by particular Web sites.

GENERAL QUILT INFORMATION WEB SITES

❧ WORLD WIDE QUILTING PAGE
http://quilt.com/MainQuiltingPage.html

All quilting roads on the Internet lead here. If you're looking for almost anything quilting related, chances are that the Traudt & Traudt World Wide Quilting Page has what you want. They feature a huge range of quilters, quilting information, and quilt-related computer facts. Unfortunately, due to demand service may be slow during peak hours, but keep trying—it's worth the wait!

❧ PLANET PATCHWORK
http://www.planetpatchwork.com/

Second only to the World Wide Quilting Page, Rob Holland's Planet Patchwork is perhaps the largest repository of quilting information on the Web. Most of the information is free, with a $5 fee for annual access to the archives of the site's regular publication, "The Virtual Quilt" (a subscription to new issues is included in the fee). One of your first and best stops on the Web.

Planet Patchwork hosts the Internet's largest collection of quilting information.

PC-PIECERS CYBERHOME
http://bankswith.apollotrust.com/~larryb/PCPiecers.htm

An enthusiastic bunch of quilters share patterns and ideas at this colorful and energetic site.

QUILTROPOLIS
http://www.quiltropolis.com/

Quiltropolis features the "Sew Ask Me" column, chat rooms, voluminous (and well-organized) message boards, a fat quarters club, and a catalog of books and supplies.

NATIONAL ONLINE QUILTERS
http://www.noqers.org/

Cheryl Simmerman's National Online Quilters started as one of the first cyberspace quilt guilds on Delphi, the commercial online service. You can now tap into their contests, galleries, and bulletin boards on the Web. Varying levels of membership (from free on up) ensure something for everyone. Incorporates some components of the now defunct "Turtle's Quilting Playground" site.

❧ THE MINING COMPANY QUILT PAGE
http://quilting.miningco.com/

Like an electronic version of a general-interest magazine, The Mining Company offers monthly features on a host of family and hobby topics, including knitting, crocheting, needlepoint, and of course quilting. Susan Druding is your "guide" on the site, posting regular columns and offering links to worthwhile quilting sites around the Web. Other quilters also contribute excellent tutorials and articles.

❧ THE ELECTRIC QUILT HOME PAGE
http://www.wcnet.org/ElectricQuiltCo/

The home of Electric Quilt is an excellent quilting site in general. EQ the Mouse guides you through sections including tech support, fun stuff, and lessons and projects.

QUILT NET
http://www.quilt.net/

Lists quilt shows, contests, local guilds, and related links.

QUILTER'S CORNER
http://www.qcx.com/

Lists the latest shows, books, magazines, vendors, and so on. Houses an interesting quilt gallery with engrossing background stories.

LOST QUILT SITE
http://www2.succeed.net/~amc/quilts.html

A page dedicated to reuniting lost and stolen quilts with their owners.

❧ QUILT BIZ
http://www.nmia.com/~ozzg/quiltbiz.htm

The premier resource for people with quilting businesses or those curious about starting one. A good launching pad when you're looking for services and products on the Web.

QUILT APPRAISALS BY DEBORAH ROBERTS
http://quilt.com/appraiser

Good information on appraisals and quilt care, with a solid list of related links.

QUILT BLOCK & PATTERN COLLECTIONS

❧ QUILTER'S HAVEN

http://www.mk.net/~coneen/quilters/index.html

An excellent and thorough archive of quilt blocks. Well-presented without being flashy, this solid and rapidly growing site also includes how-to's and tips.

You'll find lots of quilting tips, as well as block patterns and construction advice, at Quilter's Haven.

QUILT BLOCK PATTERNS

http://www.portup.com/~hjbe/quilt/qblox.html

A nice personal archive of various block patterns with instructions and illustrations for each block.

QUILLOW

http://linus.socs.uts.edu.au/~fthorne/quillow.html

Leave it to a computer scientist to come up with the directions for a "quillow"—a quilt that folds into a pillow. Fiona Thorne, of the University of Technology in Sydney, Australia, enlightens us on the elusive secrets of sewing up quilllows, and dispels once and for all the myth that quillows are actually Australian marsupials.

QUILTS & KIDS

❧ QUILTING WITH CHILDREN

http://cadvantage.com/~thompson/

Heddi Thomspon's page about the various quilting projects she has done with children. A gallery offers extensive stories and explanations of methods and techniques.

❧ ADOLESCENT QUILT PROJECT

http://galen.med.virginia.edu/~smb4v/quilts/quilthme.html

A collection of quilts made by young people in association with the University of Virginia's Children's Medical Center. Color photos of each quilt are accompanied by a story.

QUILTS TELL ALL

http://www.hipark.austin.isd.tenet.edu/home/projects/fourth/quilts/quilt.html

Students at Highland Park Elementary tell their life stories through quilts designed with KidPix, the commercial drawing software designed especially for kids.

AUNT ANNIE'S CRAFT PAGE

http://www.auntannie.com/

Every week, Aunt Annie features new craft projects for kids, ranging from finger puppets to "glitz gloves."

You'll find a wonderful library of craft projects for kids, including sewing and quilting-related ones, at Aunt Annie's.

THE ALTERNATIVE QUILT DESIGN STUDIO

http://www.visualsenses.com/quilts/quilt.htm

An online quilting coloring book. Print the designs and give them to your kids to color.

FAMILY QUILT HOMEPAGE

http://www.cd-mom.com/album/quilt.html

CD-Mom strives to foster community by allowing users to create their own electronic "patches" in the Family Quilt. While the patches in the family quilt aren't patches in the traditional sense—they can be photos, line drawings, poems, and so on—the site is still attractive and interesting.

QUILTING WEB SITES WITH AN INTERNATIONAL FLAVOR

❧ POAKALANI'S HAWAIIAN QUILTING PAGE

http://www.lava.net/~cissy/Hawaiian_Quilts/

A beautiful and content-rich site about Hawaiian quilting. One of the best quilting sites on the Web, with fascinating background stories for each quilt, detailed descriptions of patterns and methods, lovely photography, and a thoughtful layout.

Poakalani shares her secrets of Hawaiian quilting in one of the most beautiful sites on the Internet.

FCREATE

http://www2b.meshnet.or.jp/~cr-quilt/e_index.html

Home of FCREATE, the handicrafts forum on Japan's NIFTY-Serve online service. Includes information about Japanese quilting and galleries of friendship quilts.

MOLAS & MAPS

http://adams.patriot.net/~kunamola/

An interesting joint effort showcasing the Kuna Indian quilting/embroidery technique of molas and geospatial information.

MOLA ART FROM PANAMA

http://www.midtown.net/~molas/

A rundown on molas and where to find them.

CANADIAN QUILTERS RING

http://www.geocities.com/Heartland/Plains/2208/cq-ring.html

A tour of Canadian quilt sites, linked together in a ring, starts here.

DOING THE BLOCK

http://edx1.educ.monash.edu.au/~dtb/

Collected information on Australian quilters and quilt groups. Also features a picture gallery and information about antique and collectable sewing machines.

PENNY NII COLLECTION

http://www.penny-nii.com/

This commercial site exhibits unique arts and crafts from around the world. Includes new works by Michael James. Learn about the artists and the motivation behind their work.

MUSEUMS AND GALLERY WEB SITES

MUSEUM FOR TEXTILES

http://www.interlog.com/~gwhite/ttt/mtmainpg.html

This site, sponsored by Toronto's textile museum, features history and information about visiting the museum, as well as selected pictures from its galleries.

PIECES OF TIME

http://www.bslnet.com/accounts/jccraig/www/quilt.html

A collection of quilts from the mid 1800's to early 1900's on display at the Sharlott Hall Museum in Arizona. All quilts are pictured with large and small views.

In the old days quilts were relegated to the musty back rooms of museums. Today they're displayed on the Internet for all to learn from and enjoy.

QUILT EXHIBITIONS AND MUSEUMS

http://quilt.com/Museums.html

A listing of special and permanent quilt exhibits.

SMITHSONIAN QUILTS

http://www.si.edu/organiza/museums/nmah/docs/textil29.htm

A selection of quilts from the National Collection.

SMITHSONIAN—NEW AND TEMPORARY EXHIBITIONS AT THE SMITHSONIAN

http://www.si.edu/activity/exhibits/start.htm

Links to Smithsonian museum exhibits in the Washington, D.C. and New York City area.

GUIDE TO MUSEUMS AND CULTURAL RESOURCES

http://www.lam.mus.ca.us/webmuseums/

Sponsored by the Natural History Museum of Los Angeles County, this site offers a comprehensive listing of museums, acquaria, historical parks, and other cultural institutions throughout the world. Visit it to find other museums showcasing quilts.

FLORIDA QUILT COLLECTION

http://www.dos.state.fl.us/dhr/museum/quilts/

A large number of the Florida Quilt Heritage Project's registered quilts are on display here. The photographs are nice though a bit small.

FOLK ART AND CRAFT EXCHANGE

http://www.folkart.com/~latitude/index.htm

Art sources and classifications, how to exhibit and sell your art, various services, and an excellent collection of links.

Learn more about selling your crafts at the Folk Art and Craft Exchange.

KINSHIP & KOMPANY GALLERY

http://www.phoenix.net/~kinship/gallery.htm

A nice little quilt gallery.

QUILTING MAILING LIST-BASED DISCUSSION GROUPS

On the Internet, all the most worthwhile discussions transpire in what are called e-mail discussion groups. You don't have to tap into an Internet site or location to join them. All you need to do to sign up for the discussion groups is send an e-mail message to a certain computer that maintains the groups.

Some of these lists are run "by hand," which means they're run by a person—they sift through the mail and the membership requests. Others are run automatically by a computer, although there's a person responsible for managing the list (not an easy feat).

I've noted the lists that are run manually. When you send your e-mail message to sign up, type out a nice note. Don't just say "subscribe" as if you were talking to a computer.

Once you're subscribed, you'll receive a flurry of e-mail every day from other quilters. Also, the list's administrator will e-mail you instructions on how to participate in the discussion and how to unsubscribe from the list if you wish. (Read these instructions carefully and save them for future reference).

To join in the discussion, you send e-mail to a certain computer address, and your message is broadcast to the other members. (Some quilting discussion lists contain as many as a thousand or more members!)

NOTE

Don't join more than one or two of these lists initially. Some of them generate hundreds of e-mails a day which can quickly flood your inbox.

ART2WEAR

Discussions of wearable art for intermediate to advanced fiber artist.
Send mail to: **qlist@quiltropolis.com**
Subject: Leave blank
Body: **join art2wear OR digest art2wear**

BERNINA FAN CLUB

A discussion list for Bernina sewing machine users.
Send mail to: **BerninaOffice@ttsw.com**
(Run by hand by Sue Traudt.)

CRAZY QUILT

A list for crazy-quilting enthusiasts.
Send mail to: **qlist@quiltropolis.com**
Subject: leave blank
Body: **join CrazyQuilt**

ELECTRIC QUILT SOFTWARE

Discussion of the Electric Quilt design software.
Send mail to: **listserv@planetpatchwork.com**
Subject: leave blank
Body: **join info-eq**

FEATHERWEIGHT FANATICS

A list for Featherweight and other antique sewing machine fans. Sewing machine sales are not allowed on this list. Available in digest form only.
Send mail to: **FWFanatics@ttsw.com**
(Run by hand by Sue Traudt.)

THE INTERNET CULT OF THE FEATHERWEIGHT

Quilters dub it the "Cult of the Featherweight." The Internet is probably more responsible for the revival of interest in this classic little stitcher from Singer than any sewing magazine. Its devotees are as impassioned as Saturn owners. We've received e-mail from more than one Featherweight fan who's gotten sucked into brawling Internet flame-wars over the peculiarities of their favorite sewing machine. The fact is antique sewing machines in general are hot among sewers on the Net. One of the most popular Internet "FAQs" or frequently asked question files, explains how to restore that old treadle in the basement. Head to the FAQ section of this directory to learn how to get it.

FREE MOTION EMBROIDERY

Learn more about this painstaking art, which involves dropping or covering the feed dogs on a sewing machine.
Send mail to: **qlist@quiltropolis.com**.
Subject: Leave blank
Body: **join freemotions** OR **digest freemotions**

IMMERSION DYEING LIST

A list for immersion dyeing and surface application of dyes to fabric and fiber. Subscription information at:
http://www.bolis.com/L/listinfo/dyerslist
Complete the form on that page to subscribe or send mail to:
majordomo@bolis.com
Subject: Leave blank
Body: **subscribe dyerslist** OR **subscribe dyerlist-digest**
Digest version available.

KAFFEE-KLATSCH

On-topic quilt chat, digest format only.
Send mail to: **kaffee-klatsch@quilt.com**
Subject: **subscribe**
Body: **subscribe**

MACHINE EMBROIDERY LIST BBD

Discussion for users of Brother, Babyloc, and Deco embroidery machines.
Send mail to: **majordomo@embroideryclubs.com**
Subject: Leave Blank
Body: **subscribe bbd.embroidery** *your-e-mail-address*

NEW HOME/JANOME

For New Home/Janome owners.
Send mail to: **Wades@norfolk.infi.net**
(Run by hand; include a kind note.)

PFAFFIES

Pfaff sewing machine owners can chat about their machines here.
Send mail to: **majordomo@embroideryclubs.com**
Subject: **Subscribe**
Body: **Subscribe Pfaffies** *Firstname Lastname*

QUILTART-LIST

Encourages open discussion between people interested in art quilting and related topics. Maintained by Judy Smith's QuiltArt site.
Send mail to: **majordomo@quilt.net**
Subject: **subscribe quiltart** OR **subscribe quiltart-digest**
Body: leave blank

Judy Smith's QuiltArt mailing list is one of the friendliest chat groups in cyberspace.

QUILTBEE

This list attempts to foster the same sort of community as old-fashioned quilting bees. Topics range widely but usually center around quilting.
Send mail to: **majordomo@quilter.com**
Subject: **subscribe**
Body: **subscribe QuiltBee**
Or, head to **http://needlearts.dm.net/quiltbee**

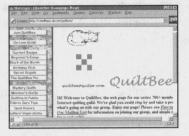

The QuiltBee Web site offers fun, information, organized quilt block swaps, and a mailing list discussion group.

QUILTBIZ

Hand run list about the business side of quilting. An "on-topic" list.
Send mail to: **OzzG@nmia.com**
Subject: **QuiltBiz**
(Run by hand; include a kind note.)

QUILTLIST

Subscribers to this list share experiences and information about foundation piecing and quilting in general.
Send mail to: **majordomo@quiltersweb.com**
Subject: **subscribe**
Body: **JOIN quiltlist**

QUILTNET

Very popular list about quilting and related topics. So popular, in fact, that it's sometimes closed to new subscribers.
Send mail to: **LISTSERV@LSV.UKY.EDU**
Subject: **subscribe**.
Body: **SUBSCRIBE Quiltnet** *yourfirstname yourlastname*.

QUILTOPIA

The official mailing list of Planet Patchwork. All quilting topics with a focus on quilting and computers.
Send mail to: **listserv@planetpatchwork.com**
Subject: leave blank
Body: **join quiltopia**

QUILTING HERITAGE

A discussion of the history and historical aspects of quilting.
Send mail to: **QHL-request@cuenet.com**
Subject: **subscribe**
Body: **subscribe**

THE SEWING LIST

Discussion of sewing related topics.
Send mail to: **qlist@quiltropolis.com**
Subject: leave blank
Body: **join sewinglist** OR **digest sewinglist**

THE SEWING PROS NETWORK

A discussion list devoted to the business of sewing, run by hand by Karen Maslowski, author of *Sew Up a Storm: All the Way to the Bank*. Includes quilters who sell their work. To sign up, send a personal message to Karen at SewProsNet@aol.com.

RAGDOLLS

A fun discussion group devoted to the creation of cloth dolls. A popular activity is "round robin" dolls in which members send each other dolls-under-construction to work on. (One member sews an arm, another paints a face, one sews the skirt, and so on.) You can see the fruit of some of these swaps at their Web site. You pay a small yearly subscription fee, but it's worth it. To learn more, drop an e-mail message to "list mistress" Melissa Bishop at mbishop@needles.com or head to **http://kbs.net/tt/ragdolls.html**.

To learn more about the Ragdolls mailing list head to its Web site.

INTERQUILT

A "cyberspace quilting guild" run by Melissa Bishop has about 600 members. You pay a yearly subscription fee, but list members feel it's well worth it. To learn more, drop Melissa a note at mbishop@needles.com or head to **http://kbs.net/tt/interquilt.html/**.

THE PFABULOUS PFAFF PFAN CLUB

Pfaffies unite! If you're puzzled by the mysteries of the rainbow buttons, or the PCD software has you down, join this lively group.

There is a yearly subscription fee. To learn more, drop Melissa Bishop a note at **mbishop@needles.com** or head to **http://kbs.net/tt/pfaff.html/pfaff.html**.

VIRTUAL DOLLIES

Whether you craft dolls of fabric or fimo, you'll love chatting with the other doll-makers who prowl the Internet. To sign up for this list head to its Web site at **http://www.wwvisions.com/dollies/**.

Even the Internet welcomes dolls. Virtual Dollies is a discussion group for doll-makers. You'll meet some pretty amazing ones too.

VIKING VENERATIONS

For the owners of Viking sewing machines.
Send mail to: **majordomo@acpub.duke.edu**
Subject: leave blank
Body: **subscribe viking-l**

WEARABLE ART LIST

Clothing as art.
Send mail to: **majordomo@embroideryclubs.com**.
Subject: Leave blank
Body: **subscribe wearable** OR **subscribe wearable-digest**

LISZT, THE MAILING LIST DIRECTORY

http://liszt.com/

If you want to find a mailing list to join, start here. Liszt shows over 71,000 lists, so you should find something!

QUILTING USENET NEWSGROUP DISCUSSIONS

You can tap into Usenet newsgroup discussions from any of the major online services, including America Online and CompuServe (use the "go" or "keyword" **INTERNET**). You can also tap in through your Internet service. These discussion groups aren't as much fun as mailing lists. They're less personal. Each group has its own culture, and sometimes a strictly defined etiquette, so you should spend some time reading the other messages in the group before writing your own.

rec.crafts.quilting
rec.crafts.textiles.quilting
rec.crafts.textiles.marketplace (A discussion group for buying and selling things)

QUILTING INTERNET RELAY CHAT, OR "COMPUTER CB" SITES

Sometimes called "computer CBing," relay chat is what you do when you type to other computer users—and they type back to you in real time. To join in a relay chat conversation you must first download and install special software, either as an add-on to your browser, or as a separate Internet tool. Then you tap your way onto the Internet, head to a specific site, log in, and start typing. Most quilt chats occur on a specific day, at a specific time. Some will even host well-known quilt artists or authors.

More and more of the family-related sites on the Internet, like Parent Soup (**http://www.parentsoup.com/**), offer extremely popular chat features.

To join the quilt related chats, head to these Web sites before the scheduled chat. You'll find directions for logging in and a link to the software you'll need to download. (Quilters on the Net like to say that quilters offer the most comprehensible computer instructions—certainly true in the case of these IRC sites.)

QUILTART IRC
http://www.his.com/~judy/quiltart.html
Learn about the QuiltArt IRC channel on the QuiltArt Web site.

QUILTCHAT
http://www.kathkwilts.com/
The home page for the #quiltchat IRC channel is also a repository of quilt information. Meet the channel operators and get some tips on quilting!

CANADIAN QUILTERS ONLINE
http://www.barint.on.ca/~wfitzger/cqolhome.html
The hot spot on the Internet for Canadian quilters. Hosts real-time chats, a question "wall," and a swap shop, among other features.

QUILT-RELATED FREQUENTLY ASKED QUESTIONS FILES

Frequently Asked Questions files are compilations of the answers and advice that quilters have provided each other through the years on the Internet. They're wonderful, wonderful storehouses of knowledge on everything from how to deal with fabrics that bleed to making a remembrance quilt (an especially good FAQ by the way). Almost every quilt mailing list and Usenet newsgroup maintains a collection of FAQs. Some Web sites have their own FAQ collections.

You can obtain these FAQs by tapping into the Web sites where they're stored. Or, if all you have is e-mail access to the Internet, you can pull them off the Web site via e-mail (see Chapter 20, "The Quilter's Guide to Cyberspace," for directions).

ANTIQUE SEWING MACHINE FAQ
http://kbs.netusa.net/tt/faq/index.html
FAQ file maintained by the Tangled Threads page.

BERNINA SEWING MACHINE FAQ
http://www.berninausa.com/forums/faq2.html
The Bernina Company's own FAQ file.

COMPUTERS & QUILTING FAQS
http://ttsw.com/ComputerQuiltingPage.html
Hosted by the World Wide Quilting page, these are all the answers to common questions about software and quilting.

PFAFF FAQS
http://www.pfaff.com/
The official Pfaff machine FAQ file, including an answer line and information on software and Creative Fantasy cards.

THE QUILT-AS-YOU-GO-FAQ
http://www.eskimo.com/~tla/qbfaq.htm
An informal FAQ file about "seat of your pants" quilting.

QUILTING FAQS
http://quilt.com/faqpage.html
Another terrific service of the World Wide Quilting page, this collection of more than 40 Frequently Asked Questions files covers everything from stain removal to purchasing a sewing machine to workspace lighting. Is there anything this site doesn't have? Here's a list of all the FAQs you can get at this site. They're all equally wonderful.

Appliqué	Australia and New Zealand
Baby Quilts	Beginner's Hints and Projects
Biased Edges	Bleeding Fabrics
Canada	Charging for Quilting
Computer Software for Quilting	Copyright FAQ
Custom Made Thimbles	Design Wall
Discharge Dyeing	Europe
Fabric Company Addresses	Fabric Dying
Fabric Dying Safety	Fabric Storage
Foundation Paper Piecing	Group Quilt Ideas
Guild Challenge Projects	Mail Order Resources
Making a Friendship Quilt	Marbled Fabrics
Metallic Threads	Mid West United States
North East United States	North West United States

The World Wide Quilting Page offers oodles of frequently asked question files that will fill you in on everything from machine quilting with metallic thread to custom-made thimbles.

Organizing an Exchange
Purchasing a Sewing Machine
Quilt Books
Quilt Magazines
Quilt Stores

Remembrance Quilts
Sewing Machine Reviews
Six Hour Baby Quilt

Participating in an Exchange
Quilt Batting
Quilt Guild Ideas
Quilt Show Reviews
Quilting Services
    & Rotary Blade Sharpening
Sashiko
Sewing/Work Rooms
South East United States

South West United States
Tea Dying
Tying a Quilt
Workspace Lighting

Stain Removal
Teachers
Wavy Edges FAQ

REC.CRAFTS.TEXTILES . . . FAQ

http://www.cis.ohio-state.edu/hypertext/faq/usenet-faqs/bygroup/rec/crafts/textiles/quilting/top.html

Lots of answers to your textile crafts questions in this large FAQ from the folks on the rec.crafts.textiles newsgroup.

SILK RIBBON EMBROIDERY FAQ

http://www.piecemakers.com/free/silk_faq.html

✿ YOUR FREQUENTLY ASKED QUESTIONS ANSWERED

http://ares.redsword.com/dduperault/qsource.htm

Dawn Duperault has put together an excellent FAQ file for beginners and veterans alike. The "Glossary of Quilting Terms" is especially useful.

QUILTING GUILDS AND OTHER ORGANIZATIONS

AMERICAN QUILTER'S SOCIETY

http://www.AQSquilt.com/

Mostly information about society events, contests, and membership.

AUSTIN AREA QUILT GUILD

http://www.io.com/~aaqg/

The Web site of this Texas guild has a gallery of members' quilts, meeting and workshop calendars, history, and so on.

CANADIAN QUILTERS ONLINE

http://www.barint.on.ca/~wfitzger/cqolhome.html

Hosts real-time chats, a question "wall," and a swap shop, among other features.

EAST BAY HERITAGE QUILTERS

http://www.straw.com/ebhq/

This Kensington, California quilt guild features workshops, meeting schedules, quilt galleries, and membership information.

NATIONAL QUILTING ASSOCIATION

http://www.his.com/~queenb/nqa/nqa.index.html

Although most of their activities occur offline, the NQA does have a Web site which chronicles their events. Some articles from their quarterly magazine are posted online, too.

QUILT ART

http://users.aol.com/hagleyss/index.htm

Unrelated to the QuiltArt mailing list and site, this is the home page of a group of professional artists who stretch the boundaries of quilting as art. Not much in the way of quilts here, but some intriguing articles and information about the artists.

QUILT RESTORATION SOCIETY

http://www.needlearts.com/quilt_restoration_society/index.html

This active group offers its members all the information you might ever want about quilt restoration.

STUDIO ART QUILT ASSOCIATES

http://isis.infinet.com/saqa/index.html

Membership information, member links, catalog, and gallery.

QUILTING CHARITY PROJECTS

ABC QUILTS PROJECT

http://www.jbu.edu/ABCQuilts/

ABC Quilts Project is home to the At-Risk Babies Crib Quilts volunteer organization. Includes news, history, and information about getting involved.

Charity projects are popular with quilters on the Internet.

CANADIAN ELECTRONIC NAMES: THE QUILT ON THE WEB

http://www.cs.utoronto.ca/~e-names/eindex.htm

Site devoted to showcasing the Canadian AIDS Memorial Quilt.

NAMES PROJECT

http://www.aidsquilt.org/

Site of the American NAMES Project Memorial Quilt. Includes online quilt display, newsletter, AIDS information.

NOVA SCOTIA HERITAGE QUILT PROJECT

http://www.total.net/~arobson/index.html

A nonprofit venture that attempts to take inventory of all quilts created before 1970 in Nova Scotia.

VIRTUAL AIDS QUILT

http://world.std.com/~MCPSys/quilt/

"Virtual Quilt" is composed of images "stitched" together on Web pages. There are some pictures of actual quilts.

QUILTING SWAP GROUPS

Quilters love to swap things—fabrics, buttons, quilt blocks, patterns. You'll find "swap groups" in every quilt mailing list discussion group. Here are a few Web sites that are devoted exclusively to swapping.

PLAID LOVERS INTERNATIONAL

http://members.aol.com/pmcdonald/pli.htm

The name says it all—lots of plaid swapping going on here.

SUE'S QUILTING BLOCK OF THE MONTH

http://www.cadvision.com/kira/bom/bomhome.htm

Lottery-style block swap allows all interested parties to participate in the monthly drawing.

QUILTING E-ZINES

An "e-zine" is an electronic magazine that's either published on the Web, or deposited in readers' e-mail boxes. They're extremely popular with quilters on the Internet. Some are boldly opinionated. You might consider them the underground fan magazines of quilting.

⚹ NINE PATCH NEWS

http://members.aol.com/ninepatchn/index.html

America Online's quilt forum sponsors this newsletter for its users. The latest issue and back issues are available here.

The premier quilt e-zine is Planet Patchwork's Virtual Quilt, e-mailed semi-monthly for a humble yearly subscription fee of $5.

PATCHWORDS

http://www.internexus.net/~silkee/pw.html

An irregular but obviously heartfelt effort, this newsletter features mostly creative and "how-to" articles, with a sprinkling of quilt fiction and Web links.

QUILTING WITH PAM

http://members.aol.com/decor8d/quilt.htm

Pam's "Quilter's Corner" is part of her larger online magazine, "Home Decorating on a Shoestring," and offers regular articles, book reviews, and contributions from readers.

⚹ THE VIRTUAL QUILT

http://www.planetpatchwork.com/tvqmain/

The Virtual Quilt is the Internet's first (and some say best) quilting newsletter. Subscribers to the newsletter, distributed via e-mail, also have access to all of the back issues in html format here. Some issues are available in Adobe Acrobat format as well.

QUILTING MAGAZINES

Paper-based magazines are in a pickle in cyberspace. They don't want to publish all their articles online because who, then, would buy them on the newsstand? These quilting magazines have bravely embraced the new media, offering article excerpts, lovely graphics, and sometimes even patterns. Visit them online, but don't forget to buy them too.

AMERICA'S FAVORITE QUILT MAGAZINES
http://www.quiltmag.com/

Online components of *Quilt, Miniature Quilt Ideas, Patchwork & Quilting Ideas*, and *Quilt Almanac* magazines. Features subscription and order forms plus article excerpts and online patterns.

MINIWORKS MAGAZINE
http://web.infoave.net/~newconcepts/miniworks.htm

A factual Web site about a print magazine for miniature quilt enthusiasts. Hosts an occasional article online from *Miniworks*.

PATCHWORK & QUILTING
http://www.traplet.co.uk/traplet/P&Q.html

Advertising for (and a sample article from) the print magazine.

❧ QUILT GALLERY MAGAZINE
http://www.quiltgallery.com/

Some good articles about quilting in general, and profiles of prominent quilters. Updated seasonally.

QUILTER'S WORLD-WIDE EXCHANGE/TRADE
http://www.cybervision-network.com/quilters-worldwide/

Free exchange and trade advertisements in the print version of *Quilter's World-Wide*.

QUILTING TRADER'S NEWSLETTER
http://www.eskimo.com/~tla/qbqtnews.htm

The Web page is spartan, but it gets the job done. Use the e-mail address you find here to subscribe and submit your ads for the twice-monthly trading e-mail newsletter.

THE CRAFTS REPORT
http://www.craftsreport.com/

The business journal for the crafts industry. Site includes feature articles, news, columns, departments, trends, back issues, craft showcase, show listing, and extensive craft-related Internet links.

SEWING MACHINE INFORMATION

Where do you go at 3 A.M. when the stitches on your crazy quilt start to become a bit crazy, and you can't find the feed dogs you dropped earlier in the day? Why, you tap your way onto the Internet where you'll find more sewing advice than just about anywhere else on the planet.

ANTIQUE SEWING MACHINE FAQ
http://kbs.netusa.net/tt/faq/index.html

FAQ file maintained by the Tangled Threads page. Membership not required for access.

BERNINA SEWING MACHINES
http://www.bernina.com/

Home of the Bernina Sewing machine.

FEATHERWEIGHT FANATICS HOME PAGE
http://quilt.com/FWFanatics/FWFanatics.html

Home of the mailing list for Featherweight enthusiasts.

ONLINE ANTIQUE SEWING MACHINE RESOURCE
http://www2.hawaii.edu/~claw/sew/

The Internet is a terrific place to find information on oiling that 1914 Singer and making it hum again.

Information about antique sewing machines, especially Singers. The Internet is a terrific place to find information on oiling that 1914 Singer and making it hum again.

PFAFF SEWING MACHINES
http://www.pfaff.com/

Pfaff's official Web site, with customer support, sales, a FAQ file, and more.

PFAFF-TALK
http://www.cwe.com/pfaff-talk/

Web-based bulletin board for owners of Pfaff sewing machines.

SEWING WITH BERNINA
http://www2.ari.net/home/rain/mln.html

Mary Lou Nall's column and Bernina information.

SINGER SEWING MACHINES
http://www.singersewing.com/

Product-by-product feature list, information about Singer publications, and more.

STITCHPOINT
http://www.wp.com/stitchpt/

The Journal for Computerized Sewing. This excellent resource for computer sewing and computerized sewing machines has templates, articles, and more.

VIKING HUSQVARNA SEWING MACHINES
http://www.vikinghusqvarna.com/

Get the lowdown on all of Viking's products, and register to win a gift certificate.

PERSONAL WEB SITES OF QUILTERS, PROFESSIONALS, AND HOBBYISTS

One of the things that makes the Internet homey are all the personal Web pages of quilters. They offer photos of themselves, their families, their quilts; they tell stories about their lives; they share advice about quilting. Scroll through someone's Web page and you'll feel like you know them. It's like stepping into someone's living room—or quilting room.

ANDERSON, SUSAN– "GRANDMA SUE'S PLACE"
http://www.northernnet.com/susanna/

See the monthly collection of quilts and read about Anderson's life, including her grandkids and her bout with cancer.

ANDERSON-SHEA, CHARLENE
http://members.aol.com/CASInc/home/Char.html

Designs and shares a block per month. Also includes tips about other fiberarts.

AUMAN, STEPHANIE
http://www.hamilton.net/subscribers/auman/index.html

Auman goes a step beyond the normal personal Web page by including her own reviews of books and software. Also included are her quilts designed using the software.

BEATTIE, MARY ANN
http://www.nb.net/~maryann/

Beattie's page is a busy one—it links to her own sewing room and a collection of mystery quilt pages, as well as the standard collection of quilting links. Worth a peek for the running commentary.

BENDESKY, COZY "COZY HOMEPAGE"
http://www.erols.com/cozy/

Useful and humorous page showcases quilting work and includes her own artistic credo.

BOWES, LISA
http://www.wam.umd.edu/~elbows/Quilts/Quilts.html

Bowes claims that quilting is "cheaper than therapy," but her quilts (and her undergraduate paper about quilts) betray the fact that she puts much thought into her life as a quilter.

BRAZY, BETSY— "UNOFFICIAL HOME PAGE"
http://www.sirius.com/~bbrazy/

Technical writer Brazy also writes book reviews for *Quilt Peddler* newsletter, and reprints them here. Also read about how she found true love.

COMBS, KAREN
http://edge.edge.net/~kcombs

A neat selection of optical-illusion quilts.

DRUDING, SUSAN
http://www.straw.com/

Visit the site of one of the first ladies of fiber arts. Be sure to ask her how her machine quilting is going.

❧ GLAES, KATHY
http://home.earthlink.net/~kglaes/

Glaes is a gifted artist. Her site is visually impressive and well-organized, and her quilt stories are fun to read.

HARMON, KATHY
http://users.sedona.net/~harmon/kathy/index.html

The eclectic quilts are worth seeing. And wow, check out that virtual quilt gallery!

HARTER, DEDE
http://fn3.freenet.tlh.fl.us/~dharter/index.html

DeDe's detailing of her autobiographical crazy-quilt vest makes her home page worth visiting.

❧ KRATOVIL, DEBBY—"A QUILTER BY DESIGN"
http://www.his.com/~queenb/

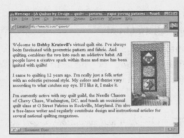

Kratovil features not only blocks and patterns, but book reviews and quilt poetry as well. One of the best personal pages around.

JONES, CATHERINE
http://majolica.com/

Jones seeks out the art in quilting, and uses her humor and writing to speak out on the "minor" arts—including quilting.

❧ MARSHALL, SUZANNE
http://www.ibc.wustl.edu/quilts/srm.html

An impressive collection of award-winning quilts, each with its own story. A must-visit.

MIGHT, JENNIFER
http://www.might.com/jmight/index.html

Visit Might's gallery, with a nice collection of wearable art, needlework, and quilting.

NEBUCHADNEZZAR, OLENA
http://cs.odu.edu/~nebuc_a/

Olena's fabulous collection of quilts as presented by her husband, Abe.

REYNOLDS, BETTY
http://www.nmt.edu/~breynold/quilts.html

Reynolds' personal gallery includes a large number of quilts and a catalog of quilt blocks. The "Whose Library?" quilt is a favorite.

SIMMS, AMI
http://quilt.com/Artists/AmiSimms/AmiSimmsV2.html

Noted quilter and author displays her own quilts and offers a free newsletter.

❧ SMITH, JUDY
http://www.his.com/~judy/

Judy's pages have received quite a bit of recognition, and for good reason. Not only does she host a large number of quilt projects and galleries on her pages, but she also maintains the QuiltArt mailing list.

STEWART, JOYCE
http://www.srv.net/~joyces/quilts.html

Features a quilt every month, along with some background on Stewart. A nice, homey site.

❧ THORPE, WENDOLYN—"QUILTS A-GO-GO!"
http://www.skep.com/wendy/quilts.htm

Be careful not to stray outside the bounds of Wendy's nicely organized quilt page—you might get sucked into the world of Wendolonia!

TILLEY, DEB—"DREAMING IN COLOUR"
http://ourworld.compuserve.com:80/homepages/deb_tilley/

Personal Web page includes gallery and information on "fantasy retreats."

TURNS, JENNIFER
http://www.isye.gatech.edu/chmsr/Jennifer_Turns/quilting.html

While not the most elaborate page ever created, it is nice to see photos of quilts together with the people for whom they were created.

VOLPICELLI, ELIZABETH—"MOTHER'S QUILTWORKS"
http://www.capecodconnection.com/quilters/

A gallery of recent works by Elizabeth Volpicelli, with detailed explanations of each quilt. Well-organized and thoughtful.

WALKER, DAVID
http://w3.one.net/~davidxix/

Walker is perhaps one of the Web's best-known quilt artists. It's no wonder; his site has both content and style that bring you back for more. Along with his personal greeting, gallery, and schedule of workshops and lectures, he includes a featured monthly artist and a bulletin board of upcoming events.

WASILOWSKI, LAURA
http://www.qcx.com/LW/main.htm

Wasilowski's quilts are some of the most humorous and personable out there. "Gus Cleans His Room" is a favorite.

WOLFROM, JOEN
http://www.mplx.com/joenwolfrom/

Like letters from an old friend, Wolfrom gives us a monthly update on her life, along with a recipe and pattern. Well organized with nice content.

FUN, WILD, AND OUTRAGEOUS QUILTING SITES

WORST QUILT IN THE WORLD CONTEST

http://quilt.com/Artists/WorstQuilt/WorstQuilt1.html

Ami Simm's annual contest searches for the world's worst quilt. Grand prize includes a paper bag for the winner to place over his or her head. Abominable mentions included.

The winner of the Worst Quilt in the World is awarded a paper bag to put over her or his head.

CAT QUILTS

http://www.execpc.com/~judyheim/catqlts.html

By our own Judy Heim. "Not quilts for cats, but patterns for quilts with cats on them," plus resources for cat-quilt-related materials.

MYSTERY QUILTERS

http://www.xyz.net/~nickf/abby/cluebees.html

"You have the right to remain clueless. Everything you sew can and will be used in your quilt." This page is for mystery quilt enthusiasts. Tips and a group mailer to get in touch with other cluebees! Inspector Cluesew.

WORST GIRLS QUILTING CLUB

http://www.wco.com/~carraher/

The best thing about this page (besides all the pictures of their quilting projects) is the story of how these four mild-mannered quilters became the Worst Girls.

STUD MUFFINS OF QUILTING

http://www.execpc.com/~judyheim/qltstud.html

A spoof on pin-up calendars in auto-repair garages, Stud Muffins of Quilting presents a monthly "quilting playboy" posing with favorite quilt blocks and revealing intimate personal details like favorite color of thread.

Oh-oh! It was inevitable, wasn't it?

MATH QUILTS

http://members.aol.com/mathquilt/index.html

Although "all quilts are math quilts," this page features those that are particularly math-related. Some neat reading here, along with the Quilts Every Day feature!

LARIE'S WEB QUILT

http://www.geocities.com/Athens/6935/quilt.html

Add your own fun electronic patch to Larie's "guest book" quilt.

FOR BOOK-LOVING QUILTERS

QUILTS, QUILTERS, QUILTING, AND PATCHWORK IN FICTION

http://www.nmt.edu/~breynold/quiltfiction.html

Bibliography of fiction which includes quilts, quilters, and the like. List is split into adult and children's sections, with some annotation.

C&T PUBLISHING

http://www.dnai.com/~ctpub/

Information about books and authors in the C&T publishing stable. Also has an excellent state-by-state listing of quilt stores.

THAT PATCHWORK PLACE

http://www.patchwork.com/

That Patchwork Place produces some of the best and most popular quilting books around. Site includes upcoming book highlights, class schedules, and an index of all TPP books.

JANE AUSTEN'S WEB SITE

http://uts.cc.utexas.edu/~churchh/janeinfo.html

Even Jane was a quilter. She used Regency period chintz's to stitch together beautiful bed quilts while writing *Pride and Prejudice*.

CHILDREN'S AUTHORS, ILLUSTRATORS, AND THEIR BOOKS

http://www.ucalgary.ca/~dkbrown/authors.html

An incredible site, with links to information on every children's author from R. L. Stine to Louisa May Alcott.

BOOK WIRE

http://www.bookwire.com/

If you're looking for a good read, this is the site to visit.

❦ AMAZON.COM

http://www.amazon.com/

The ultimate place to buy books. Search a database of every book in print; have the book in your mailbox in days.

WEB SITES FOR AND ABOUT QUILTING SOFTWARE

BARGELLO HEARTS QUILTING

http://www.ayersoft.com/bargello/

This page features an intriguing form of quilting, based on a radiating heart pattern. The site promotes the Bargello book and Bargello Designer 32, a Windows 95 program for generating your own Bargello Heart designs.

COMPUTERS & QUILTING

http://quilt.com/ComputerQuiltingPage.html

The World Wide Quilting Page offers information on computers and quilting, including a Frequently Asked Questions file.

CORELDRAW

http://www.corel.com/products/graphicsandpublishing/index.htm

Those brave enough to try CorelDraw as their quilt design software of choice can find Corel information here.

CORELNET

http://www.corelnet.com/

A treasure chest of information about using this difficult program.

If you're baffled by CorelDraw! (as most people are), head to CorelNet for enlightenment.

❦ THE ELECTRIC QUILT HOME PAGE

http://www.wcnet.org/ElectricQuiltCo/

Tech support information and advice for Electric Quilt and Blockbase users.

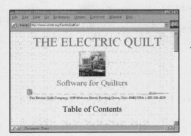

Electric Quilt users will love the EQ Web site, full of tips, advice, patterns, and projects.

HIGH TECH QUILTING

http://www.infinet.com/~jan/

Jan Cabral's self-published computer-related books and related links are available here

COMPUTER QUILTING MADE EASY BOOKS

http://www.home.earthlink.net/~mesa1/

Home of Sharla Hicks' series of quick-start books on using the different quilt design programs.

THE NEEDLECRAFTER'S COMPUTER COMPANION

http://www.execpc.com/~judyheim/needle.html

This is where you'll find Judy's book.

PCQUILT

http://www.pcquilt.com/

A very basic Web site, but it does include some screenshots so you can see what you're getting. You can also download a demo of PCQuilt for the Mac at these FTP sites:

ftp.hawaii.edu
Once at the site, you'll find the demo in /mirrors/information-mac/app/pc-quilt-demo.hqx.

ftp.luth.se
Once at the site you'll find the demo in /pub/mac/demo.

Or you can download the demo from the America Online's Macintosh software library.

QUILTDESIGN SOFTWARE

http://www.planetpatchwork.com/qltprogs.htm

Planet Patchwork offers this page with reviews of most quilting software.

QUILT-PRO

http://www.quiltpro.com/

Nothing fancy, but it has some product information and answers for users of Quilt=Pro design software.

INTERESTING AND VALUABLE GENERAL ART SITES

JIM'S FINE ART COLLECTION

http://www2.iinet.com/art/index.html

Images of thousands of classic works of art from Edward Hopper to Georgia O'Keefe and Gauguin.

WORLDWIDE ARTS RESOURCE

http://wwar.com/

Links to thousands of art galleries across the Web.

ART DECO/ERTE

http://www.webcom.com/ajarts/welcome.html

The best place on the Web to go for Art Deco.

ARTNET411

http://www.artnet411.com/

Internet access to artists, crafts people, galleries, and artists organizations.

GUERRILLA GIRLS

http://www.voyagerco.com/gg/gg.html

Women's art has always been tragically undervalued by the stodgy art world. The Guerrilla Girls decided to change that. Read about their adventures in their Internet home.

Even though they wear guerrilla masks as they plaster New York subways and streets with their posters, their messages is serious: women's art has always been undervalued. And it still is.

THE WORLD OF ESCHER

http://www.lonestar.texas.net/~escher/

Information on Escher, the graphic artist most noted for his spatial illusions and geometric patterns. This sites contains a reading room, art museum, store, and other information.

The World of Escher page.

GALLERY OF INTERACTIVE GEOMETRY

http://www.geom.umn.edu/apps/gallery.html

Interested in geometry? This site is sponsored by the University of Minnesota.

The Gallery of Interactive Geometry page.

SITES WHERE YOU CAN FIND CLIP ART TO USE IN QUILTS AND OTHER CRAFTS

✺ LORI'S COLLECTION OF CRAFT CLIP ART

http://www.geocities.com/~sewdoll/CraftClips.htm

Well-organized and LARGE! Lori has done a service to crafters everywhere. Web art and links to other clip art sites.

Lori's collection of clip art is phenomenal. Much of it she's created herself, and she shares it with the craft world.

CLIP ART CONNECTION

http://www.ist.net/clipart/index.html

Start your clip art search here! Lots of links to clip art sites all over the world.

BARRY'S CLIP ART SERVER

http://www.barrysclipart.com/

Mostly a general clip art resource, but some craft and quilt-related stuff here.

What's clip art and how can you legally use it? Read our "Quilter's Guide to Computer Graphics" appendix to learn more.

EMBROIDERY WEB SITES

❧ COUNTED CROSS STITCH, NEEDLEWORK, AND STITCHERY PAGE

http://www.wco.com/~kdyer/xstitch.html

Do you cross-stitch as well as quilt? This site is for you!

❧ CAMEOROZE'S STITCHER'S STUDIO

http://www.nidlink.com/~ddavaz/margaret/studio/studio.html

Cross-stitchers will love this homey site. You'll find articles, designs, and stitches here.

❧ MARILYN IMBLUM LEAVITT

http://www.tiag.com/

Read the stories behind the phenomenal cross-stitch designs of one of the greatest needleartists ever. See her latest patterns. Read about the designs she's currently working on. Marilyn also offers free patterns for lots of cross-stitch angels which you can download or print.

MEDIEVAL AND RENAISSANCE EMBROIDERY

http://www.uiuc.edu/ph/www/jscole/medembro.html

Gorgeous.

MACEDONIAN FOLK EMBROIDERY

http://www.auburn.edu/academic/liberal_arts/foreign/macedonia/folk-embroidery/index.html

Here's another form of intricate embroidery few stitchers have time for, but it's fun to read about and ogle the pictures.

THE BLACKWORK EMBROIDERY ARCHIVES

http://www.pacificnet.net/~pmarmor/bwarch.html

Blackwork embroidery is an ancient art that's enjoying a renaissance. Learn about it here.

You'll find patterns, pictures, and tips on mastering the age-old art of blackwork on the Internet.

THE BAYEUX TAPESTRY

http://blah.bsuvc.bsu.edu/bt

See the complete Bayeux Tapestry, including close-ups of many details not shown in history books.

DOLL-MAKING AND OTHER CRAFT SITES THAT QUILTERS TEND TO LIKE

DOLL-WEB

http://www.cascade.net/dolls/links.html

Links to over 200 doll-related sites on the Internet

ANTONETTE CELY'S DOLLS

http://www.netdepot.com/~donnybob/nonipage.html

Her dolls are breathtaking. Take a look at the one of Rita Hayward.

MARTY DONNELLAN DOLL GALLERY

http://www.donnellan.com/dolls/marty.htm

An extraordinary gallery of hand-made dolls by different doll artists on the Internet

MARIE-CLAUDE DUPONT

http://www.cam.org/~delisle/mcd.html

Wonderful links to doll artists around the world, and the Web sites of the sellers of hard-to-find doll-making supplies; also puppetry sites.

THE COSTUME PAGE

http://users.aol.com/nebula5/costume.html

If you sew dolls with period costumes, you'll love all the information and links on this site.

RUBBER-STAMPING PAGE

http://www.xmission.com/~jmabunga/stamp.htm

Who can resist trying out a few rubber stamps on their fabric on occasion? This page is a gateway to the gregarious Internet rubber stamping community. You'll find online catalogs for lots of innovative rubber stamp makers. A number of the rubber stamps in the catalogs have stitching themes.

FUN AND VALUABLE SITES NOT NECESSARILY RELATED TO QUILTING

GODEY'S LADY'S BOOK ONLINE
http://www.history.rochester.edu/godeys/

Full color pictures and text from the trend-setting 19th century ladies' journal can be found here.

⚘ HEARST HOMEARTS
http://homearts.com/cl/toc/00clhpc1.htm

Online versions of *Country Living, Bob Vila's American Home, Town & Country, Cosmopolitan, Good Housekeeping*, and *Redbook*.

You can read many complete articles from magazines like Country Living *at the Hearst HomeArts site.*

THE LIBRARY OF CONGRESS
http://www.loc.gov:80/

During the Depression, the Works Progress Adminstration interviewed quilters throughout the south. You can find full transcripts of those interviews online at the Library of Congress site. Click on "Search Our Site" and enter the word "quilt."

⚘ FAMILY PLANET
http://www.familyplanet.com/

A delightful electronic publication of articles, games, and advice for the whole family.

⚘ ONCOLINK
http://www.oncolink.upenn.edu/

The ultimate Internet cancer information site, run by the good folks at the University of Pennsylvania. This site will lead you to all the good breast cancer information and support groups on the Internet.

WALT HOWE'S INTERNET TRAINING CENTER
http://world.std.com/~walthowe

If you have any questions or confusions about the Internet you'll find the answers here.

EZ CONNECT
http://www.ezconnect.com/kj.htm

An excellent selection of links to the very best of the Internet's family-oriented sites.

ONLINE SHOPPING

QUILTSEARCH
http://www.quiltsearch.com/Quilt/index.html

Search for local stores or manufacturers. A good starting point in your hunt for supplies. Also has a HUGE (more than 800!) list of textile and sewing links, although some links may be dead.

ALL TIED UP
http://www.dev-com.com/~alltiedup/

Web site for this San Jose, California-based quilt shop.

AMERICAN BEAUTY FABRICS
http://members.aol.com/etanniru/abfhome.htm

The site is basic, but it offers some nice fabrics with online color swatches.

AMERICAN QUILTS
http://www.AmericanQuilts.com/

LARGE selection of mail-order prefab and custom quilts.

AMISH HANDMADE QUILTS
http://AmishHandmadeQuilts.com/

Mail order quilts sold by friends of the Northern Indiana Amish community.

ANTIQUE QUILTS AND VINTAGE TEXTILES
http://www.ultranet.com/~kiwi/diane.html

Antique quilts, quilt tops, and quilt squares from mid 1800 to 1945. Also fabrics, feedsacks, and more.

ARLENE'S CALICO COUNTRY
http://www.sierranet.net/~calico/

Mail order quilt supplies including beads, a Quilt PAK of the month club, and custom quilt label stamps.

BENARTEX FABRICS
http://www.benartex.com/

Previews of upcoming fabric.

C&T PUBLISHING
http://www.ctpub.com/~ctpub/

High quality quilting books and quilt-related products sold here.

CIELO AZUL ONLINE CATALOG
http://www.nmia.com/~qltshop/petchy/

Online catalog of fabrics, books, notions, and more from Santa Fe, NM.

COTTON CLUB
http://www.cottonclub.com/index.html

The Cotton Club offers a regular mailing of selected fabrics for a small annual fee. Includes different "theme" clubs for those with differing tastes.

DHARMA TRADING COMPANY

http://www.dharmatrading.com/

Our favorite catalog of painting and dyeing supplies. Request a copy of their catalog or place orders directly online.

THE DMC PAGE

http://www.dmc-usa.com/

A complete listing of DMC threads and product information together with a store search and downloadable projects.

EZ INTERNATIONAL/QUILTHOUSE

http://www.ezquilt.com/

Some unique quilting accessories for sale here, plus a useful "tool tutorial."

FABRICLINK

http://www.fabriclink.com/

Slick resource site for fabric consumers and retailers.

Head to FabricLink when you have questions about fabric.

FABRIC STASH, THE

http://fabric-stash.com/

The Fabric Stash offers a well-organized catalog with a huge selection of fabrics and quilting supplies, available for order online or by phone. Also features a chat room and regular newsletter.

Lots of quilters buy fabric on the Internet, would you believe it? You'll find a terrific selection of fabrics at the Fabric Stash.

HICKORY HILL ANTIQUE QUILTS

http://quilt.com/HickoryHillQuilts/HickoryHill.html

A catalog of antique quilts, tops, blocks, fabrics, and related items. Also promotes the Quilter's Heritage mailing list (see Mailing Lists, above).

JC QUILTS

http://home.earthlink.net/~jwestergren/

Along with JC's patterns for sale, there are some fun pages here, like the monthly free block pattern and the wall of quilt graffiti.

JINNY BEYER STUDIOS

http://www.jinnybeyer.com/

Classy site showcases Beyer's quilts and products, and includes her notes and tips.

Visit Jinny Beyer's site for information about her products, plus her notes and tips.

KIRK COLLECTION

http://www.auntie.com/kirk/

Specializing in antique quilts, fabrics, and modern reproduction fabrics. Some information about quilt conservation and restoration.

LIZANNE PUBLISHING COMPANY

http://www.evansville.net/~peter/

They claim they're "making quilting fun," and perhaps so. Their real claim to fame, however, is "Quality Quilting Quarters: The Guide to America's Quilt/Fabric Shops," which lists and maps over 1200 quilting shops in the U.S. and 10 foreign countries.

MARY GRAHAM DESIGNS

http://www.nmia.com/~mgdesign/webhome.htm

This site is mostly geared towards selling Graham's unique designs, but there is information on hand appliqué here as well.

MI-MU FABRIC CLUB

http://www.mimuclub.com/

Based in Osaka, Japan, the Mi-Mu Club offers a wide variety of Japanese 100 percent cotton fabrics for quilts. There is also a small gallery of Yasuko Takeuchi's quilts.

NANCY'S NOTIONS

http://www.nancysnotions.com/

Nancy Zieman, of the **PBS** show "Sewing With Nancy," hosts her own online store and sewing bulletin board here.

PERFECT SQUARE

http://www.webworldinc.com/perfectsquare/

Home site of the Perfect Square grid transfer, which speeds the creation of half-square triangles.

PINE LAKE FABRICS

http://www.eskimo.com/~tla/pinelakefabrics.htm

A huge and lovely selection of fabrics, including dog and cat prints, Kona Bay, Japanese prints, Aunt Gracie, and more.

❧ PINETREE QUILTWORKS
http://quilt.com/Catalogues/PTFall95/PineTree.html

PineTree has a little of everything, but they specialize in the "nuts and bolts" of quilting supplies—batting, measuring tools, hoops, needles, and notions.

QUILT IN A DAY PUBLISHERS
http://www.quilt-in-a-day.com/qiad/

Mail order books and patterns from the QIAD collection.

QUILTS: NOT JUST FOR BEDS
http://www.eskimo.com/~jlk/quilts.htm

Mail order patterns based on flowers of the Pacific Northwest. Say "Hi" to cats Tigger and BJ when you visit.

QUILT COTTAGE
http://www.buffalo.net/quilt/

Quilt store in Tonawanda, NY. Site lists classes, specials, and services available.

❧ QUILT LOFT
http://www.quiltloft.com/

Nice retail site has a personal touch and some really bright colors. Monthly tips, quilt blocks, and other regularly updated content makes it worth a return trip.

QUILTER'S COTTON BATTING

We're biased, and we love this batting. It contains no scrim, glue, or binders and is incredibly soft. send e-mail for samples: quilter@inna.net

SHAW NUF DESIGNS
http://www.shawnuf.com/

The Shaw Nuf site features their own brand of shadow appliqué and electronic versions of the *Enterprising Quilters Guild* newsletter.

TANGLED THREADS
http://kbs.net/tt/

They sell quilting books and notions, but their real claim to fame is that they stock the full line of Elinor Peace Bailey doll patterns (you know, of the crazy ladies) plus some beautiful cotton body fabrics.

THREAD & THIMBLE
http://marie.az.com/~karenm/thread.htm

A solid quilt supply store which also features quilt fiction.

WELLSPRING GALLERY: BOOKS AND ART SUPPLIES FOR FIBER ARTISTS
http://www.WellspringGallery.com/

A catalog of over 1200 titles of how-to, art books, inspiration, and pattern books and a threads and notions section.

WYNDHAM NEEDLEWORKS
http://www.WyndhamNeedleworks.com

Specializes in hard-to-find and unusual products for quilters and needleworkers.

ZIPPY DESIGNS' PATCHWORK WORLD
http://www.other-world.com/ftp/QuiltersWeb/ZippyDesigns/

The Web site for *The Foundation Piecer*, a pattern journal for foundation piecing enthusiasts. Sample patterns and more.

SHOP FOR OLD QUILT TOPS, ANTIQUE SEWING TOOLS AT INTERNET AUCTIONS

Do you haunt garage sales, scooping up old sewing baskets, sifting through stacks of yellowed linens for unfinished quilt tops? You'll *love* the Internet auction site eBay (**http://www.ebay.com/**). You can bid on literally thousands of fleamarket-style sewing finds, from jars of antique buttons, to boxes of rick-rack, darning eggs, sewing machines, and of course oodles of old quilt tops and blocks.

The items are offered for sale by antique dealers and sewing aficionados around the country. The list of merchandise offered for sale on the site changes daily. Bidders can view pictures of merchandise, write sellers with questions, and let the eBay computer bid for them in increments as low as 25 cents, up to a bidder-specified price limit.

How safe is buying from an Internet auction site? There's risk: you're buying from individuals, not companies with established reputations. You mail off a check to someone you've probably never heard of before, then wait and hope that the seller is reliable enough to ship the merchandise. One advantage of eBay is that buyers can post comments about sellers that other bidders can read when they bid. (In several months of bidding on sewing items, Judy ran into a problem only once. When she didn't receive merchandise, she e-mailed other bidders who had purchased items from that antique dealer. One sent her the e-mail address of the dealer's *mother*. The dealer's mom apologized and made her son ship out the rhinestone buttons immediately. Judy theorizes that true Internet scam artists are not likely to be selling jars of rhinestone buttons for minimum bids of $1.)

Auction Web sites like eBay can be great places to bargain hunt, but remember that caveat emptor rules. On eBay, head to the "Antiques" category for the sewing items. Don't worry, you'll find more than antiques. You'll also find old stashes of patterns, books, and notions. Here are tips for buying from Web auction sites:

- Ask questions before bidding. What condition is the item in? What are the seller's return policies?

- Familiarize yourself with the policies of the seller and the auction site. If you don't receive the merchandise, or its defective, will the auction site help you get your money back? Or will you be on your own?

- Check the seller's feedback rating to see how other customers rate their service.

- Check the site's "auctions ending today" page for the best buys.

- Nail down shipping fees before bidding. Ask that pricey items be insured when they're shipped.

- Determine at the onset the highest price that you'd be willing to pay for an item, and still consider it a bargain, then stick to that price limit. Don't get too excited by low posted bid prices. Buyers often bid items much higher in the final days or hours of an auction.

- Keep documentation of bids. Keep a copy of your bid confirmation e-mail message. If you mail a check, include with it a copy of the message sent to you to tell you of the winning bid, and add to it your shipping address. Keep copies of any correspondence with the seller.

- Pay with a credit card, if possible. Your credit card company can intervene should a despite arise. But never type your credit card number into an e-mail message. Call the seller to give it to them over the phone.

- If you have a grievance with a vendor, contact the auction site. Remember, though, that caveat emptor is often the rule for these sites.

MY FAVORITES

MY FAVORITES

MY FAVORITES

THE NEEDLECRAFTER'S COMPUTER COMPANION

Hundreds of Easy Ways to Use Your Computer for Sewing, Quilting, Cross-Stitch, Knitting, & More!

"This is the 'How-do-I-get-started-and-why?' book you've been waiting for. Don't hesitate."—THREADS MAGAZINE

by JUDY HEIM

Use your computer to create dazzling needlework designs as innovative as your imagination, or as traditional as the ones in Grandma's hope chest. You'll find opinionated reviews of quilting, cross-stitch, sewing, weaving, and knitting software; how to use your computer to convert family photos into cross-stitch patterns; how to download free craft patterns and get advice from needlework magazines online; where to find craft resources on the Internet and commercial online services (like CompuServe and America Online); how to use computers in your needlecraft business; and much more.

JUDY HEIM, *PC World* magazine columnist and contributing editor, has been an avid sewer for over 30 years. She is the author of three other No Starch Press titles: *The Needlecrafter's Computer Companion*, *Internet for Cats*, and *I Lost My Baby, My Pickup, and My Guitar on the Information Highway*. She lives in Madison, Wisconsin.

460 pp., $34.95 ($49.00 Cdn)
ISBN 1-886411-01-8

DR. BOB'S PAINLESS GUIDE TO THE INTERNET

& Amazing Things You Can Do with E-mail

". . . simple, hassle-free net surfing with a minimum of reading . . . written by Bob Rankin, the driver of the widely acclaimed Internet TourBus."—NETGUIDE MAGAZINE

by BOB "DR. BOB" RANKIN

Whether you connect to the Internet through e-mail alone or the latest Netscape beta, *Dr. Bob's Painless Guide to the Internet* will show you how to use every Internet tool—not just the Web. You'll learn how to send and receive e-mail, find the cool and useful websites, search for and download the files you want, read newsgroups and subscribe to mailing lists, chat online, and more. Includes a glossary of terms and the "Internet Mini-Yellow Pages," with lots of useful Internet resources for you to enjoy right away.

BOB RANKIN is the author of *Dr. Bob's Painless Guide To The Internet* and *The No B.S. Guide to Linux* (both from No Starch Press). Bob is a columnist for *Boardwatch Magazine* and a contributor to several computer publications. He is also well known for his "Accessing The Internet By E-Mail" FAQ (read by hundreds of thousands of people around the world and translated into more than fifteen languages) and is the publisher of the *Internet TourBus* e-zine, an e-mail "tour" of fun and interesting things on the Net.

152 pp., $12.95 ($18.25 Cdn)
ISBN 1-886411-09-3

WRITER'S INTERNET SOURCEBOOK

Reviews of hundreds of websites especially for novelists, short story writers, journalists, poets, nonfiction authors, academics, playwrights, and business writers.

by MICHAEL LEVIN

The Internet offers extraordinary opportunities for writers for researching, marketing, and selling their work. The *Writer's Internet Sourcebook* reviews hundreds of websites of interest to writers. Find out how to use the Internet to save hundreds of hours of library time; where to find online writing classes, support groups, newsgroups, and mailing lists for writers of fiction, nonfiction, drama, journalism, poetry and academic writing; descriptions and reviews of online magazines (zines); and how to use the Internet to find readers, subscribers, buyers, and online bookstores that can sell your work.

MICHAEL LEVIN is heavily involved in the teaching and business of writing: He teaches in both the UCLA and NYU Writing Programs and he is on the board of the Author's Guild. His novels have been favorably reviewed in the *New York Times Book Review,* the *Los Angeles Times,* and the *Boston Herald.* He lives in the Los Angeles area.

256 pages, $16.95 ($23.95 Cdn)
ISBN 1-886411-11-5

Distributed to the book trade by Publishers Group West

If you can't find **No Starch Press titles** in your local bookstore, here's how to order directly from us (we accept MasterCard, Visa, and checks or money orders— sorry, no CODs):

Phone:
1 (800) 420-7240 or
(415) 284-9900
Monday through Friday,
8 a.m. to 5 p.m. (PST)

Fax:
(415) 284-9955
24 hours a day,
7 days a week

E-mail:
sales@nostarch.com

Web:
http://www.nostarch.com

Mail:
No Starch Press, Dept. LX97
401 China Basin St., Ste. 108
San Francisco, CA 94107-2192
USA

ABOUT THE AUTHORS

JUDY HEIM writes a regular column for *PC World* magazine, the most widely read computer magazine in the world, and has been an avid needlecrafter for 30 years. She has written for *Family Circle, C/Net, Newsweek, PC/Computing, Cosmopolitan,* and needlework magazines like *Quilter's Newsletter* and *Sew News*. The author of the highly-acclaimed *Needlecrafter's Computer Companion; I Lost My Baby, My Pickup & My Guitar on the Information Highway;* and *Internet for Cats* (all published by No Starch Press), she lives in Madison, WI.

GLORIA HANSEN has won many significant awards nationwide for her quilts, most of which were designed using a Macintosh computer. She is a frequent contributor to *Art/Quilt Magazine* and writes the "High-Tech Quilting" column for *The Professional Quilter*. She has self-published quilt patterns, and her quilts, designs, and hand-painted fabrics have appeared in magazines such as *Quilter's Newsletter Magazine, FiberArts, McCalls Quilting,* and *Ladies Circle Patchwork Quilt*. Also a contributor to *The Needlecrafter's Computer Companion,* she lives in central New Jersey.